Crime Prevention and Security Management

Series Editor
Martin Gill
Perpetuity Research
Tunbridge Wells, UK

It is widely recognized that we live in an increasingly unsafe society, but the study of security and crime prevention has lagged behind in its importance on the political agenda and has not matched the level of public concern. This exciting new series aims to address these issues looking at topics such as crime control, policing, security, theft, workplace violence and crime, fear of crime, civil disorder, white collar crime and anti-social behaviour. International in perspective, providing critically and theoretically-informed work, and edited by a leading scholar in the field, this series will advance new understandings of crime prevention and security management.

More information about this series at
http://www.palgrave.com/gp/series/14928

Julia Muraszkiewicz • Toby Fenton
Hayley Watson
Editors

Human Trafficking in Conflict

Context, Causes and the Military

palgrave
macmillan

Editors
Julia Muraszkiewicz
Trilateral Research
London, UK

Toby Fenton
Trilateral Research
London, UK

Hayley Watson
Trilateral Research
London, UK

Crime Prevention and Security Management
ISBN 978-3-030-40837-4 ISBN 978-3-030-40838-1 (eBook)
https://doi.org/10.1007/978-3-030-40838-1

Cover illustration: TONY KARUMBA/Stringer/Getty

This Palgrave Macmillan imprint is published by the registered company Springer Nature Switzerland AG.
The registered company address is: Gewerbestrasse 11, 6330 Cham, Switzerland

Foreword

Since ancient conquerors enslaved the conquered, societies have accepted that human beings and their labours were amongst the many spoils of war that were due the victors. And while we should expect that in the modern age societies would no longer accept this, it still continues. The editors and contributors to this volume are passionate and determined that slavery and exploitation of human beings should not persist, and that all the tools available to us should be put to the purpose of preventing human trafficking during and in the aftermath of conflict and war.

The many individuals contributing to this volume have spent years focusing upon the issues underpinning human trafficking and human security. They come from a range of organisations that play a role in this space—academia, law enforcement, military and civil society. The publication of this book has been driven in large part by members of Trilateral Research, and the inter-disciplinary approach taken to unpacking the impacts of human trafficking reflects our broader efforts in the socio-technical domain. I am grateful to each of them for their openness, their energy and their dedication to those affected by the issues of human security in bringing this work forward, and for giving voice to these critical challenges.

The vision for this volume was born out of work that began in 2014 on the TRACE (Trafficking As a Criminal Enterprise) project[1] where the Trilateral Research team engaged directly with perpetrators of human trafficking and those supporting victims. The aim of the project was to support stakeholders in combating and disrupting human trafficking by assessing and consolidating information surrounding the perpetrators and the wider trafficking enterprise. That seminal project inspired Trilateral's journey to apply inter-disciplinary teams to create technology to use across the conflict arena and has fundamentally altered our direction as an organisation. It has long been a critical part of our ethos to create real-world impacts from research, and while our focus has included an emphasis on ethics, privacy and data protection, we did not initially set out to create social impacts that could so directly contribute towards human security. As we have taken this path, we have encountered many other individuals, and through them, a broader community, who are similarly committed to protecting and caring for those at risk of human trafficking.

Today, we work with hundreds of agencies, large and small, as they endeavour to create positive impacts in the arena of human trafficking, including in conflict zones—academics studying the complex socio-economic and human interrelationships that create environments ripe for exploitation and uncover new forms of this crime[2]; governmental agencies driving policy; international organizations conducting research and influencing policy[3]; law enforcement agencies[4] actively working to investigate and apprehend bad actors; and humanitarian agencies working on the front lines in origin and destination countries across the globe to provide care for the victims. All of these organisations push forward, despite incredible resource constraints and under-funding.

---

[1] EC Grant agreement ID: 607669, see [Online] https://trilateralresearch.co.uk/project/trace/.

[2] See the work done on Human Trafficking for Ransom: Van Reisen, Mirjam, and Conny Rijken. 2015. "Sinai trafficking: Origin and definition of a new form of human trafficking." Social Inclusion 3, no. 1, 113–124.

[3] Council of Baltic Sea State [Online] https://www.cbss.org/safe-secure-region/tfthb/.

[4] Programme Challenger, Manchester [Online] https://www.programmechallenger.co.uk/what_we_do/modern_slavery/.

Helping to focus resources on the key issues that need to be addressed within this book, is a broad range of researchers in academic and policy-making institutions. At the Rights Lab[5] at the University of Nottingham, a Data and Measurement Programme seeks to make advances in measuring the risk and prevalence of human trafficking. Research is underway at Hull University (UK) to better understand victims' experiences, and at the University of Balearic Islands (Spain) to grapple with international law and the responsibilities it puts on states and their agents. Issues related to the exploitation of children as soldiers are being studied at the Universidad de la Sabana. Embedded within law enforcement organisations, researchers are focused on human trafficking as it relates to organised crime, with a special focus on child sexual exploitation. The United Nations Office on Drugs and Crime (UNODC) is conducting significant research and case-gathering, some of which is available in their report entitled *Countering Trafficking in Persons in Conflict Situations.*

Informed by research, international organisations such as the UN have pressed ahead with policies aimed at creating change in this area. There are numerous UN Resolutions to specifically address human trafficking in conflict, which can be seen as part of their broader human security work (e.g. Resolution 63/156 on trafficking in women and girls). Since 2004, NATO has actively implemented policy in this area with their Policy on Combating Trafficking in Human Beings. The International Criminal Court (ICC) is setting precedent by harshly sentencing those found guilty of enslavement during war, as seen in the recent sentencing of Bosco Ntaganda of the Democratic Republic of Congo on charges that included sexual slavery and use of child soldiers.

While policy is aimed at changing the environment within which human trafficking flourishes, civil society organisations and humanitarian workers aim to prevent exploitation and to work directly with victims in its aftermath. NGOs such as War Child and Child Soldiers International seek to assist child soldiers. Association "Novi put" Bosnia and Herzegovina and many like it are working at the local level with victims of human trafficking. These organisations are supported by legal advisors

[5] Rights Lab [Online] https://www.nottingham.ac.uk/research/beacons-of-excellence/rights-lab/index.aspx.

and advocates, including some who have contributed to this volume and continue to work to raise awareness and affect policy.

Whilst not directly involved in the work against human trafficking, the media themselves have played a role with extensive reporting on the use of children as soldiers, the sexual enslavement of Yazidi women by the Islamic State in Iraq and Syria, and the kidnapping of schoolgirls by Boko Haram, amongst others. The UK Ministry of Defence (MOD), through its policy document *JSP 1325: Human Security in Military Operations*, seeks to raise awareness on human trafficking within the context of the human security work done by the military. This broader concept of human security has garnered much attention and policy development within the humanitarian and development sectors, and it is now being reviewed in greater depth. Trilateral Research is involved in this effort as well, working on an inter-disciplinary basis with social scientists, ethicists, legal advisors and technologists to help drive research, inform policymakers and create impact through methodological and technological innovations, including contributions to risk assessment in the open domain.

The editors of this book, Julia Muraszkiewicz, Toby Fenton and Hayley Watson, have brought together a wide range of perspectives from contributing authors and through this have illustrated the prevalence and scale of the problems of human trafficking. Moreover, they have shown that there is significant work that remains to be done on a global level. A key part of this is the need to communicate better across borders, jurisdictions, disciplines, and legal and political structures—communicating at a human level, in order to effect change for these most vulnerable of our fellow humans.

Trilateral Research, London, UK Kush Wadhwa

Series Editor's Introduction

Not only is this book about a topic at the forefront of official and public concerns, it covers a specific area that has received scant attention: human trafficking and the role of the military and this includes private military organisations. Human trafficking, we are told, is the third fastest growing form of crime globally. As you will read, human trafficking is in various ways a tactic of war, and while it is unsurprising that it involves organised criminals, there are many instances where state actors and not only military personnel exploit those they are supposed to protect. Examples discussed include UN peacekeepers in Congo; children from the Russian countryside being recruited to fight Russia's wars; United States military and civilian personnel availing themselves of prostitution; and Bosnia (just one case where, once tolerated in war, human trafficking has proved 'impossible to eradicate' even in peace). This is a central tenet of the book: "It cannot be denied that significant number of international peacekeepers and their contractors were frequent and the most welcome guests at the establishments where human trafficking was taking place, but also accomplices."

Those trafficked include children who end up being forced to fight or find themselves used as sex slaves to reward soldiers. There are benefits in using child soldiers in that they are less demanding, easier to control and require less recompense. Of course, these activities create human insecurity and undermine the social, psychological and economic well-being of communities.

You will read about what makes people vulnerable to human trafficking. Not just poverty and discrimination, but the effects of climate change and political/religious persecution too. Those who are alone, neither working or studying, and those have run away or had parents killed are easier to recruit. They often face a stark choice, survival alone in a conflict zone or engagement as a child soldier by 'choice' or slave by force. Child soldiers are often starved, beaten or locked away as punishment or to make them compliant. Some suffer from forced abduction; children are kidnapped or even threatened with murder or the death of parents for refusing to join. The levels of harm caused are horrendous, involving torture and even the removal of organs.

Responding to the very complexity of human trafficking requires the engagement and coordination of many organisations operating in different territories with various remits, and this has proven a challenge. Even established and respected organisations that share broad aims and work together successfully, such as the EU and NATO, have marked differences in approaches taken. State responsibilities to respond which are enshrined in law don't always have the intended impact, including on the military. For example, in Afghanistan children are disproportionately victims, and yet dealing with trafficking is a low priority and enforcement efforts remain slight, leaving children unprotected. Where governments are weak the vulnerable can more easily be exploited.

You will find many interesting discussions on key topics, for example on: whether the state can, or should, excuse the person recruited to a terrorist organisation for the purpose of exploitation; how the military should distinguish between those who are adversaries by choice and those who are adversaries because they have been trafficked and forced to fight; the role of those in charge, commanders of units, and their responsibilities for generating frontline positive action. And many more besides these.

You won't be let down at the end of the book where there are some suggestions on how to respond. It is a huge topic, and the editors of this book have skilfully brought together a range of writers with real expertise on how the problem of human trafficking flourishes and how we need to think differently to ameliorate the horrific consequences it generates. It is both a fascinating read and an important contribution to literature.

January 2020 Martin Gill

Contents

1 **Introduction** 1
Julia Muraszkiewicz, Toby Fenton, and Hayley Watson

Part I **Understanding Human Trafficking in Conflict and How Conflict Facilitates Human Trafficking** 19

2 **Typology** 21
Julia Muraszkiewicz, Olivia Iannelli, and Peter Wieltschnig

3 **Unavoidable Exploitation? Conflict, Agency and Human Trafficking** 43
Alicia Kidd

4 **Human Trafficking, Conflict and Money Flows** 61
Archana Kotecha

Part II Trafficking in Conflict: Exploring How Human Trafficking Manifests in Conflict Through the Use of Case Studies 81

5 Russia's Private Military Forces: A Dual Layer of Human Trafficking? 83
Jorn van Rij, Ágoston Mohay, and Mantas Bileišis

6 What Are the Drivers of Children's Decision to Enlist in Armed Groups? A Case Study from Antioquia, Colombia 101
Giuseppe Maio, Mónica Hurtado, Graham Hesketh, and Kush Wadhwa

7 Occurrence of Human Trafficking in a Conflict/ Peacebuilding Context: Bosnian Experience 123
Abida Pehlić

8 Helping to Keep Those Serving Honourably, Honourable: Trafficking in Persons and the United States Uniform Code of Military Justice 143
Benjamin Thomas Greer and Kymber M. Cates

Part III Addressing Human Trafficking in Conflict and Dealing with the Aftermath 171

9 The Due Diligence Duty and the Role of the Military in the Identification and Protection of Human Trafficking Victims 173
Valentina Milano

10 Legal Responsibility of the Military Commander to Prevent or Punish the Acts of Human Trafficking Under the Rome Statute 197
Michala Chadimová

11 **Applying the Non-punishment Principle to Returnees from Terrorist Organisations** 215
Julia Muraszkiewicz

12 **Trafficking and Child Sexual Violence in Afghanistan: The Military's Role in Combating Human Trafficking** 233
Olivia Iannelli

13 **How Definitions of 'Child Soldiers' Exclude Girls from Demobilisation Efforts** 257
Ally Dunhill and Alicia Kidd

14 **The Role of Regional Organizations in Addressing Human Trafficking in Conflict: The Cases of NATO and the EU** 277
Lucas J. Ruiz-Díaz

15 **Human Security Analysis for Military Planning: Lessons Learnt from Developing a Risk Assessment on Human Trafficking** 297
Hayley Watson, Toby Fenton, and Stephen Anning

16 **Incorporating Human Security Considerations into Military Planning: Some Suggestions** 317
Toby Fenton, Peter Wieltschnig, and Julia Muraszkiewicz

Index 341

List of Tables

Table 6.1 Recoding Typology 1 indicates Economic Motivations, 0 indicates Family and Political Violence Motivations 107
Table 6.2 Summary Statistics of individual-level and municipality-level variables (includes dependent variable, motive) 109
Table 6.3 Model performance metrics on train and test sets 112
Table 6.4 Model coefficients and odds ratios of Economic Motivation 112
Table 8.1 Forced Labour Contract Compliance 152

1

Introduction

Julia Muraszkiewicz, Toby Fenton, and Hayley Watson

We have seen clearly that war acts as a potent catalyst to human trafficking. It breaks down institutional and social protections. And it leaves masses of people vulnerable to traffickers. It is startlingly obvious therefore that greater focus by the international community on preventing conflicts, and stopping their reoccurrence, will have a direct impact on human trafficking.

Mr. Tim Mawe

Deputy Permanent Representative of Ireland Security Council Chamber

Introduction

The United Nations Convention Against Transnational Organised Crime (also called the Palermo Convention) was adopted through UN Resolution 55/25 (2001) with the objective of combatting transnational

J. Muraszkiewicz (✉) • T. Fenton • H. Watson
Trilateral Research, London, UK
e-mail: julia.muraszkiewicz@trilateralresearch.com; toby.fenton@trilateralresearch.com; hayley.watson@trilateralresearch.com

J. Muraszkiewicz et al. (eds.), *Human Trafficking in Conflict*, Crime Prevention and Security Management, https://doi.org/10.1007/978-3-030-40838-1_1

organised crime around the world. Within this resolution, the *Protocol to Prevent, Suppress and Punish Trafficking in Persons, Especially Women and Children* (henceforth the *Palermo Protocol*) laid the foundation for novel legislative reform for protecting victims of human trafficking, preventing the crime and prosecuting the perpetrators. Further, the protocol included an agreed definition of human trafficking (see the definition below) and aimed to put an end to state differences as to what the crime entails. Despite the undisputable legislative progress achieved following the adoption of that agreed definition, to this day much remains unresolved regarding combatting human trafficking (Reiley 2006). There is, for instance, a worrying lack of attention paid to the issue of human trafficking in conflict. Since UN Resolution 55/25, subsequent anti-human trafficking documents and policies at the regional level, such as the EU Directive *2011/36 on Preventing and Combating Trafficking in Human Beings and Protecting Its victims*, have largely neglected to focus on human trafficking in conflict. This is despite the fact that human trafficking is prevalent in conflict, as recognised, for instance, by *United Nations Security Council (UNSC) Resolution 2331. Resolution 2331* calls upon governments, the international community and all other organisations and entities that deal with conflict and post-conflict, disaster and other crisis and emergency situations to address the heightened vulnerabilities of (particularly) women and girls to human trafficking and exploitation, and also stresses the close associations between human trafficking, sexual and gender-based violence, terrorism and transnational organised crime.

The phenomenon of human trafficking in conflict is as old as conflict itself, and it has been epitomised recently in the exploitation of the minority Yazidi community in Iraq and Syria by the Islamic State (also referred to as ISIS or ISIL); or in the manner in which the ISIS in Iraq and Syria and Boko Haram in Nigeria commit yet further violations of international law (Patel 2014) through openly advocating the use of human trafficking and enslavement practices. The use of child soldiers by ISIS (the so-called "cubs of the Caliphate") or by Columbia's armed groups (see Chap. 6 for more detail), the trade in trafficked women that sprang up overnight outside the gates of UN and NATO (North Atlantic Treaty Organisation) compounds in the Balkans, the kidnaping and enslavement of school girls by Boko Haram in Nigeria and armed militias' use of forced labour to plunder rich natural resources in places such as the Democratic Republic of the Congo (DRC) provide further examples of human trafficking in conflict. The multiple manifestations of this phenomenon in a context where traditional legal, policy and law enforcement responses are likely to be inadequate—if not entirely absent—calls for concerted efforts to better understand the problem and foster context-appropriate solutions and responses. Of course, the exact number of victims of human trafficking in conflict and crisis situations remains unknown; in reality, it is incredibly difficult to calculate due to a lack of data and ineffective research methods (Weitzer 2014). Nonetheless, numerous accounts and testimonies provide ample impetus to the quest for a much stronger understanding of the nexus between human trafficking and conflict, including, importantly, the potential role of the military, who are often one of the few actors able to operate with greater degrees of agency within complex conflict environments. More broadly, the phenomenon of human trafficking in conflict and crisis warrants a stronger consideration of the potential impact of human trafficking upon multi-stakeholder efforts to promote and sustain human security, safeguard human rights, foster development and advance peace and pre–/post-conflict stabilisation.

It should be acknowledged that during conflict and crisis situations, the gap in anti-human trafficking legislation has, to an extent, been increasingly addressed by certain military actors through selected military soft law and related policy. Notably, in 2004 the North Atlantic Treaty Organisation (NATO) adopted a *Zero-Tolerance Policy on Combating Trafficking in Human Beings*. That policy commits NATO members and other troop-contributing nations participating in NATO-led operations to reinforce efforts to prevent and combat human trafficking. This, according to the policy, can be achieved through the agreement "that all personnel taking part in NATO-led operations should receive appropriate training to make them aware of the problem of trafficking and how this modern-day slave trade impacts on human rights, stability and security, as well as being informed of their own responsibilities and duties and the respective responsibilities of International Organisations in this field" (NATO 2004).

Of course, whether any existing guidance and/or policy has had a meaningful impact on the operations and planning considerations of military forces requires further study towards which this book strives, at least in part, to contribute. Indeed, this book seeks to address what is a largely understudied topic within the human trafficking literature, with few studies having sought to contemplate the broader role of the military within anti-human trafficking efforts. Scholars, policymakers and civil society recognise that conflict increases the numbers of refugees and displaced persons, and aggravates poverty, amongst other issues, thus making conflict-afflicted areas a breeding ground for human trafficking. Observers note, for instance, that existing violence leads to high rates of forced labour and sexual exploitation, and they recognise the "egregious treatment inflicted by armed and terrorist groups in areas where conflict is ongoing, the different forms of exploitation emerging in that context and the large number of people who are made vulnerable by conflicts and who are forced to flee them" (UNODC 2018). Nevertheless, the military all too often remains on the periphery of anti-human trafficking discussions, whether concerning the protection of victims, the prevention of the crime itself or the prosecution of its perpetrators. That said, there is an increasing emphasis within military thinking on understanding and addressing the range of human security issues that exacerbate, and are exacerbated by, conflict and crisis—human trafficking included. This development reflects the broader shift from a traditional state-centric conceptualisation of conflict and security (i.e. inter-state war) to a human-centric conceptualisation that focuses on security at the level of the individual and their community.

Human Trafficking and the Military and the Aim of This Book

For the editors of this book, the importance of considering the human trafficking and conflict nexus, coupled with the question of what the role of the military is in addressing this crime, is vividly apparent. Human trafficking can constitute a tactic of war that serves several purposes for organised criminal gangs, state and non-state armed actors and others actors undermining security and stability. Human trafficking facilitates the recruitment and retention of fighters, including child soldiers, and it provides rewards to combatants in the form of sex slaves. It generates illicit revenues that can support conflict financing, and it contributes to the social, psychological and economic breakdown of entire communities. It epitomises some of the worst human rights abuses. In times of conflict and crisis, this evokes numerous issues that merit the attention of legislators (domestic, regional and international), policymakers, military planners and others. Yet, despite high-level policy guidance from NATO and other military actors, as the editors embarked on the journey of exploring the potential role and contribution of the military in addressing, or at the very least understanding, human trafficking in conflict, the question heard all too often was *what is human trafficking in conflict and what does it have to do with the military?*

Human trafficking is traditionally seen as a concern of those working in fields such as human rights, criminal law, migration, gender and labour. It is seen to be situated most appropriately within the remit of a country's domestic security and justice departments (e.g. Ministry of Interior, Department of Justice, etc.), but rarely within the defence departments (e.g. Department of Defence, Ministry of Defence, etc.). Human trafficking has not traditionally been a focus of the military, whether in the context of warfighting, security operations, training, or disaster response and relief work. Nor do anti-trafficking programmes themselves necessarily self-identify as having connections with activities undertaken in the military realm. Yet, it is argued herein that there is indeed a nexus, a common trajectory.

How does human trafficking 'fit into' military operations and activities; where are the touchpoints? Noting the relative novelty of such a question, we sought to elicit some answers by way of an edited book. We invited scholars and practitioners from around the world—ensuring inclusivity regarding a range of voices and perspectives—to ponder questions such as how does human trafficking manifest in conflict; what drives it; what legislation and policy already exist; is legislation and policy effective and applied on the ground and how might military actors better respond to human trafficking in practical terms? Looking to the future, the book hopes to open up a larger space to consider *why* the military should include a stronger consideration of human trafficking within the planning and conduct of operations, and *how* this might be taken forward.

Clarification of Key Concepts and Frameworks

For a better understanding of the nexus between military operations and human trafficking, it is first necessary to situate the concepts in clear definitions and frameworks.

Human Trafficking This book defines human trafficking in line with the most internationally acknowledged definition contained within the aforementioned *Protocol*, which was adopted in 2000, entered into force on 25 December 2003 and has been signed by 117 states and regional organisations. Article 3 of the 2000 *Palermo Protocol* states that trafficking in persons shall mean:

(a) The recruitment, transportation, transfer, harbouring or receipt of persons, by means of the threat or use of force or other forms of coercion, of abduction, of fraud, of deception, of the abuse of power, or a position of vulnerability, or the giving or receiving of payments or benefits to achieve the consent of a person having control over another person, for the purpose of exploitation. Exploitation shall include, at a minimum, the exploitation of the prostitution of others or other forms of sexual exploitation, forced labour or services, slavery or practices similar to slavery, servitude or the removal or organs.
(b) The consent of a victim of trafficking in persons to the intended exploitation set forth in subparagraph (a) of this article shall be irrelevant where any of the means set forth in subparagraph (a) have been used;
(c) The recruitment, transportation, transfer, harbouring or receipt a child for the purpose of exploitation shall be considered "trafficking in persons" even if this does not involve any of the means set forth in subparagraph (a) of this article.

The definition includes three elements: an action (recruitment, transportation, transfer, harbouring or receipt), a means (threat or use of force or other forms of coercion, of abduction, of fraud, of deception, of the abuse of power, or a position of vulnerability, or the giving or receiving of payments or benefits to achieve the consent of a person having control over another person) and a purpose (at a minimum, the exploitation of the prostitution of others or other forms of sexual exploitation, forced labour or services, slavery or practices similar to slavery, servitude or the removal or organs). According to Piotrowicz (2007, 277):

> These elements indicate that [trafficking in human beings] includes a number of actors, each of whom may play a role in 'creating' a victim of trafficking, from the acquaintance in the victim's village who knows someone who can organise a job or visa, to the individual who facilitates illegal crossing of the frontier, to the person who supplies rooms to accommodate victims in transit and the bar owner who eventually 'buys' the victim.

It is important to highlight two key features of the definition. Firstly, when the victim is a child the means element does not need to be present. In addition, Article 3(b) states that the consent of a victim will be irrelevant where any of the means have been used. Article 3(b) is key as many traffickers seek to argue that victims may have consented at some point, for example, to join an armed force, to prostitution or to be transported from one place to another. By including these provisions, the law focuses on the intention and actions of the trafficker and not the intention and actions of the trafficked person. This is discussed in greater length by Kid in Chap. 3, which addresses a victim's agency, and in Chap. 12 by Muraszkiewicz, which looks at the notion of compelling victims.

Conflict Conflict is arguably as old as human history itself. In simple terms, conflict involves a disagreement between two or more parties; this can manifest in various ways, from the purely verbal argument, to physical violence, armed struggle and war. The Peace Research Institute Oslo (PRIO) defines conflict as a contested incompatibility that concerns government and/or territory where the use of armed force between two parties, of which at least one is the government of a state, results in at least 25 battle-related deaths in one calendar year. As conflict becomes increasingly people-centred, there has been a growing recognition of the need to consider the underlying social, political, economic, group and individual factors that can drive and exacerbate conflict. This has been captured, at least in part, in the concept of human security.

Human Security The core tenets of human security remain contested, as does the precise manner in which a human security approach should be utilised and operationalised in practice. In the absence of a unified interpretation of the concept, a number of often competing and conflicting interpretations have been suggested, although they are united by core principles.

The conception of the contemporary security environment has expanded beyond the traditional focus on state-based security that was predominant for most of the twentieth century. Post-Cold War intra-state instability and the ongoing processes related to decolonisation led to greater attention being placed on those issues affecting the security and well-being of individuals and their communities, as contemporary conflicts have frequently been driven and/or exacerbated by a range of factors—especially identity-based issues—manifesting within the boundaries of the state. Greater interconnectedness through globalisation and the increasing role of non-state actors in conflict and governance, including the impact of corporations and non-state armed groups upon individual lives (Spearin 2008, 363), has meant that security can no longer be understood exclusively through a state-centric prism. Armed conflict is often referred to as having undertaken a paradigm evolution from inter-state to *intra*-state conflict (Mack 2008, 2). Today, the vast majority of contemporary conflicts take place *within* the borders of a country and disproportionately impact civilians, local communities and social cohesion (Mack 2008, 5). Logically, the requirement is thus for a more people-focused framework, not only including a focus on the security and well-being of the individual, but also recognising that such human security is better understood and addressed along multiple dimensions beyond the threat of physical violence. Going even further, a people-focused framework prompts a wider consideration of the key qualitative aspects of human security including human dignity, reflecting the humanist view that people are inherently valuable by virtue of being human.

Furthermore, a growing body of research has led to a more nuanced understanding of the causes of conflict and insecurity generally (Jarvis 2018, 108–109). Global warming (Burke et al. 2009), poverty (Buhaug et al. 2011, 815), gender-based discrimination and a large number of other issues have come to be identified as salient and acute human security issues in a manner that was previously not widely accepted or understood. Under these circumstances, individuals in communities and societies across the world are impeded from developing their full human potential, particularly in instances where they are within a vulnerable demographic due to gender, age, sexual orientation, gender identity, political or religious affiliation or disability, amongst other characteristics. Within the context of this book, important is the recognition that the manner in which such issues can severely erode individuals' resilience and agency is further compounded during times of conflict and crisis, with one of many potential consequences being the increased risk of falling victim to human trafficking.

In summary, human security goes beyond traditional conceptions of security by viewing individuals, rather than states, as the key object of focus. In this respect, human security allows for a more 'subtle' and arguably 'deeper' understanding of security, with two immediate implications. Firstly, human security recognises that the security of the individual—including their security from human rights abuse such as human trafficking—is closely connected with wider peace and security. The threats and issues that affect security at the level of the individual may intersect, compound and cascade to create conditions that ultimately affect national and international security. For example, inter-ethnic tensions, economic deprivation and associated grievances may induce people to join non-state armed actors (e.g. militias and insurgent groups), thereby furthering wider and longer-term insecurity. This may also make people more vulnerable to exploitation by criminal groups, thereby fuelling organised crime.

Secondly, human security advances a normative agenda that places a premium on the survival, livelihood and dignity of the individual. In doing so, human security mandates the consideration of an array of factors that may negatively impact an individual person's well-being, beyond the purely existential threats of physical violence and force that are the focus of traditional security approaches. A natural extension of this second point ought to include human trafficking and its related dynamics.

So, what about the nexus between human security and human trafficking? Apart from erosion of the human rights of trafficked persons, human trafficking is a substantial source of revenue for, and a means to advance the agenda of, non-state armed groups, corruption, state-run security forces, criminal organisations and others, all of whose activities can thereby undermine attempts to achieve legitimate governance and can jeopardise the efforts of military activities to promote security and stability. Indeed, such is the interconnected or 'networked' nature of those issues that threaten human security that it becomes simply unrealistic and conceptually confusing to seek to understand and respond to human trafficking without understanding the manner in which these wider issues also help drive human trafficking in conflict—including for example, in the examples of sexual and gender-based violence, lack of education and government corruption, as discussed in this book. As aptly summarised by Pati (2014, 32) human trafficking is often found at the intersection of all other threats to human security.

Outline of the Book

The book brings together a number of chapters by authors with a range of expertise and interests, tying them together within a structure designed to guide the reader thematically through the myriad issues related to human trafficking in conflict. These chapters and issues discussed in this book are of course not exhaustive, but they aim to provide the reader with an introduction to the discourse, issues and case studies.

Part I of the book, entitled *Understanding Human Trafficking in Conflict and How Conflict Facilitates Human Trafficking*, is dedicated to introducing the relevant matters. It begins with Chap. 2 by Muraszkiewicz, Iannelli and Wieltschnig, who discuss the types of human trafficking that have, to date, been documented in conflict. In Chap. 3, Kidd explains why human trafficking so easily becomes a reality in conflict. She shows that a conflict's impact on agency increases the risk of being trafficked. The nature of conflict restricts the choices available, leaving people to choose between limited options which are commonly all imbued with risk. Chapter 3 also draws upon literature to provide an overview of what human trafficking looks like in the context of armed conflict. It supports the literature review by using examples from recent in-depth interviews about the experiences of people fleeing conflict, offering insight into the lived experiences of conflict-related human trafficking.

In Chap. 4, Kotecha explores the nexus between human trafficking in conflict and illicit financial flows. Human trafficking and money laundering are often intricately connected, yet money laundering charges have usually not been included in the prosecution of trafficking cases and so this aspect of human trafficking is understudied. During conflict non-state armed groups and, to a lesser extent, state militaries have been found to use human trafficking to raise revenue and fund illicit activities. Income generation takes multiple forms, from theft of salaries to the sale of trafficked people. Armed groups may use trafficked people for forced labour in mines, agriculture and factories, thus raising the prospect of introducing illicit revenues into global supply chains that stretch far beyond the conflict zone itself. The author also discusses current efforts to combat illicit financial activities and suggests ways in which existing anti-money laundering systems can be used to disrupt the activities of human traffickers in conflict zones and beyond. There is a particular need to develop stronger capabilities to gather, analyse and share more granular data on human trafficking-related illicit financial flows. Kotecha concludes by stressing the importance of collaboration between government agencies, the private sector and civil society in better mapping, analysing and understanding trafficking-related financial flows.

Part II of the book, entitled *Trafficking in Conflict: Exploring How Human Trafficking Manifests in Conflict Through the Use of Case Studies*, is dedicated to using specific case studies to further illustrate how human trafficking reveals itself in conflict and what policy and legal problems it brings up. In Chap. 5, van Rij, Mohay, Bileišis and Žemaitis focus on the example of the training and deployment of children to conflict areas by Russian private military and security companies. Many of these children are recruited through appeals to their sense of patriotism and promises of a way out of their poor socio-economic circumstances. This chapter addresses this situation as a specific, not yet described, type of human trafficking which could be seen as either labour or criminal exploitation. It leaves readers aware of a new form of exploitation and in all likelihood thinking what else remains to be uncovered.

Chapter 6 by Maio, Hurtado, Hesketh and Wadhwa takes us to Colombia and provides findings from an exploratory data analysis of cases of child recruitment trends in the country's north-western Department of Antioquia. It examines data from 554 boys and 116 girls who were illicitly recruited as children (below the age of 18) by either right-wing paramilitaries or left-wing guerrillas in Antioquia between 1994 and 2005. By doing so, the authors seek to identify why, how and under which conditions young people have joined illegal armed groups. This study provides an example of how data-driven policy strategies could be designed to tackle illicit recruitment in the context of Antioquia. The chapter concludes by showing factors that are statistically associated with children testifying to having economic motivations for joining armed groups and also identifying factors associated with children giving political violence-related motivations for joining armed groups.

In Chap. 7, Abida Pehlić explores the occurrence of trafficking in human beings and forced prostitution as a prevailing form of exploitation in the post-war Bosnia and Herzegovina of the 1990s, with a particular focus on the role of peacekeeping forces deployed to the country in fuelling demand for the provision of commercial sexual services. Chapter 8 by Greer and Cates chronicles events in the US leading up to the adoption of the *Military Extraterritorial Jurisdiction Act of 2000 (MEJA)* and the expansion of *Article 134 of the Uniform Code of Military Justice (UCMJ)* in 2005. Both are specific legislations aimed at ridding human trafficking associated with the US military. They examine military cases stemming from new laws and regulations and will discuss the extent to which US military personnel are provided substantive and adequate anti-trafficking training. Readers will find here alarming and numerous cases of different types of human trafficking in conflict zones related to the military; from labour exploitation to sexual exploitation. Through these cases, the chapter illustrates the deficiencies in the application of the law and therefore acts as a bridge to Part III of the book.

Part III is entitled *Addressing Human Trafficking in Conflict and Dealing with the Aftermath*. This is launched with Milano's Chap. 9 on 'The Due Diligence Duty and the role of the Military in the Identification and Protection of Human Trafficking Victims.' Whilst much literature has focused on the existing debate on the negative role of the military, Chap. 9 seeks to turn the discourse on its head and look at how the military can be part of the solution in contributing to the identification and protection of trafficking victims. In this chapter, Milano provides the reader with clarity on the legal standards that apply to the armed forces with regard to human trafficking, in particular in light of states' due diligence duty under human rights law.

Chapter 10 by Chadimová then turns to look at the doctrine of legal responsibility in the context of human trafficking in conflict. Focusing on the concept of command responsibility as a potential legal toolkit to further bolster responses to human trafficking, the chapter explores the responsibility of a military commander to prevent or punish acts of human trafficking under the *Rome Statute 1998*. While individual perpetrators can be held responsible for the direct commission of a crime of human trafficking under international law, the notion of superior responsibility is used to hold senior military commanders indirectly accountable. The chapter argues that a military commander (or 'superior') may be held criminally responsible for the acts of his subordinates if three general conditions are met: first, the existence of a superior-subordinate relationship, defined by the superior having 'effective control' over the subordinate; second, the knowledge of the superior that the crime was about to be, was being, or had been committed; third, the failure of the superior to take measures to prevent the crime or punish the perpetrator. The chapter also looks at what constitutes the 'necessary and reasonable' measures that a commander must take to fulfil their duty, and whether the 'remoteness' of the commander affects his responsibility to prevent human trafficking committed by his subordinates.

Chapter 11 by Muraszkiewicz focuses on considering what policy should be taken with those who return home after having spent time with a terrorist organisation. Should they be punished (if they committed crimes) or should they be perceived as victims of human trafficking and thus be protected from liability under the non-prosecution and non-punishment principle? The author examines two general philosophies of punishment—utilitarian and retributive—together with existing law to develop a guideline as to how we should treat returnees. The author agrees with Kid (Chap. 3) that agency needs to be better understood by policy-makers and the judiciary, as it is very much at the heart of understanding how victims of human trafficking may have committed crimes. Without giving careful thought to how persons end up in certain situations it is almost impossible to identify them as victims of human trafficking and subsequently offer them the required protection and assistance.

In Chap. 12, Iannelli argues that protection and assistance is needed by those most vulnerable, including minors. The author focuses on child trafficking during the conflict in Afghanistan. It analyses the legislation in this field, namely, the *Geneva Conventions* on the law of armed conflict, the *Convention of the Rights of the Child* and the *Palermo Protocol*. It also evaluates the current protection measures and practice. Iannelli demonstrates that despite the existence of strong legislation to protect children, enforcement remains weak due to the low level of priority that trafficking in conflict is awarded. Building on this analysis, the chapter explores the role of NATO in addressing human trafficking in conflict and post-conflict situations and the legality behind this role. It contends that as first responders on the ground, NATO may find ways to identify victims of exploitation and collect evidence against perpetrators, in an effort to help and protect them when they are most vulnerable and avoid issues of impunity. It suggests that this role may be consolidated through a greater focus on incorporating Women Peace and Security (WPS) within military operations while at the same time including a child-based approach and a deeper understanding of cultural contexts.

Keeping with the theme of children in armed conflict, in Chap. 13 Dunhill and Kidd examine the remit and outcomes of disarmament, demobilisation and reintegration (DDR) programmes regarding child soldiers. The chapter begins by noting that just as a human trafficking victim under the age of 18 is considered a victim regardless of the method through which they were trafficked, so too should child soldiers under the age of 18 be considered de facto victims of human trafficking. It then goes on to explore why and how DDR programmes differentiate between the gendered experiences of male and female child soldiers, and it outlines the key weaknesses in current approaches. The authors argue that in commonly failing to recognise girls as child soldier victims in conflict, DDR programmes may effectively free children from their position of trafficking victim only to place them in new positions of vulnerability to re-exploitation. The authors conclude by offering some recommendations for more effective and inclusive DDR efforts.

Chapter 14, by Ruiz, examines the role of regional organisations, specifically NATO and the EU, in addressing human trafficking in conflict. Specifically, Ruiz looks at how NATO and the EU police crime within the context of peacekeeping operations and missions and examines their contribution to the prevention and repression of human trafficking, acting under a given international UN mandate or, irrespective of the mandate, under International Law and UN Security Council Resolutions. Chapter 15 by Watson, Fenton and Anning acknowledges that law is not enough, and militaries require further analytical tools to address human trafficking, as part of wider efforts to promote security and stability. The authors offer lessons identified from the development of a risk assessment methodology concerning human trafficking in conflict and its impact on military planning. The authors conclude by considering how militaries, governments and humanitarian actors can better collaborate to drive engagement with the risks related to human trafficking in order to bolster security and stabilisation activities and the broader promotion of human security.

The book concludes in Part IV with a chapter by Wieltschnig, Fenton and Muraszkiewicz addressing the concept of human security, followed by a conclusion that summarises the thematic concerns that reveal themselves in this volume. Looking to the future, the authors consider how we ought to locate human trafficking within the wider human security space, while the editors offer some recommendations for policymakers, military planners and researchers. The authors suggest that if we unspin the tangled conceptual threads within law and policy that exist nationally and internally, it appears we are heading for a worldview of security that cannot ignore the prevalence of human trafficking in conflict and the way it is nested within a complex web of interconnected human security issues. The questions, then, are how should the broader challenge of promoting human security be addressed, who can and should contribute and how.

Notes on Contributors

As mentioned above, the chapters in this volume were sourced not exclusively from researchers and academics working in the field of human trafficking, but also from practitioners and others engaging in responding to human trafficking in conflict. This helps us to establish a space that is not bound heavily by theory, but instead transitions to 'real world' application, providing space to question and study how human trafficking manifests in conflict, its interconnection with other human security issues and why military planners should more strongly consider the phenomenon within their operational planning.

References

Buhaug, Halvard, Kristian Skrede Gleditsch, Helge Holtermann, Gudrun Østby, and Andreas Forø Tollefsen. 2011. It's the Local Economy, Stupid! Geographic Wealth Dispersion and Conflict Outbreak Location. *Journal of Conflict Resolution* 55 (5): 814–840.

Burke, Marshall B., Edward Miguel, Shanker Satyanath, John A. Dykema, and David B. Lobell. 2009. Warming Increases the Risk of Civil War in Africa. *Proceedings of the National Academy of Sciences* 106 (49): 20670–20674.

Jarvis, Lee. 2018. Toward a Vernacular Security Studies: Origins, Interlocutors, Contributions, and Challenges. *International Studies Review* 21 (1): 107–126.

Mack, M. 2008. *Increasing respect for international humanitarian law in non-international armed conflicts*. Geneva: ICRC.

NATO. 2004. *NATO Policy on Combating Trafficking in Human Beings*. Accessed November 3, 2019. [Online] https://www.nato.int/docu/comm/2004/06-istanbul/docu-traffic-app1.htm

Patel, Keshar. 2014. Boko Haram: Spotlight on Human Trafficking. *World Policy Blog*. [Online] https://worldpolicy.org/2014/05/22/boko-haram-spotlight-on-human-trafficking/

Pati, Roza. 2014. Human Trafficking: An Issue of Human and National Security. *National Security & Armed Conflict Law Review* 4: 29.

Piotrowicz, R. 2007. Trafficking of Human Beings and Their Human Rights in the Migration Context. In *International Migration Law. Developing Paradigms*

and Key Challenges, ed. R. Cholewinski, R. Perruchoud, and E. MacDoland. The Hague: Asser Press.
Protocol to Prevent, Suppress and Punish Trafficking in Persons, Especially Women and Children, Supplementing the United Nations Convention Against Transnational Organized Crime, GA Res. 55/25, Annex II, UN GAOR, 55th Sess., Supp. No. 49, at 53, UN Doc. A/45/49 (Vol. I) (2001), Nov. 15, 2000, entered into force December. 25, 2003.
Reiley, A.A. 2006. Trafficking in Human Beings: A Comparative Account of Legal Provisions for Combating Trafficking in Belgium, Italy, The Netherlands, Sweden and The United States. In *Trafficking And Women's Rights*, ed. C.L. Van Den Anker and J. Doomernik, 89–117. Palgrave: Basingstoke.
Spearin, C. 2008. Private, Armed and Humanitarian? States, NGOs, International Private Security Companies and Shifting Humanitarianism. *Security Dialogue* 39 (4): 363.
UNODC. 2018. Countering Trafficking in Persons in Conflict Situations: Thematic Paper. United Nations Office on Drugs and Crime: Vienna. [Online] https://www.unodc.org/documents/human-trafficking/2018/17-08776_ebookCountering_Trafficking_in_Persons_in_Conflict_Situations.pdf
Weitzer, R. 2014. New Directions in Research on Human Trafficking. *The Annals of the American Academy of Political and Social Science* 653: 6–24.

Julia Muraszkiewicz is a Senior Research Manager at Trilateral Research in the Applied Research and Innovation team and was the research lead of Project Solebay looking at risk assessment methodologies for human trafficking in conflict. She has a publication with Palgrave Macmillan on protecting trafficked persons from liability. Julia in her spare time volunteers with NGOs that directly help victims of human trafficking and labour exploitation. She has a PhD in Law from Vrije University of Brussels.

Toby Fenton is an associate product manager at Trilateral Research, where he works to understand the perspectives and needs of decision-makers and other stakeholders in the defence and security sectors to support innovation, applied research and technology development. From 2018–2019 he worked on Project Solebay which developed a proof-of-concept risk assessment to support the UK military's response to modern slavery and human trafficking (MSHT) as a human security issue. Fenton's background lies in research and consultancy within the defence and security space. He holds a BSc in International Relations and an MA in International Peace & Security.

Hayley Watson is Senior Practice Manager at Trilateral Research, managing business units around Applied Research & Innovation and the provision of interdisciplinary technical and research services to support data-driven decision making. Hayley's core background lies in social research that examines the positioning of citizens in relation to security-related issues. She has conducted research on the public's response to security issues (including crises), public vulnerabilities stemming from the impact of security-related issues, considerations for improving the resilience of the public, among other research projects. Hayley has a PhD in Sociology from the University of Kent.

Part I

Understanding Human Trafficking in Conflict and How Conflict Facilitates Human Trafficking

2

Typology

Julia Muraszkiewicz, Olivia Iannelli, and Peter Wieltschnig

Introduction

Vulnerabilities are arguably the key cause of human trafficking. These may stem from economic or social factors such as poverty or discrimination, natural factors such as climate change or political and/or religious factors such as persecution. Vulnerabilities distort power balances and are used by others to exploit human beings. This occurs across the globe from the UK, to Poland, to Bangladesh to Mali and to Columbia. It is true in times of peace and prosperity and in times of conflict and poverty.

Those seeking to address the crime—through prevention, protection of victims and prosecution of offenders—are in need of an agile and comprehensive picture of what human trafficking looks like on the ground. In some countries this is achieved through the use of data collection

J. Muraszkiewicz (✉) • O. Iannelli • P. Wieltschnig
Trilateral Research, London, UK
e-mail: julia.muraszkiewicz@trilateralresearch.com;
Olivia.Iannelli@trilateralresearch.com; peter.wieltschnig@trilateralresearch.com

J. Muraszkiewicz et al. (eds.), *Human Trafficking in Conflict*, Crime Prevention and Security Management, https://doi.org/10.1007/978-3-030-40838-1_2

instruments such as the National Referral Mechanism.[1] Whilst this mechanism remains partial in its assessment of the true scale of the issue—due to the hidden nature of the crime—it is able to shed some light on where intervention strategies ought to lie. A mechanism such as this does not, however, exist to map instances of human trafficking in conflict; nor is there much literature on the topic. This clearly creates a gap which this book seeks to fill.

This chapter aims to shed light on the typology of human trafficking in conflict. It thus presents an *empirical typology*, that is, one composed of types of situations that exist/existed. This typology serves to organise past research, experiences from stakeholders and reports from the media focusing on human trafficking in conflict. Thus, it helps us to find a list of examples outlining the ways in which human trafficking—due to an array of exploitation types—occurs in conflict. The different types of exploitation and the different types of victims are used in this chapter as an axis by which we carry the typological description.

N.B: The typology presented in this chapter can only reflect what is known and it would be impossible for it to copiously correspond to the reality on the ground, across time and space. However, despite difficulties in doing so, attempts ought to be made to seek "clarity" on the world of human trafficking. Organising the various experiences into a typology is not only a useful learning tool, serving as a guide for research and policy, but it also provides a launch pad for reflection.

Some types are easily recognisable such as the sexual exploitation of women; others are more difficult to categorise as human trafficking even if we may have an inherent impression that some form of exploitation has taken place. This springs from the difficulties around the definition of human trafficking and exploitation (see introduction). Notwithstanding, the one characteristic that the examples listed below have in common is that they have been mapped according to the definition of human trafficking in the Palermo Protocol outlined in the introduction to this book.

A word on methodology: a typology was developed on the basis of existent research from academic sources, international organisation and NGO

[1] Framework through which state actors fulfil their obligations to protect and promote the human rights of trafficked persons, coordinating their efforts in a strategic partnership with civil society.

reports, news stories, case law as well as through interviews that the authors conducted for project Solebay—a project conducted in 2019 which aimed to develop risk assessment tools for the UK military to support them in responding to human trafficking. Project Solebay researchers engaged in 28 semi-structured interviews which were conducted either face-to-face or via communication technology (Skype, GoToMeeting, phone, etc.). The interviews were with a variety of stakeholders including academics (experts in human trafficking and/or conflict), NGO staff, law enforcement authorities (e.g., police, including those stationed in conflict areas), military personnel and the UN Office on Drugs and Crime (UNODC). During all interviews, researchers adhered to the highest ethical standards. Semi-structured interviews lasted approximately 45 minutes to 1.5 hours.

Trafficking for Sexual Exploitation: Peacekeepers and Humanitarian Agencies

The phantom of peacekeeping forces engaging in sexual exploitation, as evidenced by the exploitation of women in Somalia in 2013–2014, continues to plague conflict today. Human Rights Watch (2014) accused AMISOM (The African Union Mission in Somalia) peacekeepers of raping women and girls as young as 12 and trading food and medicine for sex. Sexual exploitation has no agreed definition in international law although the UN has for the purpose of a Bulletin stated that the term sexual exploitation "means any actual or attempted abuse of a position of vulnerability, differential power, or trust, for sexual purposes, including, but not limited to, profiting monetarily, socially or politically from the sexual exploitation of another. Similarly, the term 'sexual abuse' means the actual or threatened physical intrusion of a sexual nature, whether by force or under unequal or coercive conditions" (UN Secretariat 2003, Section 1). We draw on this in the context of this particular typology—sexual exploitation committed by peacekeepers—and note that includes provision of sexual services to peacekeeping forces through the means described in the bulletin, usually sent under the umbrella of the UN or NATO, or humanitarian workers. As aptly summarised by Mendelson the exploitation varies in severity. "It includes peacekeepers actually trafficking in humans, that is, transporting as well as buying and selling people as chattel. Lesser but more common forms of exploitation include payments—whether wittingly or unwittingly—to traffickers for sex with women and girls, females who were trafficked explicitly for that purpose" (Mendelson 2005, 3).

However, other reports—for example, that of the UN Office on Drugs and Crime (UNODC)—group sexual exploitation under one heading, no matter who commits it; the authors of this chapter, however, felt it necessary to single this type of exploitation as one in its own right particularly as it is more specific to conflict situations. Whilst it may on the surface look similar to other forms of sexual exploitation, the nuanced factors that lead to this form of exploitation are separate to, for example, an armed group committing sexual exploitation, and, thus, require separate responses.

A plethora of accounts can be read in Prince Al-Hussein's *Comprehensive Review* (2005), documenting how UN peacekeepers in Congo have engaged in sexual exploitation when they ought to have been protecting the vulnerable. Prior to Congo the international community confronted complaints in Cambodia (Angathangelou et al. 2003), East Timor (Smith 2017) and West Africa (Smith and Miller-De La Cuesta 2011). In summary it appears that the large supply of foreign forces brings a demand for sex workers that far exceeds the local supply, a supply that can be met with consenting workers but also with those who are victims of human trafficking (note: international law takes no particular position on prostitution per se). As summarised by Smith and Miller-De La Cuesta (2011, 291), "[w]ith the injection of a large, well-paid foreign force, the economic incentives to form and expand trafficking networks to service the increase in demand are both powerful in terms of magnitude and consistent across time and geographic location." In this respect, the structural economic, social and cultural vulnerabilities present in a patriarchal society may create an environment in which women and girls are particularly vulnerable to sexual exploitation from foreign forces.

Demand is one of the reasons that we can use to explain and describe the nature and extent of human trafficking for sexual exploitation as caused by peacekeepers and humanitarian workers. However, the *raison d'etre* behind this type of exploitation, as in all human trafficking cases, is multi-layered. Certainly, the imbalance of power coupled with immunity appear to play one of the major significant roles. Allred (2006, 8) writes that "[t]here is a perception among peacekeepers that they are immune from prosecution for crimes they may commit while deployed. In many cases, this is true." Further, there continues to be poor oversight as to the conduct of personnel, inadequate training and confusion over policy. Immunity in turn is rooted in a number of explanations: countries sending troops may be shamed by reports that they are committing crimes abroad, leading to the suppression of reports on such occurrences. Those that may wish to hold the perpetrators accountable are hindered by poor criminal investigations, incomplete evidence or even lack of adequate laws.

It is acknowledged that the majority of peacekeepers serve nobly, and their work is spoiled by those who commit the crime of human trafficking and exploit others. Fortunately, there is a growing recognition of the importance of the issue, at least in soft law, as evidenced by *UN Resolution 2242* (2015), which states:

> [This resolution e]xpresses deep concern over continuing allegations of sexual exploitation and abuse by United Nations peacekeepers and non-United Nations forces, including military, civilian and police personnel, urges police and troop contributing countries to provide robust pre-deployment training on sexual exploitation and abuse and vetting of their peacekeeping personnel, to conduct swift and thorough investigations of their uniformed personnel and, if appropriate, to prosecute, and to inform the United Nations in a timely manner of the status and outcome of investigations, calls upon the United Nations to cooperate as appropriate and in a timely manner with national authorities, including courts responsible for investigating such allegations, when requested for that purpose, and requests United Nations troop- and police-contributing country meetings to address sexual exploitation and abuse whenever relevant and the United Nations Military Staff Committee to discuss these issues as part of its regular programme.

Other important steps have included NATO's *Zero Tolerance Policy* (2004), which prohibits NATO staff from engaging in or facilitating human trafficking. This is a much welcome development in international conflict practice for the cost of ignoring human trafficking by peacekeepers is too great, too great to the protection of human rights and human security.

Building on personal experience Chap. 7 looks at the peacekeeper and trafficking nexus in more detail; for now we provide one example below:

Example 1

In early 2004, The Independent, a British newspaper, sent journalist Kate Holt to Bunia in the Democratic Republic of Congo (DRC), where the United Nations has one of its largest peacekeeping operations (MONUC) with over 16,000 troops. During her interviews with the local population, Ms. Holt was told that UN peacekeeping personnel had sexually exploited and abused local women and girls. Shortly after receiving these reports, the Special Representative of the Secretary-General in charge of MONUC dispatched his officer in charge of conduct issues to Bunia to perform a fact-checking exercise into the allegations. She uncovered evidence that pointed to a widespread occurrence of sexual exploitation and abuse by UN peacekeeping personnel. These allegations marked a turning point in the UN Department of Peacekeeping Operations' (DPKO) response to allegations of sexual misconduct involving its personnel. (Shotton 2006, 97).

Trafficking for Sexual Exploitation: Armed Groups

The sexual exploitation of persons in conflict, predominantly but not only of women and girls, by armed groups has been widely reported (see, for instance, the report entitled "Destroyed from Within." Sexual violence against men and boys in Syria and Turkey by the All Survivors Project 2018). It concerns the exploitation or the prostitution of others or other forms of sexual exploitation, including forced marriage, forced impregnation, sexual slavery and sexual violence. Systematised and institutionalised human trafficking for the purpose of sexual exploitation is perpetrated by and within armed groups such as the Lord's Resistance Army in Uganda, ISIS, Boko Haram and Al-Shabaab. Indeed, the enslavement of human beings can be enshrined within the ideology of such groups. For instance, ISIS has produced pamphlets detailing why and how it is permissible to rape, attack and trade non-Muslim slaves, including young girls (Smith 2014). Human trafficking, which is often described as a clandestine crime, acted as a visible operational recruitment tool for ISIS to draw in new jihadists. ISIS' regulation and codification of sexual exploitation was expressed in its fatwa No. 64, issued in 29 January 2015. This followed the unequivocal justification of sexual enslavement presented in its pamphlet (December 2014) titled "Questions and Answers on Taking Captives and Slaves," and in volume 9 of its magazine, *Dabiq* (May 2015).

Sexual exploitation is not just a result of a demand for sex; often it is employed as a tactic of war, with widespread and deliberate sexual enslavement and rapes, committed by parties to an armed conflict. When used tactically as a form of combat, sexual exploitation dehumanises communities, creates societal divisions (e.g., victims being shunned in Yazidi communities) and creates fear and suffering amongst them. In doing so, it erodes the societal fabric by breaking up families and even whole communities. In some cases, it serves as a form of genocide in which perpetrators target members of a particular ethnic group and forcibly impregnate the women to change the community's demographics. Sexual exploitation, in all forms, affects communities long term, often in ways that traditional weapons do not.

First and foremost, like all forms of human trafficking, sexual exploitation is a human rights violation. In addition, it also presents a significant human security issue. The power imbalances that are present within conflict zones coupled with the breakdown of the rule of law create conditions in which sexual exploitation can take place with impunity. Moreover, a wider array of human insecurity issues are present in conflict settings rendering civilians particularly vulnerable to exploitation. For instance, where social and economic security is undermined, opportunistic actors (civil and military alike) take advantage. In this respect we can identify a nexus between human insecurity and the perpetration of sexual exploitation. Ultimately, human insecurity begets human insecurity. The harms that arise from such exploitation not only cause obvious impacts on victims, but they also undermine societal integrity as a whole, with structural gendered violence directly correlating with the outbreak of violence more generally. In this sense, we can recognise not only the personal human security impacts on victims, but the ways in which sexual exploitation cuts across the various categories of human insecurity and manifests itself in wider instability and conflict. As such, human security provides a valuable contribution to our understanding of human trafficking in conflict, due to the fact that it addresses human well-being within peace, crisis and conflict settings. Where it links such insecurity to instability and the outbreak or amplification of further harms, it provides for an understanding that insecurity that exists outside of conflict features prominently in the harms that arise from conflict.

Descriptions, images and accounts of sexual exploitation are widespread and can be found through an internet browser search. They can also be read in international law cases such as the case of *Prosecutor v. Kunarac* (more below). They may shock readers and can be a powerful communication, campaigning and lobbying tool. However, they will not be repeated here; instead, we ask our readers to consider the magnitude of this practice through the lens of UN resolutions:

Resolution 63/156 on trafficking in women and girls

- "Calls upon Governments, the international community and all other organizations and entities that deal with conflict and post-conflict, disaster and other emergency situations to address the heightened vulnerability of women and girls to trafficking and exploitation, and associated gender-based violence"
- "Encourages Governments, relevant intergovernmental bodies and international organizations to ensure that military, peacekeeping and humanitarian personnel deployed in conflict, post-conflict and other emergency situations are provided training on conduct that does not promote, facilitate or exploit trafficking in women and girls, including for sexual exploitation, and to raise the awareness of such personnel of the potential risks to victims of conflict and other emergency situations, including natural disasters, of being trafficked"

Resolution 2331 on the maintenance of international peace and security

- "further recognizing that trafficking in persons in armed conflict and post-conflict situations can also be associated with sexual violence in conflict"
- "recognizing the connection between trafficking in persons, sexual violence and terrorism and other transnational organized criminal activities"

- "furthermore emphasizes that survivors should benefit from relief and recovery programmes, including health care, psychosocial care, safe shelter livelihood support and legal aid and that services should include provision for women with children born as a result of wartime rape, as well as men and boys who may have been victims of sexual violence in conflict, including when it is associated with trafficking in persons in armed conflict"
- "condemns also any such trafficking in persons and violations and other abuses committed by Boko Haram, Al-Shabaab, the Lord's Resistance Army, and other terrorist or armed groups for the purpose of sexual slavery, sexual exploitation, and forced labour"

Resolution 2253 on the threats to international peace and security caused by terrorist acts.

"Condemning in the strongest terms abductions of women and children by ISIL, ANF, and associated individuals, groups, undertakings, and entities and recalling resolution 2242 (2015), expressing outrage at their exploitation and abuse, including rape, sexual violence, forced marriage, and enslavement by these entities".

Trafficking of Children into Armed Groups and for Forced Labour

The trafficking of children into armed groups and for forced labour during conflict is a violation of international human rights and humanitarian law. This violation is enshrined in various international documents including the *Convention on the Rights of the Child* (CRC) and the *Rome Statute of the International Criminal Court*, as well as various UN Security Council Resolutions. *The Cape Town Principles of 1997* define a "child soldier" as "any person under 18 years of age who is part of any kind of regular or irregular armed force or armed group in any capacity, including but not limited to cooks, porters, messengers and anyone accompanying such groups, other than family members" (UN Children's Fund 1997). The definition also includes girls recruited for sexual purposes and for forced marriage (UN Children's Fund 1997). Thus, a child does not necessarily need to be involved directly in conflict through an official combat role for a violation to take place.

Although widely accepted as a violation of human rights and humanitarian law, children continue to be trafficked into armed groups for combat and support roles, for sexual purposes and for forced labour, on a global scale. Indeed, armed groups operating in Myanmar, Sierra Leone, Colombia and Syria to name a few (Haer et al. 2019, 2) recruit children for active combat and support roles. The literature indicates that children are recruited by armed groups for a variety of different reasons. Sometimes because the group has a shortage of troops, they recruit children to increase numbers and, thus, maintain a military advantage and prolong the conflict. In addition, it is considered that children are cost-effective as they are "cheaper to feed, clothe and are satisfied with a disproportionate share of resources" (Haer et al. 2019, 4). It is also considered that they are more likely to remain loyal to armed groups and, thus, are less likely to desert (Ibid). Other times, children are used in conflict as a conscious strategy and tactic of war, to shock and destabilise the community.

The acts of ISIS in Syria are a particularly atrocious example, as they have also captured children as young as 12 to "undergo military training to join the front lines of combat, while some are deployed as human shields or made to patrol ISIL checkpoints" (US State Department 2015, 1). It is important to note, however, that other groups in Syria have also relied on child soldiers such as the Free Syrian Army, Jabhat Fateh Al-Sham and the Kurdish People's Protection Units (Johnson and Soroka 2018, 245).

According to a recent study by van der Haer et al. (2019), rebel groups that profit from natural resources are significantly more likely to forcibly recruit children than groups that do not exploit natural resources. The type of resource also has an impact, with "lootable resources, that are relatively easy to access and extract" increasing the demand for low-cost unskilled labourers which children are easily able to fill (van der Haer et al. 2019, 2). Van der Haer Haer, Faulkner and Whitaker argue that this is due to the fact that groups that profit from natural resources are less dependent on civilian populations to support them in their war effort. For this reason, they "tend to be less accountable to local communities and suffer fewer costs for abusing civilians" (2019, 5). This is particularly evident in Sierra Leone, Angola and the DRC, which are areas rich in natural resources and where children are recruited to work in mines and to traffic lootable resources such as gold, diamonds and timber to make money to support their activities (van der Haer et al. 2019, 7).

Corruption levels and economic opportunities may also impact the likelihood of children being recruited in conflict zones. Indeed, if there is a high level of impunity or if a group is receiving support from a foreign government, they are less likely to encounter repercussions (such as sanctions or prosecutions) and, thus, more likely to traffic children into armed groups and into forced labour (Bahgat et al. 2017).

Example 2: The case of *The Prosecutor v. Bosco Ntaganda*

In 2006, the International Criminal Court issued a warrant of arrest for Bosco Ntaganda who had been the Deputy Chief of Staff and commander of operations of the armed group *Union des Patriotes Congolais/Forces Patriotiques pour la Libération du Congo* (UPC/FPLC) operating in Democratic Republic of the Congo's province Ituri (The Prosecutor v. Bosco Ntaganda 2019, para 252). His alleged crimes were numerous and included crimes relating to the *enlistment, conscription, and the use of child soldiers under the age of 15 and using them to participate actively in hostilities* (The Prosecutor v. Bosco Ntaganda 2019, para 178).

In July 2019, he was found "guilty, beyond reasonable doubt of 18 counts of war crimes and crimes against humanity" (The Prosecutor v. Bosco Ntaganda 2019). Amongst these 18 counts, Mr. Ntaganda was found "responsible as an indirect co-perpetrator for conscripting and enlisting children under the age of 15 years into the UPC/FPLC between on or about 6 August 2002 and 31 December 2003 and for using children under the age of 15 to participate actively in hostilities between on or about 6 August 2002 and 30 May 2003" (The Prosecutor v. Bosco Ntaganda 2019, para 178). He was also found guilty of using children as bodyguards as well as using them to gather information about opposing forces (The Prosecutor v. Bosco Ntaganda 2019, para 178).

In its judgement the Chamber of the ICC indicated that "the UPC/FPLC imposed an obligation on families to provide one or several 'children' for military service, including by threatening them" (The Prosecutor v. Bosco Ntaganda 2019, para 181). Many children under the age of 15 were shot at, injured or killed on the battlefield. They also found it difficult to flee the battlefield after having been defeated, because of the weight of their uniforms and weapons (The Prosecutor v. Bosco Ntaganda 2019, para 181).

Trafficking for the Purpose of Slavery or Practices Similar to Slavery

Slavery is outlawed under the *jus cogens* principles of international law—fundamental, overriding principles from which derogation is never permitted. In conflict and in peace, slavery has been outlawed longer than human trafficking, and it is important to note that the two are not interchangeable. The definition of slavery has its own long history, tied to socio-political issues that led to the adoption of the 1926 *League of Nations Slavery Convention* (Forclaz 2015, 398). In the *Slavery Convention* of 1926 slavery is defined as "the status or condition of a person over whom any or all of the powers attaching to the right of ownership are exercised." The *Rome Statute*, which establishes the International Criminal Court and gives it jurisdiction over the most serious crimes of concern to the international community, includes crimes against humanity, which in turn include enslavement when committed as part of a widespread or systematic attack directed against any civilian population, with knowledge of the attack.

The definition of human trafficking includes slavery or practices similar to slavery as examples of exploitation; that is, trafficking is a process in which slavery can be the final step, and so slavery is either one of the purposes of human trafficking or a stand-alone crime.

With regard to slavery in conflict, much can be read today about the enslavement of the Yazidi women who were forced into what slavery—bought, sold or given at will. Likewise, is the case with regard to crimes committed by Boko Haram, who abducted and forced women and children into sexual slavery in Nigeria. The violent and exploitative crime of human trafficking for the purposes of slavery can also be found in the International Criminal Tribunal for the former case of *Prosecutor v. Kunarac* (2012).

Example 3

In this case the Trial Chamber confirmed that slavery does not require the purchase/trade of a person for a value, but instead "the court said that slavery was indicated by, say, the restriction or control of an individual's autonomy, freedom of choice, or freedom of movement and, often, the accruing of some gain to the perpetrator" (Turner 2015, 297). In the words of the Court, indications of enslavement include elements of control and ownership. With regard to Kunarac, he took two girls to an abandoned house; these girls were forced to do anything that the soldiers ordered them to do, they were kept in the house to be used for sex and they performed household chores for the soldiers whilst under captivity and had no control over their lives. In effect the Trial Chamber found that they were treated as personal property (Prosecutor v. Kunarac, Kovac and Vukovic, para. 738–742).

Trafficking for the Purpose of Extorting Ransom

Van Reisen and Rijken (2015) categorised human trafficking for ransom in academic literature, highlighting the practice in Sinai where trafficking takes place through torture for the purpose of extorting ransom. The authors write: "although trafficking is a crime often related to other crimes, the interconnectedness of the Sinai Trafficking with torture and other cruel and inhumane practices including sexual violence seems more ingrained in the way hostages and Eritreans specifically are treated in Sinai. The systematic torture, the severity and range of human rights violations and the aim of the whole process (the payment of ransom through abduction and extortion) makes Sinai Trafficking a specific form of trafficking not noted on a similar scale anywhere else in the world" (Van Reisen and Rijken 2015, 118).

Example 4

"According to repeated accounts, groups of approximately 200–300 Eritreans are brought to Sinai where they are held in metal containers or compounds. Captives undergo torture by burning or beating, as smugglers call their relatives demanding the immediate transfer of funds to be guaranteed transit to the Israeli border. A consequence of the high ransom price is that it often takes weeks or even months for refugees to be taken to the border. It is during this time that women are separated from the group, detained in secluded rooms and subjected to repeated sexual acts, abuse, and rape at the hands of their captors" (Van Reisen and Rijken 2015, 114).

Trafficking for the Purpose of Forced Combat (Male and Female)

Exploitation for the purpose of forcing someone to act as a combatant is another identified form of human trafficking. It is separate to child soldiers in that it concerns adults (those who are above the age of 18), but aside from that it shares many traits, including the functions the persons are expected to fulfil. People are trafficked within and into conflict zones to fulfil a number of roles from front line fighters, to vehicle drivers, cooks or suicide bombers. As identified by the Global Initiative (date unknown): "Yazidi men and boys have been forced to become militants and even suicide bombers." It is not an unusual form of human trafficking but a complex one to recognise and acknowledge. Undeniably, for many it will be hard to acknowledge, particularly in the midst of tensions in conflict, that some people are fighting not out of choice but because of the means used to recruit them (means being the second key element of the definition of human trafficking—see Introduction). In cases where someone was forced to join an armed group through actual or threatened physical abuse, they should be considered victims of human trafficking. However, as the UNODC (2018, 17) recognises, "[c]omplications arise where more subtle means are used to recruit a person, in particular in the extremely complex context of modern-day terrorist-related conflict, in which ideological means are used to manipulate people and false promises are made to deceive potentially vulnerable people." In Chap. 11,

Muraszkiewicz explores how European policy makers and the judiciary ought to treat those persons who were recruited to join groups such as ISIS, and shows that often these persons are drafted in not by force but by means such as online grooming. In Chap. 5, readers will find an example of possible forced combatants emanating out of Russia. It is accepted that in this form of human trafficking, more than in others, it is particularly hard to determine if a person is a victim, and, thus, entitled to protection, or an adversary and, thus, criminally liable. That is why as explained by the UNODC (2018, 18) "[d]etermining whether a person who joins (and is being, or is to be utilized by) an armed or terrorist group is a victim of trafficking requires careful consideration of the higher-order principles and purposes of the Trafficking in Persons Protocol." As Chaps. 5 and 11 provide examples of this type of human trafficking, below we reiterate the critical questions posed by the UNODC (2018, 18) when it comes to this form of human trafficking and in particular the means used. The questions impeccably reflect the complexity of this phenomenon:

- Are there any circumstances under which the method of imparting ideological propaganda could potentially be considered as amounting to deception as a means under the definition of trafficking in persons?
- Who is to say what is deceptive or not?
- Can the susceptibility to radicalisation of a young, impressionable mind be considered as abuse of power or of a position of vulnerability in cases where recruiters are in positions of power, for instance, because they are religious authorities or well-respected community leaders?
- Where a person is lured by promises of status or spiritual rewards, could this constitute a means of abuse of a position of vulnerability or of deception?
- What is the relevance or the veracity of such groups' belief systems and who is to establish it in the context of secular decision-making?
- If a man joins a terrorist group in order to feed his family, how dire does his family situation need to be in order for him to be considered a victim of trafficking in persons whose position of vulnerability has been exploited by a terrorist group? How viable do other options available to him need to be?

Trafficking for the Purpose of Removal of Organs (for Profit and for Injured Combatants)

Exploitation can also be for the purpose of the removal of organs, an element that only appeared towards the end of the drafting stage of the *2000 UN Protocol on Human Trafficking* (Travaux Préparatoires). A good legal source for understanding this crime is the *2014 Council of Europe Convention Against Trafficking in Human Organs*, which sets out different acts which are to be criminalised and summarises that that the Convention frames trafficking in organs as activities involving commercial transactions and lack of consent.

Trafficking in human beings for the purpose of removal of organs also occurs in conflict. Armed groups engage in this form of trafficking to help their own wounded fighters and also rely on it as a vital source of income. Cases have been reported during the Kosovo conflict (Radio Free Europe 2016) and researchers from US Berkley uncovered Fatwas (a ruling on a point of Islamic law given by a recognised authority) bearing ISIS insignia informing "ISIS combatants that harvesting organs from the bodies of the enemy-infidels or removing organs from living apostates, even if this might cause their death, was permissible" (Scheper-Hughes 2017, 168). Whilst the mere existence of the Fatwas is not proof that organ trafficking took place, stories of trafficking in human beings for the purpose of removal of organs have emerged in the press (see Example 5 below). Additionally, in 2015 the Iraqi ambassador, Mohamed Alhakim, pressed the Security Council to investigate the deaths of 12 doctors in Mosul, Iraq. He said they were killed after refusing to remove organs from bodies they were treating (Sanchez 2015).

In the case of Raïd one may ask if the case is one of trafficking, as he was paid. Yet a closer look at the definition, in particular the means used, allows us to understand why this may amount to trafficking. Raïd was deceived and his position of vulnerability was preyed upon, by those wanting to make a profit. Those responsible for the organ harvesting took advantage of Raïd's vulnerability, so that Raïd in reality was unable to make a reasonable decision. Here we see a clear example of how

Example 5

Raïd (19 at the time) "fled the embattled city of Aleppo, in Syria, to Lebanon with his parents and six siblings. The family quickly ran out of money in the capital, Beirut. Raïd heard from a relative that the solution could be to sell one of his kidneys ... Raïd had no trouble selling his left kidney because he was fit and didn't smoke. He played for the Syrian national youth soccer team. During the examinations doctors told him lies evidently meant to calm him down. With a little luck, the kidney would grow back, he was told, and there wouldn't be any after-effects. He got $7000 (€5200) for his kidney ... Raïd, sitting in the back of the car [with Abu Hussein, employed by a gang that works in the human organ trade], was feeling unwell." His kidney had been cut out from the front, seven days ago. "I need the drugs. You said you would get me the drugs," he said to Abu Hussein who just minutes earlier had been bragging how well his organisation took care of the Syrians. But when Raïd asks for painkillers, Abu Hussein shouts at him: "Shut up. I don't care if you die. You're finished anyway" (Putz 2013).

vulnerability and exploitation are interconnected; Hill (1994, 686) defined vulnerability as a "disposition of personality or circumstance of life that serve to hamper the rational-emotive process."

Conclusion and Feminist Critiques of a Conflict Focus on Human Trafficking

As a conclusion, the authors wish to acknowledge that putting together a typology of human trafficking in conflict settings does run a risk of presenting human trafficking as a phenomenon that exists in conflict, without addressing the prevalence of human trafficking and gendered violence in domestic spheres. Moreover, given the fact that the majority of conflicts occur within the Global South, these may present a depiction of these abuses existing as a problem for "uncivilised others," prompting little self-reflection on the part of states in the Global North (Cockburn 2004). Nevertheless, as highlighted above, human trafficking is exacerbated by vulnerabilities; these vulnerabilities may manifest in particular ways within conflict settings. As such, the development of a typology specifically dedicated to human trafficking in the conflict does provide a useful tool for understanding how harms may manifest and the particular vectors of vulnerability. Despite this, any attempt to actively address these issues should not treat human trafficking as unique to conflict and provide a merely reactive response. Rather, they should be identified as part of a holistic response that aims to prevent and alleviate the conditions that drive and permit human trafficking (whether this arises out of political, economic or social issues). These human security dynamics and necessary responses will be addressed in greater detail in the final chapter of this book.

References

Allred, Keith J. 2006. Peacekeepers and Prostitutes: How Deployed Forces Fuel the Demand for Trafficked Women and New Hope for Stopping It. *Armed Forces & Society* 33 (1): 5–23.

Angathangelou, Anna M., Anna M. Agathangelou, and L.H.M. Ling. 2003. Desire Industries: Sex Trafficking, UN Peacekeeping, and the Neo-liberal World Order. *The Brown Journal of World Affairs* 10 (1): 133–148.

Bahgat, Karim, et al. 2017. Children and Armed Conflict: What Existing Data Can Tell Us. *Peace research institute Oslo.*

Cockburn, Cynthia. 2004. *The Continuum of Violence: A Gender Perspective on War and Peace.* https://california.universitypressscholarship.com/view/10.1525/california/9780520230729.001.0001/upso-9780520230729-chapter-2

Forclaz, Amalia Ribi. 2015. *Humanitarian Imperialism: The Politics of Anti-Slavery.* Oxford: Oxford Scholarship Online.

Haer, Roos, Christopher Michael Faulkner, and Beth Elise Whitaker. 2019. Rebel Funding and Child Soldiers: Exploring the Relationship Between Natural Resources and Forcible Recruitment. *European Journal of International Relations*: 1–27.

Hill, John Lawrence. 1994. Exploitation. *Cornell Law Review* 79: 631–699.

Human Rights Watch Report. 2014. *The Power These Men Have Over Us, Sexual Exploitation and Abuse by African Union Forces in Somalia.* https://www.hrw.org/report/2014/09/08/power-these-men-have-overus/sexual-exploitaon-and-abuse-african-union-forces

Johnson, Whitman, and Sparwasser Soroka. 2018. Prevent to Protect: Early Warning, Child Soldiers, and the Case of Syria. *Global Responsibility to Protect* 10 (1–2): 239–259.

Mendelson, Sarah Elizabeth. 2005. *Barracks and Brothels: Peacekeepers and Human Trafficking in the Balkans*. Csis.

NATO. 2004. *NATO Policy on Combating Trafficking in Human Beings*. https://www.nato.int/docu/comm/2004/06-istanbul/docu-traffic-app1.htm

Putz, Ulrike. 2013. *Syrian Refugees Sell Organs to Survive*. https://www.spiegel.de/international/world/organ-trade-thrives-among-desperate-syrian-refugees-in-lebanon-a-933228.html#targetText=A%20young%20man%20Syrian%20refugee,illegal%20organ%20trade%20in%20Lebanon.&targetText=The%20young%20man%2C%20who%20called,%2C%20wasn't%20doing%20well.&targetText=He%20said%20he's%20employed%20by,organ%20trade%20%2D%20specializing%20in%20kidneys

Radio Free Europe. 2016. *Kosovo War Crimes Prosecutor Pledges Impartial Probe*. https://www.rferl.org/a/kosovo-war-crimes-prosecutor-vows-impartiality/27991400.html

Sanchez, Ray. 2015. *United Nations Investigates Claim of ISIS Organ Theft*. https://edition.cnn.com/2015/02/18/middleeast/isis-organ-harvesting-claim/

Scheper-Hughes, Nancy. 2017. Neo-Cannibalism and ISIS: Organs and Tissue Trafficking During Times of Political Conflict and War. *ELPAT Congress Proceedings*.

Shotton, Anna. 2006. A Strategy to Address Sexual Exploitation and Abuse by United Nations Peacekeeping Personnel. *Cornell Int'l LJ* 39: 97.

Smith, Amelia. 2014. ISIS Publish Pamphlet on How to Treat Female Slaves. *Newsweek*. https://www.newsweek.com/isis-release-questions-and-answers-pamphlet-how-treat-female-slaves-290511

Smith, Sarah. 2017. Accountability and Sexual Exploitation and Abuse in Peace Operations. *Australian Journal of International Affairs* 71 (4): 405–422.

Smith, Charles Anthony, and Brandon Miller-De La Cuesta. 2011. Human Trafficking in Conflict Zones: The Role of Peacekeepers in the Formation of Networks. *Human Rights Review* 12 (3): 287–299.

The Global Initiative. n.d. *Connecting Human Trafficking and Conflict*. http://globalinitiative.net/human-trafficking-conflict/

The Prosecutor v. Bosco Ntaganda, ICC-01/04–02/06, ICC Trial Chamber IV, November 7, 2019.

Turner, Ian. 2015. Human Rights, Positive Obligations, and Measures to Prevent Human Trafficking in the United Kingdom. *Journal of Human Trafficking* 1 (4): 296–317.

UN Children's Fund (UNICEF). 1997. The Cape Town Principles and Best Practices, Adopted at the Symposium' on the Prevention of Recruitment of Children into the Armed Forces and on Demobilization and Social Reintegration of Child Soldiers in Africa.

UN Secretariat. 2003. *Special Measures for Protection from Sexual Exploitation and Sexual Abuse.* https://www.unhcr.org/protection/operations/405ac6614/secretary-generals-bulletin-special-measures-protection-sexual-exploitation.html

United Nations Office on Drugs and Crime (UNODC). 2018. *Travaux Préparatoires of the Negotiations for the Elaboration of the United Nations Convention against Organized Crime and the Protocols Thereto.* https://www.unodc.org/unodc/en/treaties/CTOC/travaux-preparatoires.html

US State Department. 2015. Modern Slavery as a Tactic in Armed Conflicts, Civilian Security, Democracy, and Human Rights, Office to Monitor and Combat Trafficking in Persons Washington, Washington DC, US. https://2009-2017.state.gov/documents/organization/250876.pdf

Van Reisen, Mirjam, and Conny Rijken. 2015. Sinai Trafficking: Origin and Definition of a New Form of Human Trafficking. *Social Inclusion* 3 (1): 113–124.

Julia Muraszkiewicz is a Senior Research Manager at Trilateral Research in the Applied Research and Innovation team and was the research lead of Project Solebay looking at risk assessment methodologies for human trafficking in conflict. She has a publication with Palgrave Macmillan on protecting trafficked persons from liability. Julia in her spare time volunteers with NGOs that directly help victims of human trafficking and labour exploitation. She has a PhD in Law from Vrije University of Brussels.

Olivia Iannelli is a research analyst at Trilateral Research; she holds an LLM in International Human Rights and Humanitarian Law and her expertise lies in Human Trafficking, Children's Rights and Conflict. She has worked for a variety of human rights organisations both in the UK and abroad, including Amnesty International, the Council for At-Risk Academics and Leaders of Tomorrow in Jordan. She also volunteers for ECPAT UK.

Peter Wieltschnig is a research analyst at Trilateral Research. He holds an LLB in Law & Human Rights and an LLM in International Humanitarian Law. He has experience working within human rights research as he has a background in criminal defence work in the north of Ireland. His research interests relate to the protection of economic, social and cultural rights in armed conflict.

3

Unavoidable Exploitation? Conflict, Agency and Human Trafficking

Alicia Kidd

Introduction

This chapter's analysis of conflict and human trafficking argues that conflict's impact on agency increases the risk of being trafficked.

While there is a wealth of research within the social sciences which investigates conflict, and considerable literature focusing on human trafficking, there is little concentrating on the nexus between the two that contemplates whether conflict affects the risk of being trafficked. The research that does exist, and which considers victim experiences, focuses predominantly on child soldiers and post-conflict zones. In order to provide an accurate overview of the literature, this chapter discusses the experiences of both adults and children as victims of human trafficking related to conflict. Initially, the focus is on child soldiers as victims of human trafficking; attention then turns to post-conflict zones in which both adults and children are at risk of being trafficked.

A. Kidd (✉)
Wilberforce Institute, University of Hull, Hull, UK
e-mail: alicia.kidd@hull.ac.uk

J. Muraszkiewicz et al. (eds.), *Human Trafficking in Conflict*, Crime Prevention and Security Management, https://doi.org/10.1007/978-3-030-40838-1_3

This chapter draws upon literature to provide an overview of what human trafficking looks like in the context of armed conflict. It also uses examples from recent in-depth interviews about the experiences of people fleeing conflict, offering insight into the lived experiences of conflict-related human trafficking.[1]

The chapter then turns to agency to argue that conflict restricts the choices available, leaving people to choose between limited options which are commonly all imbued with risk. Whilst their choices may all be undesirable, people do exercise agency within the narrow range of options available to them, and some of these choices will lead to exploitation. As such, the chapter argues that victimhood and agency should not be understood as a binary, but on a spectrum.

Victims of Human Trafficking in Conflict Zones

A significant proportion of the literature that considers the victims of conflict-related trafficking focuses on child soldiers. While initial interpretations of child soldiers may be of boys with guns fighting on the front line, child soldiers can be boys or girls, and are not limited to combatant roles. The term 'child soldier' refers to:

> any person under 18 years of age who is part of any kind of regular or irregular armed force in any capacity, including but not limited to cooks, porters, messengers, and those accompanying such groups, other than purely as family members. It includes girls recruited for sexual purposes and forced marriage. It does not, therefore, only refer to a child who is carrying or has carried arms. (UNICEF 1997, 1)

Children are recruited in several ways: via force, offers of payment, or even 'volunteering'. These methods are summarised below, emphasising the impact that conflict has on the agency of these recruits. Regardless of

[1] The interviews were undertaken by the author as part of a larger research project identifying the links between conflict and contemporary slavery. Excerpts from interviews have been included here with permission from respondents. All references to respondents use pseudonyms.

the reason that a child becomes a soldier, conflict has left them in a situation where there is little alternative.

Recruitment of Child Soldiers

The forced abduction and recruitment of children into armed forces and groups is well documented, and there are examples of children being kidnapped, or even threatened with murder for refusing to join (David 1998; UNICEF 2002; Human Rights Watch and Brett 2003; UN Department of Economic and Social Affairs 2005; Schmidt 2007). The Lord's Resistance Army (LRA) in Uganda has been widely cited as using force and kidnapping to recruit child soldiers (Human Rights Watch 1997; Schmidt 2007). A recent interview provided an example of a young girl, Beth, kidnapped to be a 'wife' of a commander:

> And like a lot of people from that area, the LRA had come and taken all the children, the boys to be soldiers and the girls to be wives in the LRA. Beth had been quite young when that had happened and been abducted. And she'd lived as the wife of an LRA commander for about four years.

Some children are recruited on promises of payment (Coalition to End the Use of Child Soldiers 2001; UNICEF 2002). When conflict impacts on their family's ability to support itself because of a resulting lack of employment prospects, the opportunity for a child to generate an income is hugely desirable, but for many the payment never materialises. In some circumstances, child soldiers *are* paid a wage; for example, children in Colombia are recruited into the armed forces and paid 900,000–1,200,000 pesos (US$267–350) every three months (Human Rights Watch and Brett 2003). This is an attractive offer for war and poverty-stricken children and their families. However, as O'Connell Davidson (2015) states, "the fact of payment does not signal the presence of freedom."

While accessing accurate statistics is extremely difficult, 'volunteering' is a key method of recruitment for child soldiers (Dumas and de Cock 2003; Sesay 2003; Aning and McIntyre 2005). Wars alter both the social and economic roles of children, whose vulnerability to trafficking heightens if they have also suffered poverty, the death of parents, if they are runaways or live close to places with high demand for child labour or where armed forces or groups recruit new soldiers (Smucker and Murray 2004). If a child comes from a particularly impoverished area where food, employment and safe shelter are scarce, their situation may be particularly desperate if they are also living in a conflict zone which risks their basic safety. Some children see that becoming a child soldier would at least provide them with food, accommodation and some degree of protection (Verhey 2001; Human Rights Watch and Brett 2003; UN Department of Economic and Social Affairs 2005). This is the case particularly for children who have been separated from their families and are living in abject poverty with a lack of social services and no one to care for them (Watchlist 2003).

In cases of forced abduction, children's agency is severely limited; they simply have no choice in their recruitment. The lines are more blurred regarding offers of payment and 'voluntary' recruitment, as there is a suggestion that the child *wanted* to become a child soldier. However, this decision should not be taken in isolation. In these scenarios, the child is choosing between two undesirable options: try and survive in a conflict zone with limited food, shelter and support, or become a child soldier which will offer a degree of protection from the conflict. The conflict restricts children's agency, leaving them to choose between limited options which are inherently dangerous (this is discussed further in the sections below).

This gives rise to the oft-debated discussion of whether children can truly make agentic decisions. In the west, children are commonly believed not to have full agency and are prevented from making certain decisions. This is done in the name of protection of the 'innocence' of childhood and sheltering children from their own 'naivety' and 'helplessness' (Shanahan 2007). However, childhood is not a universally equal concept (Buckingham 2000) and in situations of conflict agency is limited for all. In fact:

> There is no conclusive evidence that adults are significantly better at ex-ante evaluation of the consequences of participation in war and thus better able than children to make informed decisions to volunteer. (Schmidt 2007, 67)

It is also important to recognise that a child's consent in their exploitation is irrelevant in meeting the criteria of being defined as a victim of human trafficking (see below).

Experiences of Child Soldiers

After recruitment, children's agency as soldiers continues to be limited. They are recruited into a range of roles where they are controlled by the armed forces or groups and are often fearful of repercussions should they fail to obey instructions. Invariably, they live through hugely traumatic experiences and are involved in extremely violent actions, either as perpetrators or as witnesses.

Child soldiers are often starved, beaten or locked away as punishment or to make them compliant. David (1998) provides examples of children having their skin seared with burning plastic and open wounds being doused with pepper water if they hesitated to obey orders, all experiences that these children would not have suffered if not for conflict.

McKay and Mazurana (2004) discuss child soldiers in Uganda. Here, children tend to be abducted into the forces or groups, and their initiation involves committing atrocities against those from their communities: rape, torture, maiming and even murder. Children have been forced to murder their parents or threatened with murder themselves if they fail to laugh as their family is executed. Some are sent to kidnap other children, burn down houses, shoot weapons that are bigger than the children themselves, loot, rape, terrorise. These actions serve a double purpose: they initiate the children into the armed force or group and simultaneously destroy links between them and their families and communities. Their communities deem the actions of the child soldiers unforgiveable, making it difficult, if not impossible, for children to reintegrate back into civilian society should they escape or be permitted to leave. This evidences how a child's agency can be eroded throughout the whole experience of being a child soldier, from being abducted and forced to commit actions against their will, to removing their support networks should they find a way to leave.

There are examples of girls, taken as 'wives' to commanders, being rejected by their communities on their return. Some families do not believe that the children were forced into relationships with the commanders and consider them traitors (Newman 2014). This is especially true if girls have given birth to children fathered by commanders, children the family may refuse to accept as related. These girls often have no one to look after them, are abused by relatives, unable to provide for their children, have no permanent home and no access to education (Newman 2014). If these mothers have no one to support them and their children, they must work to support themselves. If their community has rejected them, they are likely to move elsewhere in search of work. With a lack of education and assistance, they become vulnerable to exploitative offers or drawn to return to the commanders who were exploiting them. These are all situations that exist as a direct impact of the conflict.

Child Soldiers as Victims of Human Trafficking

The Palermo Protocol (UN General Assembly 2000, 2) states that:

(a) "Trafficking in persons" shall mean the recruitment, transportation, transfer, harbouring or receipt of persons, by means of the threat or use of force or other forms of coercion, of abduction, of fraud, of deception, of the abuse of power or of a position of vulnerability or of the giving or receiving of payments or benefits to achieve the consent of a person having control over another person, for the purpose of exploitation. Exploitation shall include, at a minimum, the exploitation of the prostitution of others or other forms of sexual exploitation, forced labour or services, slavery or practices similar to slavery, servitude or the removal of organs;

(b) The consent of a victim of trafficking in persons to the intended exploitation set forth in subparagraph (a) of this article shall be irrelevant where any of the means set forth in subparagraph (a) have been used;

(c) The recruitment, transportation, transfer, harbouring or receipt of a child for the purpose of exploitation shall be considered "trafficking in persons" even if this does not involve any of the means set forth in subparagraph (a) of this article;
(d) "Child" shall mean any person under 18 years of age.

Child soldiers are children—under 18 years old—recruited by armed forces or groups to be exploited for the benefit of the armed force or group. They usually experience sexual exploitation (mostly girls: David 1998; Mazurana et al. 2002; Sommers 2002; Watchlist 2003; McKay and Mazurana 2004) or labour exploitation (both boys and girls: Thompson 1999; McKay and Mazurana 2004; Becker 2017). Therefore, they fit the definition of having been trafficked. The method of recruitment into the armed force or group is irrelevant in defining them as victims of human trafficking, meaning that they should be understood as such even if they 'volunteered' to become child soldiers.

Although many of the children may have been living with vulnerabilities, it is conflict that exacerbates these vulnerabilities to an extent that makes them susceptible to being recruited as soldiers. Equally, without conflict, child soldiers would not be required. As such, their risk of being trafficked for this purpose would likely be non-existent if not for the presence of conflict.

For children, the conflict-related risk of trafficking does not end with recruitment to armed forces or groups. The conflict continues to affect their lives in the long term as they lose their pre-war societal connections. Should they leave the armed force or group, children are often left to make a life for themselves with little or no support, making them vulnerable to potentially exploitative offers of assistance.

Victims of Human Trafficking in Post-Conflict Zones

The existing published research on victims of trafficking related to conflict focuses on child soldiers and post-conflict zones. Having summarised child soldiers, the following section considers how people—both adults and children—become vulnerable to trafficking in post-conflict zones. The literature highlights a range of issues leading to human trafficking in post-conflict situations including economic and political restructuring, corruption and poverty, as well as the vulnerabilities faced by refugees, internally displaced persons (IDPs) and children. The following section summarises some of the socio-economic and social group conditions that are common in post-conflict zones and how they can lead to human trafficking. These experiences should be considered by the military when entering a post-conflict zone.

Socio-Economic Circumstances

While structural transformations (when economic activity changes between sectors) can bring about required economic and political changes, oversights can be made regarding the impact they could have on citizens. Some transitions have led to gender or ethnically based reconstruction which, in providing employment for certain sectors of the community, causes others to become vulnerable to human trafficking in a way they would not have been without the impact of conflict. Limanowska (2005) illustrates how structural economic changes in conflict zones can generate new vulnerabilities. From the mid-1990s, the transition from centrally planned to market economies in southeastern Europe, which occurred alongside conflicts in several countries, disrupted numerous societies. The resulting economic reforms were not accompanied by social policy measures and failed to anticipate the changes they would cause in social dynamics. The transitions led to the emergence of new vulnerable groups: unemployed women, unemployed youth and Roma; traffickers then had new vulnerabilities to exploit.

Cucumanova (2010) reviews Soviet states to identify how restructuring in post-conflict areas could generate new conflicts. The Soviet National Migration Policy developed social-political competition between former Soviet states over control of local power structures. This led to civil wars and ethnic conflicts in several of the new republics.

Tajikistan was hit by violent conflict in 1992, leading to the emigration of 300,000 Tajiks and 692,000 becoming internally displaced; this was in addition to the pre-existing poor security and economic conditions. The Tajiks commonly paid people to help them escape, believing them to be smugglers but discovering them to be traffickers. This exemplifies how conflict can impact agency and limit the choices of the affected populations; they must either escape in the hope of finding peace and security or wait in the conflict zone. Either choice makes them vulnerable as the mortality rate of displaced persons is second perhaps only to those who remain where the violence occurs (Bellamy 2017). In such a situation, neither choice can offer guaranteed safety and, in trying to find paid work or safety, there is an inherent risk of accepting offers from people who intend to profit from the exploitation of others.

Corruption is another factor that is rife in post-conflict zones and can impact upon agency. Human Rights Watch (2002) claims that police and government corruption in post-conflict Bosnia and Herzegovina allowed trafficking to flourish, with the Bosnian government failing, with few exceptions, to prosecute police officers directly involved in human trafficking. With government corruption being driven by organised crime (Picarelli 2002), criminals can infiltrate political and legal systems, finding people who will accept a cut of their profit in return for turning a blind eye to their crimes. In post-conflict areas, this can be relatively effortless because the difficult living situations and extreme poverty create a need for money that exceeds the desire for justice. Relatedly, conflict has the potential to increase the number of traffickers who, like victims, are trying to survive with limited options. This is particularly true in post-conflict areas where employment opportunities are scarce and poverty is rife, leading some to envisage their survival in the exploitation of others (Martens et al. 2003). The restriction of agency limits legitimate options, leading some to exploit others in order to survive themselves, and leaving others vulnerable to this exploitation with no reliable authority to turn to for support. The social breakdown caused by conflict makes it easier for traffickers to operate because the underlying factors that cause human trafficking are exacerbated and corruption allows it to be tolerated.

Social Group Circumstances

It is not only socio-economic conditions that can encourage human trafficking in post-conflict zones. For some, the circumstances of their social group can increase their vulnerabilities. For example, in post-conflict societies, parents commonly choose not to send their children to school, believing that schools are unsafe (de Watteville 2002). Land mines, military gangs and fear of rape encourage many children to stay at home rather than risk walking to school (Sommers 2002). Further, many returning child soldiers are unable to attend school because even though the school is free, their books and uniforms have been stolen or destroyed with no money to replace them. Alternatively, schools may have been closed because of rebels, or families may have been displaced to an area without schools. Other children choose not to return because they are ashamed to have to be in classes with younger children due to the schooling they missed because of their time as child soldiers (McKay and Mazurana 2004). This lack of schooling is a direct result of conflict which leaves children uneducated and naive to offers of people who may exploit them.

IDPs and refugees also suffer disproportionately as a result of conflict. The vulnerabilities they face because of war with no fixed home, secure income, legal security or confirmed future place them at severe risk of accepting the offers of people seeking to profit from their exploitation. A good example from an interview is the case of Tara who became an IDP as a result of conflict. Her circumstances as an IDP increased her vulnerabilities, and she was trafficked into sexual exploitation.

Tara became an IDP in Nigeria as a result of war. She had left everything behind, had no one to support her and job opportunities were scarce. She needed to find a way to support herself and was approached by an older woman offering her work; Tara accepted the offer, working as a cleaner for a few months. "And then the woman said I'll send you to an aunty in England and you can earn a bit more money from going abroad." Tara had no family, no secure home, and was faced with poverty, so she gratefully accepted this offer. She travelled to the UK to meet her new employer where she was forced into a brothel and kept in sexual exploitation for around nine months before managing to escape.

Refugees and IDPs are particularly vulnerable in post-conflict situations. Any pre-existing vulnerabilities are exacerbated by the conflict, which commonly restricts the options available to them and leads to poor living conditions, gender inequality, a lack of basic healthcare or education, poverty, xenophobia, a lack of security and unemployment. Particularly when there are large numbers of people in the same situation, they will likely find themselves competing for living spaces or employment opportunities. These conditions encourage people to take risks that they otherwise would not, such as looking to escape the problems by moving away. However, language barriers and a lack of awareness of migration rules can make them vulnerable to human trafficking. Traffickers can make offers of jobs in safe countries, offers that are too good not to accept. While some of those who accept these jobs may have concerns around the legitimacy of the offers, they are really left with little choice but to take the risk.

Conflict and Agency

Understandings of human trafficking often revert to an assumption that all agency must have been removed from the victim (O'Connell Davidson 2013) and that their choices leading up to the trafficking situation must have played no part in the outcome. While some victims of trafficking, like Beth, who was kidnapped by the LRA and kept as a 'wife' of a commander, have no agency in the lead-up to their trafficking experience, others have some level of choice in the decisions that lead towards their exploitation. This could be, for example, by choosing to accept a precarious job offer, or accepting the advances of a stranger who claims to be able to provide help. For some, their decisions may lead to safety, but for others the decisions could result in trafficking.

While it is clear that there is an element of agency in these situations, it is also evident that such decisions are not unconstrained. It is unlikely that if a person had a safe and stable life and was able to make an entirely free decision, that they would risk making unpredictable decisions with a high risk of danger in order to improve their living conditions. However, conflict limits agency, and while it may be a choice to accept that precarious job offer or the assistance of a stranger, the options available to them have been reduced significantly by conflict. For some it is a choice between staying in a village where there is no food, no employment opportunities and no one to support them, or making those risky decisions in the hope of a safer life. While this is a choice, it is the lesser of two evils and does not overwrite their status as a victim of human trafficking should they find themselves in a situation of exploitation.

The discussion of agency here rests on whether a person's decision that leads them towards a situation of human trafficking can be considered truly voluntary in the sense of asking whether they would make the same decision if they were not faced with poverty, violence, a lack of job opportunities, a lack of safe shelter and a breakdown in their support systems. In many of these situations, the decisions made in these scenarios are the same that any reasonable person would make in the same circumstances, but not decisions that would be made if they were living in a safe and stable environment with true autonomy.

The Victim/Agent Spectrum

There are significant flaws associated with the tendency to understand victims of human trafficking on a forced/voluntary or victim/agent binary, where only those with no agency and no level of choice leading to the situation are considered victims (Broad and Turnbull 2018). While, of course, there are examples of people who experience human trafficking as a result of a complete removal of agency, many victims have some level of agency and choice leading to their exploitation. Excerpts from interviews included below illustrate the existence of agency in a person's choices contributing to their trafficking situation.

Padma was from the Ivory Coast and was Dyula, a group targeted for their ethnicity in the Ivory Coast civil war. Her husband was a political activist who was murdered for expressing his views. Without her husband, Padma was left with no support; she had no other family and was directly at risk because of her ethnicity. Due to her vulnerability, she was approached by a man who offered to assist her in escaping the Ivory Coast, explaining that he could get her into the UK if she acted as his wife. The ethnic conflict and civil war had left Padma with little other choice; her options were to stay in the Ivory Coast where she had no support and would likely be killed, or take a risk by accepting this offer. She took the risk and posed as this man's wife, but when they arrived in the UK, it became clear that he had never intended to help her. The man locked Padma in a house and sexually exploited her for two years.

Padma's story illustrates how a person can have agency in making choices that lead to their exploitation, but that this agency is limited by conflict. Padma made the choice of accepting a stranger's offer to escape the war, but only because the conflict had reduced the legitimate options available to her after her husband was killed. Realistically, her choices were to stay and be killed, or risk a stranger's offer of help.

Andrea's story is another that demonstrates how a person can have agency but still become a victim of trafficking. She was born in Uganda where her parents were killed during the war. "She had moved to Kampala on her own. Was living in some kind of church type community, but she didn't have any family and was just told I can help you get a job abroad." Andrea was told that the job would be secretarial work in the UK, and she was keen to start. However, upon arrival, there was no job, and she was instead kept in a situation of domestic servitude.

Andrea's choices were also limited because of the conflict. If not for the war, her parents would have still been alive to support her, and she would not have needed to find a way to survive independently. As it was, being offered a job abroad provided the opportunity both to earn money and to escape the conflict. For her, the alternative was to stay in Uganda and do whatever she could to make enough money to survive and stay safe. If not for the conflict, it is unlikely that she would have accepted an offer of work abroad.

In scenarios like Padma's and Andrea's, forced and voluntary exist on a scale rather than as a binary; there is no black and white distinction between forced and voluntary trafficking situations, as a person's level of choice will depend on their circumstances. Both Padma's and Andrea's choices were constrained by conflict and they were both trafficked, yet they both had a degree of agency in the decisions they made leading up to their exploitation.

These notions of agency are not new concepts and relate to philosophical and psychological debates on free will and determinism. These debates question the extent to which anyone truly has free will or whether all decisions are constrained by outside forces from hormones, to parents, to structural conditions. In relation to this chapter, determinism would claim that all decisions made by people living through conflict would be constrained by the conflict, and that true free will is often simply unobtainable in a conflict situation. However, determinism exists in degrees and while behaviour may become predictable in the face of outside forces (like conflict), it is not necessarily certain.

In relation to human trafficking, O'Connell Davidson (2013) identifies this question of agency as the difference between autonomous and active choices. An active choice simply relates to someone making a decision; however, an autonomous choice means making a free decision without constraint. It is unlikely that in a conflict situation a person would have the opportunity to make a truly autonomous choice because of the huge restrictions that conflict places on their agency. The conflict may remove autonomy from a vast range of decisions, from where a person lives, to who they rely on for support, how much food they have, whether they are able to work, what work is available to them, and so on. While 'choosing' from a set of very limited or undesirable options is an act of agency, having this agency does not necessarily negate a person's status as a victim of human trafficking; victimhood and agency are not mutually exclusive.

Conclusion

This chapter argues that conflict leaves individuals in situations where they are faced with limited options, all of which hold inherent risk. Their choices could lead to an improved situation, but also hold the threat of leading to human trafficking. Trafficking does not always equate to a complete removal of agency, and while agency may exist to an extent, decisions are not autonomous because they are framed in the context of conflict, where conflict has restricted the available options. Understandings of human trafficking that place people as either victims or agents are unhelpful and fail to reflect the true, lived experiences of victims of trafficking. As such, this chapter encourages victimhood and agency to be understood on a spectrum as opposed to a binary.

By considering the specific way that conflict increases risk to trafficking by limiting a person's agency, this chapter expands on current knowledge of the links between conflict and trafficking, offering more than just examples of victimhood caused by conflict. By understanding the way that agency is impacted by conflict, it is possible to identify those most at risk of trafficking in conflict and post-conflict zones in order to prioritise intervention efforts and offers of support.

References

Aning, Kwesi, and Angela McIntyre. 2005. From Youth to Rebellion to Abduction: The Anatomy of Recruitment in Sierra Leone. In *Invisible Stakeholders – Children and War in Africa, Institute for Security Studies*, ed. Angela McIntyre, 67–86. Pretoria: Institute for Security Studies.

Becker, Jo. 2017. *Campaigning for Children. Strategies for Advancing Children's Rights*. California: Stanford University Press.

Bellamy, Alex. 2017. Safe Passage: An Integral Component of the Responsibility to Protect. *Beyond Slavery and Trafficking, OpenDemocracy*, March 3, 2017. https://www.opendemocracy.net/beyondslavery/safepassages/alex-bellamy/safe-passage-integral-component-of-responsibility-to-protect

Broad, Rosie, and Nick Turnbull. 2018. From Human Trafficking to Modern Slavery: The Development of Anti-Trafficking Policy in the UK. *European Journal on Criminal Policy and Research* 25 (2): 119–133.

Buckingham, David. 2000. *After the Death of Childhood: Growing Up in the Age of Electronic Media*. New York: Polity.

Coalition to End the Use of Child Soldiers (2001) *Child Soldiers Global Report*. London

Cucumanova, Vanya. 2010. *South Africa at the Crossroads of Human Trafficking: War-Pushed and Hope-Driven*. Southern African Catholic Bishop's Conference: Catholic Parliamentary Liaison Office. http://www.cplo.org.za/wp-content/uploads/2014/06/SA-at-the-Crossroads-of-Human-Trafficking.pdf

David, Kelly. 1998. *The Disarmament, Demobilisation and Reintegration of Child Soldiers in Liberia. 1994–1997. The Process and Lessons Learned.* New York: UNICEF.

de Watteville, Nathalie. 2002. Addressing Gender Issues in Demobilisation and Reintegration Programs. *World Bank Africa Region Working Paper Series* 33:1–35. http://citeseerx.ist.psu.edu/viewdoc/download?doi=10.1.1.548.2663&rep=rep1&type=pdf

Dumas, Laetitia, and de Cock, Michaëlle. 2003. *Wounded Childhood: The Use of Child Soldiers in Armed Conflict in Central Africa.* Geneva: International Organization for Migration. https://www.ilo.org/wcmsp5/groups/public/%2D%2D-ed_emp/%2D%2D-emp_ent/%2D%2D-ifp_crisis/documents/publication/wcms_116566.pdf

Human Rights Watch. 1997. *The Scars of Death – Children Abducted by the Lord's Resistance Army in Uganda.* New York: Human Rights Watch.

———. 2002. Hopes Betrayed: Trafficking of Women and Girls to Post-Conflict Bosnia and Herzegovina for Forced Prostitution. *Human Rights Watch* 14(9):1–75. https://www.hrw.org/reports/2002/bosnia/Bosnia1102.pdf

Human Rights Watch and Brett, Sebastian. 2003. *You'll Learn Not to Cry: Child Combatants in Colombia.* New York: Human Rights Watch.

Limanowska, Barbara. 2005. *Trafficking in Human Beings in South Eastern Europe.* Sarajevo: UNDP.

Martens, Jonathan, Pieczkowski, Maciej, and van Vuuren-Smyth, Bernadette. 2003. *Seduction, Sale and Slavery: Trafficking in Women and Children for Sexual Exploitation in Southern Africa.* 3rd edn. Pretoria: International Organization for Migration. http://www.unicef.org.mz/cpd/references/40-TraffickingReport3rdEd.pdf

Mazurana, Dyan, Susan McKay, Khristopher Carlson, and Janel Kasper. 2002. Girls in Fighting Forces and Groups: Their Recruitment, Participation, Demobilization, and Reintegration. *Peace and Conflict: Journal of Peace Psychology* 8 (2): 97–123.

McKay, Susan, and Dyan Mazurana. 2004. *Where Are the Girls? Girls in Fighting Forces in Northern Uganda, Sierra Leone and Mozambique: Their Lives During and After War.* Montreal: International Centre for Human Rights and Democratic Development.

Newman, Carter. 2014. No One to Stand by Us: Reintegrating Formerly Abducted Child-Mothers in Uganda. *Journal of Intervention and Statebuilding* 8 (4): 357–380.

O'Connell Davidson, Julia. 2013. Troubling Freedom: Migration, Debt and Modern Slavery. *Migration Studies* 1 (2): 176–195.

———. 2015. *The Margins of Freedom*. London: Palgrave Macmillan.

Picarelli, John T. 2002. Trafficking, Slavery and Peacekeeping: the Need for a Comprehensive Training Program. *A Conference Report Hosted by the Transnational Crime and Corruption Centre, American University and the UN Interregional Crime and Justice Research Institute*. Turin, May 9–10, 2002. http://traccc.gmu.edu/pdfs/publications/human_trafficking_publications/TIP&PKO_EWG_Report_Final.pdf

Schmidt, Alice. 2007. Volunteer *Child* Soldiers as Reality: a Development Issue for Africa. *New School Economic Review* 2 (1): 49–76.

Sesay, Amadu. 2003. *Civil Wars, Child Soldiers and Post Conflict Peace Building in West Africa*. Ibadan: College Press & Publishers.

Shanahan, Suzanne. 2007. Lost and Found: The Sociological Ambivalence Towards Childhood. *Annual Review of Sociology* 33: 407–428.

Smucker, Glenn R., and Gerald F. Murray. 2004. *The Uses of Children: A Study of Trafficking in Haitian Children*. Port-au-Prince: USAID.

Sommers, Marc. 2002. *Children, Education and War: Reaching Education for All (EFA). Objectives in Countries Affected by Conflict*. Washington, DC: The World Bank.

Thompson, Carol B. 1999. Beyond Civil Society: Child Soldiers as Citizens in Mozambique. *Review of African Political Economy* 26 (80): 191–206.

UN Department of Economic and Social Affairs. 2005. World Youth Report: Young People Today and in 2015. July 30, 2005, ST/ESA/301. New York: United Nations.

UN General Assembly. 2000. Protocol to Prevent, Suppress and Punish Trafficking in Persons, Especially Women and Children, Supplementing the UN Convention Against Transnational Organized Crime (15 November 2000, Res 55/25). http://www.ohchr.org/EN/ProfessionalInterest/Pages/ProtocolTraffickingInPersons.aspx

UNICEF. 1997. *Cape Town Annotated Principles and Best Practices*. April 30, 1997. Cape Town: UNICEF.

———. 2002. *Adult Wars, Child Soldiers. Voices of Children Involved in Armed Conflict in the East Asia and Pacific Region*. Bangkok: UNICEF East Asia and Pacific Regional Office.

Verhey, Beth. 2001. Child Soldiers: Preventing, Demobilizing and Reintegrating. *Africa Region Working Paper Series,* 23:1–31. http://web.worldbank.org/archive/website00523/WEB/PDF/CHILD_SO.PDF

Watchlist. 2003. *The Impact of Armed Conflict on Children in the Democratic Republic of Congo (DRC)*. New York: Watchlist.

Alicia Kidd is a postdoctoral researcher at the Wilberforce Institute, part of the University of Hull. Her PhD focused on identifying the links between conflict and contemporary slavery, and she continues to undertake research on exploitation, human trafficking and 'modern slavery.' Alicia also works with practitioners through her role as Vice Chair of the Humber Modern Slavery Partnership.

4

Human Trafficking, Conflict and Money Flows

Archana Kotecha

Introduction

Human trafficking is the third fastest growing form of crime globally and an extremely lucrative business estimated to be worth US$150 billion annually (ILO 2014, 13). Yet detecting the proceeds of trafficking-related crimes within existing anti-money laundering and counter-terrorist financing frameworks has proven difficult. One reason is that practitioners and policymakers lack a clear understanding of money flows from human trafficking. This shortfall is especially pronounced in the context of conflict situations. The local population of conflict zones and those on the fringes, living in precarious situations and in a perpetual state of fear, unable to work and earn money and often without access to necessities such as food or medicine, can be particularly susceptible to trafficking. Traffickers and organised crime groups view those living in areas where there is conflict or social instability as easy targets. Further, armed groups use trafficking as a

A. Kotecha (✉)
Liberty Shared, Hong Kong, Hong Kong
e-mail: Archaba@libertyshared.org

J. Muraszkiewicz et al. (eds.), *Human Trafficking in Conflict*, Crime Prevention and Security Management, https://doi.org/10.1007/978-3-030-40838-1_4

means to raise funds to advance their activities and/or as a tool to maintain control over the areas they occupy (UNODC 2018a, 11).

The importance of detection and disruption of money flows arising from trafficking crimes in areas of conflict arises as a direct consequence of the fact that conflict zones are likely to be areas where the rule of law is weak or non-existent. In situations where the legal system and supporting actors such as law enforcement agencies no longer function effectively it is unlikely that traditional methods of deterrence and redress such as investigation, arrest and prosecution under domestic law for crimes committed will be available. Identifying and following money flows from these crimes and subsequent actions such as asset freezes and seizures can be used as an effective tool to disrupt the actions of traffickers and to send a message that their actions have real life consequences. Ultimately, the proceeds of criminal enterprises involving trafficking are subject to anti-money laundering laws and controls. It follows therefore that any efforts to curb trafficking of vulnerable people in conflict must necessarily involve addressing the money that is generated by such activities and also highlighting the role of exploitation in global supply chains.

This chapter examines the nexus between human trafficking and conflict and connected financial flows, the challenges associated with identifying and disrupting financial flows connected to human trafficking crimes originating or occurring in or close to conflict affected areas and possible ways to address those challenges. To supplement the prevalent focus with the literature upon conflict in the Middle East and North Africa region (MENA), this chapter points its analytical lens more towards Southeast Asia, although not to the exclusion of the former. It is suggested herein that identifying illicit funds linked to trafficking in and around conflict zones provides an opportunity to identify and seize ill-gotten gains whilst also offering better insights into network characteristics and modus operandi. This approach offers complementarity to the criminal justice effort which focuses on the commission of the crimes and the experience of victims rather than accountability for proceeds of crime. Accountability of proceeds of crime and their seizure is essential for identification and disruption of trafficking networks and may also provide opportunities to identify victims and compensate them from seized assets.

Since the international standard definition of the crime of trafficking was coined in 2000, trafficking has often been talked about as a single crime when in fact it is a "crime of many crimes" (United Nations 2000). Trafficking and its related forms of exploitation are, in reality, the ultimate manifestation in many respects of offences of deceit, fraud, bribery, trespass, assault, battery, wage theft, money laundering, rape and many other crimes coupled with related coercive and deceptive practices carried out with the intention of exploiting and abusing vulnerable persons (Hoffman 2004, 80). Many of these crimes are already predicate offences that trigger the application of anti-money laundering laws. However, anti-trafficking efforts have until very recently focused on investigation and prosecution of the crime as defined in legal frameworks with a heavy focus on victim testimony (OSCE 2014, 16). Often, trafficking is perpetrated through highly organised criminal networks that sustain themselves through corruption (UNODC 2011) and money laundering (OSCE 2014, 12). Historically, the corruption and money laundering aspects that are so inherent to the offence of trafficking have not figured heavily into the prosecution of trafficking cases. It is only relatively recently that asset seizures and money laundering charges are being prosecuted in trafficking cases—yet these still tend to be quite rare. As a result of the growing recognition of human trafficking as an illicit business enterprise, the pressure on existing anti-money laundering infrastructure to deliver better detection and investigation of money flows linked to trafficking is increasing. There is an acknowledgement, however, that given the many forms of trafficking and its constituent crimes and their tendency to take place alongside or within legitimate commercial activities, detection is not always simple or achievable (OSCE 2014, 13). Nor is it impossible.

The difficulties of grappling with money flows linked to trafficking are further compounded by the multiple forms that human trafficking can take within conflict situations and in moments of social instability. Conflict, natural disasters, poor economic opportunities make for an ideal breeding ground for the illicit business of human trafficking. Given their income generating capacity it was no surprise when the first links were made between human trafficking and armed conflict, both profitable enterprises. Although the relationship between human trafficking and conflict was highlighted in the context of Islamic State of Iraq and the Levant (ISIL's) trafficking of Yazidi women, exploitation of vulnerable people caught up within, on the fringes of or fleeing from conflict zones, is common practice (UNODC 2018a, 13). In particular, sex trafficking (UNODC 2018a), the use of children in forced labour in mines in conflict areas (Sjöström 2016), trafficking for the purpose of engaging vulnerable people in criminal activities such as child soldiering (Tiefenbrun 2007) or terrorism are well-documented. In 2017 there was a large increase in the number of children forced into armed conflict as compared to the previous year, with at least 6000 verified violations by government forces and more than 15,000 by a range of non-state armed groups (United Nations 2018, para. 5). If one considers the trafficking of Rohingya fleeing from ethnic violence in Myanmar for forced labour on fishing boats, for ransom or in other exploitative situations (Gunia 2019), it is very clear that the vulnerabilitiess of those fleeing conflict and the existence of corrupt transnational networks that spread across multiple jurisdictions make the exploitation of thousands of vulnerable individuals possible. The discovery of mass graves in Thailand and Malaysia (Stoakes et al. 2015) and the subsequent prosecution and conviction in Thailand of a high-level military general among more than 60 people responsible for this organised transnational crime highlights the network dimension and the breadth and depth of criminality involved in the exploitation of vulnerable people fleeing regional conflicts (Fortify Rights 2017). The asset seizures in the Rohingya case in Thailand were also very telling of the profitability of this criminal enterprise and is also one of the first cases of asset seizures by a government in a large-scale regional trafficking context (Manager 2015; Thai Rath 2015).

An interesting aspect of the Rohingya case is how easily criminality penetrated global supply chains (Stoakes et al. 2015). Human trafficking must be viewed beyond a narrow examination of its perpetrators and victims to a more extensive understanding of supply chain liability. An increased demand for cheap products/services and thus cheap labour is met by trafficked persons. Given the ready access to vulnerable people in or around conflict areas and the strong demand for cheap labour across poorly regulated sectors such as mining and fishing, opportunities for exploitation are there and trafficking groups or other networks operating in or around conflict zones are extremely well-placed to take advantage of the same. The trafficking of those caught up in or on the fringes of conflict hence feeds into supply chains tainting the goods or services they are engaged in or contributing to. Those forced onto fishing boats worked excessive hours, suffered poor treatment and ill-health to supply fish to consumers under well-known brands sold in supermarkets and restaurants around the world (Murphy 2018). In a similar vein, children and others forced to work in diamond mines in conflict areas in the Democratic Republic of Congo (Sjöström 2016) or forced labourers in jade and ruby mines owned by the Tatmadaw conglomerates in Kachin and Shan states in Myanmar (United Nations 2019, 4) also contributed to global supply chains, hence extending the reach of the criminal activity and its income generating capacity.

Intersection Between Human Trafficking and Conflict

Armed conflict, persecution and human rights violations are notably large drivers of migration, particularly if the rule of law in a source country has been ignored or is weak (UNHCR 2018, 2). Migration is a major driver for human trafficking as populations on the move are often vulnerable and those displaced by conflict are easy prey for sexual exploitation, forced and child labour, forced marriage and other forms of extortion (UNODC 2016). Where legal avenues for migration are unavailable or hard to access, refugees, asylum seekers and internally displaced people fleeing armed conflict often have no other option but to resort to illegal channels in their search for safety. In exchange for the promised passage out of conflict-affected areas, traffickers exploit men, women and children from refugee camps for both sex and labour trafficking (United Nations 2016, 6–9). For instance, Somali and Sudanese refugees fleeing conflict have been kidnapped or lured from their camps or caravans and held captive and sold in Libya or the Sinai desert for the purposes of exploitation (United Nations 2018, 9). In Libya the complicity of security services assists with the flourishing of these smuggling and exploitation networks (United Nations

2019, 19). Libya is an example of a jurisdiction where terrorist groups work increasingly with organised crime syndicates who often extract a proportion of the profits to commit or facilitate crimes (FATF-GIABA-GABAC 2016, 10; GITNOC 2015, 4–5). This makes for a very complex web of financial relationships between militias, organised crime groups and terrorist groups (Baker 2019). Although an organised crime group would actually force people into exploitation, terrorist or armed groups may receive a certain portion of the monetary gains (Sizer 2017). One can but imagine how complex the detection of money flows in this intricate web of criminality is likely to be.

To better understand money flows generated by trafficking in conflict situations, it is important to explore a little further the intersection between human trafficking and conflict and in particular the modus operandi of different groups profiting from it. Trafficking flows related to armed conflict can include human trafficking within the conflict zone, into the conflict zone and on the fringes of conflict areas especially where there are displaced populations on the move seeking safer ground (FATF-APG 2018, 12). Human trafficking is used by armed groups—both terrorist and military—as a means of raising funds to further their activities even though human trafficking is still not the dominant form of financing for terrorists (FATF-APG 2018, 16). This is a forever evolving space and changes to adapt to the evolving needs of armed groups. For example, ISIL previously derived the majority of its funding from acts of robbery, extortion, illegal trading of antiquities and exploitation of natural and economic resources. With ISIL losing much of the territory under its control, activities such as human trafficking, hostage taking and ransom are becoming more important sources of income generation (United Nations 2016c, para. 16). ISIL has its own publication, Al Dabiq, which details its involvement in human trafficking of women and children (FATF 2015, 13). In addition, there are recent reports documenting the use of palm oil plantations located in Sumatra and Kalimantan to fund terrorist activities by the terrorist group Jemaah Islamiyah (The Jakarta Post 2019). Using palm oil farms in this manner is a new development and also a potential nexus with human trafficking as Indonesian palm oil is a sector where there are already strong trends of exploitation in the form of forced labour and human trafficking (Amnesty International

2016). Any use of palm oil plantations to generate funds for terrorist activities would be an important change in revenue generation and would clearly be within the purview of anti-money laundering and counter-financing of terrorism regulations (AML/CFT regulations).

Income generation through human trafficking happens in a multitude of ways. In Somalia, it is reported that Al-Shabaab is involved in the exploitation of victims who are promised employment and whose salaries are paid directly to Al-Shabaab (FATF-APG 2018, 15). Boko Haram in Africa uses children in forced begging to raise funds and forces women into domestic servitude or forced marriages to Boko Haram militants (United Nations 2019, 26). The use by ISIL of displaced children in Syria in conditions of forced labour as part of organised begging rings is also well-documented (FATF-APG 2018). The most prolific trafficking activity of ISIL was the sale of Yazidi women at "slave auctions" and extortion and ransom payments exacted from the Yazidi community by ISIL (Wood 2014). In fact, the United Nations reported that in 2014 ISIL earned between US$35 million and US$45 million from extorting the Yazidi community and in January 2016 ISIL received payments of US$850,000 from the Yazidi community for the return of 200 kidnapped members of their community (United Nations 2016b, para. 20).

In addition to trafficking for the purpose of forced marriage, extortion and exploitation in prostitution, vulnerable people are trafficked for forced labour within conflict areas to generate revenue or sustain military activity (UNODC 2018a, 13). In Myanmar, the Tatmadaw reportedly trafficked villagers including children to porter army supplies (Child Rights Forum of Burma 2011, 21). The Tatmadaw has also used forced labour to increase mining revenue. Ruby and jade mines in the Kachin state guarded by the Tatmadaw and the armed ethnic groups are reported to be rife with abuses such as rape and forced labour (International Labour Conference 2019, 16). Furthermore, when women labourers are working and living in mining areas, they are at a particularly heightened risk of experiencing sexual violence by the Tatmadaw (Idem; United Nations 2019, 36). In addition to direct Tatmadaw involvement, the significant involvement of companies affiliated with Tatmadaw in the ruby and jade industries means parts of the US$31 billion revenue (Global Witness 2015, 26–27) from the jade trade and US$56.2 million from rubies and other precious stones exported to the European Union (United Nations 2019, 34) are illicit proceeds (United Nations 2019, 33).

Trafficking for forced labour also occurs out of conflict-affected areas where refugees or displaced persons living in camps near conflict zones or on smuggling routes are also at risk of trafficking for forced labour (UNODC 2018a, 13). For example, Syrian refugees fleeing conflict have been trafficked into labour in agriculture, manufacturing, catering and other sectors in neighbouring countries (United Nations 2016, para. 22). Militant and terrorist groups have reportedly forced people into labour in the construction, cleaning, mining, trench-digging and agricultural sectors, as well as domestic servitude (UNODC 2018b, 15). Little information is available about the actual money flows connected to these different forms of revenue generation and whether the funds remain within the country where they are generated, or if they are sent abroad.

Where militant or terrorist groups control large territories, they also generate revenues by taxing those who operate lucrative trafficking rings or smuggling networks within their territories (Liang 2016, 3). Although the erosion of territory controlled by terrorist groups globally suggests that human trafficking is unlikely to be a dominant form of income generation for terrorist groups (FATF 2018, 16), its capacity to generate revenue cannot be underestimated. Terrorist groups reportedly orchestrate attacks on civilians in refugee camps in order to increase the flow of migrants and subsequently profit from taxation revenues (Liang 2016, 3). Human trafficking is also a "perceived benefit for fighters in conflict" and "is likely opportunistic and could be for the benefit of individual terrorists or for the terrorist organisation at large" (FATF 2018, 16). Human trafficking sponsored by militaries is similar in practice, save that militaries tend to control larger territories and infrastructure and for longer periods of time. For example, the trafficking of the Rohingya travelling via Thailand to Malaysia to escape persecution in Myanmar or the Tatmadaw-used forced labour in mining. The ransom, extortion and forced labour patterns amongst those under the control of the authorities and military is also well-documented (Fortify Rights 2017).

Identifying Money Flows

Having established that there are clear patterns of human trafficking within, into and at the fringes of conflict as an income generating activity for both military and terrorist groups, it is worth asking whether this is adequately addressed in the existing counter-terrorism financing legal frameworks or anti-money laundering frameworks. It is vital to point out that human trafficking does arise on a wide scale that stretches beyond, and is unconnected to, conflict situations. Money flows generated therefrom are equally worthy of investigation. However, for the purpose of this chapter, the focus is on money flows generated by conflict-induced trafficking.

This question is important because where financial flows can be detected and disrupted using anti-money laundering mechanisms, this presents an opportunity to identify traffickers, seize their assets and disrupt their illicit activities. Over the last few years, a significant amount of attention has been dedicated at the international level to analysing financial flows associated with human trafficking within the context of armed conflict and beyond. The *United Nations Convention Against Transnational Organised Crime* requires state parties to criminalise the laundering of proceeds of human trafficking offences (UNODC 2004, Art. 6). It follows that states must not only establish a robust legal framework criminalising human trafficking but also criminalise human trafficking as a predicate offence in their national anti-money laundering/counter-financing of terrorism (AML/CFT) legislation (United Nations 2019, 41). In *Security Council Resolution 2331* (2016), the UN Security Council emphasised the connection between financing of terrorism and trafficking in persons and encouraged the analysis of financial flows stemming from human trafficking. It also called upon member states to develop the expertise of their Financial Intelligence Units (FIUs) to analyse cases of trafficking that are associated with terrorism financing. The Resolution draws attention to the need for states to reinforce legal and regulatory measures to help identify and regulate suspicious financial activity related to such abuse (United Nations 2016, para. 6). This was underscored again by *Security Council Resolution 2388* (2017) which calls upon states to "strengthen their compliance with international AML/CFT standards and enhance their capacity to conduct proactive financial investigations to track and disrupt human trafficking and identify potential linkages with terrorism financing" (United Nations 2017, para. 7).

Of the 28 national AML/CFT risk assessments, 14 specifically identified human trafficking as a money laundering risk and none identified it as a terrorism financing risk (FATF-APG 2018, 16). It is worth noting that, as per Financial Action Task Force (FATF's) explanation, in completing the risk assessments jurisdictions will take into account proceeds of crime from predicate offences that are the most prevalent in their jurisdictions. FATF notes that for those jurisdictions that did report on human trafficking as a money laundering risk, there was very little information about financial flows or laundering of funds from trafficking in persons (FATF-APG 2018, 17). Gathering the relevant information across different jurisdictions will allow for a better understanding of the movement of funds from trafficking, the network complicit in aiding, abetting and facilitating the commission of this crime and associated crimes. This actionable information provides the relevant enforcement authorities across different jurisdictions with an opportunity to collaborate on investigations and take incisive action in the form of asset seizures in order to disrupt the ability of traffickers to and their facilitators from benefiting from the proceeds of crime. This approach offers great complementarity to the criminal justice approach that is focused on criminalising actions of perpetrators rather than focusing on their illicit gains. However, given the complexity of facilitator relationships between different organised crime, military and terrorist groups and the hyper-efficient co-mingling of legitimate and illegitimate income and activities, financial institutions face many challenges in detecting and disrupting money flows linked to trafficking. FATF and FATF-Style Regional Bodies (FSRBs) have issued typologies to help relevant actors to identify suspicious activities and transactions which have highlighted the important role that cash couriers, straw men and cash-intensive businesses usually play in human trafficking networks (Cockayne and Walker 2016, 19).

Income generated by human trafficking is laundered through various channels and in conflict-affected contexts cash and commodity-based transactions are likely to play an important role where informal remittance systems such as the Hawala have emerged as an important form of payment for human trafficking in the context of conflict (Cockayne and Walker 2016, 19). Known as the system of informal alternative banking, Hawala allows for the immediate physical transfer of funds between two distant geographical regions through a broker who must have the capital available to advance those funds because settlement comes after the fact. Trust underpins this process since there is rarely any physical proof to substantiate a transaction and this little or lack of paper trail has made this informal remittance system very attractive for criminals (Martis 2018, 10). Informal money or value transfer channels such as remittance providers who are not regulated and not subject to AML/CFT supervision are often misused for money laundering and terrorism financing purposes (FATF 2010). For instance, ISIL reportedly relies heavily on informal money/value transfer services where money is transferred via money remitters who have agents operating in border areas close to ISIL-held territory (FATF 2015, 27–28). Boko Haram is also known to receive payments via cash couriers and Hawala transactions (Caulderwood 2014).

Hawala agents settle the accounts by use of cash couriers to transport the cash from one end to the other. For instance, Iraqi money-exchange operators pay Shi'ite militias to guard cash shipments via ground transportation from Baghdad across their front lines to militant-controlled territory in Anbar province (Cooker 2016). Balances may also be settled through wire transfers, anonymous prepaid cards, trade transactions, money services business. Emerging channels such as crowdfunding platforms (Hall 2019) and virtual currencies (Stalinsky 2018) are increasingly exposed to AML/CFT risks (European Commission 2017, 4). Most Hawala agents operate other legitimate businesses such as (mobile) pawn shops, grocery stores, nail salons, travel agencies, cafeteria/deli, import/export where income generated from these types of business are co-mingled with the criminally derived cash (Martis 2018, 4) and integrated into the financial system. These proceeds of crimes are difficult to detect when the transactions are bundled and hence leave a limited information trail (European Commission 2017, 8).

Reduced exposure to the formal financial sector and cash-intensive transactions that take place outside the formal banking system can make it difficult to identify signs of money laundering from human trafficking and to use existing AML/CFT tools to disrupt money flows. In light of the informal channels used to launder money and the growing threat of terrorist groups, FATF's revised recommendations provide that:

> [c]ountries should take measures to ensure that natural or legal persons that provide money or value transfer services ("MVTS") are licensed or registered, and subject to effective systems for monitoring and ensuring compliance with the relevant measures called for in the FATF Recommendations. Countries should take action to identify natural or legal persons that carry out MVTS without a license or registration, and to apply appropriate sanctions … Countries should take measures to ensure that MVTS providers that use agents include them in their AML/CFT programmes and monitor them for compliance. (FATF 2012–2019, 15)

In addition, Special Recommendation VI further adds that persons or legal entities that carry out this service illegally should be subject to administrative, civil or criminal sanctions (FATF 2010, 15). Furthermore, in jurisdictions where the Hawala system exists in parallel to the formal financial sector, the International Monetary Fund strongly recommends that Hawala agents should be registered and should keep adequate records in line with FATF Recommendations in order to improve transparency and bring the Hawala system more in line with the standards of the formal financial sector (El Qorchi et al. 2003).

The Need for Granular Data

Over the last couple of years, significant efforts have been made to bring granularity to the indicators of suspected money laundering related to human trafficking. The financial sector is slowly but surely coming to better understand financial flows connected to trafficking both as a predicate offence to money laundering and as a form of terrorism financing. Granularity is particularly important in this case as indicators of human trafficking-connected money flows are very generic and not always helpful. Granularity added by typologies such as those set out in the FATF report "Financial Flows from Human Trafficking" (FATF report) are extremely helpful in providing financial institutions with a better understanding of what money flows connected to trafficking look like. Viewing the indicators in light of the typologies enhances understanding of money flows that are tainted by trafficking. The FATF report does not provide examples of financial flows linked to human trafficking arising in connection with conflict but it does set out helpful guidance in relation to trafficking for sexual exploitation and trafficking for labour exploitation and organ trafficking. There is a need for creativity on the part of financial institutions to apply these indicators and knowledge across money flows that originate from circumstances that do not squarely fit a particular form of trafficking. Conflict situations and money flows stemming therefrom can present such difficulties.

In order to effectively apply indicators and identify tainted money flows, it is vital to have access to reliable data sets that are credible and provide a comprehensive linkage from the underlying crimes to the income generated. Ideally, information should not rely on victims' testimony alone and must take into account financial transactions and various other forms of corroborative evidence such as evidence of financial transactions that document the activities of traffickers and logistics expenses that may be consistent with victims' accounts of how they were trafficked. As highlighted above, the emergence of informal remittance agencies and the complexity of criminality and networks of opportunistic criminality in conflict do make it difficult to summon compelling and reliable evidence. Information sharing partnerships are more critical today than ever before. Recent years have seen the emergence of partnerships between law enforcement and financial institutions such as the UK's Joint Money Laundering Intelligence Task Force (JMLIT) or multi-stakeholder working groups to share information and typologies. Such partnerships focus on developing typologies and a better shared understanding of risk so that the illicit money flows from trafficking can be addressed. More research is needed to understand how proceeds that stem from the exploitation of vulnerable people in conflict situations are used. For example, are such funds invested beyond conflict zones in other sectors with a view to laundering the proceeds and increasing profits or do these funds remain within the territory controlled by terrorists and other armed groups? Better information will allow for a more targeted response to identifying and disrupting these money flows. In cases where individuals are trafficked for sexual and/or labour exploitation it is also important to have an estimate of the value of these services for the purposes of measuring and, in some cases, compensating victims for damages suffered in monetary terms.

Leadership from FIUs is required as they are an important player in investigations into illicit money flows based upon Suspicious Transaction Reports (STRs) from financial institutions. FIUs have a very important role to play in providing guidance on the nature of risk, the content of STRs and the granularity of information required for a good quality STR that is of use to law enforcement. Such guidance from FIUs can help financial institutions with recognising the materiality of human trafficking in conflict as an AML/CFT risk and lead to the implementation of better risk management systems. Guidance can also take the form of a tick-box approach relating to human trafficking or guidance around the elements of an STR narrative that are helpful in a trafficking case (FINTRAC, Project Protect n.d.). The filing of STRs relies on good quality information that allows for identification of corresponding indicators. Good quality and credible information are vital for customer onboarding processes and for ongoing transaction monitoring. Information sharing partnerships with key front-line NGOs can be a powerful source of information, particularly as they often capture information from victims and witnesses on the ground. This type of information is often impossible to obtain from routine sources due to the distance between the front line, where trafficking takes place, and the financial institutions where transactions are processed, and accounts banked.

The Way Forward

The vulnerability of those caught up in conflict situations or on the fringes of conflict is as undeniable as the opportunistic income generated by armed groups which profit in order to further their activities. The complex meshing of various organised crime, in some cases the military and terrorist cross-border networks and their increasing use of cash-intensive transactions and informal remittance services to escape detection, makes it a daunting task to track money flows linked to human trafficking in conflict. However, the mingling of legitimate and illegitimate funds often creates a trail in the formal financial system, while investment or expenditures of cash also leave trails that can be followed and developed into typologies that can lead to detection and disruption of illicit money flows when viewed in conjunction with indicators of crime. The traceability of goods and services tainted by trafficking and forced labour within global supply chains also offers an opportunity to identify the exploited and the exploiters and may help to achieve a better understanding of the movement of people in conflict into labour exploitation. The mapping of migration patterns and the movement of tainted goods can in turn offer an opportunity to trace money flows by tracking the movement of people into such industries. The need to nurture the flow of information from the ground to the front desk of those monitoring account openings or ongoing transactions is vital. More incisive action in this space requires more cross-border information sharing partnerships, collaboration across government agencies, partnerships with NGOs on the ground and creativity in looking at the different crimes that exist and constitute human trafficking such as deceit, fraud, trespass that may offer different opportunities to engage with disruption of this heinous crime. Each may provide different but equally fruitful avenues to identify and disrupt the financial backbone of exploitation of vulnerable people in conflict.

References

Amnesty International. 2016. *The Great Palm Oil Scandal: Labour Abuses Behind Big Brand Names*. London: Amnesty International. https://www.amnesty.org/download/Documents/ASA2152432016ENGLISH.PDF

Baker, Aryn. 2019. 'It Was As if We Weren't Human.' Inside the Modern Slave Trade Trapping African Migrants. *Time*, March 14, 2019. https://time.com/longform/african-slave-trade/

Caulderwood, Kathleen. 2014. Fake Charities, Drug Cartels, Ransom and Extortion: Where Islamist Group Boko Haram Gets Its Cash. *International*

Business Times, May 16, 2014. https://www.ibtimes.com/fake-charities-drug-cartels-ransom-extortion-where-islamist-group-boko-haram-gets-its-1585743

Child Rights Forum of Burma. 2011. *The Plight of Children Under Military Rule in Burma.* The Child Rights Forum of Burma. http://www.burmapartnership.org/wp-content/uploads/2011/05/CRC-Shadow-Report-Burma_29thApril_2011-and-photos.pdf

Cockayne, James and Summer Walker. 2016. *Fighting in Conflict Human Trafficking, 10 Ideas for Action by the United Nations Security Council.* United Nations University. http://collections.unu.edu/eserv/UNU:5780/UNUReport_Pages.pdf?utm_source=UNU%20Campaign%20page&utm_medium=Web&utm_campaign=Human%20Trafficking

Cooker, Margaret. 2016. How Islamic State's Secret Banking Network Prospers. *The Wall Street Journal,* February 24, 2016. http://www.wsj.com/articles/how-islamic-states-secret-banking-network-prospers-1456332138

El Qorchi, Mohammed, Munzele Maimbo, Samuel and John F. Wilson. 2003. *Informal Funds Transfer Systems: An Analysis of the Informal Hawala System.* The World Bank and the International Monetary Fund. http://documents.worldbank.org/curated/en/410351468765856277/pdf/multi0page.pdf

European Commission. 2017. *Report from the Commission to the European Parliament and the Council on the Assessment of the Risks of Money Laundering and Terrorist Financing Affecting the Internal Market and Relating to Cross-border Activities,* COM(2017)340 final 26 June, 2017. https://publications.europa.eu/en/publication-detail/-/publication/ce3cb15d-5a5a-11e7-954d-01aa75ed71a1

FATF. 2010. *FATF IX Special Recommendations.* Paris: FATF. https://www.fatf-gafi.org/media/fatf/documents/reports/FATF%20Standards%20-%20IX%20Special%20Recommendations%20and%20IN%20rc.pdf

———. 2012–2019. *International Standards on Combating Money Laundering and the Financing of Terrorism & Proliferation.* Paris: FATF. http://www.fatf-gafi.org/media/fatf/documents/recommendations/pdfs/FATF%20Recommendations%202012.pdf

———. 2015. *Financing of the Terrorist Organisation Islamic State in Iraq and the Levant (ISIL).* Paris: FATF. http://www.fatf-gafi.org/media/fatf/documents/reports/Financing-of-the-terrorist-organisation-ISIL.pdf

———. 2018. *FATF Monitoring of Terrorist Financing Risks and Actions Taken to Combat ISIL, Al-Qaeda and Affiliates Financing.* FATF, October 19, 2018.

https://www.fatf-gafi.org/publications/methodsandtrends/documents/isil-alqaeda-affiliates-financing-update.html

FATF-APG. 2018. *Financial Flows from Human Trafficking*. Paris: FATF. https://www.fatf-gafi.org/media/fatf/content/images/Human-Trafficking-2018.pdf

FATF-GIABA-GABAC. 2016. *Terrorist Financing in West and Central Africa*. Paris: FATF. http://www.fatf-gafi.org/media/fatf/documents/reports/Terrorist-Financing-West-Central-Africa.pdf

FINTRAC, Project Protect. n.d. *Public Service Renewal in Action*. https://www.fintrac-canafe.gc.ca/emplo/psr-eng.pdf

Fortify Rights. 2017. Thailand: Government Officials Convicted of Human Trafficking, Organized Crime. *Fortify Rights*, July 20, 2017. https://www.fortifyrights.org/publication-20170720.htm

Global Initiative against Transnational Organized Crime. 2015. *Libya: A Growing Hub for Criminal Economies and Terrorist Financing in the Trans-Sahara*. New York: GITNOC. https://globalinitiative.net/wp-content/uploads/2015/05/2015-1.pdf

Global Witness. 2015. *Jade: Myanmar's "Big State Secret"*. London: Global Witness Limited. https://www.globalwitness.org/en/campaigns/oil-gas-and-mining/myanmarjade/

Gunia, Amy. 2019. Human Traffickers Accused of 'Crimes Against Humanity' in Thailand and Malaysia. *Time*, March 28, 2019. https://time.com/5560095/malaysia-thailand-rohingya-crimes-against-humanity/

Hall, Richard. 2019. Isis Suspects in Syrian Camp Raise Thousands Through Online Crowdfunding Campaign. *Independent*, July 25, 2019. https://www.independent.co.uk/news/world/middle-east/isis-syria-camp-al-hol-paypal-telegram-online-crowdfunding-a9021006.html

Hoffman, Richard L. 2004. *Effective Countermeasures Against the Trafficking in Human Beings and Smuggling of Migrants*. Tokyo: United Nations Asia and Far East Institute for the Prevention of Crime and Treatment of Offenders. https://www.ncjrs.gov/App/Publications/abstract.aspx?ID=206392

International Labour Conference, Committee on the Application of Standards. 2019. *Myanmar (ratification 1955), Forced Labour Convention, 1930 (No. 29)*, C.App./PV.4/Myanmar/C29, 13 June 2019. https://www.ilo.org/wcmsp5/groups/public/%2D%2D-ed_norm/%2D%2D-relconf/documents/meetingdocument/wcms_711208.pdf

International Labour Office. 2014. *Profits and Poverty: The Economics of Forced Labour*. Geneva: ILO. https://www.ilo.org/wcmsp5/groups/

public/%2D%2D-ed_norm/%2D%2D-declaration/documents/publication/wcms_243391.pdf

Liang, Christina Schori. 2016. *The Criminal-Jihadist: Insights into Modern Terrorist Financing*. Geneva Centre for Security Policy. https://dam.gcsp.ch/files/2y10TflBzyeiQACfYZl2yYpaGuBhSe3KV8jrljD8vV3iRFQyrikhop2

Manager. 2015. "ปปง.ยึดทรัพย์แก๊งค้ามนุษย์ อ.หัวไทร กว่า 100 ล้าน" [AMLO confiscated more than 100 million from human trafficking gang in Hua Sai District]. *Manager*, May 12, 2015. https://mgronline.com/crime/detail/9580000054166

Martis, Genesis J. 2018. *A guidance to Understand Hawala and to Establish the Nexus with Terrorist Financing*. ACAMS. https://www.acams.org/aml-white-paper-understand-hawala-nexus-terrorist-financing/

Murphy, Daniel. 2018. *Hidden Chains, Rights Abuses and Forced Labor in Thailand's Fishing Industry*. New York: Human Rights Watch, 2018. https://www.hrw.org/report/2018/01/23/hidden-chains/rights-abuses-and-forced-labor-thailands-fishing-industry

Organization for Security and Co-operation in Europe. 2014. *Leveraging Anti-Money Laundering Regimes to Combat Trafficking in Human Beings*. Vienna: OSCE. https://www.osce.org/secretariat/121125?download=true

Sizer, Lydia. 2017. *Libya's Terrorism, Challenge Assessing the Salafi-Jihadi Threat*. Washington, DC: The Middle East Institute. https://www.mei.edu/sites/default/files/publications/PP1_Sizer_LibyaCT_web.pdf

Sjöström, Therese. 2016. *Childhood lost: Diamond Mining in the Democratic Republic of the Congo and Weaknesses of the Kimberley Process*. Stockholm: Swedwatch. https://swedwatch.org/wp-content/uploads/2016/12/83_swedwatch_drc_diamonds_0.pdf

Stalinsky, Steven. 2018. Terrorists Have Been Using Bitcoin for Four Years, So What's the Surprise? *The Hill*, August 3, 2018. https://thehill.com/opinion/cybersecurity/377415-terrorists-have-been-using-bitcoin-for-four-years-so-whats-the-surprise

Stoakes, Emanuel, Kelly, Chris and Annie Kelly. 2015. Sold from a Jungle Camp to Thailand's Fishing Industry: 'I Saw 13 People Die'. *The Guardian*, July 20, 2015. https://www.theguardian.com/global-development/2015/jul/20/sold-from-jungle-camp-thailand-fishing-industry-trafficking

Thai Rath. 2015. "ไล่อายัด 75 ล. คดีค้ามนุษย์ ออกหมายจับแล้ว 61 คน ประสานมาเลย์ล่าโกโต้ง" [Confiscated 75 million in Human Trafficking Case; 61 Arrest Orders; Coordinated with the Malay to Search for Ko Tong]. *Thai Rath*, May 13, 2015. https://www.thairath.co.th/news/local/498454

The Jakarta Post. 2019. Police Track Funding of Jamaah Islamiyah Terror Group. *The Jakarta Post*, July 2, 2019. https://www.thejakartapost.com/news/2019/07/02/police-track-funding-of-jamaah-islamiyah-terror-group.html

Tiefenbrun, Susan. 2007. Child Soldiers, Slavery and the Trafficking of Children. *Fordham International Law Journal* 31(2, Article 6):415–486. https://ir.lawnet.fordham.edu/cgi/viewcontent.cgi?article=2091&context=ilj

United Nations, General Assembly. 2000. *Protocol to Prevent, Suppress and Punish Trafficking in Persons, Especially Women and Children, Supplementing the United Nations Convention Against Transnational Organized Crime.* New York: United Nations. https://treaties.un.org/Pages/ViewDetails.aspx?src=IND&mtdsg_no=XVIII-12-a&chapter=18&clang=_en

United Nations, General Assembly. 2016a. *Trafficking in Persons, Especially Women and Children: Note by the Secretary-General*, A/71/303, 5 August 2016. https://undocs.org/A/71/303

———, Security Council. 2016b. *Report of the Secretary-General on Conflict-Related Sexual Violence*, S/2016/361, 20 April 2016. https://undocs.org/en/S/2016/361

———, Security Council. 2016c. *The Threat Posed by ISIL (Da'esh) to International Peace and Security and the Range of United Nations Efforts in Support of Member States in Countering the Threat: Report of the Secretary-General*, S/2016/92, 29 January 2016. https://undocs.org/S/2016/92

United Nations, Security Council resolution 2331. 2016. S/RES/2331 (2016), 20 December 2016. http://unscr.com/en/resolutions/doc/2331

United Nations, Security Council resolution 2388. 2017. S/RES/2388, 21 November 2017. http://unscr.com/en/resolutions/doc/2388

United Nations, Human Rights Council. 2018. *Report of the Special Rapporteur on Trafficking in Persons, Especially Women and Children*, A/HRC/38/45, 14 May 2018. https://undocs.org/A/HRC/38/45

United Nations, Security Council. 2018. *Children and Armed Conflict: Report of the Secretary-General*, A/72/865–S/2018/465, 16 May 2018. https://undocs.org/s/2018/465

United Nations, Counter-Terrorism Committee Executive Directorate. 2019. *Identifying and Exploring the Nexus Between Human Trafficking, Terrorism, and Terrorism Financing*, February 2019. https://www.un.org/sc/ctc/wp-content/uploads/2019/02/HT-terrorism-nexus-CTED-report.pdf

United Nations, Human Rights Council. 2019. *The Economic Interests of the Myanmar Military, Independent International Fact-Finding Mission on*

Myanmar, A/HRC/42/CRP.3, 5 August 2019. https://www.ohchr.org/Documents/HRBodies/HRCouncil/FFM-Myanmar/EconomicInterestsMyanmarMilitary/A_HRC_42_CRP_3.pdf

United Nations Office on Drugs and Crime. 2004. *United Nations Convention against Transnational Organized Crime and the Protocols Thereto*. New York: United Nations. https://treaties.un.org/Pages/ViewDetails.aspx?src=TREATY&mtdsg_no=XVIII-12&chapter=18&clang=_en

———. 2011. *The Role of Corruption in Trafficking in Persons*. Vienna: UNODC. https://www.unodc.org/documents/human-trafficking/2011/Issue_Paper_-_The_Role_of_Corruption_in_Trafficking_in_Persons.pdf

———. 2016. *Global Report on Trafficking in Persons 2016*. New York: UNODC. https://www.unodc.org/documents/data-and-analysis/glotip/2016_Global_Report_on_Trafficking_in_Persons.pdf

———. 2018a. *Global Report on Trafficking in Persons – in the Context of Armed Conflict 2018, Booklet 2: Trafficking in Persons in the Context of Armed Conflict*. New York: UNODC. https://www.unodc.org/documents/data-and-analysis/glotip/2018/GloTIP2018_BOOKLET_2_Conflict.pdf

———. 2018b. *Countering Trafficking in Persons in Conflict Situations*. Vienna: UNODC. https://www.unodc.org/documents/human-trafficking/2018/17-08776_ebook-Countering_Trafficking_in_Persons_in_Conflict_Situations.pdf

United Nations High Commissioner for Refugees. 2018. *Global Trends: Forced Displacement in 2017*. Geneva: UNHCR. https://www.unhcr.org/5b27be547.pdf

Wood, Paul. 2014. Islamic State: Yazidi Women Tell of Sex-Slavery Trauma. *BBC News*, December 22, 2014. https://www.bbc.com/news/world-middle-east-30573385

Archana Kotecha is the Asia Region Director and Head of Legal for Liberty Shared. She has extensive experience in the areas of advocacy, casework and policy work relating to trafficking in persons. Archana has authored extensively and advises governments, financial institutions and other businesses on human trafficking including legal and anti-money-laundering frameworks and human rights risks.

Part II

Trafficking in Conflict: Exploring How Human Trafficking Manifests in Conflict Through the Use of Case Studies

5

Russia's Private Military Forces: A Dual Layer of Human Trafficking?

Jorn van Rij, Ágoston Mohay, and Mantas Bileišis

Introduction

In 1997, the *Cape Town Principles* were the result of a symposium organised by UNICEF and the NGO Working Group on the *Convention on the Rights of the Child* to develop strategies for preventing recruitment of children, demobilising child soldiers and helping them to reintegrate into society (UNICEF 1997). As a follow-up in 2005–2006, UNICEF undertook a review which has led to an agreement on the need for two documents—the first, a short and concise document, *The Paris Commitments*

J. van Rij (✉)
Netherlands National Police, The Hague, The Netherlands
e-mail: Jorn.van.rij@politie.nl

Á. Mohay
Faculty of Law, University of Pécs, Pécs, Hungary
e-mail: mohay.agoston@ajk.pte.hu

M. Bileišis
General Jonas Žemaitis Military Academy of Lithuania, Vilnius, Lithuania
e-mail: mantas.bileisis@mil.lt

J. Muraszkiewicz et al. (eds.), *Human Trafficking in Conflict*, Crime Prevention and Security Management, https://doi.org/10.1007/978-3-030-40838-1_5

to Protect Children Unlawfully Recruited or Used by Armed Forces or Armed Groups, known as *The Paris Commitments*, and the second, *The Principles and Guidelines on Children Associated with Armed Forces or Armed Groups*, known as *The Paris Principles* (UNICEF 2007, 4–5).

The Paris Principles (UNICEF 2007) gives an outline of the role of children in combat. This is based on international law and standards and on the original *Cape Town Principles*. By doing so, this document incorporates knowledge and lessons learned, and in particular emphasises the informal ways in which boys and girls both become associated with and leave armed forces or armed groups. *The Paris Principles* states that children are often trained and used for combat, assigned to support roles such as porters or messengers or used for tactical advantage as human shields or for political advantage in propaganda (UNICEF 2007, 4).

Children are defined by the *Convention on the Rights of the Child* (CRC 1989) as persons under the age of 18. These children can be associated with military organisations, such as state armed forces and non-state armed groups. These non-state armed groups vary widely in their goals, size and methods. They may include narcotics cartels, popular liberation movements, religious and ideological organisations, corporations like private military and security companies (hereinafter PMSCs), self-defence militias and paramilitary groups established by state governments to further their interests (Hofmann and Schneckener 2011). For this chapter special interest is devoted to PMSCs and paramilitary groups as both are being used by Russia.

Through history many countries have made use of child soldiers in combat roles and up until the present day this is a common practice in conflict areas (Singer 2005). Violent non-state actors have drawn international condemnation for relying heavily on children under the age of 18 as combatants, scouts, porters, spies, informants and in other roles (Child Soldiers International 2017) although many state armed forces also recruit children (Child Soldiers International 2012). There are no accurate statistics available on the true number of child soldiers, with estimates running from 250,000 to 300,000 globally (Waschefort 2018, 136).

This practice can also be addressed from a different perspective, namely, that of human trafficking. The adoption in 2000 by the United Nations General Assembly of the *Protocol to Prevent, Suppress and Punish Trafficking in Persons, Especially Women and Children* marked a significant milestone in international efforts to stop the trade in people and within this legal framework the conditions for addressing the issue of child soldiers as a form of trafficking are also met. Due to its nature, the recruitment and deployment of children associated with armed groups "nearly always constitutes trafficking in persons" according to the UN Secretary-General's Special Representative on Children and Armed Conflict (United Nations Human Rights Council, Annual Report of the Special Representative of the Secretary-General for Children and Armed Conflict, A/HRC/37/47, paras 15–16). This chapter addresses the concept of child soldiers as being a special type of human trafficking and will examine the exploitation of children in and during military service in both state military and working for PMSCs; we suggest that this is in breach of international rules. In order to do so, a case study of the position of Russia as a state actor and the Wagner group as a PMSC has been taken as an example due to the relation between Russia and Wagner, but of course other examples which link human trafficking with child soldiers, like in the Yemen conflict (MEMO 2019), are also possible. Because of the novelty of describing the link between child soldiers and human trafficking but also more generally the link between PMSCs and human trafficking, much of the information is based on news articles and other non-scientific materials. The aim of this chapter is to outline the relation between child soldiers, PMSCs and the associated risk of human trafficking.

The Position of the Russian Federation

In the wake of the end of the Cold War, many were optimistic about Russia becoming a democratic state that would fully participate in international institutions. Even after the South Ossetia war some believed that President Medvedev would lead the country towards created democratisation (White 2018). With the return of Putin, Russia is currently profiling itself more and more as a military superpower and is therefore involved in several global and local conflicts. On some occasions a Russian military force is present and visible but in other conflict areas their presence is less visible, and they operate less conspicuously. Within these regions of conflict, Russian presence runs from deploying military personnel for combat (e.g., in Syria) to intelligence support in proxy warfare situations like in Eastern Ukraine.

Because of this, Russia openly places itself in opposition with the West and by doing so evades or even ignores obligations to international institutions or rules (Allison 2017). Equally, Russia does not have the capabilities to project power in ways similar to those of the United States. Its relative economic and military weakness forces it to try to find alternative ways, like the deployment of PMSCs, to achieve its goals (Thomas 2015). PMSCs are a useful tool for the Russian government as they are not bound to international regulations on warfare (Komar et al. 2017). On the other hand, these organisations may have a self-sustaining business model, where they sell their services internationally at a competitive price and with little to no regulation in their host state (Spearin 2019). The two types of activities are clearly distinct from the point of view of motivation, but the recruitment of operators is unlikely to be separate for the different operations.

There is proof that in many of these conflict areas, Russian military personnel are replaced by forces consisting of private military forces (units) who officially may or may not be fighting for the Russian Federation.[1] In order to fill the ranks of these units young underprivileged men and children as young as 15 (Child Soldiers International 2008) from the Russian countryside are mostly being recruited to fight Russia's wars. This is usually under the false pretence of joining the official Russian armed forces. This can be seen as a type of coercion as it entails the exploitation of one's vulnerability which is a specific condition for the crime of human trafficking. Of course, some of them will be injured or killed in action but these kills and injuries formally do not count as Russian casualties as they are not enlisted as military personnel (Tsvetkova 2015). This in turn means that when these private contractors are being injured or killed in action, they or their next of kin cannot rely on governmental financial support and recognition (Eckel and Zakharov 2018) like normal military personnel can (Roth 2019).

[1] Information out of three interviews with officers located in Vilnius (names are known by the authors).

These private contractors usually receive limited training and have little combat experience and lack accountable supervision which could easily lead them to commit violations of fundamental human rights or even war crimes (Rempfer 2019). At the same time, the presence of these young men and children in conflict areas is enough to lead to an increase in human trafficking as conflict areas create vulnerability and dependency, which will always lead to the exploitation of this vulnerability, that is, by forced prostitution (Van Rij 2019) by the ones in and with power (Zimbardo 2008).

Human Trafficking

Human trafficking has been on the international agenda ever since the beginning of the twentieth century but after a lull in interest due to the two great wars, interest was renewed in the early 60s–70s of the previous century and from that moment on it has been high on the political agenda and the subject of continuous debate (Aranowitz et al. 2010).

In 2001 the definition for human trafficking was formulated in the (Palermo) *Protocol to Prevent, Supress and Punish Trafficking in Persons, Especially Women and Children* (2000) and states: "*Transnational Human trafficking is the recruitment, moving or reception, of a person under coercive or deceptive conditions for the purpose of exploitation.*" This now widely accepted definition of human trafficking (Rijken 2009) has been supplemented by the elements of act, means and purpose (Werson and Goutbeek 2005), which are as follows:

- recruitment, transportation, transferring, harbouring or receipt of a person (act);
- means of threat, use of force, coercion, abduction, fraud, deception (means);
- purpose or act of exploitation, including sexual exploitation, forced slavery and slavery-like practices (purpose).

This addition, just like the definition provided in the Palermo Protocol, uses the term exploitation which in itself is seen as an unclear concept.

The current European Union standard and definition on the trafficking of human beings has been set out in Directive 2011/36/EU Article 2(1) which states:

> The recruitment, transportation, transfer, harbouring or reception of persons, including the exchange or transfer of control over those persons, by means of the threat or use of force or other forms of coercion, of abduction, of fraud, of deception, of the abuse of power or of a position of vulnerability or of the giving or receiving of payments or benefits to achieve the consent of a person having control over another person, for the purpose of exploitation.

Paragraphs 2 and 3 of *Article 2 of Directive 2011/36/EU* define the two key elements of vulnerability and exploitation as follows: "Vulnerability is a situation in which the person concerned has no real or acceptable alternative but to submit to the abuse involved" (§2) and "exploitation is prostitution or other forms of sexual exploitation, forced labour or services, including begging, slavery or practices similar to slavery, servitude, or the exploitation of criminal activities or the removal of organs" (§3).

Due to the cunningness of the malicious people who are responsible for the exploitation of vulnerable victims, new victims and methods and ways to exploit them are being sought and thought of constantly (Van Rij and McAlister 2019). This is one of the reasons why clear and comprehensive numbers on the nature and extent of the different types of exploitation which can be legally defined as human trafficking are missing. For example, 958 possible victims were reported to the Dutch coordination centre on human trafficking (CoMensha). The Dutch National Rapporteur on Trafficking in Human Beings and Sexual Violence Against Children uses this data to give an overview of the nature and extent of the exploitation. The Rapporteur, however, estimates that this number is much higher in reality. In a joint research with the United Nations Office on Drugs and Crime (UNODC), the Dutch National Rapporteur (2017, 16) on Trafficking in Human Beings and Sexual Violence Against Children states that the actual number of possible victims of human trafficking could be five times higher, that is, around 6250 possible victims. The registered data, therefore, should only be used as an indicator for the detection of possible victims rather than a definite number of victims. This detection is of the utmost importance but is usually difficult due to the lack of knowledge concerning newly applied methods and types of victims.

In recent years the focus of trends has shifted from mere sexual exploitation via forced prostitution towards labour exploitation and even more recently interest has risen regarding criminal exploitation, especially illicit drug trading (Robinson and McLean 2018). These types of exploitation, however, are not easily recognised, confirmed as being exploitation and acted upon consequently, due to the fact that these types are legally more difficult to prove due to the nature in comparison to sexual exploitation. Even more difficult is to detect and describe more unconventional ways in which men, women and children (Europol 2018) are—unknowingly—exploited. This chapter, thus, is interested in whether the actions by the Russian government in the indirect recruitment of young boys to fight in their proxy wars without any legal military status can be defined as a specific type of human trafficking.

As mentioned previously, Russia is present in different conflicts around the world from Georgia to Venezuela (Tsvetkova and Zverev 2019). In some regions the Russian military is operating in general within the limits of international law, like in Syria. In other conflicts Russia denies the presence of its troops, for example, Eastern Ukraine or states where (according to Russia) their presence is necessary to protect the Russian minorities, for example, in Moldova's Transnistria and the Georgian regions of Abkhazia and Ossetia (Pugsley and Wesslau 2016). The Vice News documentary entitled *The Kremlin's Secret War: Russia's Ghost Army in Ukraine* gives insight into Russia's military presence in Eastern Ukraine. This, however, is officially being denied and countered with the statement that these fighters are volunteers who have joined different separatist movements in Eastern Ukraine (Maynes 2018). Russia also uses the Russian Private Military Company Wagner to be deployed in conflict zones in Syria and Africa. Several Wagner veterans have requested the International Criminal Court (ICC) to investigate the possibility of the prosecution of Wagner for being a criminal enterprise acting in contravention of the International Committee of the Red Cross (ICRC's) Montreux Document (Nieuwsuur 2019). The *Montreux Document on pertinent international legal obligations and good practices for states related to operations of private military and security companies during armed conflict* was adopted in 2008 and is the first document of international significance to define how international law applies to the activities of private military and security companies (PMSCs) when they are operating in an armed conflict zone.

Wagner is also allegedly operating with the full support of the Russian government (Giglio 2019), in at least the conflict in Syria and Eastern Ukraine, but it is also stated that *de jure* PMSCs are not allowed or present in Russia (Shurogradsky et al. 2016). At the same time, there is a rise in members of the Russian Yunarmia—youth army—which is a youth military-patriotic movement with members aged 8–18 (Gershkovich 2019). The Yunarmia is best known for its summer camps (MacFarquhar 2018) but the question of how voluntary these camps actually are may be raised (Lockett 2019). More recently in Donetsk a children's army was installed as well (Coynash 2019). Apart from this there are different Military Sport Clubs which provide children as young as five battlefield training and hand-to-hand combat training. One of these clubs is Berkut (Golden Eagle) which teaches children from the age of 12 how to handle fully automatic weapons (Bennet 2014). Comparison between the Yunarmia and youth associations like Berkut and the Hitler Jugend under the Nazi regime can be made as the aim of both organisations is/was to create loyalty for the authorities, instilling patriotic values and combat exercises. Child soldiers have been active in the Ukrainian conflict from the start and, in putting this in perspective and in relation to the definition on human trafficking, it can be stated that the use of children in conflict situations or even in the preparation for a conflict can be considered to be human trafficking (Shevchenko 2014). This is confirmed by the UN Secretary-General's Special Representative on Children and Armed Conflict (United Nations Human Rights Council, Annual Report of the Special Representative of the Secretary-General for Children and Armed Conflict, A/HRC/37/47, paras 15–16).

It must also be emphasised that—sadly—it is not unheard that PMSCs would be to a certain degree involved in different types of human trafficking like labour and sexual exploitation in conflict situations as is described by Cole and Vermeltfoort (2018) who have done case studies on human trafficking in Iraq and Bosnia-Herzegovina. Thus, the recruitment and deployment of children in the service of PMSCs represents a risk for a dual layer of human trafficking.

Putting this into perspective, it is possible that Russia is luring and conscripting young children aged 8–18 from deprived regions in Russia into a military career via the Yunarmia or is engaged in similar initiatives. The question, however, is, if these children are officially registered as military in due time as there are set age requirements and the fact that Russia is not officially deploying military personnel to certain conflict zones. It is possible that these children are going to be enlisted by government-supported private military contractors, like Wagner, to become involved in frontline warfare. In this situation the government is responsible for the exploitation of the vulnerability of these children by using deception on the basis of patriotism in order to become child soldiers.

The following subsection will focus on the case of the Wagner group in the situations described above—with an international law focus.

PMSCs, International Law and the Case of Wagner

The activities of the Wagner group in this context raise a number of international law concerns which we will briefly elaborate upon. These issues are (1) the status of private military and security companies in relation to the aforementioned context; (2) the recruitment of child soldiers and (3) possible violations of international humanitarian law and international human rights law.

Ad 1. The international law status of PMSCs is a difficult question in and of itself, regardless of the fact that privatisation of activities related to armed conflict is quite frequent and can be considered a quite significant factor for many states' military capabilities, and is increasing in size and scope (Sossai 2009). Yet there is no commonly accepted, legally binding definition of what PMSCs even are. One may find a proposed definition in the *UN Draft Convention on Private Military and Security Companies* (hereinafter Draft Convention) and a (similar but not identical) one in the *Montreux Document*—however, neither of these documents are binding treaties, and they, furthermore, operate with concepts which are themselves disputed and not easily interpreted; see, for example, the use of "inherently state functions" or "direct participation in hostilities". Mercenarism is forbidden under international law, but the definition of mercenaries according to *Additional Protocol I to the Geneva Conventions* is complex and requires that all six definitional requirements are met cumulatively; therefore, it is actually not that difficult *not* to fall under the definition and conversely quite difficult to prove that someone *is* a mercenary. PMSCs, however, are in principle not regarded as mercenaries although this does not preclude a case-by-case analysis of this question, especially as PMSCs are not defined in international law (Tonkin 2011). The case of Wagner is rendered even more difficult as Russia officially does not acknowledge them, and, moreover, PMSCs are not legally allowed or regulated in Russia (Eklund and Elfving 2017). Most analysts in any case regard Wagner as a quasi-PMSC anyway, one that is formally a private company but one that is at the same time supported and controlled by the Russian state military (Marten 2019).

Ad 2. International humanitarian law clearly prohibits the recruitment of children into armed forces or armed groups. This is obvious with regard to *Additional Protocols I and II* to the *Geneva Conventions* (Article 77[2] of Additional Protocol I Article and Article 4[3][c] of Additional Protocol II), the *Convention on the Rights of the Child* (Article 38[3] and its *Optional Protocol on the Involvement of Children in Armed Conflict*) as well as customary international law and national legislation in numerous states—including Russia (Child Soldiers Global Report—Russian Federation 2008). The prohibition to conscript children applies regardless of the classification of the conflict, that is, in international and non-international armed conflicts, even if Additional *Protocols I and II* regulate the issue somewhat differently (Waschefort 2018, 139).

Conscripting children into armed groups could thus raise state responsibility under international law and individual criminal responsibility for *delicta juris gentium*, that is, acts defined as crimes by international law. Going into a detailed analysis of the responsibility issues related to PMSCs would be beyond the scope of this chapter (see Van Rij and Kis Kelemen 2019 for a theoretical analysis), but some statements can be made in this regard. Firstly, the direct responsibility of PMSCs—which are essentially companies—is not a legal possibility under current international law (Van Rij and Kis Kelemen 2019). Secondly, attribution of PMSC conduct to states—although not undisputed—is possible under general rules of attribution of state responsibility in line with customary international law in case the PMSC can be considered a *de facto* state organ or in case it exercises elements of governmental authority; or in other cases subject to the "effective control" test on a case-by-case basis (Van Rij and Kis Kelemen 2019, 110–111). Thirdly, individual criminal responsibility of PMSC staff for recruitment of child soldiers as a war crime is possible (see in this regard the case law of the Special Court for Sierra Leone and the judgement of the International Criminal Court in Lubanga [2012]) (Waschefort 2018, 13). It needs to be mentioned in this context that Russia has only signed but not ratified the *Rome Statue of the International Criminal Court* (1998) and has officially announced the withdrawal of its signature to the Statue in 2016 (Reuters).

Ad 3. Obviously the violation of international humanitarian law is only possible if international humanitarian law is indeed applicable to a situation, which depends on the question of whether an armed conflict exists at all—something which itself can be disputed, either in its entirety or as regards the classification of the conflict (Szpak 2017). However, even if an armed conflict does not exist, child labour and recruitment of children may still entail a violation of international human rights law—of relevance are *inter alia* the *European Convention on Human Rights* (ECHR 1950), more specifically Article 4 on forms of slavery, which has been ratified by both Russia and Ukraine. Other Council of Europe Treaties such as the *European Social Charter* (revised in 1996), more specifically Article 7 on the right of children and young persons to protection, were also ratified by both Ukraine and Russia. Next to this in terms of relevance are the *Convention on Action Against Trafficking in Human Beings* (2005), which has been ratified by Ukraine but has not even been signed by Russia, and the *ILO Convention on the Worst Forms of Child Labour* (1999), which was ratified by both Russia and Ukraine. Other non-Council of Europe treaties such as the International Covenant on Civil and Political Rights (*ICCPR*) (Article 8 and Article 24), which have been ratified by both Russia and Ukraine, can also be mentioned in this connection.

However, the enforcement of the relevant fundamental human rights and freedoms in the abovementioned context of a disputed conflict and a Russian quasi-PMSC and the probable use of child soldiers would no doubt be extremely difficult, aggravated further by the otherwise also not overly effective or "soft" enforcement mechanisms of the relevant human rights treaties other than the ECHR (Milanovic 2015). What is quite significant is that Ukraine had filed four interstate complaints (Applications no. 20958/14; 8019/16; 42,410/15 and 70,856/16) against Russia before the European Court of Human Rights—following relinquishment of jurisdiction by a chamber, the complaints will be examined by the Grand Chamber. In support of its claims the Ukrainian government relies on numerous ECHR articles which had allegedly been infringed by Russia. The ongoing cases could potentially carry significant relevance as regards the much discussed and disputed relationship between international humanitarian law and international human rights as well.

Conclusion

Russia is working hard on once again becoming a military superpower and it is involved in many conflicts worldwide. It is hard to imagine that Russia would abandon recruiting and dispatching private military forces under its current regime. Furthermore, various militias and PMSCs are an integral part of Russia's military doctrine and are one of the means for the government to coerce its own population (Persson 2016). For Russia, private military forces are a key instrument of power and influence projection. Irregular forces that Russia can employ offer it the benefit of plausible deniability of its activities when in clear breach of international law (Colby and Solomon 2015). Therein lies the danger as these irregular forces evade international supervision and by doing so are more likely to be guilty of the recruitment and deployment of child soldiers. The use of child soldiers by PMSCs can be seen as a new type of human trafficking in which socially vulnerable minors are being recruited, while they think that they can contribute if they fight for their country. These feelings and thoughts are being strengthened by a system of indoctrination visible within the Yunarmia and other similar initiatives which also offer them training with the regular Russian military. Out of patriotic belief these minors are willing to accept being recruited by PMSCs to fight in Russia's unknown wars while believing they are actually fighting for the Russian military instead of a PMSC. Because in all honestly who can tell the difference, they trained together, uniforms are alike as are weapon systems, and so on. Too little research has been done on the topic of the role of PMSCs and the use of child soldiers let alone research into the topic of child soldiers as a specific type of human trafficking.

The substantial benefits that private military forces offer the Russian government means that compelling the Russian government to abandon its use and support of private military forces would be very unlikely to succeed. Therefore, tackling the problem of recruitment of irregulars has to be a part of a complex Russia policy and strategy, which would need to be closely coordinated between the EU, NATO and its member states (Gressel 2015). One important aspect that this brings forth is that plausible deniability is in fact oftentimes implausible and serves Russia just as much as Western leaders by allowing them to avoid taking costly measures and to save face measures and saving their faces when something clearly contradictory to declared values is committed (Cormac and Aldrich 2018).

Ironically, there is a benefit for the West in the use of private military forces in that it allows them to ignore Russia's interventions in the post-Soviet space, and this would be quite impossible if regular forces were developed. Because the West is complicit in the proliferation of the use of private military forces by Russia a response is not to be expected. Therefor other venues need to be researched to tackle the problem. One obvious course of action is an explicit recognition in policy documents that Russia uses private military forces to achieve its political goals and that they are in contradiction to international law and then creating a reporting system that would serve as a sanctions trigger. Also, this would result in recognising some of the belligerents as victims of human trafficking, sponsored by the Russian state, and open venues to granting these persons political asylum and possibilities for future legal action towards

Russia. A resolution of this sort could uphold values of international law, ratchet up the cost of using human trafficking in international conflict for Russia and create a systematic data collection system, which could be used by multiple states and institutions in their Russia policy. The convoluted responsibility issues of PMSCs in general, and the quasi-PMSC Wagner specifically, however, contribute to the difficulty of effective policy responses and/or legal action. In line with Waschefort's (2018, 143) conclusion it needs to be said that human trafficking in itself is already a type of transnational crime, which is usually conducted in an organised manner, due to its complexity. When one combines this with the exploitation of children in the military, this gives an additional possibility as an avenue of response for international frameworks and governments to act upon.

References

Allison, R. 2017. Russia and the Post-2014 International Legal Order: Revisionism and Realpolitik. *International Affairs* 93 (3): 519–543.

Aranowitz, A., G. Theuermann, and E. Tyurykanova. 2010. *Analysing the Business Model of Trafficking in Human Being to Better Prevent the Crime.* Ueberreuter: OSCE.

Bennet, O. 2014. Putin's Tiny Army: Russian Children Taught to Use Guns and Skills in Combat Camps. *Express*, March 24, 2014. https://www.express.co.uk/news/world/466582/Putin-s-Tiny-Army-Russian-children-taught-to-use-guns-and-combat-skills-in-training-camp

Child Soldiers International. 2008. Global Report 2008 – Russian Federation. https://www.refworld.org/docid/486cb1282d.html

———. 2012. Louder Than Words an Agenda for Action to end State Use of Child Soldiers. https://www.child-soldiers.org/Handlers/Download.ashx?IDMF=da92581e-7130-40e6-bf3a-a86b944f17dd

———. 2017. A Law Unto Themselves? Confronting the Recruitment of Children by Armed Groups. https://www.child-soldiers.org/Handlers/Download.ashx?IDMF=38e90749-3a76-4441-82dc-bd49f1217599

Colby, Elbridge, and Jonathan Solomon. 2015. Facing Russia: Conventional Defence and Deterrence in Europe. *Survival* 57 (6): 21–50.

Cole, C., and R. Vermeltfoort. 2018. *U.S. Government Contractors and Human Trafficking. Two Case Studies of Iraq and Bosnia-Herzegovina*. Springer.

Cormac, R., and R.J. Aldrich. 2018. Grey Is the New Black: Covert Action and Implausible Deniability. *International Affairs* 94 (3): 477–494.

Coynash, H. 2019. Russian-controlled "Donetsk Republic" Creates "Children's Army" to Install "Correct Views". *Kyiv Post*, April 10, 2019. https://www.kyivpost.com/article/opinion/op-ed/halya-coynash-russia-led-donetsk-republic-creates-childrens-army-to-instill-correct-views.html

Eckel, M., and Zakharov, A. 2018. After Syria Deaths, Creeping Anger – and Kremlin Silence – Over Mercenaries in *Radio Free Europe/Radio Liberty February* 16, 2018. https://www.rferl.org/a/russia-syria-deaths-creeping-anger-kremlin-silence-mercenaries/29044248.html

Eklund, N., and Elfving, J. 2017. Russian Private Military Companies – Redwater? in Eurasia Daily Monitor 14 (39). https://jamestown.org/program/russian-private-military-companies-redwater/

Europol. 2018. Situation Report: Criminal Networks Involved in the Trafficking and Exploitation of Underage Victims in the European Union. REF No. 1001370.

Gershkovich, E. 2019. Russia's Fast-Growing "Youth Army" Aims to Breed Loyalty to the Fatherland. *The Moscow Times* April 17, 2019. https://www.themoscowtimes.com/2019/04/17/russias-fast-growing-youth-army-aimst-to-breed-loyalty-to-the-fatherland-a65256

Giglio, M. 2019. Inside the Shadow War Fought by Russian Mercenaries. *BuzzFeedNews* April 17, 2019. https://www.buzzfeednews.com/article/mikegiglio/inside-wagner-mercenaries-russia-ukraine-syria-prighozhin

Gressel, G. 2015. Russia's Quiet Military Revolution, and What It Means for Europe. European Council on Foreign Relations.

Hofmann, C., and Schneckener, U. 2011. Engaging Non-state Armed Actors in State and Peace-Building: Options and Strategies. *International Review of the Red Cross* 89 (93, 883): 1–19.

ICRC. 2008. The Montreux Document on Pertinent International Legal Obligations and Good Practices for States Related to Operations of Private Military and Security Companies During Armed Conflict. https://shop.icrc.org/document-de-montreux-sur-les-entreprises-militaires-et-de-securite-privees-2637.html

Komar, R., Borys, C. and Woods, E. 2017. The Blackwater of Jihad. *Foreign Policy* 10-02-2017.

Lockett, J. 2019. Vlad's Child Soldiers. *The Sun* Mach 20, 2019.

MacFarquhar, N. 2018. Patriotic Youth Army Takes Russian Kids Back to the Future. *The New York Times*, March 22, 2018. https://www.nytimes.com/2018/03/22/world/europe/russia-soviet-youth-army.html
Marten, K. 2019. Russia's Use of Semi-state Security Forces: the Case of the Wagner Group. *Post-Soviet Affairs* 35 (3): 181–204.
Maynes, C. 2018. Russia's Shadow Armies: Soldiers, Mercenaries or Volunteers? *PRI's The World* 15-03-2018.
MEMO. 2019. Report: Saudi Arabia Using Human Trafficking Networks to Recruit Child Soldiers. https://www.middleeastmonitor.com/20190902-report-saudi-arabia-using-human-trafficking-networks-to-recruit-child-soldiers/
Milanovic, M. 2015. Ukraine Derogates from the ICCPR and the ECHR, Files Fourth Interstate Application Against Russia. EJIL: Talk 05-10-2015. https://www.ejiltalk.org/ukraine-derogates-from-the-iccpr-and-the-echr-files-fourth-interstate-application-against-russia/
Nieuwsuur. 2019. Veteranen dienen klacht in tegen geheimzinnig Russisch privéleger, 01-04-2019.
Persson, G. 2016. Russian Military Capability in a Ten-Year Perspective–2016. FOI, December.
Pugsley, S., and Wesslau, F. 2016. Russia in the Grey Zones. *ECFR.EU* September 1, 2016. https://www.ecfr.eu/wider/specials/russia_in_the_grey_zones
Rempfer, K. 2019. Why This US General Says Russian Wagner Mercenaries in Africa "Concern Me Greatly". *Military Times*, April 4, 2019.
Reuters World News. 2016. Russia Withdraws Backing for International Criminal Court Treaty, 16-11-2016. https://www.reuters.com/article/us-russia-icc-withdrawal/russia-withdraws-backing-for-international-criminal-court-treaty-idUSKBN13B1KJ
Rijken, C. 2009. A Human Rights Based Approach to Trafficking in Human Beings. *Security and Human Rights* 11 (3): 212–222.
Robinson, G., and R. McLean. 2018. Working County Lines: Child Criminal Exploitation and Illicit Drug Dealing in Glasgow and Merseyside. *International Journal of Offender Therapy and Comparative Criminology* 63 (5): 694–711.
Roth, A. 2019. "There's No One to Help": Russian Mercenary Industry's Toll on Families. *The Guardian*, August 26.
Shevchenko, V. 2014. Ukraine Conflict: Child Soldiers Join the Fight. *BBC News*, November 26, 2014.
Shurogradsjy, A., Gostev, A., and Krutov, M. 2016. Сирийские потери "Славянского корпуса." https://www.svoboda.org/a/27642396.html

Singer, P.W. 2005. Children at War. Pantheon.
Sossai, M. 2009. 1 Status of PMSC Personnel in the Laws of War: The Question of Direct Participation in Hostilities. EUI Working Paper AEL 2009/6.
Spearin, C. 2019. Russian Military and Security Privatization: Implications for Canada. *Canadian Military Journal* 19 (2): 5–14.
Szpak, A. 2017. Legal Classification of the Armed Conflict in Ukraine in Light of International Humanitarian Law. *Hungarian Journal of Legal Studies* 58 (3): 261–280.
Thomas, T. 2015. Russia's Military Strategy and Ukraine: Indirect, Asymmetric—and Putin-led. *The Journal of Slavic Military Studies* 28 (3): 445–461.
Tonkin, H. 2011. *"State Control Over Private Military and Security Companies" in Armed Conflict.* Cambridge University Press.
Tsvetkova, M. 2015. Special Report: Russian Soldiers Quit Over Ukraine. *Reuters World News*, May 10, 2015. https://www.reuters.com/article/us-ukraine-crisis-soldiers-specialreport-idUSKBN0NV06Q20150510
Tsvetkova, M., and Zverev, A. 2019. Exclusive: Kremlin-linked contractors help guard Venezuela's Maduro – sources. *Reuters World News*, January 25, 2019. https://www.reuters.com/article/us-venezuela-politics-russia-exclusive/exclusive-kremlin-linked-contractors-help-guard-venezuelas-maduro-sources-idUSKCN1PJ22M
UNICEF. 1997. "Cape Town Principles and Best Practices: Adopted at the Symposium" on the Prevention of Recruitment of Children into the Armed Forces and on Demobilization and Social Reintegration of Child Soldiers in Africa." https://www.unicef.org/emerg/files/Cape_Town_Principles(1).pdf
———. 2007. The Paris Principles: Principles and Guidelines on Children Associated with Armed Forces or Armed Groups. https://www.unicef.org/emerg/files/ParisPrinciples310107English.pdf
UNODC and National Rapporteur on Trafficking in Human Beings and Sexual Violence Against Children. 2017. Monitoring Target 16.2 of the United Nations Sustainable Development Goals a Multiple Systems Estimation of the Numbers of Presumed Human Trafficking Victims in the Netherlands in 2010–2015 by Year, Age, Gender, Form of Exploitation and Nationality. https://www.nationaalrapporteur.nl/binaries/An%20estimation%20of%20the%20numbers%20of%20presumed%20human%20trafficking%20victims%20in%20the%20Netherlands_tcm23-282157.pdf
Van Rij, J. 2019. The Fight Against Human Trafficking and the (Absent) Role of the Military. General Jonas Zemaitis Military Academy.
Van Rij, J., and B. Kis Kelemen. 2019. Private Military and Security Companies on E.U. Borders: Who Will Take Responsibility for Their Human Rights Violations? – A Theoretical Analysis. In *EU Justice and Home Affairs Research*

Papers in the Context of Migration and Asylum Law, ed. B. Kis Kelemen and Á. Mohay. University of Pécs Faculty of Law, Centre for European Research and Education.
Van Rij, J., and R. McAlister. 2019. Using Criminal Routines and Techniques to Predict and Prevent the Sexual Exploitation of Eastern-European Women in Western-Europe. In *The Palgrave International Handbook of Human Trafficking*, ed. J. Winterdyk and J. Jones. Cham: Palgrave Macmillan.
Waschefort, G. 2018. Child Soldiering in Relation to Human Trafficking. In *Routledge Handbook of Human Trafficking*, ed. Ryszard Piotrowicz, Conny Rijken, and Baerbel Heide Uhl. Routledge.
Werson, H., and Goutbeek, F. 2005. Protocol for Identification and Assistance to Trafficked Persons and Training Kit. *Anti-Slavery International.*
White, D. 2018. State Capacity and Regime Resilience in Putin's Russia. *International Political Science Review* 39 (1): 130–143.
Zimbardo, P. 2008. *The Lucifer Effect, How Good People Turn Evil.* London: Ebury Publishing.

Jorn van Rij is a senior researcher at the intelligence unit of the Netherlands National Police working on human trafficking and organised crime. Before this he was an associate professor in Criminology at Inholland University of Applied Sciences. In the past he was also an appointed expert for several European anti-trafficking projects and he was a member on the advisory committee for the pilot project 'Advising on the Victimhood of Human Trafficking' by the Dutch Ministry of Justice. He holds a PhD from the University of Pécs.

Ágoston Mohay is an associate professor at the Faculty of Law University of Pécs where he is the head of the Department of International and European Law and the director of the Centre for European Research and Education. He also works for the Office of the Commissioner for Fundamental Rights of Hungary as legal adviser. His research interests include EU citizenship and fundamental rights, EU migration and asylum law and the relationship between EU law and international law. He is a member of the Hungarian branch of the Fédération Internationale Pour Le Droit Européen (FIDE) and the European Migration Network.

Mantas Bileišis is the vice-rector for Research and Studies of General Jonas Žemaitis Military Academy of Lithuania. He conducts research in areas of public administration related to civil and uniformed services regulation and institutional cooperation and conflict among public sector agencies.

6

What Are the Drivers of Children's Decision to Enlist in Armed Groups? A Case Study from Antioquia, Colombia

Giuseppe Maio, Mónica Hurtado, Graham Hesketh, and Kush Wadhwa

Introduction

The Colombian armed conflict has lasted more than 50 years and illicit recruitment[1] has been a regular practice amongst illegal armed groups, including right-wing paramilitaries and left-wing guerrillas. For decades, the department of Antioquia, one of Colombia's 32 sub-national

[1] The Optional Protocol on the Involvement of Children in Armed Conflicts (2000) established that neither state parties nor illegal armed groups should recruit or use in hostilities persons under the age of 18 years (art. 2 and 4). Illicit recruitment, child recruitment, and child soldiering are used as synonyms in this chapter.

G. Maio (✉) • G. Hesketh • K. Wadhwa
Trilateral Research, London, UK
e-mail: giuseppe.maio@trilateralresearch.com

M. Hurtado
Universidad de La Sabana, Campus Universitario del Puente del Común, Chia, Colombia
e-mail: monicahl@unisabana.edu.co

J. Muraszkiewicz et al. (eds.), *Human Trafficking in Conflict*, Crime Prevention and Security Management, https://doi.org/10.1007/978-3-030-40838-1_6

administrative units, has been the epicentre of child recruitment (CNMH 2018; Defensoría del Pueblo 1996, 2001, 2006).[2] Here, as in other conflicts worldwide (such as those in Sri Lanka, Angola, Sierra Leone, and the Philippines), more than 70% of child soldiers claimed to have joined armed groups 'voluntarily' (CNMH 2018; Defensoría del Pueblo 1996, 2001, 2006).[3]

While enlisting in an illegal armed group may be seen as a life-disrupting event for a child, it may also represent an opportunity for vulnerable populations. In prolonged armed conflicts like that of Colombia, enlisting in an illegal armed group in some specific areas may be considered as the 'norm' and even the safer option for some children whose parents, neighbours, and friends are part of these groups (Lugo 2018). Not joining such groups may furthermore represent an even greater risk for these children, as they may be stigmatised and considered supporters of some rival illegal armed organisation, while lacking the means to defend themselves. In addition, for many girls and women, joining an armed group could be a form of empowerment, that is, a way of achieving some form of equality with boys and men—a very different experience from their daily lives (Herrera and Proch 2008).

In this chapter, children's decision to enlist in an armed group is assumed to be 'voluntary', but not free. For these children, a regrettable decision was enlisting in an illegal group, but an even worse decision was remaining in the same situation prior to enlistment. The main drivers of the decision to enlist in an armed group are investigated in this chapter.

What factors drive a child's decision to enlist in an illegal armed group? A number of studies have helped to understand the complexity and

[2] Of the 1387 victims of illicit recruitment heard in the tribunals of Justice and Peace between 2011 and 2018, at least 660 came from Antioquia. The 27 sentences pronounced in these tribunals include the following paramilitary groups within the United Self-Defence Forces of Colombia (AUC): the "Elmer Cardenas" blocks that recruited 322 children; the Miners blocks 336, Bananero block with 7 recruited children, and Heroes of Granada block with 3, all of which operated in Antioquia (see *Sentencias Justicia and Paz*).

[3] It is difficult to establish with certainty how many children have been recruited in an armed conflict like that in Colombia; not only due to its duration, but also due to the multiple illegal armed actors involved that have systematically used illicit recruitment. It is estimated that the number of child soldiers range between 6000 and 18,000, including children and adolescents (Centro Nacional de Memoria Histórica 2018; Human Rights Watch 2003).

nuances of illicit recruitment by armed groups in Colombia. Qualitative studies have identified some of the conditions and factors that influence children's decision to enlist in armed groups. These include, but are not limited to, socio-economic factors such as poverty, lack of education, and lack of job opportunities (Brett 2002; Brett and Specht 2004; Reich and Gates 2010; Downing 2014; Hurtado et al. 2018). Furthermore, the family situation can also impact this decision. For example, children may join an armed group to escape domestic violence and sexual abuse (Brett and Specht 2004; Lugo 2018; Hurtado et al. 2018). In addition to socio-economic factors, authors have identified enlistment drivers related to political violence, for example, children's desire for revenge following the death of a relative, children's need to protect themselves from physical violence, but also living in close proximity to illegal armed groups (Iranzo et al. forthcoming). Quantitative studies have found that the amount of illicit recruitment varies greatly by municipality (Arjona and Kalyvas 2012): areas characterised by rural poverty and the presence of illicit cultivations (such as coca plantations) are more prone to being used as a recruiting ground (Vargas and Restrepo-Jaramillo 2016).

This chapter aims to combine these two approaches to draw statistical connections from the circumstances in which children lived prior to recruitment to their self-identified motivations to join the illegal armed group, whether due to economic or family reasons, and/or political violence (often studied qualitatively). Doing so provides a unique insight into the study of child soldiers, enhancing our understanding of what motivates a child to join an armed group, and may lead to targeted prevention policies that can be more effective than a one-size-fits-all approach.

This is an important line of enquiry following the signing of the peace agreement between the Colombian President Juan Manuel Santos and the Revolutionary Armed Forces of Colombia (FARC) guerrillas in 2016, through which about 10,000 adult combatants laid down their weapons, although some of them had been enlisted as children (International Crisis Group 2017). It is important to understand the patterns and dynamics of recruitment that characterised these young ex-combatants—not only in the context of the current Colombian peace-building process, but also because illicit recruitment continues to affect children in post-conflict zones. Through studying the Colombian case of Antioquia, the authors of this chapter seek to contribute towards the prevention of illicit recruitment in Colombia and beyond.

Illicit recruitment and human trafficking are seen by the authors as being characterised by similar patterns: they are both forms of unfree labour, with a supply and a demand side (Iranzo et al. forthcoming). On the demand side, illegal armed groups look for inexpensive young soldiers to participate directly and indirectly in the war. On the supply side, children living in poverty are 'willing' to join illegal armed groups because this might help them improve their socio-economic conditions (Downing 2014; Brett and Specht 2004; Reich and Gates 2010).

The chapter continues with the following sections: first, a description of the background situation in Antioquia is provided; second, the chapter explains the methods employed in this study; third, the results of the study are presented and discussed; finally, the chapter considers its impact and concludes with a reflection on the extent to which the drivers of children's decision to enlist in an armed group that were identified continue to pose a risk to the current Colombian peace-building process.

The Background Situation in Antioquia

This section provides contextual information about the circumstances in which the children that make up the sample used in this study lived prior to their recruitment. These will be explored, in next sections, as the factors that may drive children's decision to enlist in armed groups.

Regarding the socio-economic context, between the late 1990s and early 2000s (the time span of illicit recruitment covered by the sample used in this chapter), Antioquia was the thirteenth most developed Colombian department out of a total of 32, according to Human Development Index (HDI) data (UNDP 2003). Between 1991 and 2001, Antioquia's illiteracy rate went down from 10.6% to 5.26%, and the department achieved almost universal primary education (UNDP 2003). However, it was characterised by a high unemployment rate, which reached 28% in 2001 (DANE 2001), as well as various forms of inequalities, such as income inequality and inequality in land ownership (UNDP 2003).

Between the 1980s and 2000s, Antioquia suffered high levels of political violence. For instance, in the 1980s in Urabá, an Antioquian subregion characterised by a high volume of illicit recruitment into armed groups (Hurtado et al. 2018), there was a strong presence of two communist guerrilla groups: the Popular Liberation Army (EPL) and the FARC. These armed groups undermined the state's legitimacy and extorted money from local entrepreneurs. Seeking to protect their businesses, the latter financed right-wing paramilitaries in order to curb guerrillas' activities. The FARC and the EPL also clashed over territorial disputes. In 1991, the EPL guerrilla signed a peace agreement and demobilised but was soon accused of 'treason of the revolution' by both the FARC and by a splinter faction of the EPL that did not demobilise (OPPDH 2006). In this situation, the ex-combatants of the EPL rearmed in order to defend themselves and formed the so-called Popular Commands, which forged an alliance with right-wing paramilitaries operating in Antioquia under the name United Self-Defence Forces of Colombia (AUC). The AUC battled for years against guerrilla organisations to gain territorial control. Rather than confronting the guerrillas directly, however, the AUC often attacked the civilian population that formed the guerrillas' support base, causing mass displacement and massacres as a result (Nasi 2018). Between 1990 and 2000, Antioquia had the highest rate of homicides per 100,000 inhabitants in the country (UNDP 2003).

Since the 1980s in Antioquia, illegal armed actors on the extreme left (communist guerrillas) and extreme right (paramilitaries) have controlled and/or engaged in various illicit economic activities, such as illegal mining, the production of illicit crops, cocaine trafficking, weapons trade, and small-scale drug trafficking (Sánchez et al. 2003; Thoumi 2011). Both illegal armed groups have directly or indirectly benefited from and protected the interests of drug traffickers (Adams 2011; Sánchez et al. 2003). In turn, the presence of illicit crops used for drug production and trafficking was found to increase the probability of children enlisting in the ranks of Colombian illegal armed groups (Vargas and Restrepo-Jaramillo 2016). Between 1991 and 2007, cocaine-related revenues in

Colombia were estimated to range between US$ 600 million and US$ 1.2 billion; between 1991 and 1999, this represented between 0.56% and 1.61% of Colombia's GDP (O'Connor 2009).

Methods

This section presents the data used and the model employed to explore the factors that may drive children's decision to enlist in armed groups.

Child Soldier and Municipality Data from Antioquia

The 2019 study conducted by the authors employed a sample of 554 boys and 116 girls who were illicitly recruited as children (below the age of 18) by either right-wing paramilitaries or left-wing guerrillas in the Colombian department of Antioquia between 1994 and 2005. The children in the sample resided in 59 Antioquian municipalities prior to their recruitment, and they all discharged as adults (aged 18 or above). Information about the children was obtained from their post-demobilisation testimonies; 601 of these testimonies were gathered by the Public Prosecutor's Office that specialises in transitional justice, and the remaining 59 were gathered by the Colombian ordinary justice system. Testimonies were converted from text to numerical data by Iranzo et al. (forthcoming). The present study builds on the work carried out by those authors, analysing a subset of the dataset they built from the testimonies of 1928 children illegally recruited in 290 Colombian municipalities. In order to understand which factors, drive a child's decision to enlist in an illegal armed group, the variable *Motivation to join the illegal armed group (according to the victim)* was selected as the dependent variable. This was originally constructed by extracting the numerous motivations of enlistment in the armed group that the victims provided in their testimonies. For the purpose of this study, the various motivations were divided into two typologies and recoded as shown in Table 6.1. Reducing the number of categories in this way boosts the number of children in each category, thus improving confidence in the patterns identified.

Table 6.1 Recoding Typology 1 indicates Economic Motivations, 0 indicates Family and Political Violence Motivations

Initial value	Recoded value
Employment opportunity	1
Shortage of economic means or emotional deprivation	1
Family economic situation	1
Offered a sum of money	1
Earning money in the armed group	1
In order to generate an income	1
Intra-family violence	0
Through family connections	0
Fell in love with a member of the group	0
Consent given by parents	0
Invitation by a cousin who was part of the group	0
Lover was a member of the guerrilla group	0
His/her brothers were members of the paramilitary group	0
As a protection mechanism from intra-family violence	0
Interest in weapons/attracted by the ideology of the group	0
Protection mechanism from attacks or threats from rival group	0
Threats against him/her or family by the group	0
Revenge against member of rival group	0
Demand for young participants	0
Easy access to hallucinogenic substances	0
For belonging to the rival group	0
The guerrilla group was based in the street where he/she resided	0
His/her mother was assassinated	0
Interest in weapons	0
As a protection mechanism from rival groups	0
Desire for revenge resulting from the assassination of his/her sister by the paramilitary group	0
Desire for revenge resulting from the assassination of his/her brother by the paramilitary group	0
Interest in the uniforms of the guerrilla groups	0
Was obliged to join by the commander of the guerrilla group	0
The paramilitary group was based in the street where he/she resided	0
The paramilitary group obliged him to run errands	0
Desire for revenge as the guerrilla murdered one of his/her uncles	0
Was obliged to join by the commander of the paramilitary group	0

As a result of the recoding above, the dependent variable, renamed *motive*, consists of the following values: 1 for economic motives, and 0 for family or political violence motives. This recoding results in a standard binary classification problem, with the aim then being to explain the circumstances under which a child would join the armed group because of either of these motives.

As far as the independent variables are concerned, the following individual-level variables were included in the analysis:

- child's gender (0 = male; 1= female), renamed *gender*;
- child's age (ranging from 7 to 17 years), renamed *age*;
- child's previous activity (0 = children in employment or education or both; 1 = for inactive children who neither work nor study), renamed *inactive*;
- child's recruiting group (0 = paramilitary; 1 = guerrilla), renamed *illegalGroup*;
- child's family composition (0 = biparental families; 1 = non biparental families), renamed *nonBiparental*.

These are socio-economic, demographic, and recruitment-related variables that provide information on the recruited child, thanks to the granularity of the data available.

Respondents with missing values in the *motive*, or *age* or municipality of residence variables were removed thereby reducing the sample size to 514 children nested within 57 municipalities. Additionally, the municipality-level independent variables below were considered:

- mean number of hectares of cultivation of coca in each municipality between 2001 and 2005 (UNODC 2018), renamed *illicitCrops;*
- political killings in each municipality, computed by summing the total number of town councillors, mayors, trade unionists, unionised teachers, and journalists murdered between 1990 and 2005 (*Observatorio del Programa Presidencial de DDHH y DIH* 2013), renamed *polKillings;*
- labour formality calculated as percentage of workers contributing to health and pension (FILCO 2017), renamed *labourForm*.

These are economic, political violence, and criminality-related indicators that provide information on the municipality where the child lived prior to recruitment.

To help the interpretation of the model results as well as the model convergence (i.e. the model's ability to compute consistent and reliable estimates), all the independent variables that take more than two values were transformed into binary categorical variables. These variables' median values were used as cut-off points for constructing the categories (1 indicates above the median value, while 0 indicates below the median value; for *labourForm,* 1 indicates below the median value, while 0 indicates above the median value). Independent variables that take two values (e.g. *gender*, *inactive*, *illegalGroup* and *nonBiparental*) were not transformed. Table 6.2 describes the data used in the analysis and provides summary statistics of the dependent and independent variables. It should be noted that the proportion of children in the sample who stated they joined the armed group for family reasons was only 3%. Hence, in order

Table 6.2 Summary Statistics of individual-level and municipality-level variables (includes dependent variable, motive)

Overall (n = 660)			
Variable	Missing val.	Level	Freq. (Perc.)
Age	29	Above Median (16)	153 (30)
		Below Median	361 (70)
Gender	0	Male	554 (83.9)
		Female	106 (16.1)
Inactive	112	Inactive	220 (40.2)
		Working, Studying, Both	328 (59.2)
illegalGroup	0	Paramilitary	552 (83.6)
		Guerilla	108 (16.4)
nonBiparental	327	Non Biparental	190 (57)
		Biparental	143 (43)
motive	127	Family and Political Violence	196 (36.8)
		Economic	337 (63.2)
illicitCrops	0	Above Median (30.5 hectares)	255 (49.7)
		Below Median	259 (50.3)
polKillings	0	Above Median (1)	252 (49)
		Below Median	262 (51)
labourForm	0	Below Median (4.9)	260 (50.6)
		Above Median	254 (49.4)

to avoid reducing the sample size further, family motivations were absorbed into political violence motivations; findings will be thus discussed in terms of economic or political violence motivations only (see the Results, Discussion and Conclusion sections).

In order to avoid reducing the sample size further, the missing values in two independent variables were imputed: 112 values were imputed in *inactive* and 327 in *nonBiparental*. The missing values in these variables were filled using the information provided by the other variables in the dataset, excluding the dependent variable *motive*.[4]

Modelling Children's Decision to Enlist in Armed Groups

This study performed a logistic regression analysis using the *scikit-learn* Python library (scikit-learn 2019a, b, c) to explore children's self-declared reasons to join the armed group. This type of analysis is appropriate because it allows researchers to account for the relationship between a binary dependent variable (e.g. *motive*) and multiple independent variables,[5] whilst also being easily interpretable, thus allowing conclusions to be drawn regarding the role played by each variable. The equation for the logistic regression model is shown in Eq. (6.1). This equation models how the motivation to join the armed group is statistically linked to the circumstances of the child's life prior to recruitment. In Eq. (6.1), p_i is the predicted probability of the ith child joining the armed group for economic reasons (dependent variable), b_0 is the intercept of the model, b_j is the model coefficient for the jth independent variable, $x_{i,j}$ is the value of the jth independent variable for the ith child, and N is the number of independent variables. The values for the intercept, b_0, and coefficients, b_j, are to be obtained by fitting the model to the data using Python *scikit-learn* (scikit-learn 2019a, b, c).

Logistic Regression Equation

[4] Imputation was carried out using Python *sklearn*'s *Iterative* Imputer (scikit-learn 2019a, b, c).

[5] More information on logistic regression models can be found in Chap. 15 of Agresti et al. (2009). See also Chap. 3 of Kary and Schaub (2011).

$$\ln\left(\frac{p_i}{1-p_i}\right) = b_0 + \sum_N^j b_j x_{i,j} \tag{6.1}$$

By studying the coefficients of the model, it is possible to explain how the motivation to join the armed group depends on each aspect of the child's circumstances prior to recruitment. To be explicit, for a unit increase in the independent variable $x_{i,j}$, the odds of a child joining for economic reasons increases by $\exp(b_j)$ as indicated in Eq. (6.2):

Odds ratio gives an indication of the importance of a variable on the child's motivation to join an armed group

$$\frac{odds\left(x_{i,j}+1\right)}{odds\left(x_{i,j}\right)} = \exp\left(b_j\right) \tag{6.2}$$

The model was trained on 70% of the dataset (363 observation randomly selected) and tested on the remaining 30% (151 observations). Due to the class imbalance in the data (the *Economic* to *Political Violence* class ratio of the dependent variable was 63:37), it was felt that the outcome would be most insightful if the model was optimised to maximise balanced accuracy. This was achieved by setting *scikit-learn*'s scoring method to '*balanced_accuracy*' (scikit-learn 2019a, b, c). In order to regulate against overfitting, the logistic regression model to the training data, a penalty term known as the C regularisation parameter (scikit-learn 2019a, b, c) was optimised within a five-fold cross-validation routine.[6] The optimal value of the C parameter was 2. Cross-validation also provides a 95% confidence interval on the model performance during the training stage. Once the optimal value of the C parameter had been found, the model was retrained on the entire training dataset. The model performance was finally re-tested using the test dataset.

[6] More information on cross-validation can be found in Wong (2015), but the key point is that large values of C give more freedom to the model, which can lead to overfitting, while small values constrain the model more, introducing more bias, but sometimes improving the model's ability to generalise to unseen data.

Results

Table 6.3 shows the accuracy, recall of economic motivations, and recall of political violence motivations, computed on both the training and test sets. The mean and 95% confidence interval of the accuracy score of the five-fold cross validation on the training set was 0.65 (+/– 0.073), while the accuracy score on the test set was 0.67. This indicates that the model predicts motivations to join almost seven out of 10 times. As far as the model's ability to predict economic motivations, the recall scores for this class on the training and test set are 0.61 and 0.62 respectively, showing the model successfully predicts economic motivations over 6 out of 10 times. Finally, with regards to political violence class, the model predicts this 72% of the times on the training set and 79% of the times on the test set.

Table 6.4 shows the coefficients, b_j, of the logistic regression model (Eq. 6.1) associated with children's motivations to join the armed group as derived when fitting the model to the training data. Coefficients with negative values indicate those factors that were identified as statistically

Table 6.3 Model performance metrics on train and test sets

	Accuracy	Recall-economic	Recall-political violence
Training set (CV)	0.65	0.61	0.72
Test set	0.67	0.62	0.79

Table 6.4 Model coefficients and odds ratios of Economic Motivation

Logistic Regression Model			
Variables	Coefficients	Odds ratios	p-values
inactive	1.255566***	3.5098	0.0000007022
illicitCrops	0.882124***	2.4160	0.0000555257
nonBiparental	0.633700*	1.8846	0.0201246532
age	−0.109396	0.8964	0.0981617564
polKilling	−0.207340**	0.8127	0.0020111854
gender	−0.252527	0.7768	0.4835458126
labourForm	−0.346791*	0.7070	0.0252028244
illegalGroup	−1.007704***	0.3650	0.0011982138
model intercept	−0.802625	0.4482	–

***$p < 0.001$, **$p < 0.01$, *$p < 0.05$

significant drivers of political violence-driven recruitment (i.e. they reduce the likelihood of joining for economic reasons). These are: *age*, *gender*, living in a municipality characterised by an above-median (over 1) number of political killings (*polKillings*), living in a municipality with below-median (below 4.9%) levels of formal labour (*labourForm*), and joining guerrillas (*illegalGroup*). Coefficients with positive values indicate those factors that were identified as statistically significant drivers of economic recruitment. These are: neither working nor studying (*inactive*), living in a municipality with an above-median (over 30.5 hectares) presence of illicit cultivations (*illicitCrops*), and living in a non-biparental household (*nonBiparental*). All the independent variables of this model, apart from *age* and *gender*, are statistically significant with a p-value of 0.05[7] or below. In order to understand how much influence each of the variables has on the child's motivation to join the armed group, the model coefficients, b_j, were transformed into an odds ratio of economic motivations using Eq. (6.2) as shown in Table 6.4 below. Each of these will be discussed in detail in the next section.

Discussion

With regards to socioeconomic factors related to illicit recruitment, results show that being inactive, for example, neither working nor studying (*inactive*), increases children's odds of economic-driven recruitment by a factor of almost 4. This is a valuable insight which could inform policy makers about the potential economic recruitment-related risks in the current peace-building process. Between the mid-1990s and the early 2000s (the timeframe of illicit recruitment covered by this sample), a child living in an Antioquian municipality which had long been plagued by the armed conflict, was not left with many options. If they had ever studied, these children were likely to have obtained only a primary school-level qualification; often, they dropped out of school, as with almost 40% of the children in this study's sample. For some, joining paramilitary groups and earning a monthly salary of US$ 85

[7] P-value ≤ 0.05 conventionally indicates that a relationship is statistically significant.

(200,000–250,000, Colombian Pesos) was an option (Hurtado et al. 2018; Gutiérrez Sanín 2008, 14).[8] The fact that inactive children were found to be more prone to join the armed group for economic reasons rather than due to political violence supports this reasoning. Furthermore, this might provide support for the argument that illicit recruitment functions as a labour market: for those who neither work nor study, economic-driven recruitment may be a way to improve their life conditions. A similar scenario may unfortunately materialise today: the *Ejército de Liberación Nacional* (ELN) guerrilla organisation, FARC dissidents, and Criminal Gangs (BACRIM) continue recruiting young children and adolescents in Antioquia (CIPRUNNA 2018). To prevent economic-driven recruitment, policies that aim to boost local economies and provide job opportunities to young people should target those who have prematurely interrupted their studies and are not in any form of employment. This demographic was identified as being particularly at risk of economic-driven recruitment.

Interestingly, the results of the model suggest that living in a municipality characterised by an above-median presence of illicit crops (over 30.5 hectares) increases children's odds of economic-driven recruitment by a factor of more than 2. Although Colombia is undergoing a peace-building process, drug-trafficking continues to be a lucrative activity and continues to offer economic opportunities (UNODC 2018). In fact, between 2016 and 2017, the production of coca leaves increased by 25,000 hectares—and Antioquia was one of the departments characterised by an above average increase (UNODC 2018, 13). This data warns of the dangers of economic-driven recruitment associated with the increase in the presence of illicit crops. To reduce illicit recruitment, when carrying out economic reforms it seems appropriate to start with those municipalities characterised by a high prevalence of illicit crops. Giving precedence to these areas when boosting economic growth may also reduce the risk of economic-driven illicit recruitment.

Children living in a non-biparental household (*nonBiparental*) tend to join armed groups more for economic than political violence reasons

[8] See also Justice and Peace Sentences: Tribunal Superior del Distrito Judicial de Bogotá, Sala de Justicia y Paz (2011) and Tribunal Superior de Medellín, Sala de Justicia y Paz (2015).

(their odds of economic recruitment increase by 88%). Living in non-biparental families, where sources of income can be scarcer than in biparental ones, may render children less economically secure and thus more prone to join the armed group for economic reasons, as this result seems to suggest. This finding may also draw attention to the role that children's carers in non-biparental families may play in children's decisions to join armed groups. Therefore, policy interventions that aim to provide economic support to these carers may reduce the risk of economic-driven child recruitment.

Children living in below-median (below 4.6%) municipalities for labour formality (*labourForm*) are more prone to join for political violence than economic reasons (their odds of political violence recruitment increase by 30%). The significant relationship between municipal low levels of formal labour (*labourForm*) and children's political violence-driven motivations to enlist is surprising. Considering that poverty was found to be a driver of illicit recruitment (Vargas and Restrepo-Jaramillo 2016), low levels of formal labour were expected to be associated with economic-driven motivations. Nonetheless, this finding may shed light on the complexities characterising the interplay of economic issues and political grievances in Antioquia and Colombia more broadly. The results from the model also show that children who enlist in guerrilla groups (*illegalGroup*) do so more for political violence than economics (their odds of political violence-driven recruitment increase by 64%). This is consistent with previous studies (e.g. Gutiérrez Sanín 2008) which have found that paramilitaries offer more economic incentives than guerrillas, and that the latter tend to subject children to forced recruitment more than the former (Gutierrez 2010).

Finally, living in a municipality with an above median (over 1) incidence of political homicides (*polKillings*) was found to increase children's odds of political violence-driven recruitment by 19%, although this was the weakest predictor of political violence-driven motivations. This finding is particularly relevant in post-conflict Colombia, where "between January 2016 and January 2019, 343 civil society leaders and human rights activists were murdered: 49 of these homicides, happened in Antioquia" (Defensoría del Pueblo 2019). This finding may inform policy makers of the risks of political violence-driven recruitment in areas affected by political homicides; a number of recent homicides have taken place in territories formerly controlled by the now-demobilised FARC, found to be associated with political violence-driven recruitment (INDEPAZ 2019). The model's results suggest the importance of ensuring that FARC-perpetrated political violence-driven recruitment in those territories is not simply being replaced by the activities of drug-traffickers or FARC dissidents.

Impact and Conclusion

This chapter demonstrated a rigorous methodology to analyse children's decision to enlist in illegal armed groups through the use of logistic regression. This supports qualitative researchers who focus on studying children's motivation to join the armed group by quantifying the contributions that socio-economic, demographic, political violence and criminality indicators make to children's decision to enlist. This application of logistic regression can be extended to other data sources (e.g. *Observatory of Peace and Conflict*'s data, *Family Welfare Institute*'s data, *Unit for Victims' Care and Integral Reparation*'s data, etc.) in order to investigate quantitatively children's motivation to enlist in armed groups. With larger sample sizes, the confidence in the patterns identified will increase, and it will be also possible to employ more advanced and insightful techniques to study this aspect of child soldiering. Hence, this chapter represents a useful proof of concept and, focussing on Antioquia, can be used to draw comparisons with trends in children's self- declared reason to join the armed group in other Colombian departments.

In addition, this study provides an example of how data-driven policy strategies could be designed to tackle illicit recruitment in the context of Antioquia. For instance, the data suggests that in order to reduce the risk of economic-driven child enlistment, it is important to target young adolescents who neither work nor study (found to be almost four times more prone to enlist for economic motivations), live in non-biparental households (found to be 88% more prone to enlist for economic motivations), within municipalities characterised by an above median (30.5 hectares) presence of illicit crops (these areas were found to render respondents over two times more prone to economic recruitment).

To conclude, the study discussed in this chapter identified the various factors statistically associated with children's decisions to enlist in illegal armed groups during the period 1994–2005 in the department of Antioquia, Colombia. Factors that are statistically associated with children testifying to having economic motivations for joining armed groups include being inactive, for example, neither working nor studying prior to recruitment (*inactive*), living in a municipality with an above-median presence of illegal cultivations (*illicitCrops*), and living in a non-biparental family (*nonBiparental*). Factors associated with children giving political violence-related motivations for joining armed groups include living in a municipality with an above-median number of political homicides (*polKillings*) and living in an area characterised by below-median levels of formal employment (*labourForm*).

The municipal-level political violence and criminality-related factors identified to be statistically associated with economic- and political violence-driven recruitment, for example, presence of illicit crops (*illicitCrops*) and political homicides (*polKillings*) respectively, persist in the current peace-building process. These, in turn, constitute a risk for children because many criminal organisations still attempt to fill the void left by the now-demobilised illegal armed groups in Colombia. Hence, although the armed groups representing the demand side of illicit recruitment may have changed, factors driving the supply of children who 'willingly' join these groups for economic and political violence reasons may continue.

Acknowledgements We are thankful to Jose Vinaixa Kinnear for his contribution to the translation, cleaning, and harmonisation of the datasets used in this chapter.

References

Adams, D. 2011. Vínculos entre paramilitares y drogas: antes y después de la desmovilización. *La desmovilización de los paramilitares en Colombia: entre el escepticismo y la esperanza, Bogotá: Univresidad de Los Andes* 69–87.

Agresti, A., B. Finlay, and J. Miller. 2009. *Statistical Methods for the Social Sciences*. Upper Saddle River, NJ: Pearson.

Arjona, A.M., and S.N. Kalyvas. 2012. Recruitment into Armed Groups in Colombia: A Survey of Demobilized Fighters. In *Understanding Collective Political Violence. Conflict, Inequality and Ethnicity*, ed. Y. Guichaoua. London: Palgrave Macmillan.

Brett, R., and Specht, I. 2004. Young Soldiers: Why the Chose to Fight? Geneva: International Labour Office; Boulder, C.O Lynne Reinner Publishers.

Brett, R. 2002. *Girl soldiers: Challenging the Assumptions*. New York, NY: Quaker United Nations Office.

Centro Nacional de Memoria Histórica -CNMH. 2018. Una guerra sin edad. Informe nacional de reclutamiento y utilización de niños, niñas y adolescentes en el conflicto armado colombiano. Bogotá, Colombia (nota).

Defensoría del Pueblo. 1996. *Víctimas de la violencia: el conflicto armado en Colombia*. Bogotá: Defensoría del Pueblo.

———. 2001. *La niñez en el conflicto armado colombiano*. Bogotá: Defensoría del Pueblo.

———. 2006. *Caracterización de las niñas, niños y adolescentes desvinculados de los grupos armados ilegales*. Bogotá: Defensoría del Pueblo.

———. 2019. *Homicidios de líderes sociales y defensores de DDHH*. http://www.defensoria.gov.co/es/public/contenido/7399/Homicidios-del%C3%ADderes-sociales-y-defensores-de-DDHH.htm

Departamento Administrativo Nacional de Estadística. 2001. Informe de Coyuntura Económica Regional de Antioquia III TRIMESTRE DE 2001. https://www.dane.gov.co/files/icer/2001/antioquia/t3.pdf

Downing, C. 2014. Child Recruitment to Illegal Armed Groups in Colombia: Peacebuilding and Development Challenges. *Journal of Peacebuilding & Development* 9 (3): 33–49.

Fuente de Informacion Laboral de Colombia (FILCO). 2017. "Porcentaje de ocupados que cotizan a salud y pension 2017". Available at: http://filco.mintrabajo.gov.co/FILCO/faces/estadisticas.jsf

Gutierrez, S.F. 2010. Organizing Minors: The Case of Colombia. In *Child Soldiers in the Age of Fractured States*, ed. S. Gates and S. Reich. Pittsburgh: University of Pittsburgh Press.

Gutiérrez Sanín, F. 2008. Telling the Difference: Guerrillas and Paramilitaries in the Colombian War. *Politics and Society* 36 (1): 3–34.

Herrera, N., and D. Porch. 2008. 'Like Going to a Fiesta' – the Role of Female Fighters in Colombia's FARC-EP. *Small Wars & Urgencies* 19 (4): 609–634.

Human Rights Watch (HRW). 2003. "You'll Learn Not to Cry: Child Combatants in Colombia". Available at: https://www.hrw.org/reports/2003/colombia0903/colombia0903.pdf

Hurtado, M., Á. Iranzo Dosdad, and S. Gómez Hernández. 2018. The Relationship Between Human Trafficking and Child Recruitment in the Colombian Armed Conflict. *Third World Quarterly* (5): 941.

Instituto para de estudios para el Desarrollo y la paz (INDEPAZ). 2019. "Fuente de la información "566 líderes sociales y defensores de derechos humanos han sido asesinados desde el 1 de enero de 2016 – al 10 de enero de 2019" Available at: http://www.indepaz.org.co/566-lideres-sociales-y-defensores-de-derechos-humanos-han-sido-asesinados-desde-el-1-de-enero-de-2016-al-10-de-enero-de-2019/

International Crisis Group. 2017. *Colombia's Armed Groups Battle for the Spoils of Peace. Preventing War. Shaping Peace.* https://d2071andvip0wj.cloudfront.net/063-colombias-armed-groups-battle-for-the-spoils-of-peace_0.pdf

Iranzo, A., Hurtado, M., and Escobar L. (Forthcoming). Labor Markets in Contexts of War: Recruitment and Trafficking of Child Soldiers in Colombia.

Kary and Schaub. 2011. *Bayesian Population Analysis using WinBUGS: A Hierarchical Perspective*. Amsterdam: Elsevier.

Lugo, V. 2018. Niños y jóvenes excombatientes en Colombia: ¿por qué se vinculan y separan de la guerra? *Athenea Digital* 18 (2): e1933.

Nasi, C. 2018. La economía política del conflicto armado en Colombia: Algunas hipótesis sobre el contraste entre los sectores bananero y floricultor. En Rettberg, A., Leiteritz, R., Nasi, C., and Prieto, D. *¿Diferentes recursos, conflictos distintos?: La economía política regional del conflicto y la criminalidad en Colombia. Ediciones Uniandes*-Universidad de los Andes, 83–134.

O'Connor, D. 2009. *The Political Economy of Colombia's Cocaine Industry.* http://www.scielo.org.co/pdf/papel/v14n1/v14n1a05.pdf

Observatorio de Derechos Humanos (DDH) y Derecho Internacional Humanitario (DIH) (2013). *Estadísticas.* http://2014.derechoshumanos.gov.co/Observatorio/Paginas/Estad%C3%ADsticas-2012.aspx

Observatorio del Programa Presidencia de Derechos Humanos y DIH - OPPDH. 2006. *Dinámica reciente de la confrontación armada en el Urabá antioqueño.* http://historico.derechoshumanos.gov.co/Observatorio/Publicaciones/documents/2010/Estu_Regionales/uraba.pdf

Recruitment, Use/Utilization and Sexual Violence against Children and Adolescence by Armed Groups on the Margin of Law and by Organized Crime Groups--CIPRUNNA, July, 2018.

Reich, S., and S. Gates. 2010. *Child Soldiers in the Age of Fractured States.* Pittsburgh, Pennsylvania: University of Pittsburgh Press.

Sánchez, F., Díaz, A.M., and Formisano, M. 2003. Conflicto, violencia y actividad criminal en Colombia: un análisis espacial. CEDE.

scikit-learn. 2019a. 5.4. *Imputation of missing values*—scikit-learn 0.21.3 documentation. https://scikit-learn.org/stable/modules/impute.html#iterative-imputer
———. 2019b. *Balanced Accuracy Score* — scikit-learn 0.21.3 documentation. https://scikitlearn.org/stable/modules/generated/sklearn.metrics.balanced_accuracy_score.html
———. 2019c. *Penalty and Sparsity in Logistic Regression*—scikit-learn 0.21.3 documentation. https://scikitlearn.org/stable/auto_examples/linear_model/plot_logistic_l1_l2_sparsity.html
Thoumi, F. 2011. Paramilitares, crimen organizado y tráfico de drogas: son sus raíces endógenas o exógenas a Colombia? In *La desmovilización de los paramilitares en Colombia: entre el escepticismo y la esperanza*, 2301–2326. Bogotá: Univresidad de Los Andes.
Tribunal Superior del Distrito Judicial de Bogotá, Sala de Justicia y Paz (16/12/2011). 2011. Sentencia 110016000253200782701. [MP. Uldi Teresa Jiménez López].
Tribunal Superior de Medellín, Sala de Justicia y Paz (02/02/2015). 2015. Sentencia 110016000253200680018. [MP. María Consuelo Rincón Jaramillo].
United Nations Development Programme. 2003. *OCCASIONAL PAPER: Background paper for HDR 2003*. http://hdr.undp.org/sites/default/files/colombia_2003.pdf
United Nations Office on Drugs and Crime. 2018. *Colombia Coca Cultivation Survey 2017 – Executive Summary* (English). https://www.unodc.org/documents/crop-monitoring/Colombia/Colombia_Survey_territories_affected_illicit_crops_2017_Summary.pdf
Vargas, G.A., and N. Restrepo-Jaramillo. 2016. Child Soldiering in Colombia: Does Poverty Matter? *Civil Wars* 18 (4): 467–487.
Wong, T. 2015. Performance Evaluation of Classification Algorithms by k-fold and Leave-One-Out Cross Validation. *Pattern Recognition* 48 (9): 2839–2846.

Giuseppe Maio is a senior data analyst at Trilateral Research. His research interests lie where data, political science and new technologies meet. He has developed a data-driven Modern Slavery risk assessment tool for the UK's Ministry of Defence (MOD) as part of Project Solebay.

Mónica Hurtado is an associate professor in the Faculty of Law & Political Sciences, Universidad de La Sabana, Colombia. She holds an MA in Latin

American studies from Stanford University and an MA in international peace studies from the University of Notre Dame. She worked as a consultant for the Trafficking in Persons Program of the International Organization for Migration (IOM) and the International Labor Organization (ILO). She has done research on human trafficking, sexual exploitation, child recruitment, historical memory and forced displacement in Colombia.

Graham Hesketh is the Head of Data Science at Trilateral Research, where he leads a technical team developing a data-driven cloud-based web application for risk analysis. As part of MOD projects, he applies machine learning methods to Human Security and Modern Slavery risk assessment for the UK military.

Kush Wadhwa is Director at Trilateral Research where he leads product strategy for the transfer of research to methodologies and tools that enable data-driven decision-making and risk identification, assessment and management.

7

Occurrence of Human Trafficking in a Conflict/Peacebuilding Context: Bosnian Experience

Abida Pehlić

Introduction

The term "trafficking in human beings" had become very prominent in Bosnia and Herzegovina (B&H) immediately after the end of the last war in the late 1990s, when B&H used to be predominantly a country of transit and destination for girls and women from the Eastern European countries. They were forced to provide commercial sexual services at numerous nightclubs and brothels located near major international military bases established in the country to stabilize peace. Ethnic conflicts in the former Yugoslavia have contributed significantly to the vulnerability of women to sex trafficking. Nikolic-Ristanovic (2003) states their impact is mostly connected to specific war and post-war situations, but human, and especially sex, trafficking may also be the consequence of the very presence of military in the region, regardless of whether there is war going on or not. She further added that examples from recent history showed that the expansion of prostitution due to the extended presence of

A. Pehlić (✉)
Association "Novi put", Mostar, Bosnia and Herzegovina

J. Muraszkiewicz et al. (eds.), *Human Trafficking in Conflict*, Crime Prevention and Security Management, https://doi.org/10.1007/978-3-030-40838-1_7

military forces has got long-term consequences on the development of sex trafficking at both the local and global levels.

At the time when the term first came into use, a vast majority of B&H's population and officials could not comprehend the actual meaning of the phrase, let alone accept the fact that it was happening in the country. Unfortunately, the author was not an exception and at the time when she was redeployed to the UNMIBH (United Nations Mission in Bosnia and Herzegovina) STOP Team in 2000, she was struggling to accept that something like that existed at all, and particularly in B&H. However, almost 20 years later she has been struggling with a different problem—how to successfully combat the issue in B&H. The war ended almost 25 years ago; however, human trafficking has still remained a big issue in B&H, also showing up in other forms. The 2019 Trafficking in Persons Report of the U.S. Department of State reads that

> "Bosnian women and girls are subjected to sex trafficking within the country in private residences, motels, and gas stations. Marginalized Romani children are subjected to forced begging, sex trafficking, and domestic servitude in forced marriages…Bosnian victims are subjected to sex trafficking and forced labour in construction and other sectors in countries across Europe … Bosnia and Herzegovina remained on Tier 2 Watch List for the second consecutive year" (2019, 105).

The 2017 report of the Group of Experts on Action against Trafficking in Human Beings responsible for monitoring the implementation of the Council of Europe Convention on Action against Trafficking in Human Beings by the Parties (GRETA) on B&H stated that due to the difficult economic situation in B&H, an increasing number of people has been seeking jobs abroad, exposing themselves to the risk of falling victim to human trafficking (Council of Europe 2017).

The aim of the chapter is to explore the occurrence of trafficking in human beings and forced prostitution as a prevailing form of exploitation in the post-war B&H of the 1990s, with a particular focus on the role of peacekeeping forces deployed to the country in fuelling demand for the provision of commercial sexual services. The chapter will show how corruption within the local police forces allowed the trafficking of women and girls to flourish and will examine the engagement of the UNMIBH Special Trafficking Operations Program (STOP) in light of identification of potential trafficking victims during raids of brothels and nightclubs. The chapter analyses the legal immunity and impunity for international community members involved in trafficking, and both, law enforcement efforts of the B&H authorities in prosecuting traffickers and their failure to prosecute police officers involved in trafficking of human beings. In conclusion, the chapter will assess the role of the relevant actors to shed light on the reasons why over 20 years, B&H has evolved from a country of destination and transit for the trafficking of foreign women and girls subjected to sexual exploitation, into a Tier 2 Watch list country of origin for the trafficking of women, men and children subjected to various forms of exploitation in the country and abroad.

The B&H example shows that increased presence of military/peacekeeping forces has contributed to both the occurrence and expansion of human trafficking, that has affected not only the country itself but the region and beyond as well. Evidently, not enough efforts have been invested so far to combat the issue at the earliest stage, when the international community used to be both, the key demand factor and the key elimination factor of the phenomenon.

Occurrence of Trafficking in Human Beings in Bosnia and Herzegovina

As pointed out by Gamino (n.d.), during the conflict in B&H around 20,000 to 30,000 women and girls suffered sexual abuse and violence in camps and in the cities. Nikolic-Ristanovic (2003) elaborates that although sex trafficking that was closely connected to ethnic conflicts stayed mainly within the borders of war-affected and neighbouring countries, it contributed to the expansion of prostitution and made good basis for these countries to become attractive destination for trafficking in women from other parts of Eastern Europe.

Existence of human trafficking phenomenon was officially confirmed in B&H in 1999, when the first official statistics were collected. A number of key reports by watch groups in the early 2000s brought national and international attention to the issue of sex trafficking in B&H (HRW 2002; Muftić and Pehlić 2015). In May 2000, UNMIBH and the Office of the High Commissioner for Human Rights (OHCHR) published a report entitled Trafficking in Human Beings in B&H which described B&H as "a significant destination for women trafficked from Eastern Europe," stating that the International Organization for Migration (IOM) estimated range from 6000 to 10,000 (ICG 2002).

Sex trafficking was the first form of the phenomenon in B&H and it became widespread immediately after the end of the war. However, the issue had not been dealt with at all, despite the rumours that hundreds of Moldova, Ukrainian, Romanian prostitutes came to work in the country. Gamino (n.d.) states that after the deployment of thousands of peacekeepers in B&H, the business of sex trafficking started to flourish. Lalić (2007) points out that girls were bought at one of the world's slave markets, in Hungary, Yugoslavia, Romania or Ukraine. There were more or less "women's markets," and many girls the author talked to at that time stated they were auctioned after spending a while in a nightclub/brothel and were replaced by "fresh goods."

During the height of the sex trade in B&H, traffickers ran the businesses openly and only a few of them were prosecuted. This was primarily the result of a lack of proper legislation governing the issue of human trafficking within the country. Of the few traffickers that were prosecuted, the majority were charged with "enticing to prostitution," which is a minor offense in B&H. Furthermore, victims of sex trafficking were also arrested and prosecuted for a variety of offenses, including illegal entry in the country and disturbance of "peace and order," whilst traffickers mostly enjoyed impunity; this is in contradiction to the non-prosecution and non-punishment principle discussed in this book. With the UN threatening to sanction B&H, law enforcement cracked down on the sex trade by conducting a string of raids on nightclubs and cafes, where sex trafficking was believed to be taking place across the country. However, traffickers just changed their *modus operandi* and continued with the sex trade underground, operating in private homes and hotels, what was in direct contrast to the flagrant and brazen nature of the commercial sex trade in the late 1990s that was designed, for the most part, to catch the attention of the growing number of foreigners in the country in the immediate post-war years (Muftić and Pehlić 2015).

During her work on combating the issue in the period 1999–2003, the author met hundreds of girls from Moldova, Rumania, Bulgaria, Russia and even neighbouring Serbia forced to provide sexual services and they all testified the same—they were promised well-paid jobs in Western Europe, but found themselves in B&H as victims of sex trafficking in a debt-bondage. Almost all survivors stated to be forced to starvation, drugs and alcohol use, they were physically and emotionally abused in parallel with sexual exploitation and many of them had cigarette marks on their skin, even breasts.

Role of Peacekeeping Forces in Fuelling Demand

On December 14, 1995, the Dayton Peace Agreement was signed to end the conflict between the republics of the Socialist Federation of Yugoslavia. In order to enforce peace in the region, the presence of international peacekeepers, international police and civilian contractors was necessary. The objective of the United Nations Mission in B&H (UNMIBH) was the implementation of the Peace Agreement on B&H and the establishment of "the rule of law by assisting in reforming and restructuring the local police, assessing the functioning of the existing judicial system and monitoring and auditing the performance of the police and others involved in the maintenance of law and order." In 1996, after a one-year mandate, the Stabilization Force (SFOR), led by NATO came to support the Implementation Force (IFOR) due to the unstable situation (Gamino date unknown).

Since the end of the war in 1995, B&H has become a major trafficking destination. With the arrival of about 50,000 mainly male international peacekeeping personnel in 1995, the small already existing local sex industry in Bosnia boomed (Wölte 2004). While trafficked women and girls there reported that approximately 70 per cent of their clients were local citizens, with internationals making up the remaining 30 per cent, local NGOs believed that the presence of thousands of expatriate civilians and soldiers was a significant motivating factor for traffickers to "invest" in B&H (Vandenberg 2002a, b). Mendelson (2005) emphasized many experts pointed to the locations and names of the bars as evidence that traffickers not only targeted but also responded to the demand of international peacekeepers, suggesting that "While SFOR was stationed in Bosnia, activists claimed that one could drive through Bosnia and know which international contingent had responsibility for the region." Tony Robson wrote in 2002 (Chap. 1, Section "Introduction") that "[t]here is mounting evidence that the United Nations has carried out a cover-up of the role played by its personnel in human trafficking and prostitution in Bosnia—a trade that has grown astronomically since the establishment of the Western protectorate seven years ago."

Sadly, from the experience of this author, none of those statements were exaggerations. During all raids, it was very evident that internationals were major clients. Rooms were full of various items that could be bought only in a military base; girls barely spoke the local language but were able to communicate in Spanish or English which they admitted to have learned while staying in B&H.

Whistle-blower Kathryn Bolkovac (a human rights advocate, consultant, former US police investigator of 12 years, who also served as a human rights investigator for the UNIPTF in B&H) stated there were many cases of sexual abuse and exploitation committed by UN Peacekeepers in Bosnia in the 1990s, but they were never prosecuted: "[y]oung girls from Romania, Ukraine, Moldova and other Eastern European countries being brought in to service the UN and military bases as sex-slaves. The cases involved the officers from many foreign countries, including the USA, Pakistan, Germany, Romania, Ukraine, government contractors and local organized criminals. The human rights investigators were never allowed to fully investigate, the suspects were immediately removed from the mission or transferred to other missions. The young women were simply sent back to their home countries" (Deutsche Welle Interview with Kathryn Bolkovac 2016, Answer No. 2). In her interview with *The Telegraph* (February 06, 2012), Bolkovac stated that 1800 officers from 45 countries of the UN Police were "not only using trafficked women for sexual services but also they were on the traffickers' pay roll. They were also giving warnings on raids to the brothels owners, returning girls who escaped from the bars or when rescued girls were repatriated letting the traffickers know where they could find them to recovered them and put them back into the system."

Vandenberg (2002a, b, 49) states: "Human Rights Watch found evidence—including internal UNIPTF reports, interviews with monitors, and verbatim transcripts of testimony by five trafficking victims—that UNIPTF monitors in B&H purchased the services of trafficked women in brothels. Some monitors also arranged for trafficked women to be delivered to their residences. Most striking, however, was the evidence that at least three UNIPTF monitors purchased women and their passports from traffickers and brothel owners." In October 2002, the UNMIBH spokeswoman, Kirsten Haupt, announced that UNMIBH had found that 11 local police officers—including a STOP team leader—had used sexual services in the nightclubs (Human Rights Watch Report on Bosnia 2002, Chap. 5).

In her book "Hopes betrayed," Vandenberg (2002a, b) writes that in 2000, UNIPTF monitors conducted raids of three nightclubs in Prijedor city. Thirty-four women trafficked into these three brothels in that city were freed and six UNIPTF officers were repatriated—two Americans, two Spaniards and two British nationals. The official reason given for the disciplinary measures was exceeding the mandate of the UNIPTF; however, the girls reportedly pointed out that the men driving them had been their clients. In her testimony on Trafficking of Women and Girls to Bosnia and Herzegovina for Forced Prostitution, Vandenberg (2002a, b, 5) also added that: "Allegations of purchase of trafficked women have also been raised in relation to U.S. military contractors providing support services to the U.S. contingent of the Stabilization Force (SFOR). In 1999, the direct employer of these contractors, DynCorp, repatriated a group of contractors after allegations emerged that the men had purchased women from the brothels."

It was not a secret that numerous foreigners working at international organizations present in B&H at that time, including those from SFOR and UNIPTF were frequent visitors at nightclubs and brothels offering commercial sexual services. Many survivors stated they were discouraged from seeking any assistance from the UNIPTF STOP teams by the very presence of international soldiers and peace officers as clients and their obvious good relations with traffickers.

Mendelson (2005) suggests that until the summer of 2003, civilian and military leadership at NATO headquarters and in Bosnia (and Kosovo)[1] avoided addressing the links between human trafficking and peacekeeping operations. Senior officers treated trafficking as peripheral to peacekeeping missions even when they were tracking organized crime, and even when they were presented with concrete evidence of the involvement of their troops. Her report finds that the way in which peacekeepers and those supporting peacekeepers perceived human trafficking inhibited their ability to respond to it. Mendelson pointed out: "This research confirms what an earlier UN report found in Bosnia, that 'trafficking in human beings is seen as substantially less important than other crimes. There is a tendency to look at these as isolated cases and overlook the transnational character of the criminal enterprise'" (Mendelson 2005, p. 5), even though it was stated by the UN (2004) that the use of trafficking victims by peacekeepers for sexual and other services was a source of major embarrassment and political damage to UN Peace Keeping Operations (PKOs).

Gamino (n.d.) points out that the lack of efforts and strategies from member states to prevent this behaviour in their troops have created a chain of corruption and have had a domino effect in other peacekeeping operations like in Haiti, Liberia or in the Democratic Republic of Congo.

[1] In July 1999, the Kosovo Protection Force (KFOR) entered Kosovo, the war-torn province of Serbia, in order to protect ethnic Albanians. This United Nations (UN) force was large by UN standards. More than 20,000 troops were on the ground within days of the passage of the authorizing UN Security Council Resolution. Within months, the global human rights community drew attention to the establishment and intensification of human sex trafficking into Kosovo (Smith and Smith 2011).

Impact of Corruption Within the Local Police Forces on Sex Trafficking

UNIPTF STOP Teams were supposed to assist the local police during raids of numerous nightclubs and brothels that were mushrooming within the country. The author participated in many raids conducted in the period 2000–2003, however, in most of the cases, police failed to find any evidences against traffickers. Later we learned that many police officers were actually directly involved in exploitation of the girls and even used their services free of charge, hence they used to inform bar owners about the date and time of a raid. Also, during one raid, we found two foreign girls in a house used by a former police officer, who were forced to provide commercial sexual services whilst the trafficker's wife and underage daughter were staying in the living room. Due to the fact that police officers were also frequent at those establishments, trafficked girls and women were hesitant to seek any assistance during a raid. In fact, they fiercely denied that any form of exploitation or abuse was taking place.

Vandenberg (2002a, b, 26) points out that: "Trafficking in persons flourishes in conditions of state complicity and with the involvement of state officials. Human Rights Watch uncovered evidence of such corruption among local police in B&H. Some police officers accepted money or free sexual services from traffickers and bar/brothel owners in exchange for protection…, others gave bar/brothel owners tip-offs before raids, allowing the owners to hide under-age girls and women without documents. A small number of police officers participated in trafficking directly as owners or staff of bars and brothels. Finally, some trafficking victims alleged that officials in the foreigners' departments in some police stations engaged in document fraud, facilitating trafficking. Testimony provided to Human Rights Watch by UNMIBH and NGOs indicated that local police officers who engaged in trafficking-related crimes rarely faced disciplinary or criminal charges."

After the first few raids the author took part in, it became evident that there was a strong link between the traffickers and local law enforcement officers. The owners of the raided establishment showed no fear or worry during the site investigations, just on the contrary—they were quite arrogant and some of them even laughed into faces of the raid executors. Mujanović et al. (2016) emphasized that cooperation of criminals from the countries of origin of victims with those from transit countries and destination sites in B&H was fully harmonized. As a result, a chain of criminals established links with B&H border police and customs services.

Gamino (n.d.) stated that the Foreign Affairs Office of Bosnia was cooperating by issuing false passports to the trafficked women with false data, and Vandenberg (2002a, b) pointed out that in other cases, police pretended not to recognize obviously fake documents or assisted directly in the creation of fraudulent documents. During the raids, UNIPTF officers established that many girls had fraudulent B&H ID cards which were supposed to facilitate their movement within B&H but also to enable them to easily cross the border with Croatia and go further into the EU.

Vandenberg (2002a, b) elaborates that a lack of political will, state incompetence and outright corruption coalesced in B&H, allowing traffickers to violate the law with impunity. The Bosnian authorities largely failed to criminally prosecute traffickers, failed to discipline or prosecute corrupt police officers, and not infrequently prosecuted the victims of trafficking. The government has failed to make it possible for witnesses to remain in Bosnia to testify. Without shelter, government protection, legal sources of income, or witness protection, women and girls opted quickly to return home. Unfortunately, such an approach to the issue has had a long-lasting adverse impact on the state of human trafficking in B&H until now.

Engagement of the UNMIBH in Combating Sex Trafficking

After being accused that their own personnel were involved in sex trafficking, the UNIPTF Mission in B&H established a special team called STOP Team, aimed not only at preventing human trafficking in B&H, but also at maintaining the reputation of the international community.

STOP Teams contributed a lot to closing the nightclubs where sex trafficking took place. They were composed of police officers with prior experience in combating human trafficking. The head of the STOP Team Mrs. Celhia de Lavarene was very familiar with the issue which enabled the teams to effectively advise local colleagues resulting in rescuing of hundreds of victims from traffickers' claws. Unfortunately, this was still a dead-end for many girls as the moment they were repatriated local traffickers immediately forced them to go to another country where their exploitation continued.

However, Vandenberg (2002a, b) is of the opinion that in theory, UNIPTF monitors supervised internal investigations by local police and ensured that corrupt and complicit officers faced disciplinary, and even criminal proceedings, but in reality, had minimal impact on internal local police investigations. High turnover among UNIPTF monitors, combined with the desire to close cases and maintain good relations with local police, stymied supervision of investigations and often precluded follow up on existing cases…" Pressing local police to investigate their own personnel often met resistance" (Vandenberg 2002a, b, 33). Local police exploited UNIPTF officers' short tenure in the country by delaying punitive action against fellow officers. Once an UNIPTF officer went home or was transferred, disciplinary cases often died. However, as concluded by Vandenberg, UNMIBH officials did report the occasional success in establishing accountability for local police.

The STOP Team that the author worked in assisted three Moldovan girls identified by the B&H border police during an attempt to cross the border with Croatia with forged B&H ID cards. They were driven by the man who was exploiting them in B&H and who wanted to sell them to "friends" in Croatia. During the investigation, they described the entire process from recruitment by promising well-paid jobs in Italy to exploitation in B&H, where they served dozens of clients a day. After testifying before the court in B&H, they were immediately repatriated, and the trafficker was sentenced only to probation. However, some six months later, the author learned that Moldovan traffickers arranged their forcible return to B&H immediately upon their arrival in Moldova under severe threats to their family members.

Eventually, engagement of the UNIPTF resulted in shutting down almost all nightclubs throughout B&H. However, Muftić and Pehlić (2015) pointed out that repeated raids, tighter border control and visa requirements and increased prosecution of trafficking offenders did not result in the elimination of the problem—rather, the sex trade has moved underground; operating in private homes and hotels and with the shift in the market, B&H has become a source country.

Legal Immunity and Impunity for International Community in the Context of Human Trafficking

After the Vienna Convention of 1961, diplomatic immunity has been given to any individual who has served as peacekeeper in extraterritorial missions in order to achieve his or her duties. In the case of the peacekeepers in B&H, their involvement in sex trade was obviously not part of their duties during the UNMIBH, and the crimes committed must not be ignored or justified by diplomatic immunity jurisdiction. Vandenberg (2002a, b) points out that internal investigations undertaken by the Criminal Investigation Division (CID) of the U.S. Army uncovered evidence of direct contractor involvement in trafficking within B&H. "UNMIBH officials could not point to any cases where the U.N. secretary-general had waived immunity. They stated that repatriation served as the only punishment for involvement in trafficking-related misconduct, but they also could not point to any prosecutions in home countries" (Vandenberg 2002a, b, 60) Mendelson (2005, 7) emphasizes that: "The active engagement of peacekeepers in trafficking is especially harmful when followed by rapid repatriation of the implicated peacekeeper—whether it is a uniformed service member in a NATO-led operation, a civilian contractor, or a police officer detailed to the UN—with no consequence to the peacekeeper except losing that particular job, no domestic trial, and no prosecution. The norm of impunity is strengthened."

One of the biggest SFOR bases was located in Mostar, a city severely affected by the war and requiring a huge presence of the international stabilization forces. However, in the vicinity of the SFOR base, numerous establishments were opened overnight offering commercial sexual services provided by mostly foreign girls and women, but some local girls too. The author talked to one of the underage girls who used to work at such a nightclub. She stated she had been forced by her own mother to provide sexual services. She asked some of her SFOR and UNIPTF clients for help but nobody helped her until she run away from home. It was well known among SFOR soldiers that the girls were forced to provide sexual services, and still it did not stop them from buying the services. Even though it was not a secret that numerous SFOR officers were visiting those establishments almost on a daily basis, no sanctions were imposed on them, which in turn encouraged them to continue with buying sexual services from human trafficking victims.

Gamino (n.d.) quoted a senior political affairs officer from the UN headquarters B&H who in summary stated that the UN could not prosecute the officers for the crimes committed and left the responsibility to the contributing countries to do it. Gamino (n.d., 10) points out that: "Until 2002 was that no UNIPTF's monitors faced criminal investigation or charges in their home countries, according to the NGO Human Rights Watch and personnel involved in that time." Gamino further questioned the limits between immunity and impunity and its consequences in the fight against Human Trafficking and stated it was important to remember each of the members involved in peacekeeping operations that the legal system was created to protect all people not only on a daily basis but also in times of vulnerability. What is more, the diplomatic immunity jurisdiction was created to protect the diplomatic personnel, who are head of states or in charge of extraterritorial missions, to realize their duties under unstable or difficult situations but not to cover up or tolerate crimes in extraterritorial missions. She well noted that: "[f]ortunately, this jurisdiction has also established the expulsion from diplomatic immunity when the person commits a crime not related to his or her duty. This exception in the jurisdiction should be taken as a sufficient reason to prosecute ex-officers. Through the involvement of peacekeepers, diplomats and head of states among others, who are supposed to be enforcing human rights law and provide security to others, human trafficking becomes more difficult to combat. As a consequence, the international community has not only to fight against private traffickers but also against their own representatives. Peacekeeping operations have been created with the intention of relief the host society of the problems after a conflict. It should not be the case that during their stay peacekeeping missions generate other social sicknesses to combat such as sex trade…The tolerated impunity covered by the diplomatic immunity is a pull factor for peacekeepers to get involved in human trafficking. It also creates a notion in host countries of peacekeeping operations that law is beside the people who transgress it or have political influence and power, instead of the victims and the most vulnerable" (Gamino n.d., 13).

Current Situation Regarding Human Trafficking in Bosnia and Herzegovina

As stated at the beginning, in the period to 2004, B&H used to be primarily a country of transit and destination for victims coming from Eastern Europe. As of 2004, B&H has predominantly become a source country experiencing internal recruitment of women and girls, but also boys and men, trafficked for purposes of sexual and labour exploitation to Western European and beyond, as well as a transit country for trafficking routes from the East and South towards the North and West (Rizvo and Mujanović 2016).

The U.S. State Department 2019 TiP Report reads: "As reported over the past five years, human traffickers exploit domestic and foreign victims in B&H, and traffickers exploit victims from B&H abroad.… Law enforcement lacked capacity and knowledge and continued to regularly investigate trafficking under lesser offenses, while judges issued sentences that fell short of the trafficking statutes' minimum penalties and cited unreasonable 'mitigating circumstances' to decrease the sentences. In addition, the government identified fewer victims and lacked victim protection efforts, particularly efforts to proactively screen victims and provide assistance, which led to penalization of victims for unlawful acts that traffickers compelled them to commit, due to which B&H remained on Tier 2 Watch List for the second consecutive year."

2017 GRETA report on B&H states the number of child victims has been on the rise, in particular those trafficked for the purpose of forced begging, forced criminality and sexual exploitation.

Poor prosecution and lack of convictions of traffickers create fertile ground for traffickers who become even bolder and start openly recruiting new victims, such as issuing fraudulent vacancies without any fear of possible legal sanctions. However, almost all arrests of traffickers in human beings are done either in joint international police actions such as a joint police operation of France and B&H resulting in the arrest of B&H Consul in Paris (Council of Europe 2017), a joint operation of German, Austrian, Serbian and B&H police (Sito-Sucic 2016) or abroad (arrest of B&H traffickers in Barcelona, Spain) and hardly ever in B&H.

Conclusion

As well observed by Gamino (n.d.), peacekeeping forces travel with the purpose to "provide security and the political and peacebuilding support to help countries make the difficult, early transition from conflict to peace (…) but also to facilitate the political process, protect civilians, assist in the disarmament, demobilization and reintegration of former combatants; support the organization of elections, protect and promote human rights and assist in restoring the rule of law." Tragically, most of the time this purpose has been disputed due to the involvement of troops in transnational crimes like human trafficking.

However, Mendelson (2005, 13) points out that the historical legacy from the war in Bosnia bestows trafficking with a special horror: the war crime of rape. "When peacekeepers, deployed to help stabilize and rebuild societies, purchase women and girls as chattel, they continue the grim sexual slavery of the war years."

Would the human trafficking issue have become a serious problem if there was no war in B&H? If it had not been for the sudden and more important huge presence of foreign peacekeepers? Most probably, it would have still become an issue but not to such an extent as it really happened. B&H authorities burdened with an everlasting complex political situation, hundreds of thousands of refugees and internally displaced persons, unsolved ethnical tensions, destructions, poverty and many other adverse impacts of the war have never properly put the issue on the agenda. B&H, as mostly affected by the last Balkan wars, required increased presence of foreign peace stabilization forces, what evidently fuelled human, and especially sex trafficking.

It cannot be denied that significant numbers of international peacekeepers and their contractors were frequent and the most welcome guests at the establishments where human trafficking was taking place, but also accomplices. After four years of war, local men did not have money to use commercial sexual services that were offered almost on every corner in B&H, and foreigners were actually those who were the prime target of traffickers. However, once the situation in the country became stabilized and after the vast majority of internationals were gone, local traffickers have realized that such activity is very lucrative and requires hardly any investments. Learning from the example of lack of prosecution of both local and foreign perpetrators, they have realized they should not fear any serious prosecution and hence, have continued with it, recruiting not only women and girls, but also men and children for all known forms of human trafficking.

Another important question is what would have happened if the foreign officers had been trained in human trafficking before deployment to B&H, or even better, if they had been properly prosecuted and sanctioned if involved in human trafficking. Sadly, the role of the international community in both the creation of demand and failure to tackle it was diminished. Moreover, the evident corruption of the international community whose members were either directly fuelling demand by using sexual services of trafficking victims, profiting therefrom or were obstructing anti-trafficking actions of local police were mostly ignored. However, as well noted by Gamino, the most concerning issue is that the people who represent the law or the image of the United Nations, an organization recognized worldwide as the guardian of Human Rights protecting any person in any situation of vulnerability, are becoming the perpetrators in this organized crime. This aspect would put in question the credibility of international law in terms of protection and prosecution, and of many other institutions that day by day are actually working to create possible solutions to punish trafficking in people and for the same propose as the United Nations peacekeeping missions. This kind of attitude was not evident only in B&H, but in other later peacekeeping operations.

The Bosnian experience has demonstrated that once it occurs in a post-conflict country, human trafficking is difficult or better to say impossible to eradicate. Stricken with destruction, poverty, never-ending ethnical tensions, but more importantly, lack of any previous experience in the issue, the B&H authorities have not been able to properly tackle the issue. The international community who used to have all the legal and administrative power in the hands at that time could and should have done way more to stop the issue immediately when it had occurred. It is obviously too late for B&H to start asking any of these questions. The human trafficking, and not only sex trafficking, has become a serious issue which still has not been dealt with adequately. However, our sad example could and should help both the international community and all war-affected countries throughout the world to prevent human trafficking in a conflict/peacebuilding context, as supply would not occur without the creation of demand for commercial sexual services.

References

Council of Europe, Report Concerning the Implementation of the Council of Europe Convention on Action Against Trafficking in Human Beings by Bosnia and Herzegovina. Second Evaluation Round, 2017. https://rm.coe.int/greta-2017-15-fgr-bih-en/1680782ac1

Department of State, United States of America, Trafficking in Persons Report, June 2019. https://www.state.gov/wp-content/uploads/2019/06/2019-Trafficking-in-Persons-Report.pdf

Deutsche Welle Interview with Kathryn Bolkovac. 2016. https://www.dw.com/en/bolkovac-un-tries-to-cover-up-peacekeeper-sex-abuse-scandal/a-19082815

Gamino, Dulce. n.d. Peacekeepers as Unpunished Perpetrators: "The Invisible Line Between Impunity and Diplomatic Immunity in Human Trafficking." http://www.fight-human-trafficking.org/wordpress/wp-content/uploads/Peacekeepers-and-Human-Trafficking_Dulce-Gamino.pdf

Human Rights Watch Report on Bosnia. 2002. https://www.hrw.org/reports/2002/bosnia/Bosnia1102-06.htm

International Crisis Group (ICG). 2002. Policing the Police in Bosnia: A Further Reform Agenda. https://www.esiweb.org/pdf/bridges/bosnia/ICG_PolicingthepoliceinBiHMay02.pdf

Lalić, V. 2007. Trgovina ljudima u Bosni i Hercegovini. Defendologija centar za bezbjednosna, sociološka i kriminološka istraživanja.

Mendelson, S.E. 2005. Barracks and Brothels: Peacekeepers and Human Trafficking in the Balkans. Csis.

Muftić, L.R., and A. Pehlić. 2015. Sex Trafficking in Bosnia and Herzegovina: A Descriptive Analysis Based on Law Enforcement Officers' Accounts. *Sarajevo: Kriminalističke teme* 5–6: 3–16.

Mujanović, E., E. Muratbegović, M. Budimlić, and V. Obradović. 2016. *Trgovina ljudima u Bosni i Hercegovini.* Sarajevo: CPRC.

Nikolic-Ristanovic, V. 2003. Sex Trafficking: The Impact of War, Militarism and globalization in Eastern Europe. *Michigan Feminist Studies* 17: 1.

Nisha Lilia, Diu. 2012. What the UN Doesn't Want You to Know. *The Telegraph.* 06 February 2012. https://www.telegraph.co.uk/culture/film/9041974/What-the-UN-Doesnt-Want-You-to-Know.html

Rizvo, S., and E. Mujanović. 2016. Trafficking in Human Beings in Bosnia and Herzegovina: State of the Art and Associated Puzzles. *Kriminalističke teme* 5–6: 75–93.

Robson, T. 2002. Bosnia: The United Nations, Human Trafficking and Prostitution. *World Socialist Web Site.* 21 August 2002. https://www.wsws.org/en/articles/2002/08/bosn-a21.html

Sito-Sucic, D. 2016. Balkan Police Help Smash Ring Trafficking Women to Western Europe. *Reuters.* 10 November 2016. https://www.reuters.com/article/us-balkans-arrests-smuggling/balkan-police-help-smash-ring-trafficking-women-to-western-europe-idUSKBN1351I6

Smith, C.A., and H.M. Smith. 2011. Human Trafficking: The Unintended Effects of United Nations Intervention. *International Political Science Review* 32 (2): 125–145.

United Nations. 2004. Human Trafficking and United Nations Peacekeeping DPKO Policy Paper. https://www.un.org/womenwatch/news/documents/DPKOHumanTraffickingPolicy03-2004.pdf

Vandenberg, M. 2002a. Hopes Betrayed: Trafficking of Women and Girls to Post-conflict Bosnia and Herzegovina for Forced Prostitution.

Vandenberg, M.E. 2002b. Testimony on Trafficking of Women and Girls to Bosnia and Herzegovina for Forced Prostitution.

Wölte, S. 2004. *Armed Conflict and Trafficking in Women*: Desk Study. Deutsche Gesellschaft für Technische Zusammenarbeit (GTZ).

Abida Pehlić is an anti-trafficking expert, with 20 years of work experience in prevention and combatting the issue. Her portfolio includes work with various international agencies and she is a co-founder and Vice-President of the Association 'Novi put' Bosnia and Herzegovina. Mrs. Pehlić holds an MA in sociology and an MA in German Language and Literature.

8

Helping to Keep Those Serving Honourably, Honourable: Trafficking in Persons and the United States Uniform Code of Military Justice

Benjamin Thomas Greer and Kymber M. Cates

Introduction

War, conflict, and government instability play a significant role in the vulnerability of a populace. While military and civilian peacekeeping forces are deployed to protect, stabilize, and support the affected citizenry, research shows troops' demand for prostitution-based sexual services and civilian contractors with unscrupulous and exploitative business practices continue to, directly or indirectly, support human trafficking. Human trafficking is best described as the exploitation of a person for profit. Commonly referred to as modern day slavery in the UK, Australia, and the US, trafficking persists in all countries and regions of the world.

B. T. Greer (✉)
California Govenor's Office of Emergency Services – California Specialized Training Institute, Elk Grove, USA

University of Cambridge's Centre for Applied Research in Human Trafficking (CCARHT), Cambridge, UK
e-mail: benjamin.greer@caloes.ca.gov

J. Muraszkiewicz et al. (eds.), *Human Trafficking in Conflict*, Crime Prevention and Security Management, https://doi.org/10.1007/978-3-030-40838-1_8

Tied with the illegal arms trade, it is the second largest criminal industry in the world and the fastest growing crime in the twenty-first century (US Department of Health 2004); with the most common forms being sexual exploitation, forced manual labour, and domestic servitude. Traffickers seek out vulnerable populations, typically using atrocious techniques of fear and intimidation to exert control over their victims. Some traffickers keep their victims under lock and key or use less obvious methods, specifically debt bondage whereby the trafficker asserts fictitious or erroneous financial obligations the victims feel honour-bound to repay. A central component of human trafficking is the exploitation of economically vulnerable people. Traffickers lure victims into their web with deceptive promises of good jobs and better lives, in order to force them to work under brutal and inhumane conditions, depriving them of their freedom and power of self-determination. Victimization is not only economic loss, but often includes extreme physical and mental abuse, including rape, sexual exploitation through forced prostitution, torture, beatings, starvation, and death threats to the victim and their family.

United States military personnel, along with their civilian counterparts, availing themselves of prostitution while overseas has a long and sordid history (Mendelson 2005). Since the passage of the *Trafficking in Person Protection Act* (TVPA) in 2000, the US Congress and the office of the President of the United States have taken specific actions to eliminate its continued practice. The *Military Extraterritorial Jurisdiction Act* (MEJA) and Article 134 of the *Uniform Code of Military Justice* (UCMJ) are the foundational statutes and regulations seeking to hold military personnel and civilian contractors accountable for trafficking and exploitative labour practices. This chapter will chronicle the events leading up to the adoption of the MEJA and the expansion of Article 134 of the UCMJ in 2005; will examine military cases stemming from these laws; and will discuss the extent military personnel are now provided substantive and adequate anti-trafficking training.

K. M. Cates
California Govenor's Office of Emergency Services – California Specialized Training Institute, Elk Grove, USA

Judge Advocate General for the United States Navy, Sacramento, California, USA

The South Korean Incident and the Birth of "Zero-Tolerance"

Whilst a vast majority of deployed soldiers and civilian contractors serve and work without incident, historically there has been consistent entwinement of military action and sexual exploitation. In 2002, after numerous media outlets reported about US troop activity at brothels near military bases in South Korea, many began accusing the military's "unquenchable demand" for prostitutes in tandem with leadership ignoring such exploitation as condoning sex trafficking. Upon release of the news story, the leaders of US Forces Korea took immediate action, developing trafficking in persons awareness training and a prevention program to stop personnel from feeding the demand for commercial sex. The political and societal fallout from this reporting was swift and wide-ranging. US President George Bush immediately issued a National Security Presidential Directive (NSPD-22) establishing a zero-tolerance policy towards US military involved in trafficking and trafficking-related activities abroad (White House 2003; Department of Defense 2003). NSPD-22 expressly covered all US government employees and contracted personnel representing the US abroad who engage in trafficking and trafficking-related activities. Specifically stating the "policy of the United States is to attack vigorously the worldwide problem of trafficking in persons, using law enforcement efforts, diplomacy, and all other appropriate tools" (White House 2003; Department of Defense 2003).

The emerging "zero-tolerance" policy/program provided two tangible affects: (1) it increased and better defined areas known or suspected areas of exploitation, classifying them as "off limits" and "no go" zones; and (2) it mandated an aggressive anti-trafficking awareness training program that all US military personnel and civilian contractors must complete in advance of deployment (Department of Defense 2014–2018). Since 2003, this program has been expanded to include a 24-hour TIP (Trafficking in Persons) hotline where military personnel and civilian contractors can report suspicious activity. In September 2003, the US Secretary of Defense reinforced the statements in a memorandum by directing military commanders to:

1. Establish a systematic method to evaluate anti-trafficking in persons efforts;
2. Ensure Department of Defence personnel are trained to recognize trafficking in persons indicators; and
3. Use all tools available to combat trafficking in persons.

In 2004, the Department of Defense (DoD) furthered the "zero-tolerance" policy by updating the *Uniform Code of Military Justice* (UCMJ) to expressly prohibit patronizing houses of prostitution. The UCMJ went on to clarify that the US military will neither condone nor permit such activity, regardless of whether the encounter is consensual and/or legal in the country in which that activity occurs. Before the House Armed Services Committee and the Commission on Security and Cooperation in Europe, Principal Deputy Undersecretary of Defence Charles Abell stated:

> We are confident that the various offences currently within the UCMJ are sufficient to address misconduct that constitutes, or is associated with, human trafficking activities. However, the Department has taken several steps to strengthen its resolve in combating such misconduct. The Military Departments have been asked to examine their regulations and procedures for placing off-limits those places that may contribute to conditions that support such activities, and have made clear that violations are offenses punishable under the UCMJ. Through the auspices of the Joint Service Committee on Military Justice, the Department has drafted a clearly stated Article 134, UCMJ, offense that prohibits military members from patronizing prostitutes. The draft offense will be submitted as part of the 2004 Annual Review [of] proposed amendments to the Manual for Courts-Martial (Abell 2004).

In October 2005, "patronizing a prostitute" was officially adopted as a specific chargeable offence for service members under Article 134 of the UCMJ. This expansion of the UCMJ was, in part, to rebut the reporting from South Korean media indicting US troops' role in fuelling the commercial sex trade. The DoD's mantra became that it is the *demand* for commercial sex which drives the sex trafficking industry; DoD is therefore striving to end such demand by making it a criminal offence. The year 2005 also saw the issue spread beyond commercial sexual exploration when the DoD Inspector General—the DoD's chief internal investigatory service—confirmed new media allegations of multiple abuses committed by defence contractors or subcontractors employing third country national (TCN) workers in Iraq. Some of these abuses were indicative of human trafficking, such as withholding workers' passports and deceptive hiring practices. The commander of Multinational Forces Iraq implemented an order directing all contractors to stop withholding employee passports, provide employees a signed copy of their work contract, and require contractors and subcontractors to use certified recruiting firms.

US Department of Defence Reporting and Mandatory Training

The US DoD is the nation's largest domestic employer with over 1.4 million active duty personnel and 1.1 million reservists. However, it is also the nation's largest employer of contractors within the US and overseas. It also employs 861,000 civilians, with 450,000 employees stationed overseas in 163 countries (Amadeo 2019). The DoD's reach and volume of work makes forced and exploited labour a high exposure threat. There were approximately 1.3 million total active-duty US military personnel in 2016. Of these, 193,442—or 15%—were deployed overseas. The five countries with the largest active-duty US military presence in 2016 were Japan (38,818), Germany (34,602), South Korea (24,189), Italy (12,088), and Afghanistan (9023) (Bialik 2017). The US maintains nearly 800 military bases in more than 70 countries and territories abroad (Vine 2015).

In 2006, the DoD was the first federal agency to require a clause in defence contracts prohibiting human trafficking codified in Federal Acquisition Regulation 22.1705 (FAR 22.1705). FAR 22.1705 was expanded in 2015 requiring contractors to develop a compliance plan and to make employees aware of their rights. A major goal of the DoD Combating Trafficking in Persons program is to educate every member of

DoD about human trafficking (Department of Defense 2014–18). In its Strategic Plan for Combating Trafficking in Persons (CTIP) 2014–2018, the DoD provides a vision and mission for the Department in its collective effort to eliminate trafficking across the defence enterprise (Department of Defense 2014–18). The DoD touts this Strategic Plan as a "blueprint for the way forward" (Department of Defense 2014–18). The Department published DoD Instruction 2200.01 "Combating Trafficking in Persons" in 2007 and revised it in 2010 and 2015 to reinforce the message that trafficking destroys lives and poses a threat to national security (Department of Defense 2014–18).

The DoD CTIP Strategic Plan is supported by seven guiding principles and four strategic goals focusing on partnerships as foundations for developing policies, training, programs, and procedures that prevent trafficking in persons.

The guiding principles are as follows:

1. Reduce the risk and incidence of trafficking in persons within DoD's garrison and deployed military operations
2. Identify victims and help alleviate suffering
3. Improve monitoring and reporting
4. Identify criminal activity
5. Educate stakeholders and clients on DoD's stance on trafficking in persons
6. Train all DoD personnel on combating trafficking in persons
7. Inform contractors of DoD about CTIP policies and best practices

The strategic goals are as follows:

1. Partner with internal and external stakeholder communities to coordinate prevention efforts and bring consistency to the DoD CTIP program.
2. Issue DoD-wide policy on CTIP that conforms to law and executive orders and integrates with U.S. Government (USG) stakeholder approaches.

3. Institute synchronized training, education, and outreach programs that ensure trafficking in persons awareness and support identification, prevention, protection, and prosecution activities.
4. Implement standardized CTIP monitoring and enforcement processes and procedures that enhance compliance and improve incident tracking and reporting (Department of Defense 2014–18).

This report "mark[ed] a clear milestone for the Department... [T]his plan presents a comprehensive, integrated way ahead for combating this serious problem. The Plan provides a focused and systematic framework for making measurable improvements in DoD policy, programs, and practices ... that will result in the effective prevention of trafficking in persons, strong protection of trafficked victims, and appropriate accountability for traffickers." (Department of Defense 2014–18). While the DoD's training provides an adequate reflection of law and regulation, if the laws are poorly or rarely enforced, the training becomes unmoored to reality and is likely to be disregarded by the student as irrelevant.

Trafficking in Persons Laws Applicable to US Military and Civilian Contractor Personnel

The US "Military CTIP Trinity" and the Path Forward

US personnel and civilian contractors have a long-standing and notorious reputation for patronizing brothels for sexual services when serving and working abroad. The breadth and scope of US personnel's exposure makes education and compliance challenging. Congress and the President have addressed past ingressions with three primary legal tools. Coinciding with the passage of *United Nations Convention against Transnational Organized Crime* and its associated protocols, the US Congress concurrently passed the bipartisan *Trafficking Victims Protection Act* (TVPA). The design of the TVPA was to ensure just and effective punishment for traffickers, while assisting and protecting their victims. The TVPA serves as the centrepiece and a living framework of US governmental efforts in combating human trafficking domestically and abroad. The legislative scheme aims to increase cooperation among nations, provide education and economic opportunities for potential trafficking victims from all three country classifications (origin, transit, and destination); and provides grants and economic assistance to non-governmental organizations (NGOs) through programs aimed at assisting victims and educating the public (US Department of State 2018). Additionally, the TVPA sets minimum identification, prosecution, and victim assistance standards for foreign governments in the fight against trafficking (US Department of State 2018). The original legislative framework was organized into three main categories: (1) Protection, (2) Prosecution, and (3) Prevention. The TVPA is periodically re-authorized and expanded in its protections. In 2009, a fourth P (Partnership) was added to the framework to encourage and is recognizing the benefit public/private partnerships play in combatting human trafficking. TVPA increased the maximum penalties for trafficking and trafficking-related crimes, including the potential for life imprisonment terms. It also enhanced provisions safeguarding victim restitution and refined federal criminal law permitting a civil right of action against the trafficker in federal court. The law also requires the Secretary of State to submit a detailed report to Congress describing measures taken to prevent employees, contractors, and peacekeepers from human trafficking, exploiting victims of trafficking, or committing acts of illegal sexual exploitation (*Victims of Trafficking and Violence Protection Act*, 22 U.S.C. §7101, §104(e)(2)(A) 2000).

Military Extraterritorial Jurisdiction Act (MEJA)

As corporate globalization expands, more opaque and complex supply chains place a heavy burden on a country's oversight, regulatory, and transparency safeguarding against exploitation (Greer and Purvis 2016). Ensuring contractors maintain proper vigilance and act according to the values and laws of the US are exceedingly difficult. The military's growing dependence on civilian contractors poses a unique oversight challenge. The number of active-duty US military troops stationed overseas is at its lowest levels in decades. Troops stationed overseas fell below 200,000 for the first time since the late-1950s (Bialik 2017). The US military has reduced the number of active troop levels from 2.9 (Diamond 2017) million at the end of the Cold War to approximately 1.3 million troops (Bialik 2017). Despite having a "zero-tolerance" policy, ensuring forced labour is not used by a TCN is exceedingly difficult, if not impossible. Jurisdictional limitations or the inability to prosecute foreign subcontractors alone, almost immediately frustrate any investigation (*Adhikari v. Daoud & Partners* 2013). While the FAR 22.1705 is incorporated into all federal contracts (Garcia-Oscasio 2015), TCNs are often defrauded, indebted, stripped of their personal travel documents, and are forced to endure dangerous living and working conditions (Garcia-Oscasio 2015, 551). TCNs are more susceptible to exploitation due to "distance and isolation from their home communities, the possibility of language barriers, and dependence on their employers to procure and maintain current visas and work permits" (Wyler 2013). In 2012, it was estimated that US contractors in Iraq and Afghanistan utilized approximately 70,000 TCNs (American Civil Liberties Union 2012a, b). While the FAR framework includes a compliance plan and reporting of suspicious activity, very few reports of suspected exploitation have been submitted or investigated.

Around the world, trafficked people are forced to work in controlled environments of isolation and domination, such as: remote farms, mineral quarries, raw material mines, offshore fishing platforms, and industrial sweatshops (Greer and Purvis 2016). In an attempt to address the globalization and military nexus, Congress passed the *Military Extraterritorial Jurisdiction Act* (MEJA) specifically targeting civilian contractors' criminal activity overseas (STATEMENT-LEAHY 2000). MEJA created a legal framework whereby contractors accompanying the armed forces overseas could be charged for felonious activity committed abroad, as if the offences were committed in US territory. MEJA was enacted to help provide an enforcement answer to the difficult jurisdictional issues presented when host nations refuse to investigate or charge contractors due to the political and monetary influence that the US military poses. Federal Acquisition Regulation (FAR) Section 22.1703 states the following:

(a) Prohibit contractors, contractor employees, subcontractors, and subcontractor employees from

1. Engaging in severe forms of trafficking in persons during the period of performance of the contract;
2. Procuring commercial sex acts during the period of performance of the contract; or
3. Using forced labour in the performance of the contract;

(b) Require Contractors and Subcontractors to notify employees of the prohibited activities described in paragraph (a) of this section and the actions that may be taken against them for violations; and
(c) Impose suitable remedies, including termination, on Contractors that fail to comply with the requirements of paragraphs (a) and (b).

Since the passage of MEJA in 2000, there have only been a handful of investigations for malfeasance. Between 2000 and 2012 only 27 former military members, civilian dependents, and civilian contractors have been held to account for their criminal actions and only 15 of these prosecutions or attempted prosecutions were against civilian contractors working in Iraq or Afghanistan (Warren 2012). Statistical data on compliance, reported violations, and punitive actions taken are especially difficult to uncover. In his testimony for "The Final Report of the Commission on Wartime Contracting in Iraq and Afghanistan," the Principal Deputy Undersecretary of Defence for Acquisition, Technology, and Logistics disclosed to Congress that out of the 7997 active contracts, 99.11% included the required clause. There were only 71 contracts found to be noncompliant [see Table 8.1: the mathematical error of 84

Table 8.1 Forced Labour Contract Compliance

	# Contracts	# Noncompliant	Percent Noncompliant	# Compliant	Percent compliant
Afghanistan	5423	37	0.68	5386	99.32
Iraq	2574	34	1.32	2540	98.68
Total	7997	84	.89	7926	99.11

Source: The Final Report of the Commission on Wartime Contracting in Iraq and Afghanistan, October 19, 2011, [Online] https://www.govinfo.gov/content/pkg/CHRG-112shrg72564/pdf/CHRG-112shrg72564.pdf

noncompliant contracts list in the chart below is in the original document. In order to reach the 99.11%, complaint 84 should be corrected to read 71 noncompliant contracts].

He further stated:

> "The Army had two cases where the issue was raised in the past 3 years. The first was not substantiated, so no suspension or debarment action was taken. The second was a contractor accused of harboring an illegal alien and extracting cheap labor under threat of exposure. In this case, both the principal and the entity were debarred. This case was Stateside and not in the contingency environment" (US Congress 2011).

Inclusion of mandatory language in a contract does not guarantee compliance. The "compliance" percentages stated by the DoD only reflects the inclusion of the language in the underlying contract and do not indicate faithfulness of action. MEJA has been in effect for approximately 18 years and has produced little to no investigative or prosecutorial results, despite the tens of thousands of contracts during that timeframe, indicating MEJA either is written perfectly or is completely ineffective. A failure to hold contractors fully accountable for their criminal actions emboldens bad actors, knowing their nefarious activities are likely to go unnoticed or un-investigated.

United States Code of Military Justice (Article 134) Offence "Patronizing a Prostitute"

With its roots found in the Articles of War established by the Second Continental Congress for the Continental Army in 1775, the UCMJ serves as the modern-day mechanism for both punishment of criminal activity and the maintenance of good order and discipline (Joint Services Committee 2016). Passed by Congress in 1950, the UCMJ has jurisdiction over all members of the uniformed services of the US Military and its personnel are subject to UCMJ jurisdiction at all times, on or off duty, or on or off military reservation, worldwide. In addition, retired members of the armed forces entitled to retirement pay are subject to the UCMJ. The UCMJ, the Rules for Courts-Martial, and the Military Rules of Evidence have evolved since their implementation, often closely paralleling the developments in society and the civilian criminal justice system. The UCMJ is implemented through Presidential Executive Orders (*President may prescribe rules. US Code* 10 (2006), §836). On October 14, 2005, President Bush, as Commander-in-Chief, signed Executive Order (EO) 13,387 "*2005 Amendments to the Manual for Courts-Martial, United States*" enumerating the UCMJ Article 134 offence of "*Patronizing a Prostitute.*" In part, Article 134 provides all disorders that are "to the prejudice of good order and discipline in the armed forces" or are "conduct of a nature to bring discredit upon the armed forces" are to be punished by the discretion of the court according to the "nature and degree of the offence" (*General Article. US Code* 10 [2016], §934).

Article 134 is solely focused on sexual exploitation, more specifically prostitution. Article 134 reads as follows:

Article 134—(Pandering and prostitution)... b. *Elements.*

1. *Prostitution.*
   - (a) That the accused engaged in a sexual act with another person not the accused's spouse;
   - (b) That the accused did so for the purpose of receiving money or other compensation;
   - (c) That this act was wrongful; and.
   - (d) That, under the circumstances, the conduct of the accused was to the prejudice of good order and discipline in the armed forces or was of a nature to bring discredit upon the armed forces.
2. *Patronizing a prostitute.*
   - (a) That the accused engaged in a sexual act with another person not the accused's spouse;

(b) That the accused compelled, induced, enticed, or procured such person to engage in a sexual act in exchange for money or other compensation; and.
(c) That this act was wrongful; and.
(d) That, under the circumstances, the conduct of the accused was to the prejudice of good order and discipline in the armed forces or was of a nature to bring discredit upon the armed forces.

3. *Pandering by inducing, enticing, or procuring act of prostitution.*

(a) That the accused induced, enticed, or procured a certain person to engage in a sexual act for hire and reward with a person to be directed to said person by the accused;
(b) That this inducing, enticing, or procuring was wrongful;
(c) That, under the circumstances, the conduct of the accused was to the prejudice of good order and discipline in the armed forces or was of a nature to bring discredit upon the armed forces.

4. *Pandering by arranging or receiving consideration for arranging for a sexual act.*

(a) That the accused arranged for, or received valuable consideration for arranging for, a certain person to engage in sexual act with another person;
(b) That the arranging (and receipt of consideration) was wrongful; and.
(c) That, under the circumstances, the conduct of the accused was to the prejudice of good order and discipline in the armed forces or was of a nature to bring discredit upon the armed forces.

...

e. *Maximum punishment.*

1. *Prostitution and patronizing a prostitute.* Dishonourable discharge, forfeiture of all pay and allowances, and confinement for one year.
2. *Pandering.* Dishonourable discharge, forfeiture of all pay and allowances, and confinement for five years.

US Personnel and Civilian Case Summary and Analysis

The following case summaries will examine the application and effectiveness of the "*military CTIP trinity*." Are these statutes and regulations having their desired effect? Each of these laws, if applied independently would be insufficient or non-effective. It is in their interconnectivity and design where success might be found.

TVPA-Related Cases

Case 1—*Adhikari v. Daoud & Partners* was originally dismissed for lack of jurisdiction (DODIG 2012), but was refiled in US District Court of Texas in 2009 (*Adhikari v. Daoud & Partners* 2013). The two defendants, Daoud & Partners (Daoud) and Kellogg Brown & Root Incorporation (KBR) were Jordanian corporations, which had entered into numerous contracts with the US for military base services (*Adhikari v. Daoud & Partners* 2013). Nepalese men and women ranging from age 18–27 were recruited by a company in Nepal, to work in a luxury hotel in Amman or at an American military camp, which the workers assumed to be in the United States (*Adhikari v. Daoud & Partners* 2013). All of the workers were promised $500 per month, but instead incurred substantial brokerage fees (*Adhikari v. Daoud & Partners* 2013). None of the workers believed they would be placed in dangerous areas and assumed their employer would protect their wellbeing. This was not the case. First, the workers were transported to Jordan, held by Daoud, and required to turn in their passports (*Adhikari v. Daoud & Partners* 2013). Daoud's agents told the workers they were being sent to work in Iraq at Al Asad Air Base (AAAB), causing them "concern and fear about their futures" (*Adhikari v. Daoud & Partners* 2013). Many stated that they were kept as captives in Jordan and forced to go to Iraq (*Adhikari v. Daoud & Partners* 2013). While in Jordan, one man reported to his family that he and the other men were kept in isolated barracks (*Adhikari v. Daoud & Partners* 2013). The workers were also informed they would not be earning $500 per month as promised, but would be receiving only three-quarters of their promised pay (*Adhikari v. Daoud & Partners* 2013). They were then moved to AAAB in an unprotected caravan along the treacherous Baghdad highway (*Adhikari v. Daoud & Partners* 2013). No security was given to the caravan by Daoud, despite risks of the highway (*Adhikari v. Daoud & Partners* 2013). During travel, two of the cars were stopped by members of the Ansar al-Sunna Army, an Iraqi insurgent group (*Adhikari v. Daoud & Partners* 2013). The kidnapping and holding of the workers was broadcast on the Internet by the insurgent group and all were later killed live on video by gunshot and one beheading (*Adhikari v. Daoud & Partners* 2013). One man in the caravan made it to AAAB where he was supervised by KBR as a warehouse loader and unloader (*Adhikari v. Daoud & Partners* 2013). He learned about the deaths of the others in the caravan and requested to return to Nepal (*Adhikari v. Daoud & Partners* 2013). His request was denied until completion of his work in Iraq. Fifteen months later after working in dangerous conditions, including mortar fire without protection, he was allowed to return to Nepal (*Adhikari v. Daoud & Partners* 2013). The survivor and the families of the other men brought suit against Daoud and KBR (Defendants) under the *Trafficking Victims Protection Reauthorization Act* (TVPRA), the *Racketeering Influenced and Corrupt Organizations Act* (RICO), and the *Alien Tort Statute* (ATS) (*Adhikari v. Daoud & Partners* 2013). For the purposes of this analysis, the focus will be on the TVPRA claim. The defendants claimed the court did not have jurisdiction to hear the case due to a lack of extraterritoriality and the presumption against retroactive application of laws (*Adhikari v. Daoud & Partners* 2013). The court disagreed. It found because the defendants never had the right to traffic humans, regardless if the trafficking occurred domestically or not, no additional substantive duties would be created by applying the extraterritoriality of the act retroactively (*Adhikari v. Daoud & Partners* 2013). The retroactivity only enlarges the court's jurisdiction, but does not change the substantive law against trafficking (*Adhikari v. Daoud & Partners* 2013). In addition, the purpose of TVPRA would be "severely undermined" if the extraterritoriality provision was not used retroactively because human trafficking by nature is an international crime (*Adhikari v. Daoud & Partners* 2013). Therefore, the Court found jurisdiction under the TVPRA (*Adhikari v. Daoud & Partners* 2013). The ability of the Court to find jurisdiction over this case under TVPRA demonstrates its potential effectiveness. The Court's analysis finding jurisdiction allows the American legal system to charge traffickers under TVPRA, despite their location, due to the inherent wrongness of trafficking as a crime.

Case 2—Naval Petty Officer Second Class, Shane Allan Childers responded to an online advertisement seeking sex with an 11-year-old girl (US Attorney's Office of Western District of Missouri 2009). He used his government computer, communicated via his government email account, and then used his government issued cell phone to arrange the transaction (US Attorney's Office of Western District of Missouri 2009). When Mr. Childers arrived at the meeting location, he wore his Navy uniform, minus his blouse (US Attorney's Office of Western District of Missouri 2009). Once at the location, he paid an undercover law enforcement officer $60 to have sex with the child with an additional $20 not to use a condom (US Attorney's Office of Western District of Missouri 2009). Mr. Childers pleaded guilty and admitted to attempting to pay for sex with a child (Kendall 2009). During his arrest, he admitted he had previously paid for and used prostitutes when serving in Hong Kong in 1998 (Kendall 2009). The Western District of Missouri's US District Court sentenced Mr. Childers to 15 years, without parole, for being a customer of child prostitution in violation of the TVPA (US Attorney's Office of Western District of Missouri 2009).

These two cases demonstrate the potential effectiveness of the TVPRA. Unfortunately, cases later discussed will reveal TVPRA is not used enough in order to achieve such results, as many traffickers in the military are charged under Article 134 or Article 120, sexual assault, of the UCMJ.

MEJA-Related Cases

In 2007, the US State Department hired Armor Group North America Inc. (AGNA) to provide armed guard services for the US embassy in Kabul, Afghanistan. Shortly thereafter, AGNA employees were patronizing nearby brothels disguised as Chinese restaurants utilizing sexually exploited victims. In response, AGNA agreed to pay $7.5 million to settle and resolve all claims including violations of the TVPA. The settlement also absolved AGNA of allegations management knew of the guards' activities and AGNA's misrepresentation of work experience of 38 guards it hired to guard the US Embassy (US Department of Justice 2011).

UCMJ-Related Cases

When examining human trafficking investigations, specifically labour trafficking, there is a significant dearth of litigated cases involving the US military or civilian contractors. Many, if not all of these investigations were closed for lack of evidence. There are many contributing factors in an indicting agency's decision to move forward with the prosecution of a case or to seek terms of settlement. However, the value of seeking a final judgment is often discounted. If an indicting agency constantly and consistently seeks monetary settlements as the favoured resolution, especially where criminal conduct is suspected, the subjects of scrutiny begin to treat the rules and regulations as suggestions, and monetary fines are seen as the cost of business. When the administrative and legislative intent for violations is disbarment of future business and/or jail time for criminal activity, routinely obtaining settlements should be scrutinized. Further, where investigations are consistently set aside for lack of evidence of a trafficking violation, it prevents prosecution under the UCMJ, TVPRA, or MEJA; thus, this inhibits these laws from having their desired effect on the human trafficking industry. In the following three cases, none of investigations were deemed to merit a violation of human trafficking under any viable statute, thus diminishing the value of the statute for deterrence and prevention.

Case 1—One case that did not result in a hearing also dealt with KBR in Baghdad, Iraq. This incident of labour trafficking was documented in a 2009 report as a Special Interest Case for the Department of Defense Inspector General's (DODIG) Defense Criminal Investigative Service (DCIS) branch at Camp Victory (Isenberg and Schwellenbach 2011). Around 1000 South Asian (Sri Lanka, Nepal, and Bangladesh) workers came to Iraq to work for Najlaa International Catering Services (Najlaa), a subcontractor of KBR's contract (Isenberg and Schwellenbach 2011). The men came to Iraq being promised "the moon and stars" by the company. Rather, their passports were taken from them; they were confined to a windowless warehouse without money for three months and were charged $2000–$3000 for the costs of transportation, medical exams, and visas. These services typically cost approximately $500 (Isenberg and Schwellenbach 2011). The living conditions for these men were substandard, requiring them to share bedding, three to four men per twin bed, their sewage drained to a "cess-pool" 100 yards from their camp, sickness spread without any medical treatment, and they were given very little food and water (Isenberg and Swchwellenbach 2011). After investigating, DCIS concluded no implication of a human trafficking violation due to the fact that workers were technically allowed to leave (ACLU 2012a, b, 25). Najlaa sustained no substantial negative repercussions for its treatment of the men. Najlaa continues to bid and fulfil US government contracts. Subsequently, KBR conducted an internal investigation concluding the living conditions were abysmal, cancelling its contract with Najlaa (ACLU 2012a, b, 25). Due to the lack of any evidence indicating trafficking was afoot in the base this case, like many others, never made it to court in order to be tried in accordance with UCMJ or any other of the comparable statutes.

Case 2—KBR appears again in 2008 with Kulak Construction Company (KCC), a Turkish subcontractor. KCC was accused of using deceptive practices to hire 10 women and 100 men from Fiji to work in Iraq (ACLU 2012a, b, 1). At the time of the investigation, the women were working at the Army and Air Force Exchange Services (AAFES) at Forward Operating Base (FOB) Sykes, earning a significantly lesser amount than promised (ACLU 2012a, b, 1). The DODIG investigation focused specifically on the treatment of the Fijian women hired as beauticians (ACLU 2012a, b, 1). The women were originally told they would be taken to Dubai and were promised $3033 per month (ACLU 2012a, b, 8). However, upon arrival, their passports were confiscated, and they were forced onto a plane destined for a military base in Iraq. Once in Iraq they were charged a fee to return home (ACLU 2012a, b, 8). They were subjected to verbal and sexual harassment, poor living conditions, and coercive fees to keep them indebted and working (ACLU 2012a, b, 9). In addition, they earned considerably less than promised. One of the women signed a contract for one year for $350 per month, allowing her to keep her tips (ACLU 2012a, b, 10). One victim was sent home when Kulak discovered she had spoken to the authorities about the living and working conditions (ACLU 2012a, b, 2). Yet, DODIG's investigation once again came to the conclusion of no human trafficking violations (ACLU 2012a, b, 10). First, after various interviews with the women, DODIG found most of the women wished to stay employed at AAFES because they were allowed to keep their tips, which ranged from $15 to $50 per day, making the monthly salary closer to $850. The women believed business would increase soon, and they were making more money in Iraq than they would in Fiji (ACLU 2012a, b, 10). In addition, DODIG found the Kulak contract indicated the working location would be anywhere in Iraq, not Dubai, therefore the change in service location was not improper (ACLU 2012a, b, 10).

Case 3—A similar situation occurred at Bagram Air Field (BAF) in Afghanistan at their AAFES. Amina Enterprise Group (AEG) recruited women from Fiji to work at AAFES's beauty salon (ACLU 2012a, b, 37). They were charged $700 for their flight to BAF and received $150 per month to work at the salon (ACLU 2012a, b, 38). Yet, they were conveniently charged $150 per month "rental" fee for the use of the beauty chair used (ACLU 2012a, b, 38). The only monies they were permitted to keep were tips (ACLU 2012a, b, 38). In addition, AEG was accused of providing prostitutes to the engineers and contractors at the BAF as a sexual bribe, in hopes of continued contracts with BAF (ACLU 2012a, b, 38).

Sexual Exploitation: At Home and Abroad

Sexual exploitation and sex trafficking cases are more prominently investigated among members of the military than labour exploitation cases. Many of these cases have been handled by prosecuting the military member individually. However, these prosecutions are not normally conducted through the court-martial process under the UCMJ. Typically, US District Attorneys under Title 18 of the US Code conduct these prosecutions. Cases prosecuted under the UCMJ are typically sexual assault and not trafficking-related cases. This phenomenon contributes to the lack of a human trafficking article in the UCMJ. Though the TVPRA may not have an effect on sexual exploitation cases within the military, the UCMJ is successful in its prosecution of violators of Article 120 of the UCMJ, dealing with sexual assault. The UCMJ charges service members with sexual assault regardless of whether the assault was the result of exploitation by traffickers. The most common form of punishment for Article 120 violations is discharge from service and time in prison. Yet, the difficulty remains in connecting the UCMJ prosecutions with those under TVPRA in order to create a comprehensive weapon to attack human trafficking at home and abroad.

Case 1—Jeffrey Chadwick Wright, a former Navy sailor, pleaded guilty in 2014 to traveling across state lines to enable underage prostitution (Mitchell 2014). Mr. Wright was found by Naval Criminal Investigative Service (NCIS) with a 17-year-old girl in his on-base housing whom he had helped run away from her foster home (Mitchell 2014). He then prostituted her in Virginia, North Carolina, and Maryland and facilitated the creation of advertisements on backpage.com (Navy Times 2014). As a result, Mr. Wright was discharged from the Navy and sentenced to five years in prison for the offence (The Associated Press 2014).

Case 2—In 2010, Craig Allen Corey II, a 23-year-old Army soldier, was investigated by the Maryland Human Trafficking Task Force for running a sex and drug trafficking business. Mr. Corey was stationed at Fort Meade in Maryland where he knowingly recruited a 16-year-old girl and transported her from Ohio to Maryland in order to solicit her for sexual services (US Attorney's Office of Maryland 2010). Mr. Corey, with other defendants, enticed 12 girls to join this ring (US Attorney's Office of Maryland 2010). The men photographed the girls naked, putting their photographs on various social media platforms, including Craigslist, MySpace, and YouTube, offering sex for money (US Attorney's Office of Maryland 2010). Mr. Corey received a percentage of the money the girls made and used it to buy drugs to re-sell (US Attorney's Office of Maryland 2010). The US District Court sentenced Mr. Corey to 210 months in prison followed by supervised release for life (US Attorney's Office of Maryland 2010). He also plead guilty to trafficking by force, sex trafficking of a minor, drug charges, enticement to travel in interstate commerce to engage in prostitution, interstate transportation for prostitution, and conspiracy to prostitute (US Attorney's Office of Maryland 2010).

Case 3—In an investigation led by the Central California Internet Crimes Against Children Taskforce, ICE, Homeland Security, NCIS along with the Porterville, Tulare, and Lemoore Police Departments, it was found that Charles Ray Benavidez, a 33-year-old Aviation Ordinanceman Second Class engaged in commercial sex acts with a minor (US Attorney's Office Eastern District of California 2015). The investigation revealed Mr. Benavidez met the victim, a 17-year-old girl, on a social media website, and then drove to engage the victim in a sexual act (US Attorney's Office Eastern District of California 2015). Mr. Benavidez returned multiple times to have sex with the victim and on a third time, coerced her to have sex with another person (US Attorney's Office Eastern District of California 2015). The US District Court found Mr. Benavidez knowingly recruited a 17-year-old to engage in commercial sex and was sentenced to 10 years for sex trafficking of a minor (US Attorney's Office Eastern District of California 2015).

Case 4—In 2008, Retired Marine Corps Captain Michael Pepe, 60 years old at the time, was investigated by Immigration Customs and Enforcement (ICE) and Homeland Security Investigations regarding accusations of sexual abuse of minors in Cambodia (ICE 2014). The investigation found girls Mr. Pepe abused were between the ages of 9 and 13 (ICE 2014). These girls had been drugged, bound, beaten, and raped by Mr. Pepe (ICE 2014). They also told investigators they were forced to give Mr. Pepe sexual massages and perform oral sex on him every day (ICE 2014). Mr. Pepe was able to "use" these girls via a Cambodian prostitute who acted as his broker (ICE 2014). The broker, with the knowledge and assistance of the victims' families, would bring young girls to Mr. Pepe's house and he would pay the families for their "continued use of them." (ICE 2014). When investigating the case, rope, cloth strips, sedatives, and child pornography were found and seized from Mr. Pepe's apartment (ICE 2014). Mr. Pepe was sentenced to 210 years by the US District Court for violent sexual abuse of young girls and was required to pay $247,000 in restitution to the victims (ICE 2014).

Case 5—Since 2009, Navy Commander Jose Luis Sanchez, Commander Michael Vannak, and NCIS Supervisory Special Agent John Bertrand were providing information to Leonard Glenn Francis, the CEO of Glenn Defense Marine Asia (GDMA), in exchange for money, vacations, and prostitutes (US Department of Justice 2013). GDMA is a government contractor set in Singapore that provides "husbanding" services (US Department of Justice 2013). Specifically, Sanchez received bribes and in return used his authority to recommend to the Navy that it hire GDMA for contracts (US Department of Justice 2013). Francis hired female escorts for Sanchez and his friends on multiple occasions. Mr. Sanchez would attend meetings with his "wolf pack." (US Department of Justice 2013). At one point, Mr. Francis asked for pictures of prostitutes he could disseminate to the "wolf pack" for motivation (US Department of Justice 2013). Finally, in 2011, Francis contacted Mr. Sanchez and asked him to "swing" business his way, referencing a US Navy ship that needed to refuel in Thailand (US Department of Justice 2013). Mr. Sanchez was able to get Francis the contract, costing the Navy an unnecessary $1 million dollars (US Department of Justice 2013).

Conclusion

The *Trafficking Victims Protection Reauthorization Act* (TVPRA), the *Military Extraterritorial Jurisdiction Act* (MEJA), and the *Uniform Code of Military Justice* (UCMJ) can best be seen as the "*military CTIP trinity*" for the enforcement and the prosecution of trafficking-related offences. The complexity of human trafficking and sexual exploitation is so deeply nuanced that for these laws to have maximum impact, further evaluation of their interplay and harmonization is required. The evolution of these laws will need to keep pace with societal understanding of trafficking's modus operandi, evolve with contractors' patterns and practice of artful concealment of forced labour exploitation, and evolve to anticipate future exploitative schemes.

US personnel and military contractors often find themselves helping a country rebuild infrastructure or are assisting local governments secure a stable legal and social framework. It is extremely well documented how exploitation thrives in chaotic, lawless, and post-conflict areas. Lack of awareness, oversight, and law enforcement priority provide the shadow required for this crime to prosper. If US personnel are to be seen as a welcomed and stabilizing force, it is imperative its soldiers are not directly or indirectly complicit in human exploitation. Sexual exploitation has a unique and deeply rooted historical connection with military actions. Past patterns of practice and accepted socio-historical norms concerning soldiers in-theatre greatly inhibit military leaders' ability to honestly and faithfully hold subordinates fully accountable for their actions. As global society learns more about this crime, including its connection to organized and transnational crime and its growing nexus to the funding and recruitment of international terrorism, we must not permit our fighting men and women to contribute to this heinous human rights violation.

The US' inability to prevent its personnel and civilian contractors from continuing these relationships threatens the credibility and reputation of the US. In the past, when utilizing prostitution was discouraged, the primary concern was based in personal health and maintaining the health of the fighting force, avoiding venereal disease. Now, in the twenty-first century, the concern is rightfully grounded in its repugnancy and its human rights violations. In President George W. Bush's Executive Order, he states "our policy is based on an abolitionist approach to trafficking in persons, and our efforts must involve a comprehensive attack on such trafficking, which is a modern day form of slavery" (White House 2003). Yes, the TVPA, UCMJ, and MEJA laws have structural and definitional deficiencies; however, the current and future President and the US Congress have an obligation to continue to perfect and harmonize these statutes, ensuring their full and proper application and thereby progressing the fight against exploitation.

References

ACLU. 2012a. Military Contractor Human Trafficking - Documents Released Under FOIA. *ACLU.* https://www.aclu.org/other/military-contractor-human-trafficking-documents-released-under-foia

———. 2012b. Victims of Complacency: The Ongoing Trafficking and Abuse of Third Country Nationals by U.S. Government Contractors. *ACLU.* https://www.aclu.org/report/victims-complacency-ongoing-trafficking-and-abuse-third-country-nationals-us-government

Adhikari v. Daoud & Partners, 697 F. Supp. 2d 674, 680 (S.D. Tex. 2013).

Amadeo, Kimberly. 2019. Department of Defense and its Effect on the Economy. *The Balance*, 25 June 2019. https://www.thebalance.com/department-of-defense-what-it-does-and-its-impact-3305982

Bialik, Kristen. 2017. U.S. Active-duty Military Presence Overseas Is at Its Smallest in Decades. *Pew Research*, 22 August 2017. http://www.pewresearch.org/fact-tank/2017/08/22/u-s-active-duty-military-presence-overseas-is-at-its-smallest-in-decades/

Department of Defense Office of Inspector General. 2012. Military Contractor Human Trafficking. DODIG Release 29–31. https://www.aclu.org/other/military-contractor-human-trafficking-documents-released-under-foia

Department of Defense Office of the Inspector General. 2003. Assessment of DoD Efforts to Combat Trafficking in Persons: Phase II – Bosnia-Herzegovina and Kosovo. http://www.dodig.osd.mil/fo/foia/HT-Phase_II.pdf

Department of Defense. 2014. Strategic Plan for Combating Trafficking in Persons 2014–2018. https://ctip.defense.gov/Portals/12/Documents/Strategic_Plan_FINAL.pdf

Diamond, Christopher. 2017. Report: U.S. Military's Shrinking Size and Growing Equipment Age Reflect DoD Policies. *Military Times*, 15 March 2017. https://www.militarytimes.com/news/your-military/2017/03/15/report-u-s-military-s-shrinking-size-and-growing-equipment-age-reflect-dod-policies/

Garcia-Oscasio. 2015. How Tolerant is Zero Tolerance? The Loopholes in Anti-Trafficking Federal Contract Regulations. *Public Contract Law Journal* 44: 551–554.

General Article. U.S. Code 10 (2016), §934.

Greer, Benjamin, and Purvis, Jeffery. 2016. [See Generally] "Corporate Supply Chain Transparency – California's Seminal Attempt to Discourage Forced Labor." *The International Journal of Human Rights* 20(1).

Isenberg, David, and Schwellenbach, Nick. 2011. Documents Reveal Details of Alleged Labor Trafficking by KBR Subcontractor. *POGO*. June 14, 2011. https://www.pogo.org/investigation/2011/06/documents-reveal-details-of-alleged-labor-trafficking-by-kbr-subcontractor/

Joint Service Committee on Military Justice. 2016. Part IV, Article 134: Pandering and Prostitution. *Manual for Courts-Martial United States*. https://jsc.defense.gov/Portals/99/Documents/MCM2016.pdf?ver=2016-12-08-181411-957

Kendall, Justin. 2009. Navy Recruiter Admits to Trying to Pay $80 to Have Unprotected Sex with an 11-Year-Old Girl. *The Pitch KC*. July 17, 2009. https://www.thepitchkc.com/news/article/20588196/navy-recruiter-admits-trying-to-pay-80-to-have-unprotected-sex-with-an-11yearold-girl

Mendelson, Sarah. 2005. Barracks and Brothels – Peacekeepers and Human Trafficking in the Balkans. *Center for Strategic and International Studies.* https://csis-prod.s3.amazonaws.com/s3fspublic/legacy_files/files/media/csis/pubs/0502_barracksbrothels.pdf

Mitchell, Becca. 2014. Former Navy Sailor Pleads Guilty to Sex Trafficking HIV-Positive Child. *WKTR.* July 31, 2014. https://wtkr.com/2014/07/31/former-navy-sailor-pleads-guilty-to-sex-trafficking-child/

Navy Times. 2014. Ex-Sailor Pleads Guilty to Sex Trafficking Child. *Navy Times,* July 24, 2014. https://www.navytimes.com/news/your-navy/2014/07/30/ex-sailor-pleads-guilty-to-sex-trafficking-child/

President may prescribe rules. U.S. Code 10 (2006), §836.

Principal Deputy Under Secretary of Defence, Personnel and Readiness Charles S. Abell, speaking at the House Armed Services Committee and the Commission on Security and Cooperation in Europe. 2004. https://www.c-span.org/person/?charlesabell

Senator Patrick Leahy, Speaking on S11, 146th Cong., *Congressional Record* 183 (October 26, 2000).

The Associated Press. 2014. Ex-Sailor Gets 5 Years for Sex Trafficking Child. *The Associated Press,* December 10, 2014. https://www.navytimes.com/news/your-navy/2014/12/11/ex-sailor-gets-5-years-for-sex-trafficking-child/

U.S. Attorney's Office Eastern District of California. 2015. Service Member at U.S. Naval Air.

U.S. Attorney's Office of Maryland. 2010. U.S. Army Soldier Sentenced to Over 17 Years in Prison for Operating a Brothel from Millersville Apartment and to Drug Trafficking. USAO Archive, April 28 2010. https://www.justice.gov/archive/usao/md/news/archive/U.S.ArmySoldierSentencedtoover17YearsinPrisonforOperatingaBrothelandtoDrugTrafficking.html

U.S. Attorney's Office Western District of Missouri. 2009. Former Naval Recruiter Sentenced for Attempted Sex Trafficking of a Child. *FBI Archives,* October 19. https://archives.fbi.gov/archives/kansascity/press-releases/2009/kc101909.htm

U.S. Congress. Senate. Subcommittee on Readiness and Management Support. *The Final Report of the Commission on Wartime Contracting in Iraq and Afghanistan.* 112th Congress, 1st Sess, October 2011.

U.S. Congress. House of Representatives. Subcommittee on Technology, Information Policy, Intergovernmental Relations and Procurement Reform. *Are Government Contractors Exploiting Workers Overseas? Examining Enforcement of the Trafficking Victims Protections Act.* 112th Congress, 1st Sess, November 2011.

U.S. Department of Health and Human Services. 2004. *Human Trafficking Fact Sheet*. http://www.acf.hhs.gov/trafficking/about/fact_human2004.pdf
U.S. Department of Justice. 2011. Armor Group North America and Its Affiliates pay $7.5 Million to Resolve False Claims Act Allegations. July 7. https://www.justice.gov/opa/pr/armor-group-north-america-and-its-affiliates-pay-75-million-resolve-false-claims-act
———. 2013. Navy Commander Charged with Accepting $100,000 Cash and Prostitutes in Widening International Bribery Scheme. DOJ Office of Public Affairs, November 6. https://www.justice.gov/opa/pr/navy-commander-charged-accepting-100000-cash-and-prostitutes-widening-international-bribery
U.S. Department of State Office to Monitor and Combat Trafficking in Persons. 2018. *Trafficking in Persons Report*. https://www.state.gov/documents/organization/282798.pdf
U.S. Immigration and Customs Enforcement. 2014. Ex-Marine Receives 210-year Federal Prison Term for Drugging and Raping Girls in Cambodia. *ICE,* February 28. https://www.ice.gov/news/releases/ex-marine-receives-210-year-federal-prison-term-drugging-and-raping-girls-cambodia#wcm-survey-target-id
Victims of Trafficking and Violence Protection Act, 22 U.S.C. §7101 2000.
———, 22 U.S.C. §104(e)(2)(A) n.d..
Vine, David. 2015. Where in the World is the U.S. Military? https://www.politico.com/magazine/story/2015/06/us-military-bases-around-the-world-119321
Warren, Brittany. 2012. If You Have Zero-Tolerance Policy, Why Aren't You Doing Anything?: Using the Uniform Code of Military Justice to Combat Human Trafficking Abroad. http://www.gwlr.org/wp-content/uploads/2012/07/80_4_Warren.pdf
White House. 2003. Trafficking in Persons National Security Presidential Directive. Office of the Press Secretary Press Release, February 25. Accessed July 24, 2019. www.whitehouse.gov/news/releases/2003/02/20030225.html
Wyler, Liana Sun. 2013. Trafficking in Persons: International Dimensions and Foreign Policy Issues for Congress. *Congressional Research Service*, R42497.

Benjamin Thomas Greer works at the California Governor's Office of Emergency Services (Cal OES) as Subject Matter Expert in the field of human trafficking and child sexual exploitation. Before joining Cal OES, he served as a Special Deputy Attorney General with the California Department of Justice—

Office of the Attorney General where he led a team of attorneys and non-attorneys in writing a comprehensive report for the California Attorney General entitled 'The State of Human Trafficking in California 2012.'

Kymber M. Cates obtained her Juris Doctor from the University of the Pacific, McGeorge School of Law. She previously internd with both the Judge Advocate General Corps (JAGC) of the United States Air Force and United States Navy. Since passing the BAR she is now serving as a Judge Advocate General for the United States Navy.

Part III

Addressing Human Trafficking in Conflict and Dealing with the Aftermath

9

The Due Diligence Duty and the Role of the Military in the Identification and Protection of Human Trafficking Victims

Valentina Milano

Introduction

Human trafficking stems from existing vulnerabilities, such as poverty, unemployment, lack of socioeconomic opportunities, gender-based violence and discrimination, which are exacerbated during and after conflicts because of the general breakdown of the rule of law and higher levels of violence (SR trafficking 2018, 5). Human trafficking in conflict, which still disproportionately affects women and girls (SR trafficking 2018, 7 and 12; IOM 2015, 15), takes various forms: sexual exploitation by armed state and non-state actors, use of trafficked children as combatants, trafficking for the removal of organs to treat wounded fighters or finance war, and enslavement as a tactic of terrorism (UNODC 2018a, vii; Nagle 2003, 18–28). Victims are also put into servitude as porters, cooks, domestic workers or to work in mines, plantations or drugs crops

V. Milano (✉)
Universidad de las Islas Baleares, Facultad de Derecho,
Palma de Mallorca, Spain
e-mail: valentina.milano@uib.es

J. Muraszkiewicz et al. (eds.), *Human Trafficking in Conflict*, Crime Prevention and Security Management, https://doi.org/10.1007/978-3-030-40838-1_9

as reported during the conflicts in the DRC, Angola, Sierra Leone and Colombia (UNODC 2018b, 13–14; Martin and Callaway 2009, 50–51).

In this complex scenario, what is the role of the military? In the last two or three decades, the military have regrettably been known either for recruiting labour force through trafficking networks, as happened with South Asian migrant workers in conflicts in the Middle East (SR trafficking, 2016, 35–36) or for buying the services of trafficking victims, in particular women and girls forced into prostitution in, for example, Kosovo, Haiti or Sierra Leone (UNODC 2018a, xiii; Godec 2010, 245; Smith and Miller-de la Cuesta 2011, 292–297). As of today, members of the military have been identified not as part of the solution but as part of the problem. Acknowledging the existing debate on the negative role of the military, this chapter seeks to turn the discourse on its head and look at how the military can be part of the solution in contributing to the identification and protection of trafficking victims. Indeed, as a frontline actor in times of conflict, the military is ideally placed to contribute to national efforts to identify traffickers and their victims. But is such a role for the military actually provided for under international law? To what extent have international bodies expressly referred to it? In this chapter, we will try to provide more clarity on the legal standards that apply to the armed forces in this area, in particular in light of States' due diligence duty under human rights law.

The first section of this chapter examines the prevailing weakness of international instruments as far as the identification and protection of trafficking victims is concerned, both in times of peace and in times of conflict, and how the due diligence duty broadens State obligations in this regard. Section 2 explores the extent to which international law and policy establish a mandate for militaries' engagement in identification and what the main requirements attached to this identification are, including proactivity and multi-stakeholders' cooperation. Finally, conclusions are drawn and proposals are formulated on how to address current gaps.

The International Framework on the Protection of Trafficking Victims and the Role of the Military

Human trafficking *per se* is far from being comprehensively addressed in international human rights conventions, as only the *Convention on the Elimination of all Forms of Discrimination against Women* and the *Convention on the Rights of the Child* prohibit it. Although of course slavery is addressed. Similarly, international criminal law shortly refers to it as an element of the crime against humanity, while international humanitarian law does not address it at all. Only recent specialized anti-trafficking instruments provide for the substantive regulation of this serious human rights violation. In turn, human rights law has subsequently taken on an essential role in supplementing anti-trafficking instruments by addressing its weaknesses, not based on a new human rights treaty but on a principle that reflects the essence of human rights law: the doctrine of States' positive obligations and its related standard, the due diligence duty.

The *UN Protocol to Prevent, Suppress and Punish Trafficking in Persons, especially Women and Children* (Palermo Protocol) is the treaty that regulates trafficking at the international level. Even if it is the first anti-trafficking treaty that is structured around the so-called three Ps—States' duties to *prevent* and *prosecute* trafficking and to *protect* its victims—as opposed to an approach focused on prosecution, the Protocol in fact fails to adequately address the three Ps. A closer look at it shows that victim protection is only addressed in a marginal way and prevention in very general terms (Gallagher 2001, 990–991 and 995; Milano 2018c, 107–108). The approach is still a criminal law one: its marked focus on prosecution results in an unbalanced three P approach that neglects protection and prevention.

Indeed, the idea of a balanced three Ps framework finds its origins in international human rights law and more precisely in the "positive obligations" doctrine, also referred to by several international bodies as the "due diligence" duty, as it is measured by the due diligence standard. How did this doctrine emerge? Human rights treaties mostly include negative obligations that require abstaining from interfering with the enjoyment of rights, which proved insufficient to protect human rights, in particular—but not only—in relation to abuses perpetrated by non-state actors. The development of the positive obligation doctrine has thus been essential to identify States' duty to take a number of positive measures aimed at ensuring the practical and effective enjoyment of rights even where treaties only provide for a succinct prohibition.

Positive obligations were initially identified by the European Court of Human Rights (ECtHR) (Mowbray 2004). However, the Committee on the Elimination of Discrimination against Women (CEDAW) was the first body to use this notion to identify States' obligations in relation to trafficking. In its 1992 General recommendation number 19 on gender-based violence, the Committee established that trafficking in women is a form of gender-based violence prohibited under the Convention (paras 13–16) and that:

> States may be responsible for private acts if they fail to act with due diligence to prevent violations of rights or to investigate and punish acts of violence, and for providing compensation (para 9)

It reiterated this concept in General recommendation n. 28 (para 13) and again in latest General recommendation n. 35 on gender-based violence, where it extensively refers to States' due diligence duties in the area of prevention, protection and prosecution. The Human Rights Committee and the Committee on Torture also referred to this duty in relation to trafficking as a violation of the prohibition of slavery, servitude and forced labour and of the prohibition of torture respectively (HRC 2000, 12; CAT 2008, 18). Finally, as of the 2010 *Rantsev v Cyprus and Russia* case, the ECtHR applied this doctrine to the right not to be subjected to trafficking. It recognized that States' positive obligations in this area shall include, in addition to measures to punish traffickers, measures to prevent trafficking and to protect victims (*Rantsev*, 285). In that context, it established that such comprehensive approach requires States to comply with three main positive obligations: to put in place an appropriate legislative and administrative framework to prevent and punish trafficking and to protects its victims, to take operation measures to protect victims, and to investigate and prosecute trafficking (*Rantsev*, 285; Stoyanova

2017, 319–426). While the ECtHR's subsequent trafficking case law has not always been coherent (Milano 2017; Milano 2018a), *Rantsev* is certainly a landmark judgment as it established the existence of comprehensive State obligations in the area of trafficking based on human rights law and, more specifically, on the positive obligations doctrine and the corresponding due diligence duty.

As far as anti-trafficking instruments are concerned, only some of them have incorporated broader duties that reflect this doctrine. In fact, it is only in the European continent that States agreed to commit to a broader human rights perspective based on a balanced three Ps framework, as reflected in the 2005 *Council of Europe Convention on Action against Trafficking in Human Beings* and, even if less comprehensively, in the 2011 *EU Trafficking Directive* (2011/36/EU). Indeed, treaties adopted in other regions, such as the 2015 ASEAN *Convention Against Trafficking in Persons, Especially Women and Children*, failed to incorporate such a framework as they very much reproduce the text and spirit of the Palermo Protocol. However, the instrument that more clearly incorporates States' positive obligations to act with due diligence is a UN soft law instrument: the 2002 *Recommended Principles and Guidelines on Human Rights and Human Trafficking* ("Trafficking Principles and Guidelines"). They constitute the first "codification" in an international anti-trafficking instrument of a balanced three Ps approach that expressly refers to States' due diligence duties, as follows:

> States have a responsibility under international law to act with due diligence to prevent trafficking, to investigate and prosecute traffickers and to assist and protect trafficked persons (Principle 2)

As opposed to the Palermo Protocol, which is an example of international law fragmentation that persists in separating transnational criminal law and international human rights law commitments, the Trafficking Principles and Guidelines, together with the European Trafficking Convention, demonstrate that commitments under these two regimes—in particular protection and prosecution—are not contradictory but complementary and shall be comprehensively addressed (Milano 2018c).

Is the Role of Militaries Addressed?

In conflict, the role of the military in trafficking is more relevant in relation to prevention and protection as opposed to prosecution, which is foremost an area for the judiciary. However, international anti-trafficking instruments do not directly address the military's role in these two areas, nor do they refer to trafficking in times of conflict. Of course, militaries are agents of the State and are as such bound by State obligations under international law. However, anti-trafficking instruments include several references to other categories of State agents, such as police, border guards or prosecutors, underlining their role in, for example, identification or prosecution. This does not happen with the military.

In fact, the Trafficking Principles and Guidelines are the only instrument that refers to the military, although indirectly. Guideline 10 calls for eradicating the involvement of peacekeepers in trafficking through regulations and codes of conducts, pre-deployment trainings and reporting and investigation mechanisms. As can be seen, this provision only refers to a particular group of militaries: peacekeepers. As will be highlighted further in this chapter, in anti-trafficking instruments and policies there are many more references to peacekeepers than to the broader category of the military. Moreover, this guideline only refers to preventing their involvement in human trafficking. Indeed, the issue of peacekeepers' involvement in trafficking clearly attracts more attention (UN DPKO 2004, 12–15; NATO 2004a, 4(d) and f; UNODC 2018a, xiii; IOM 2015, 4) than the positive role peacekeepers or, more broadly, the military can have in the identification and protection of victims.

The State Obligation to Identify Trafficking Victims

Victim Identification: Main Concerns

Identification is crucial since victims can only exercise their rights if they are identified properly and at an early stage. However, very few of those caught in trafficking are identified in relation to the magnitude of the phenomenon (UNODC 2015, 20; GRETA 2016a, 4–5 and 33–43). The challenges and shortcomings in identification are numerous (Gallagher 2010, 278–280; McAdam 2013, 33–49; Surtees 2007, 49–105). First, literature points at the persistence of a criminal law approach principally or exclusively aimed at fighting crime and irregular immigration at the expense of a human rights approach aimed at victims' identification and protection (GRETA 2016a, 4–5 and 33–43; Rijken and Bosma 2014, 23, 99, 121–122). Second, too many States still rely on victims' self-identification instead of engaging in proactive identification, while it has been documented that those caught up in trafficking generally refrain from revealing their situation, including because of the fear of violent retaliation by traffickers, deep feelings of mistrust towards official bodies, as well as their trauma and embarrassment due to the extreme violence and humiliation they experience (UNODC 2008, 273–4; IOM 2009, 9; *Rantsev* 2010, 320).

In light of these challenges, it is crucial that all public officials that are likely to come into contact with victims are involved in identification and protection efforts. As mentioned, in a conflict situation, the military are certainly a major frontline actor that holds the capacity to monitor situations in communities and to be in contact with local groupings and leaders and, possibly, with non-governmental armed groups. Therefore, they are uniquely placed to identify situations that may amount to trafficking and to protect those in need. One could also argue that, as a still prevalently male group, the military continue to be an ideal target for traffickers to offer the services of trafficking victims. This reality should be used by the military for the benefit of anti-trafficking efforts, that is, as an opportunity to pinpoint locations where trafficking networks operate and thus to get hold of information that is vital to locate victims.

The Obligation to Identify Trafficking Victims

While the Palermo Protocol is silent on States' obligation to identify victims and on the procedures to be followed, the UN Working Group on Trafficking in Persons, which is in charge of advising States' Parties on its implementation, quickly reacted to this far-reaching omission and recommended that States "develop, disseminate to practitioners and systematically use criteria for the identification of victims" (UN WGTIP 2009, 13.a and e and 9). Many other relevant UN documents refer to this duty (UNODC 2009a, 11; UNODC 2009b, 53–54; UNODC 2004, 289). Clearly, the current interpretation of the Protocol includes the obligation to identify victims as a central duty (Gallagher 2010, 282).

As opposed to the Palermo Protocol, the Trafficking Principles and Guidelines refer to the identification of trafficked persons as a central obligation (Guideline 2) and describe how this obligation should be implemented, as will be addressed in more detail below. Importantly, it also states that "States are also obliged to exercise due diligence in identifying traffickers". In the same line, the 2005 Council of Europe Convention on Action against Trafficking in Human Beings devotes Article 10 exclusively to identification and places clear obligations on States in this area, including the duty to train competent authorities adequately, to adopt legal and other measures necessary to identify victims, to collaborate with other States and relevant support organizations, to guarantee non-removal and assistance to all suspected victims until the identifications process has been finalized, as well as special measures for unaccompanied children identified as victims. In *Rantsev*, the ECtHR also confirmed that the positive obligation to adopt operational measures to protect victims includes the obligation to identify victims as soon as "a credible suspicion that an identified individual had been, or was at real and immediate risk of being, trafficked" arises (para 286) and to have competent authorities that are sufficiently trained to do so.

However, it has already been mentioned that none of these instruments refer to identification in times of conflict or to the militaries as state officials that have to be involved in identification and protection efforts. Nevertheless, the argument we developed so far demonstrates that, notwithstanding the lack of reference to a role in identification efforts for the military in anti-trafficking instruments, international human rights law imposes on States a positive obligation to act with due diligence to identify and protect trafficking victims and that the military as agents of the State are bound to comply with this obligation. Clearly, this is particularly so in times of conflict where the presence of the military as state agents in charge of law enforcement is greater and often even prevalent. In such contexts, the State's failure to provide military personnel with the capacity to identify and protect victims might constitute a breach of its due diligence obligation to protect trafficking victims.

On that basis, we will now explore to what extent international bodies and policy documents have referred to that mandate for the military or made it more explicit, thereby supporting our argument, and which legal standards apply to the armed forces in this area in terms of when and how such identification shall be carried out.

The Role of the Military in Identifying and Protecting Trafficking Victims

Instruments and Pronouncements by International Monitoring Bodies

As mentioned, the Trafficking Principles and Guidelines do not expressly refer to the military. They refer to "State authorities and officials such as police, border guards, immigration officials and others" as well as "prosecutors, judicial authorities and social and public health workers". Of course, many provisions refer to "law enforcement authorities", which, depending on the interpretation, might include the military. But, most importantly, the list of State authorities and officials is an open one: "such as" makes it clear that it is not a closed list. It is thus for States to decide which authorities are relevant.

Similarly, the Council of Europe Convention on Action against Trafficking in Human Beings refers to States' duty to have "competent authorities" that are trained and qualified in identifying and helping victims, and the Explanatory report does not refer to the military when providing examples of such authorities. However, two points in the Explanatory Report clearly point to the inclusion of the military. First, competent authority shall be "the public authorities which may have contact with trafficking victims", which, in times of conflict, would hardly justify the exclusion of the military. Second, when interpreting Article 29 of the Convention that requires States to have persons or entities specialized in the fight against trafficking, the Report says that this "covers persons and services liable to have contact with trafficking victims, such as … soldiers or police on international peacekeeping missions" (CoE 2005, 297). This is a welcome clarification that can only be criticized for being too narrow, as it only refers to international peacekeepers: what about militaries operating outside this context, such as those acting at the national level or in a military base abroad? The positive aspect is that the report insists on their potential contribution:

> it is extremely important that staff of the services concerned be trained in recognizing signs of a trafficking offence and collecting and circulating information relevant to anti-trafficking action, and also that they be fully aware of their potential importance for identifying and helping victims (297).

Through its Explanatory Report, the Council of Europe Convention on Action against Trafficking in Human Beings thus recognizes that peacekeepers have a key role in identifying victims and that they shall be adequately trained for that purpose. In the same spirit, the UN Working Group on Trafficking listed "soldiers involved in peacekeeping missions" among the front-line officers who shall receive training that will enable national authorities to respond effectively to trafficking, especially by identifying victims (UN WGTIP 2009, 9). Also, the Special Rapporteur on trafficking, in addition to highlighting that States must "build the capacity of front-line officials from all agencies that might encounter trafficking crimes or victims for quick and accurate identification of trafficking victims" (SR on trafficking 2012, 88; SR on trafficking 2014, 83), more specifically recommended to "adequately train all stakeholders, including peacekeepers and humanitarian personnel working in conflict zones, in refugee camps and in areas of arrival of large influxes of people fleeing conflict, to identify trafficking or risks of trafficking, in cooperation with United Nations agencies and programmes, international organizations, host countries and civil society organizations" (SR trafficking 2016, 64(f)).

These explicit recognitions of the role of soldiers in anti-trafficking efforts in general or more specifically in times of conflict are certainly important. However, the scope is too narrow as it is limited to peacekeepers. References to peacekeepers are important but clearly insufficient to cover the entire spectrum of situations that concern the military.

Policy Documents

The role of the military in anti-trafficking efforts in times of conflict is reflected in more specific and far-reaching terms in a number of policy documents. First of all, the UN General Assembly's Global Plan of Action to Combat Trafficking in Persons points to the need to mainstream the issue of trafficking in UN policies aimed at addressing post-conflict reconstruction and includes peacekeepers among the officials likely to encounter and identify possible victims of trafficking and whose capacity shall be strengthened (UNGA 2010, 14 and 29). A few years later, the Political Declaration on the implementation on this Global Plan recognizes that the issue of trafficking in situations of armed conflict requires further attention and recommends "the training of humanitarian and peacekeeping personnel ... on responding to trafficking in persons" (UNGA 2017, 20).

In fact, this idea was first introduced in documents produced by organizations and offices that are directly managing soldiers being sent abroad: UN Department of Peacekeeping Operations (DPKO) and NATO. The DPKO Human Trafficking Resource Package identifies as its second objective the development of the capacity of peacekeepers to "support national efforts to prevent and counter trafficking" where mandated and requested (UN DPKO 2004, 13). There are two aspects of this DPKO tool that make it probably the most far-reaching document on this topic. First, it points to a number of areas where peacekeepers are more likely to be required to assist local efforts and on which they should be trained: detection and identification of trafficking activities, reporting procedures, the mapping of key partner agencies in the field and their respective roles, and the training of local police forces. Second, it establishes that "the overall approach must be to help develop and support sustainable national anti-trafficking structures" (UN DPKO 2004, 15–16). This is the first recognition that, beyond short-term assistance in the identification and protection of trafficking victims in a conflict setting, a foreign military presence can also contribute to the improvement of the national anti-trafficking capacity in the long term.

The NATO policy and guidelines on trafficking similarly identify as a main objective that NATO deployed forces "support, within their competence and mandate, the efforts of responsible authorities in the host country in their efforts to combat trafficking in human beings" (NATO 2004b, 4; see also NATO 2004a, 1 and 4(e)) and require NATO to develop pre-deployment training modules on how to combat trafficking that include "guidelines to detect instances of trafficking or identify trafficked people, and how to deal with such events", including for the military police in charge of investigating trafficking (NATO 2004c, 3(c) and 4(b)), and an evaluation mechanism on the implementation of this policy (NATO 2004b, 8).

In sum, the mentioned instruments, pronouncements and policy documents recognize that in conflict settings, military personnel shall have a role in identifying trafficking victims and shall be trained for that purpose. Very few of them provide more details on how this shall take place. For example, who identifies officially? To whom should military officers report suspected cases? If the militaries are posted abroad, do they refer cases to the local national referral mechanisms? What if this mechanism is totally ineffective and fails to conform to basic international standards (e.g. multi-stakeholder participation in the mechanism)? If military in a country other than their own use their own identification procedures, which standards shall these fulfil? Most policy documents simply recommend that States adhere to and implement the applicable international legal framework, in particular the Palermo Protocol. Therefore, it is necessary to explore the extent to which the due diligence duty informs the general obligations set out in international law, in particular the Palermo Protocol, in order to obtain more guidance on when and how such identification duty shall be fulfilled by the military.

Multi-stakeholder Cooperation

Except for the Palermo Protocol, anti-trafficking instruments and international monitoring bodies require that States put in place a national identification and referral mechanism based on a multi-stakeholder's approach. As the Group of Experts on Action against Trafficking in Human Beings (GRETA) very clearly states:

> Proper identification requires the existence of a nationwide system of identification and referral of victims to assistance, commonly known as a "National Referral Mechanism" (NRM), which defines the roles and responsibilities of different actors and provides clear procedures, guidance and operational indicators (GRETA 2015, 41)

In the same line, the UN Working Group on Trafficking in Persons invited States to provide a formal identification role to a variety of governmental and non-governmental actors, taking into consideration "the need for a multi-stakeholder approach and the specific roles of potential actors in combating trafficking in persons" (UN WGTIP 2011, 25). Indeed, a multi-disciplinary and cross-sector approach is required in order to integrate a sufficiently high level of expertise in an exercise as complex as the identification of trafficking victims who are threatened, afraid and traumatized.

The Trafficking Principles and Guidelines also refer to this aspect. They recommend "ensuring cooperation between relevant authorities, officials and nongovernmental organizations to facilitate the identification and provision of assistance to trafficked persons" and that such cooperation should be formalized (Guideline 2.3). In the same line, the Special Rapporteur on trafficking recommends the conclusion of bilateral agreements and memorandums of understanding between all relevant actors, as this promotes dialogue and helps building trust among partners (SR trafficking 2012, 95).

The call to formalize cooperation is in the view of this author essential. Formalization guarantees pre-established and effective coordination, as opposed to improvised cooperation. In the same way that it is essential to identify all actors that must participate in identification in times of peace and to formalize their role, States should have regulations and protocols that formalize the participation of the armed forces in identification processes in times of conflict jointly with other actors, establishing the role of each actor. The NATO guidelines, for example, reflect this requirement when it calls upon NATO Authorities to "identify within the Area of Operations, local and international organisations with capacity for protecting and housing adult and child victims of trafficking and the establishment of appropriate liaison arrangements with such organisations" (NATO 2004b, 9(d)). However, this is insufficient: there is a need to establish how local referral mechanisms shall, in times of conflict, adapt to integrate national and foreign militaries and how these shall interact with the system.

Proactive Identification as a Key Requirement

Even if this is still not reflected in the reality on the ground, all international monitoring bodies agree that proactivity is an essential requirement of identification. The UN Working Group on trafficking recommends that States develop a proactive and systematic approach to identification as well as tailor-made indicators for different practitioners (UN WGTIP 2011, 24–25). GRETA consistently insists on the need to proactively identify victims (GRETA 2016b, 146) and increase relevant officers' outreach work (GRETA 2014, 135). In relation to this fundamental requirement, the ECtHR's pronouncement in *Rantsev* provides important guidance on when this proactive identification duty is triggered (Milano 2017, 716–721; Stoyanova 2017, 400–404). The Court considers that the positive obligation to identify a victim and take protective measures is triggered when:

> State authorities were aware, or ought to have been aware, of circumstances giving rise to a credible suspicion that an identified individual had been, or was at real and immediate risk of being, trafficked or exploited within the meaning of Article 3(a) of the Palermo Protocol and Article 4(a) of the [European] Anti-Trafficking Convention (*Rantsev*, 286).

If this precondition for the due diligence duty to be activated is fulfilled, which relates to States' level of awareness, the Court will find a violation of the positive obligation to protect trafficking victims if the authorities "failed to take appropriate measures within the scope of their powers to remove the individual from that situation or risk", adding that this duty "shall not impose an impossible or disproportionate burden on the authorities" (*Rantsev*, 286 and 287). Interestingly, as opposed to cases on the right to life where the Court requires that authorities knew or ought to have known of the "existence" of a real and immediate risk to the individual, what is required in trafficking cases is awareness of "circumstances giving rise to a credible *suspicion*" [emphasis added] of that risk. Indeed, this higher level of diligence is appropriately required in trafficking cases since States, claiming their ignorance, too often fail to act with regard to situations that respond to well-known trafficking patterns that should raise a suspicion, while attacks to the right to life do not very frequently respond to such well-established patterns. However, the Court has regrettably not been consistent in the way it implemented this principle in its subsequent case law: it fully departed from it in *L.E. v Greece* (*L.E.*, para 75) to then come back to it, although not as comprehensively, in *Chowdury and others v Greece* (*Chowdury*, para 111–115; Milano 2017, 716–721; Milano 2018a, 102–106; Milano 2018b, 14).

On this issue, the Special Rapporteur on trafficking even brings her reasoning a step further and reaches arguably the most comprehensive formulation of proactive identification duties:

> The identification of victims is very often post hoc and too closely tied to the need to identify victims for criminal or immigration processes, rather than being pre-emptive in circumventing situations of exploitation that may increase susceptibility to trafficking. Instead, a meaningful due diligence approach broadens the scope of identification to address a wider class of potential or presumed victims, as part of a comprehensive approach to prevention rather than a solely reactive or post-hoc due diligence measure (SR trafficking 2015, 24-25)

Indeed, a coherent interpretation of the due diligence duty requires that risks be assessed and addressed proactively in order to prevent or stop abuses in situations where these can be reasonably foreseen based on circumstances that raise a suspicion. Therefore, far from waiting for victims to come forward, as is too often the case, States must monitor areas and groups that are more at risk and proactively detect and preventively address circumstances that point to a risk of trafficking.

As the Rapporteur highlights in a report devoted to this topic, in conflicts and post-conflict situations, large sectors of the population become more vulnerable to trafficking: therefore, proactive identification is even more crucial to protect large portions of the population which become at risk of falling in the hands of traffickers. In these exceptional contexts, she insists on the fact that States are required to take positive steps to identify victims accurately and in a timely manner. States should, for example, adopt proactive measures to protect children caught in conflict when indications of child trafficking or risk of child trafficking are identified (SR trafficking 2016, 56(a) and 66(b)). Undoubtedly, patterns of trafficking in conflict situations have been established in a number of studies and reports we have referred to. On that basis, a number of indicators of vulnerability to trafficking in times of conflict should be collected in order to assist States in identifying when their duty to proactively identify victims or persons at risk is triggered.

A number of UN human rights treaty bodies have taken a similar position. The Human Rights Committee called upon States "to identify and protect persons who may be vulnerable to human trafficking" (HRC 2016, 33). CEDAW also raised this point, referring to early identification and warning systems as effective measures to prevent trafficking (CEDAW 2015, 23(c); CEDAW 2014, 21(b)). Similarly, the CRC welcomed the adoption of programmes focusing on "the identification of vulnerable groups and potential victims of trafficking, especially children without parental care, children in street situations, children involved in child labour, children who are foreign citizens or who belong to ethnic minorities, and children living in poverty" (CRC 2015a, 24). Although not specifically targeted at a conflict setting, the CRC recommended to undertake research on the extent and root causes of the exploitation of children in order to identify children at risk and assess the extent of the problem and undertake targeted preventive measures (ibid., 25). In other cases, it found that "there are insufficient mechanisms in place to identify and monitor children at risk of becoming victims" (CRC 2015b, 17(b)).

Some Committees identified vulnerabilities that are specific to armed conflicts. In relation to conflict-related sexual violence and sexual slavery in Sri Lanka, CEDAW indicates that victims were mainly Tamil women, women heads of households, former combatants, war widows and women family members of the disappeared who searched for justice and women human rights defenders (CEDAW 2017, 24(b)). When urging Colombia to strengthen "early warning systems" to address the continuous recruitment of children by non-state armed groups, the CRC pointed to the particular vulnerability of rural, indigenous and Afro-Colombian children and children from marginalized urban areas (CRC 2015c, 57 and 65; see also Nagle 2003, 23). These approaches rightly focus on a pre-emptive notion of identification, bringing identification and protection efforts much closer to the realm of prevention. They urge States to identify persons who, according to a number of indicators or risk factors, but also based on national or international reports that may have put the State on notice, may potentially become trafficking victims and to protect them from that risk.

In sum, this analysis allows us to reach some preliminary conclusions. The different ways in which international bodies interpret States' proactive duties highlight the existence of different types—or degrees—of obligations. The critical element relates to the point in time when we consider that the proactive identification duty is triggered. A proactive identification duty is clearly triggered when indicators are present in relation to one or more persons in the absence of any self-reporting. But isn't this duty also triggered in a situation where elements that may raise a suspicion have been brought to the attention of authorities, even if they do not relate to a group of identified individuals but to a more general situation, such as child abduction by armed groups, happening in a specific area?

In order to fully conform with States' duty to act with due diligence in protecting victims or potential victims from trafficking, all of these dimensions of proactive identification should be taken on board. The more we place the moment when the identification duty is triggered back in time, the more preventive aspects become relevant to the entire identification and protection system. When we take a broader approach to identification that focuses on its proactive and preventive duties, we highlight the existence of another aspect that adds to the individual identification duties: we could refer to it as systemic identification duties, or systemic due diligence duties, a concept that was first developed to by the Special Rapporteur on violence against women (SR violence against women 2013, 20, 70 and 71). Systemic due diligence appears to be particularly relevant in times of conflict where vulnerabilities are exacerbated for large portions of the populations. It requires an identification strategy that is pre-emptive and addressed to a wide range of actual and potential victims. It requires monitoring pre-emptively systemic situations of vulnerability to trafficking that arise in conflict settings, in conformity with pre-established but periodically updated strategies and indicators. The military as key frontline actors in times of conflict shall be involved the development of such strategy and trained on its implementation. Also, international cooperation in the development of guidelines for such early warning strategies and indicators would certainly be helpful.

Conclusions

The militaries as public officials that are likely to be in contact with victims or potential victims of trafficking in conflict settings need to be fully integrated into victims' identification and protection strategies in such contexts. Although almost no international instrument refers to their role, international bodies' pronouncements and policy documents by the UN and NATO recognized them as key State authorities in identification efforts. As a consequence, general anti-trafficking commitments, including those that stem from States' due diligence duty, are applicable to them. Therefore, States have a duty to train them on victims' identification and on how to report suspicious situations and take protective measures according to pre-established procedures.

States due diligence duty as reflected in a number of instruments requires that identification and protection take place at an early stage. Militaries have a duty to engage in proactive identification, that is, to detect circumstances that raise the suspicion of a risk that a person or a group of persons might be trafficked. A fully coherent interpretation of the due diligence duty requires departing from a solely individual protection paradigm and endorsing a more systemic approach to vulnerabilities to trafficking in conflict setting. For that purpose, indicators shall be developed—general indicators but also specific indicators for a country or region in conflict—as well as monitoring and early warning systems. In addition to making militaries' identification work easier, these are also essential to trigger their due diligence duty as these tools would raise the military's level of awareness about potential risks and would prevent them from alleging ignorance of these risks.

Second, the military cannot do this on its own. Multi-stakeholder cooperation is key, including with UN agencies, such as the United Nations High Commissioner for Refugees (UNHCR) or IOM, with specific expertise on identification and referral to protection systems. As trafficking situations are extremely complex, a failure by the militaries to coordinate their action with partners specialized in protecting and assisting victims would most likely cause their re-victimization.

Finally, a number of gaps need to be addressed. First, standards and recommendations on the role of the military shall not be limited to peacekeepers but shall apply to all militaries that operate in conflict settings, including national military and foreign military not on a peacekeeping mission. While the focus on the contribution of foreign forces is important, more attention should be devoted to the role of national militaries in times of conflict. On the need to make them aware of their role and train them, but also on the need to establish specific protocols on identification and protection in times of conflict that clarify the role of each actor, in particular on how the national military will coordinate with foreign military presences, UN agencies and other national actors.

Related to that is another main challenge: how will national identification and referral systems be adapted in times of conflict? How will new actors such as national and foreign militaries be integrated? Also, what happens when national systems are weak, ineffective and/or not human rights-based? This might be one of the big challenges for both national and foreign forces. As far as foreign forces are concerned, in such a situation shall they follow their own trafficking identification system and attempt to coordinate it with the national one? Indeed, this is a difficulty but, at the same time, an opportunity: the opportunity to engage in the enhancement of national referral mechanism in accordance with international standards. However, more guidance is required in this regard. Indeed, it would be extremely important to develop a strong normative framework to address trafficking in conflict. There is a need for anti-trafficking standards and guidelines that are specific to conflict settings and that clarify, among others, how the military and other actors should coordinate their efforts and how such work can be incorporated in peacebuilding efforts in order to influence anti-trafficking strategies in the long term. In that normative effort, the due diligence standard should always remain the main guiding principle.

References

Chowdury and Others v Greece, Application no. 21884/15, Merits and Just Satisfaction, 30 March 2017.

Committee on the Rights of the Child (CRC). 2015a. Concluding Observations on Turkmenistan CRC/C/OPSC/TKM/CO/1.

———. 2015b. Concluding Observations on Switzerland, CRC/C/OPSC/CHE/CO/1.

———. 2015c. Concluding Observations on Colombia, CRC/C/COL/CO/4–5.

Committee on torture (CAT), General Comment n. 2, CAT/C/GC/2, 2008.

Council of Europe. 2005. *Explanatory Report to the Council of Europe Convention on Action Against Trafficking in Human Beings*. https://www.coe.int/en/web/anti-human-trafficking/about-the-convention

Council of Europe Convention on Action against Trafficking in Human Beings, 16 May 2005, CETS n° 197.

Directive 2011/36/EU of the European Parliament and of the Council of 5 April 2011 on Preventing and Combating Trafficking in Human Beings and Protecting its Victims, O.J. L 101/1, 15.04.2011.

Gallagher, Anne T. 2001. Human Rights and the UN Protocols on Trafficking and Migrant Smuggling: a Preliminary Analysis. *Human Rights Quarterly* 23 (4): 975–1004.

———. 2010. *The International Law of Human Trafficking*. New York: Cambridge University Press.

Godec, Samantha T. 2010. Between Rhetoric and Reality: Exploring the Impact of Military Humanitarian Intervention Upon Sexual Violence – Post-Conflict Sex Trafficking in Kosovo. *International Review of the Red Cross* 92 (877): 235–258.

GRETA (Group of Experts on Action against Trafficking in Human Beings), CoE. 2014. Report on Italy, GRETA(2014)18. https://www.coe.int/en/web/anti-human-trafficking/greta

———. 2015. Fourth General Report on GRETA's activities.

———. 2016a. Fifth General Report on GRETA's Activities.

———. 2016b. GRETA (Group of Experts on Action against Trafficking in Human Beings), CoE Report on the United Kingdom, GRETA(2016)21.

Human Rights Committee (HRC). 2000. General Comment n. 28, CCPR/C/21/Rev.1/Add.10, 2000.

———. 2016. Concluding Observations on South Africa CCPR/C/ZAF/CO/1.

IOM (International Organization for Migration). 2009. Caring for Trafficked Persons, Guidance for Health Providers.

———. 2015. Addressing Human Trafficking and Exploitation in Times of Crisis.

L.E. v. Greece, Application no. 71545/12, Merits and Just Satisfaction, 21 January 2016.

Martin, Susan, and Amber Callaway. 2009. Women, Conflict and Trafficking: Towards a Stronger Normative Framework for Protection. In *Women, Migration, and Conflict*, ed. Susan F. Martin and John Tirman, 47–61. Dordrecht: Springer.

McAdam, Marika. 2013. Who's Who at the Border? A Rights-based Approach to Identifying Human Trafficking at International Borders. *Anti-Trafficking Review* 2: 33–49.

Milano, Valentina. 2017. The European Court of Human Rights' Case Law on Human Trafficking in Light of L.E. v. Greece: a Disturbing Setback? *Human Rights Law Review* 17 (4): 701–727.

———. 2018a. Uncovering Labour Exploitation: Lights and Shadows of the Latest European Court of Human Rights' Case Law on Human Trafficking. *Spanish Yearbook of International Law* 21: 83–117.

———. 2018b. Human Trafficking by Regional Human Rights Courts: An Analysis in Light of Hacienda Brasil Verde, the First Inter-American Court's Ruling in This Area. *Revista Electronica de Estudios Internacionales* (36): 1–29.

———. 2018c. The International Law of Human Trafficking: At the Forefront of the Convergence Between Transnational Criminal Law and International

Human Rights Law? In *Convergences and, Divergences Between International Human Rights Law, International Criminal Law and International Humanitarian Law*, ed. Paul De Hert, Stefaan Smis, and Mathias Holvoet, 101–132. Cambridge: Intersentia.

Mowbray, Alastair R. 2004. *The Development of Positive Obligations Under the European Convention on Human Rights by the European Court of Human Rights*. Oxford: Hart Publishing.

Nagle, Luz Estella. 2003. How Conflict and Displacement Fuel Human Trafficking and Abuse of Vulnerable Groups. The Case of Colombia and Opportunities for Real Action and Innovative Solutions. *Groningen International Law Journal* 1 (2): 1–53.

NATO. 2004a. NATO Policy on Combating Trafficking in Human Beings.

———. 2004b. NATO Policy on Combating Trafficking in Human Beings, Appendix 1: NATO Guidelines on Combating Trafficking in Human Beings for Military Forces and Civilian Personnel Deployed in NATO-led Operations.

———. 2004c. NATO Guidance for the Development of Training and Educational Programmes to Support the Policy on Combating the Trafficking in Human Beings. https://www.nato.int/cps/en/natohq/official_texts_71856.htm?selectedLocale=en

Rantsev v. Cyprus and Russia, Application no. 25965/04, Merits and Just Satisfaction, 7 January 2010.

Rijken, Connie, and Bosma, Alice. 2014. *A Review of the Implementation of the EU Strategy on Human Trafficking by EU Members*. TRACE (EU Project). https://pure.uvt.nl/ws/portalfiles/portal/5078137/TRACE_D1.1_A_review_of_the_implementation_of_the_EU_strategy_on_Human_trafficking_by_EU_members.pdf

Smith, Charles Anthony, and Brandon Miller-de la Cuesta. 2011. Human Trafficking in Conflict Zones: The Role of Peacekeepers in the Formation of Networks. *Human Rights Review* 12: 287–299.

Stoyanova, Vladislava. 2017. *Human Trafficking and Slavery Reconsidered: Conceptual Limits and States' Positive Obligations in European Law*. New York: Cambridge University Press.

Surtees, Rebecca. 2007. *Listening to Victims: Experiences of Identification, Return and Assistance in South-Eastern Europe*. Vienna: International Centre for Migration Policy Development (ICMPD).

UN Department of Peacekeeping Operations (DPKO). 2004. Human Trafficking Resource Package. https://www.un.org/ruleoflaw/files/

DPKO,%20Human%20Trafficking%20Resource%20Package,%20 2004.pdf
UN General Assembly (UNGA). 2010. United Nations Global Plan of Action to Combat Trafficking in Persons, A/RES/64/293.
———. 2017. Political Declaration of the Implementation of the United Nations Global Plan of Action to Combat Trafficking in Persons, A/RES/72/1.
UN Special Rapporteur on Trafficking in Persons, in Particular Women and Children. 2012. Report to the Human Rights Council, A/HRC/20/18.
———. 2014. Report to the Human Rights Council, A/HRC/26/37/Add.2.
———. 2015. Report to the General Assembly, A/70/260.
———. 2016. Report to the Human Rights Council, A/HRC/32/41.
———. 2018. Report to the General Assembly, A/73/171.
UN Special Rapporteur on Violence Against Women, Its Causes and Consequences. 2013. Report to the Human Rights Council, A/HRC/23/49.
UN Treaty Bodies: Committee on the Elimination of Discrimination Against Women (CEDAW). 2014. Concluding Observations on Venezuela CEDAW/C/VEN/CO/7–8.
———. 2015. Concluding Observations on Eritrea CEDAW/C/ERI/CO/5.
———. 2017. Concluding Observations on Sri Lanka, CEDAW/C/LKA/CO/8.
UN Working Group on Trafficking in Persons (UN WGTIP). 2009. Report of the First Session, CTOC/COP/WG.4/2009/2.
———. 2011. Report of the Fourth Session, CTOC/COP/WG.4/2011/8.
UNODC (United Nations Office on Drugs and Crime). 2004. Legislative Guide for the Protocol to Prevent, Suppress and Punish Trafficking in Persons, Especially Women and Children.
———. 2008. Toolkit to Combat Trafficking in Persons.
———. 2009a. International Framework for Action to Implement the Trafficking in Persons Protocol.
———. 2009b. Model Law against Trafficking in Persons.
———. 2015. Regional Strategy for Combatting Trafficking in Persons and Smuggling of Migrants in West and Central Africa 2015–2020.
———. 2018a. Countering Trafficking in Persons in Conflict Situations.
———. 2018b. Global Report on Trafficking in Persons – Booklet 2: Trafficking in Persons in the Context of Armed Conflict.

Valentina Milano is a lecturer in Public International Law at University of Balearic Islands (UIB), Spain. She has worked as a human rights lawyer in

UNESCO (2000–2001), WHO (2002–2004) and the Office of the High Commissioner for Human Rights (2004–2010), where she was in charge of coordinating the mandate of the Special Rapporteur on trafficking in persons (latest assignment). She is also an adviser to the Spanish government on human trafficking.

10

Legal Responsibility of the Military Commander to Prevent or Punish the Acts of Human Trafficking Under the Rome Statute

Michala Chadimová

Introduction

This chapter will discuss the legal responsibility of the military commander to prevent or punish acts of human trafficking under the *Rome Statute*.[1] In July 2019, the first conviction for human trafficking in the form of sexual slavery was rendered by the International Criminal Court (ICC) (*Prosecutor v. Ntaganda* 2019). Bosco Ntaganda, the former Congolese rebel commander, was held responsible for sexual slavery as a crime against humanity (Article 7(1)(g) of the Statute) and as a war crime (Article 8(2)(e)(vi) of the Statute). He was found responsible as an indirect co-perpetrator under Article 25(3)(a) of the Statute, moreover,

[1] Unless otherwise specified, the author employs the term 'command responsibility' in a relation to military commanders or persons effectively acting as military commanders as defined by Article 28 of the Rome Statute. The term 'superior' refers to military commander, as well as civilian superior.

M. Chadimová (✉)
Palacky University, Olomouc, Czech Republic

J. Muraszkiewicz et al. (eds.), *Human Trafficking in Conflict*, Crime Prevention and Security Management, https://doi.org/10.1007/978-3-030-40838-1_10

command responsibility was submitted by the Prosecution as an alternative form of responsibility. This alternative has fewer evidentiary roadblocks to prove superior's omission than direct participation in the commission of the crime. This case highlights the necessity of including responsibility of commanders in the discussion on responsibility for human trafficking and the obligation of commanders to prevent and punish the acts of human trafficking. Needless to say, this case may be also regarded as a message from the ICC about its willingness and capability to deal with human trafficking as an international crime.

The command responsibility is derived from Article 28 of the *Rome Statute* that refers to "Responsibility of commanders and other superiors" (*Rome Statute* 1998, Article 28). The Article sets out the parameters as to how the ICC should apply the doctrine of superior responsibility, under which military commanders, persons effectively acting as military commanders and other superiors are held accountable for the crimes undertaken by their subordinates. The elements of command responsibility under the *Rome Statute* were analysed in the *Bemba* case (*Prosecutor v. Bemba* 2009, 2016, 2018). In 2016, the Trial Chamber (TCH) of the ICC found Jean-Pierre Bemba guilty of crimes against humanity and war crimes committed by his troops in the Central African Republic (CAR) from 2002 to 2003 and sentenced him to 18 years imprisonment based on command responsibility. This was a ground-breaking decision as Bemba was the first person, and so far the only one, sentenced by the ICC on the basis of command responsibility (*Prosecutor v. Bemba* 2016). Nevertheless, in 2018, the Appeals Chamber (ACH) reversed that decision and acquitted Bemba arguing that Bemba lacked effective control over the subordinates committing the crimes. This final judgment in *the Bemba* case caused controversy and confusion. Not only amongst judges of the ACH who decided the case by a narrow majority of 3/2 (*Prosecutor v. Bemba* 2018). Despite its controversy, the *Bemba* case provides a powerful view into the applicability of command responsibility for international crimes.

This chapter provides legal analysis of the requirements for command responsibility in relation to human trafficking as a crime against humanity under Article 7 and war crime under Article 8 of the *Rome Statute*.[2] Legal responsibility for human trafficking can be discussed either as the state's responsibility to prevent or stop the crime, or as the individual's responsibility for commission of the crime. Nevertheless, employing commanders' responsibility may be an additional powerful tool in addressing human trafficking in conflict. As opposed to direct commission of the crimes, command responsibility is used to hold commanders accountable for their omission to prevent or punish crimes committed by their subordinates. Thus, command responsibility has a lower evidentiary burden, as a commander's direct participation in the commission of the crime does not have to be proven. A commander can also be held responsible for a failure to prevent a crime which creates a demand for effective preventive measures and as such contributes to the general fight against human trafficking. Command responsibility can also be used in relation to human trafficking committed as part of widespread policy when the subordinates are not precisely identified. In such a scenario, the perpetrators of human trafficking cannot be held responsible for acts of human trafficking, but their commander can be held responsible for the failure to prevent or punish their conduct.

Military commanders' individual criminal responsibility has been recognised in domestic law, in jurisprudence since the aftermath of the Second World War, and was subsequently reflected in Article 86 of *Additional Protocol I to the Geneva Conventions* (AP). Command responsibility is also firmly established within customary international law and as such it is reflected in the founding documents of all *ad hoc* international tribunals, hybrid tribunals and also the ICC.[3] Nowadays, invoking

[2] The Rome Statute does not contain the wording human trafficking. By referring to the crime of human trafficking under the Rome Statute, reference is made mainly to the crime of enslavement (Article 7(1)(c)), sexual slavery as a crime against humanity (Article 7(1)(g)) and sexual slavery as a war crime (Article 8(2)(b)(xxii), and Article 8(2)(e)(vi) and of the Statute). This chapter will purposefully omit the possibility of defining human trafficking as a crime of genocide; as such an approach would acquire proving special intent on the part of the perpetrator which causes controversy in relation to superior responsibility (Schabas 2009, 363).

[3] The terms 'superior' and 'command' have been historically employed in different contexts, particularly to distinguish between a military superior—commander—and a civilian superior. The term command responsibility gives a more accurate impression of the origin and purpose of the doctrine, whereas the term superior responsibility has been preferred during the last decade because of its neutrality, referring to both civilian and military superiors.

command responsibility is not conditioned by a war nexus. If a command responsibility is used in connection to war crimes, it is irrelevant whether the armed conflict is international or national (*Prosecutor v. Hadžihasanović and Kubura* 2003, para 31). Even though the doctrine of command responsibility originally applied only to military commanders, which is related to its origin in military law, it is also applied to the responsibility of non-military persons, for instance a person with authority over other individuals, such as a city mayor (O. Triffterer 2008, 279).[4] However, Article 28 of the *Rome Statute* distinguishes between the responsibility of military superiors and other superiors.

Command responsibility is notable in several aspects, but mainly in criminalising the commander's failure to act.[5] The superior may be held criminally responsible for the conduct of his subordinates if three general conditions are met. Firstly, the existence of a superior-subordinate relationship, defined by effective control, must be established. Secondly, knowledge of the superior that the crime was about to be, was being, or had been committed, must be proven. Lastly, there must be a failure of the superior to take the necessary and reasonable measures to prevent or stop the crime, or to punish the perpetrator (*Rome Statute* 1998, Article 28).[6]

The requirement of a superior-subordinate relation will be defined, with the focus on the definition of military commander, the issue of unidentified subordinates and the requirement of effective control. The most controversial proposal for command responsibility, as introduced in the *Blaškić* case, is the positive obligation upon the superior to actively search for information leading to a conclusion that the crime has been committed or is about to be committed (*Prosecutor v. Blaškić* 2000).[7] The

---

[4] In the *Akayesu* case (ICTR), it was found that Akayesu, in his capacity as mayor, had effective control over the communal police and found him responsible based on his superior responsibility (*Prosecutor v. Akayesu* 2001).

[5] In other word, failure to prevent or punish acts of human trafficking (commander's failure to act) as opposed to committing human trafficking (acts of human trafficking committed by commanders' subordinates).

[6] Elements of superior responsibility were defined for the first time in the *Celabici case (Prosecutor v Mucić et al.* 1998, para. 346.)

[7] The approach imposing a duty upon the superior to actively acquire information about whether subordinates have committed or are about to commit crimes was introduced by the TCH in the

duty to search will be defined in the light of the *mens rea* requirement and latest ICC case law. The chapter will also demonstrate what constitutes "necessary and reasonable" measures in the context of command responsibility as analysed in the *Bemba* case. As such, the existing legal framework to address human trafficking under Article 28 of the *Rome Statute* will be identified and analysed under the most recent ICC case law.

Establishment of Commander-Subordinate Relation

The first condition that has to be satisfied in order to trigger legal responsibility of the military commander is the proven existence of a superior-subordinate relation. Such a relation may be created by law or by factual and personal factors connecting the accused superior and the perpetrators. The *Rome Statute* brought a distinction between the legal obligation of military commanders and civilian superiors, and introduced the new term, "person effectively acting as a military commander" (*Rome Statute* 1998, Article 28). The distinction between military commander and civilian superior is critical as the *Rome Statute* sets up different elements that have to be proven in order to hold a commander responsible.

According to the *Rome Statute*'s commentary, a military commander is generally a member of the armed forces who is assigned authority to issue orders to subordinates either directly or through a chain of command (Triffterer and Arnold 2016, 1085). In the *Bemba* case, the Pre-Trial

---

Blaškić case in 2000 (*Prosecutor v. Blaškić* 2000). According to the interpretation of the TCH, the requirement *had a reason to know* is also fulfilled when the superior fails to carry out his duty to actively search for information suggesting that his subordinates commit or have committed criminal acts (*Prosecutor v. Blaškić* 2000, paras 309–332). This approach is much stricter and imposes higher standards on the superior, namely to establish an effective reporting system. As noted by J. Fuchs, "the standard applied by the Tribunal in the *Blaškić* case corresponds to the 'should have known' standard" (Fuchs 2001, 17, see also Keith 2001, 617). However, the ACH in the *Celabici* case rejected this argument stating that "it comes close to the imposition of criminal liability on a strict or negligence basis" (*Prosecutor v. Mucić* 2001, para 226). The ACH *Celabici* case stated that the superior is only held criminally responsible for failing to take necessary and reasonable measures to prevent or to punish, for example, failure to commence investigation, but not for failure to gather information suggesting that his subordinates commit or committed crimes under international law.

Chamber (PTCH) interpreted the term 'military commander' as a *de jure* commander who is formally or legally appointed to carry out military functions, whereas a "person effectively acting as military commander covers superiors not elected by law to carry out a military commander's role" (*Prosecutor v. Bemba* 2009, para 409).

The Trial Chamber (TCH) in the *Bemba* judgment provided further distinction between a military commander and a person effectively acting as military commander. In this context, a military commander is usually part of the regular armed forces and is appointed by and operates according to domestic laws (*Prosecutor v. Bemba* 2016, para 176). On the other hand, a person effectively acting as a military commander was described as someone who is not formally or legally appointed as military commander, but who effectively acted as a commander over the military forces that committed the crimes. The TCH also emphasised that the term "military commander or person effectively acting as a military commander," includes individuals who do not perform exclusively military functions (*Prosecutor v. Bemba* 2016, para 177). It is clear from the findings of the PTCH and the TCH that the definitions of 'military commander' and 'person effectively acting as a military commander' are quite extensive and can cover a range of different subjects—not only members of regular military forces, but also members of militia groups with structures similar to those in regular military forces, or even members of terrorist groups.

Crime Committed by the Forces

A person who commits the underlying crime has been traditionally referred as a 'subordinate.' However, in Article 28(a) of the *Rome Statute*, the subordinates are referred to as 'forces,' as opposed to Article 28(b) which also uses the traditional term 'subordinates.' The precise significance of the choice to use this term is not clear. According to Triffterer and Arnold, the term 'forces' ought to be interpreted along the lines of Article 43 of *Additional Protocols I* of 1977, and may thus signify the armed forces of a party to a conflict, that is, all organised armed forces, groups and units which are under a command responsible to that party for the conduct of its subordinates (Triffterer and Arnold 2016, 1093). In the *Bemba* case, the PTCH used the terms 'forces' and 'subordinates' as synonyms (*Prosecutor v. Bemba* 2009, para 428) and nothing in the TCH judgment and Appeals Chamber judgment suggests a different approach.

To apply the doctrine of command responsibility, the accused must be in a superior position with respect to the perpetrators of the underlying crime. Two possible scenarios might occur in the relation to human trafficking. In the first scenario, the perpetrators who committed the acts of human trafficking are not known. In the second scenario, the perpetrators of the act itself were identified, but the commander didn't know the identity of the perpetrators of human trafficking at the time when he failed to prevent or punish the crime committed by that subordinate. The main question is whether the superior-subordinate relation requirement is fulfilled in those scenarios, and thus whether the question of the command responsibility arises.

The TCH in the *Bemba* case held that proof of a superior-subordinate relationship does not require the identification of principal perpetrators by name. It is sufficient to identify the perpetrators by group or unit in relation to a particular crime site (*Prosecutor v. Bemba* 2016, para 186). As such, a superior may be held responsible for crimes committed by an anonymous person.[8] The TCH, however, maintained that the perpetrators need to be identified at least to the extent necessary to assess the existence of the superior-subordinate relationship with the commander. The identification of the individual subordinates by name may assist in this verification; however, it is not a legal requirement (*Prosecutor v. Bemba* 2016, para 186). Regarding the second scenario, the TCH in the *Bemba* case concluded that Article 28 of the *Rome Statute* does not require that the commander knew the identities of the specific subordinates who committed the crimes (*Prosecutor v. Bemba* 2016, para 194). The broad definition of subordinates enables applicability of command responsibility when the identification of individual perpetrators of the crime is evidentiary almost impossible, for example, a human trafficking in a form of sexual slavery committed as a widespread policy of military groups.

[8] In context of the *Orić* case (*Prosecutor v. Orić* 2006, para 315), Mettraux expressed concerns that opening superior responsible in relation to crimes committed by anonymous person creates a danger that the link between superiors and subordinates can be loosening while the punishment is still based on this relation between them (Mettraux 2009, 135).

Effective Control Requirement

Article 28 of the *Rome Statute* explicitly requires the effective control of superiors over subordinates. For military commanders, the *Statute* states that a superior is responsible for the crimes committed "by forces under his or her effective command and control" (*Rome Statute* 1998, Article 28). The military commander can be held liable for the misconduct of subordinates that occurred outside of working hours or which were not related to their working activities, so long as 'effective control' is proven (Triffterer and Arnold 2016, 1103).

In the *Bemba* case, the PTCH followed the concept of effective control given by the *ad hoc* tribunals (*Prosecutor v. Bemba* 2009, para 414–417). The PTCH also stressed that the term 'effective command and control' which is applicable to military commanders, and the 'effective authority and control' which is applicable to civilian superiors, both have "close but distinct meaning" (*Prosecutor v. Bemba* 2009, para 413). The PTCH confirmed that the term 'effective command' reveals or reflects effective authority, using an interpretation of the term 'command' which can be defined as "authority, especially over armed forces" (*Prosecutor v. Bemba* 2009, para 414–417). The exact meaning of this conclusion made by the PTCH is, however, unclear, so it is not certain whether this is just one of the possible interpretations. The TCH concurred with the PTCH insofar as stating that the terms 'command' and 'authority' have "no substantial effect on the required level or standard of 'control,' but rather denote the modalities, manner, or nature in which a military commander or person acting as such exercises control over his or her forces" (*Prosecutor v. Bemba* 2009, para 412–416). The TCH in the *Bemba* case held that it is not relevant whether or not there are intermediary subordinates between the commander and the forces that committed the crimes. The question is simply whether or not the commander had effective control over the relevant forces (*Prosecutor v. Bemba* 2016, para 184). The TCH also found that Article 28 contains no requirement that a commander have sole or exclusive authority and control over the forces that committed the crimes (*Prosecutor v. Bemba* 2016, para 185).

Required *mens rea* of the Commander in Order to Be Held Responsible

In order to apply superior responsibility, it must always be proved that the commander had some level of knowledge about the crimes committed (known as the *mens rea* requirement). The *mens rea* (state of mind) requirement must be identified with respect to the criminal acts committed by the subordinates. In general, superior responsibility is not a case of strict liability. The *mens rea* required for command responsibility may have the following forms: (a) actual knowledge implying that the "superior knew about the conduct of the subordinates"; (b) constructed knowledge, which is defined in different ways; the statutes of the International Criminal Tribunal for Former Yugoslavia (ICTY) and the International Criminal Tribunal for Rwanda (ICTR) define it as "the superior had a reason to know" (*ICTR Statute*, Article 6; *ICTY Statute*, Article 7). The *Rome Statute* differentiates between two categories of superiors. For military commanders or persons effectively acting as military commanders, the constructed knowledge is defined as 'should have known,' and a civilian superior can be held responsible only if it can be proven that he "consciously disregarded information" (*Rome Statute* 1998, Article 28). It is unclear whether constructed knowledge (the 'should have known' standard) can be interpreted as an open door for requiring there to be a duty to actively search for information on the part of superior. In other words, the issue is whether commander responsibility includes a duty to actively search for information or whether a commander can be held responsible only when he already possessed information that was sufficiently alarming to put him on notice of the crimes of his subordinates.

Positive Duty to Search

The PTCH clarified that the 'should have known' standard requires more of an active duty on the part of the superior to take "the necessary measures to secure knowledge of the conduct of his troops and to inquire, regardless of the availability of information at the time on the commission of the crime" (*Prosecutor v. Bemba* 2009, para 433). Unfortunately, in the *Bemba* case the TCH did not explicitly follow up on findings made by the PTCH regarding active duty to secure knowledge about and inquire into the conduct of troops. However, the TCH listed numbers of indicia suggesting that a commander had knowledge that the forces were committing or about to commit such crimes. One of the indicia suggesting the commander's knowledge is the notoriety of the illegal acts. The TCH clarified that notoriety of the illegal act can prove required knowledge on the part of the commander if the illegal acts were reported in the media coverage "[…] of which the accused was aware" (*Prosecutor v. Bemba* 2016, para 193). The TCH add that such awareness may be established by evidence suggesting that a commander, based on these reports, "[…] took some kind of action" (*Prosecutor v. Bemba* 2016, para 193). The *mens rea* requirement was not subjected to the appeal.

The TCH in the *Bemba* case did not follow the findings of the PTCH and required the information to be available to the commander. Under the ICC approach, in order to hold a commander responsible, the commander must be aware of information leading him to a conclusion that the crimes have been committed or about to be committed. Such information may have different forms and need not be directly implied by a written or spoken report on the conduct of the subordinates (*Prosecutor v. Bemba* 2016, para 193). Thus, whenever a commander has been in possession of information leading him to the conclusion that his subordinates committed or are committing human trafficking decided not to act upon that, he might be held responsible for his failure to stop them or failure to punish the subordinates for committing human trafficking. Whenever a commander has been in possession of information that by itself does not lead him to that conclusion without further investigation, he cannot be held responsible under command responsibility.

Duty to Prevent or Punish the Crime Committed by the Subordinates

Under command responsibility, it is necessary to prove that the commander failed to fulfil at least one of the duties listed under Article 28 of the *Rome Statute*. It has to be proven that the commander failed to prevent a crime, failed to repress crimes or failed to submit the matter to the competent authorities for investigation and prosecution.[9] The key issue is whether the military commander took necessary and reasonable measures to prevent or repress the commission of the crimes or to submit them to the competent authorities for investigation and prosecution.

The measures to prevent or repress the commission of the crimes by subordinates has to be necessary, reasonable and within the commander's power. To a certain extent, the matter as to what can be considered necessary and reasonable measures within the superior's powers is connected to the requirements of effective control (Triffterer 2008, 301). It was confirmed in the *Bemba* case by the TCH, when the Chamber ruled that the duty of the commander to take all necessary and reasonable measures to prevent or repress the crimes committed by his forces "rests upon his possession of effective authority and control" (*Prosecutor v. Bemba* 2016, para 199).

Article 28 of the Statute does not define any specific measures required by the duty to prevent or punish the crimes. Nevertheless, in the *Bemba* case the PTCH presented some factors that could be taken as such measures. According to the PTCH, the duty to prevent encompasses the duty to (i) ensure adequate training in international humanitarian law; (ii) to secure reports that all military actions were carried out in accordance with international law; (iii) to issue orders aiming at bringing the relevant practices into accord with the rules of war; and (iv) to take disciplinary measures to prevent the commission of atrocities by the troops under the superior's command (Prosecutor v. Bemba 2009, para 438). Duty to prevent arises not only before commission of the crime but also during commission of the crime and arguably after the crime is committed. Once the crime of human trafficking is committed, the primary obligation of the commander is to punish the crime. As clarified by the TCH, the minimum standard for measures that may fulfil the duty to punish are whether any steps were taken to secure an adequate investigation capable of leading to the criminal prosecution of the perpetrators (*Prosecutor v. Bemba* 2016, para 207). The duty to punish includes, at least, the obligation to

[9] Article 28 of the Rome Statute. Although the Statute uses alternative language ('or') it is clear that failure to discharge any of these duties may attract criminal responsibility.

investigate possible crimes in order to establish the facts. The obligation to punish the crime should also be accompanied by preventive measures. However, a superior can be held responsible for failure to conduct preventive measures after the commission of the crime only in relation to subsequent crimes. If the circumstances of the crime suggest that it was not an isolated incident and other acts of human trafficking may be committed in the future, the commander is required to also fulfil his preventive duties. This creates obligation towards the establishment of general preventive measures against human trafficking.

Remoteness of a Commander

A commander's remote location from his troops played a key consideration in the assessment of a command responsibility in the *Bemba* case. The TCH held that "despite his remote location, Mr. Bemba had the authority and ability to take measures to prevent and repress the commission of crimes" (*Prosecutor v. Bemba* 2016, para 738). However, the ACH disagreed with the TCH's findings and concluded that Mr. Bemba took all necessary and reasonable measures within his power to prevent or repress the commission of crimes by his subordinates. The majority found that the TCH paid insufficient attention to the fact that the Movement for the Liberation of the Congo (MLC) troops were operating in a foreign country and the difficulties on Bemba's ability to take measures (*Prosecutor v. Bemba* 2018, para 171). It held that "the Trial Chamber failed to appreciate that, as a remote commander, Mr. Bemba was not part of the investigations and was not responsible for the results generated [...]"(*Prosecutor v. Bemba* 2018, para 192) and "[...] Trial Chamber paid insufficient attention to the fact that the MLC troops were operating in a foreign country with the attendant difficulties on Mr. Bemba's ability, as a remote commander, to take measures" (*Prosecutor v. Bemba* 2018, para 171).

Nevertheless, the majority itself fails to set out comprehensively those limitations, or explain in detail why the TCH had reached the wrong conclusion in this regard.[10] It is not clear whether the majority has made

[10] See also Remoteness in itself cannot serve as a defence to command responsibility. *Amnesty International. Opinion*. 10. 10. 2018. [online] [20-01-2019]. Available at: https://hrij.amnesty.nl/

a distinction between remote commander and commander present at the grounds, and whether there are different sets of requirements for both categories. The Concurring Separate Opinion of Judge Eboe-Osuji[11] suggested that the findings of the majority should be interpreted as a factor all on its own, which would not necessarily insulate perpetrators from criminal responsibility. Judge Eboe-Osuji clarified that "geographic remoteness is only a factor to be considered among other circumstances or peculiarities of a given case. It serves its greatest value in the assessment of what is reasonable as a measure to prevent or repress violations to submit them to competent authorities for investigation and prosecution [...]" (*Prosecutor v. Bemba,* Separate Opinion, 2018, para 258). Dissenting judges held that "[...] remoteness of the commander is part of the factual considerations that the Trial Chamber must assess in order to determine whether the accused had the material ability to prevent, repress or report the commission of crimes" (*Prosecutor v. Bemba,* Dissenting Opinion, 2018, para 127). As such, the remoteness of a commander should be seen as a relevant fact, rather than the entire basis of a legal distinction.

From reading the decision in connection to dissenting judges' findings, it seems that no distinction between remote and non-remote commander in relation to the assessment of measures taken (or measures that should have been taken) was either drawn or contemplated. As correctly noted by Jackson, the assumption that the remoteness would have made responding more difficult cannot be held across the full range of measures assessed by the TCH, such as the mandates of the two investigative commissions to allegations of pillage (Jackson 2018). Karnavas suggests that geography may play a role in the overall assessment of the facts and evidence in determining a commander's awareness and any failures to act. He suggests that this assessment, taken into account with proper context—geography being one of the factors—was missing from the TCH's analysis (discussion at Jackson 2018). The author of this chapter supports Karnavas's interpretation of the ACH Judgment. There is nothing in the ACH judgment and the opinions suggesting an interpretation that

remoteness-command-responsibility-icc/

[11] The Concurring Separate Opinion of Judge Eboe-Osuji is his written opinion attached to the majority judgment in which he agrees with the judgment made by the majority of the Chamber, but states different or additional reasons as the basis for his decision.

supports a distinction between requirements for reasonable and necessary measures for remote commanders and non-remote commanders. On the other hand, the reading suggests that remoteness of the commander is one of the factors that may play a role in the overall assessment of the facts and evidence into determination of a commander's effective control and any failures to act. The dissenting judges also point out that the majority decision comes from losing sight of Article 28 of the *Rome Statute*. The dissenting judges stress that the manner the majority interpreted the requirement of a necessary and reasonable measure suggests that a commander is responsible for not his failures but for his actions (*Prosecutor v. Bemba,* Dissenting Opinion, 2018, para 45).

The remoteness of the commander should be part of the factual considerations as to whether a commander failed to prevent or punish human trafficking. However, the majority of the ACH may also suggest that a remote commander has a distinctive position compared to a commander present in lieu of the crime. This interpretation would be denying the nature of commander responsibility and as such, the remoteness of the commander should only have impact on the factual assessment of effective control requirement and measures taken.

Conclusion

The definition of a commander who can be responsible for the crimes committed by his subordinates is quite extensive. The *Rome Statute* uses, in addition to the term 'military commander,' a new term: 'acting as a military commander.' It does not bring into creation a whole new category, rather a clarification that a person responsible does not have to be only a commander appointed as part of a regular military force. The person responsible under Article 28(a) of the *Rome Statute* might be also a commander within a non-regular militia group or a terrorist group. It is argued that the ICC confirmed that under Article 28 of the *Rome Statute,* the precise identification of principal perpetrators is not required in order to hold the commander responsible, as long as the perpetrators can be identified by a unit or group in connection to the crime The requirement of a superior-subordinate relationship can be satisfied not only within the forces which report to a single chain of command but also to forces made up of troops from several nations. Effective control is the key element that proves the existence of a superior-subordinate relationship. It refers to the possibility of the commander to exercise command or control over his forces. The commander does not have to be a direct superior to the subordinate nor does he have to be performing exclusive authority and control over the subordinate. Proving effective control of the commander over the subordinates is more a matter of evidence than law and it might be particularly difficult in conflict settings.

The command responsibility is not a strict liability and, at minimum, some commanders' knowledge about the crimes committed or being committed by his subordinates is required. In the *Bemba* case, the PTCH opened the door for requiring an active duty to search for information. However, the findings of the TCH seem to opt out of requiring such a duty. It might be argued that under the ICC approach, in order to hold a commander responsible, the commander must be aware of information leading him to a conclusion that the crimes are committed or about to be committed. Such information may have different forms and need not be directly implied by a written or spoken report on the conduct of the subordinates. Thus, whenever a commander is in a possession of information leading him to the conclusion that his subordinates committed or are committing human trafficking and he decides not to act upon that, he might be held responsible for his failure to stop them or failure to punish the subordinates for committing human trafficking. Article 28 of the *Rome Statute* does not explicitly list what constitutes necessary and reasonable measures in order to prevent or punish the crimes committed by subordinates. This has been detailed in the *Bemba* case, whereas the duty to prevent and punish includes everything from adequate trainings, taking disciplinary measures to proper investigation that is capable of leading to the criminal prosecution of the perpetrators. In the *Bemba* case, the remoteness of a commander was a highly discussed issue. The majority of the ACH, and as far the only interpretation of Article 28 of the *Rome Statute* in this manner, may also suggest that a remote commander has a distinctive position than a commander present in lieu of the crime. This interpretation would be denying the nature of commander responsibility and as such, the remoteness of the commander should only have an impact on the factual assessment of effective control requirement and whether or not a commander failed to prevent or punish human trafficking.

As shown, the applicability of command responsibility follows fulfilment of strict conditions, however, it is applicable in various scenarios. Under fulfilment of previously presented conditions, command responsibility may apply for the international peacekeepers missions and their personnel. On top of potential responsibility of an organisation (typically the UN) and the state of the personnel involved for not preventing or punishing the commission of the crimes, individual responsibility for not preventing or punishing the acts of human trafficking should not be omitted. It is not relevant that the mandate of the peacekeeping mission was not focused on the fight against human trafficking or that the mandate did not establish *de jure* relationship between the peacekeeping personnel and the alleged perpetrators of human trafficking. As shown in the analysis, the *de facto* relationship is enough to establish the condition required for the commander's responsibility. Taking a closer look at the military, countries such as Syria, Iraq, Afghanistan or Libya are ranked highly in the Global Slavery Index (GSI) and several countries have their military personnel deployed there. Command responsibility opens a possibility to hold deployed military personnel responsible for not preventing or punishing acts of human trafficking, not conducted only within the own ranks but possibly committed by the local military or civilians, as long as all the elements, including effective control, are proven. Command responsibility brings another avenue for establishing responsibility for acts of human trafficking, and not only when the military itself is involved or implicated in the direct commission of human trafficking.

Importantly, command responsibility must be conceived as a type of personal responsibility for a failure to act. Thus, the commander will not be convicted for crimes committed by his subordinates—such as human trafficking—but for failing in his obligation to prevent the crimes or punish the perpetrators. Alongside the responsibility of the direct perpetrators and state responsibility, command responsibility provides a powerful legal toolkit with which to respond to human trafficking in conflict.

References

UN General Assembly. Rome Statute of the International Criminal Court. 17 July 1998.

Fuchs, Jiří. 2001. Trestní odpovědnost velitelete za opomenutí v současném mezinárodním právu. [Criminal Responsibility of Superior for Omission in Current International Law]. *Trestni pravo* 6 (12): 14–20.

Jackson, Miles. Geographical Remoteness in Bemba. *EJIL: Talk! Blog of the European Journal of International Law*. 30 July 2018. https://www.ejiltalk.org/geographical-remoteness-in-bemba/

Keith, Kirsten M.F. 2001. The Mens Rea of Superior Responsibility as Developed by ICTY Jurisprudence. *Leiden Journal of International Law* 14 (3): 617–634.

Mettraux, Guénaël. 2009. *The Law of Command Responsibility*. Oxford: Oxford University Press.

Prosecutor v. Bemba, ICC-01/05–01/08 A, ICC, Appeals Chamber Judgment, 8 July 2018.

———, ICC-01/05–01/08–3343, ICC, Trial Chamber Judgment, 21 March 2016.

———, ICC-01/05–01/08, ICC, Decision Pursuant to Article 61(7)(a) and (b) of the Rome Statute, 3 July 2009.

Prosecutor v. Blaškić, IT-95-14, ICTY, Trial Chamber Judgment, 3 March 2000.

Prosecutor v. Akayesu, 2001, ICTR-96-4-T, ICTR, Trial Chamber Judgment, 1 June 2001.

Prosecutor v. Mucić, IT-96-21-T, ICTY, Trial Chamber Judgment, 16 November 1998.

———, IT-96-21-A, ICTY, Appeals Chamber Judgment, 20 February 2001.

Prosecutor v. Hadžihasanović and Kubura, IT-01-47, ICTY, Decision on Interlocutory Appeal Challenging Jurisdiction in Relation to Command Responsibility, 16 July 2003.

Prosecutor v. Ntaganda, ICC-01/04–02/06–2359, ICC, Trial Chamber Judgment, 8 July 2019.

Schabas, William. 2009. *Genocide in International Law: The Crime of Crimes*. Cambridge: Cambridge University Press.

Triffterer, Otto, and Arnold, Roberta. 2016. Article 28. In *The Rome Statute of the International Criminal Court. A Commentary*, by Triffterer, Otto. Ambos, Kai. C. H. Beck.

Triffterer, Otto. 2008. Commentary on the Rome Statute of the International Criminal Court: Observers' Notes, Article by Article. München: Beck.

Michala Chadimová is Legal Advisor at La Strada Czech Republic, a PhD candidate at Palacky University Olomouc researching on International Criminal Responsibility for Special Intent Crimes. She holds an LLM in International Public and European Law (University of Amsterdam). She participated in the prosecution of Bosco Ntaganda at the International Criminal Court and also served at the Office of the Co-Prosecutor in the Extraordinary Chambers in the Courts of Cambodia.

11

Applying the Non-punishment Principle to Returnees from Terrorist Organisations

Julia Muraszkiewicz

Introduction

Human trafficking, as defined by the *UN Protocol to Prevent, Suppress and Punish Trafficking in Persons, Especially Women and Children*, is known to be committed by a range of terrorist groups, including the Lord's Resistance Army in Uganda, the Revolutionary United Front in Sierra Leone, ISIS, Boko Haram and Al Shabaab. Indeed, the enslavement of human beings can be enshrined within the ideology of such groups, with ISIS producing pamphlets detailing why and how it is 'permissible' to have sexual intercourse with, attack and trade non-Muslim slaves, including young girls (Smith 2014).

The core of the crime of human trafficking has three elements: (1) an act, such as the recruitment, movement, harbouring, or receipt of a person; (2) a means, such as the use of force, fraud, or coercion (this is not required for those under the age of 18); and (3) the intention of

J. Muraszkiewicz (✉)
Trilateral Research, London, UK
e-mail: julia.muraszkiewicz@trilateralresearch.com

J. Muraszkiewicz et al. (eds.), *Human Trafficking in Conflict*, Crime Prevention and Security Management, https://doi.org/10.1007/978-3-030-40838-1_11

exploitation. There is little doubt in the anti-human trafficking discourse that victims of this crime, for instance, members of the enslaved Yazidi population, require protection. But it also ought to be remembered that terrorist groups recruit vulnerable people through the means contained in the definition of human trafficking and who, in turn, go on to commit crimes on their behalf, or be seen to facilitate the activities of a terrorist group, or be suspected of communicating statements that knowingly advocate or promote the commission of terrorist offences. At times, these people may not even commit crimes directly, they might not engage in violence or criminal activity, but instead might fulfil the role of an obedient spouse, undertaking duties that are expected of this position. For example, ISIS uses the promised reward of access to women and girls as wives as a method to recruit fighters from across the globe (Watson 2014).

Currently, it does not appear to occur to policy makers that the acts they call terrorism could, in some contexts, be described otherwise. And yet, some people will be recruited using the same techniques by which victims of human trafficking are lured. As highlighted by writers such as Binetti (2015), recruiters befriend, flatter and praise their targets, often exploiting their vulnerabilities, whether related to psychological well-being, age, circumstances or other, or preying on their loneliness, making promises of a better life. This raises an important question. What happens, for example, to a citizen of the European Union (EU) who is recruited through cyberspace or grooming into a terrorist organisation and is induced to travel to a conflict area and to live amongst an armed group, but then wishes to return home? Categorising these persons as victims of human trafficking has implications for how they are (or should be) treated in conflict situations, how they should be considered upon their return, and even how national counter-terrorism policies and the criminal justice agenda should be informed.

A key component of protecting victims of human trafficking is ensuring that they are not criminalised or otherwise punished for acts they have committed as a direct result of being trafficked. This chapter explores the questions of what should be done with those persons who were recruited, compelled to join a terrorist group and who return home. Should they all be punished under criminal law (if they committed crimes)? Or are some of them victims of human trafficking, in which case should they thus receive protection under the non-punishment principle, which is enshrined in Article 26 of the 2005 *Council of Europe Convention on Action Against Trafficking in Human Beings*? The approach outlined in this chapter is both a legal and a philosophical one, whereby the author examines the two general philosophies of punishment—consequentialism and retributivism—in order to explain why returnees who were trafficked and compelled into committing crimes should be excused from liability. This chapter also acknowledges that there exists an inherent tension between the victimhood-centred human rights narrative on the one hand, and on the other hand, the recognition of a person's independent ability to make autonomous, rational decisions, and thus be liable for their own actions. Are they victims of human trafficking, or are they perpetrators of violence, or both? Importantly, the chapter seeks to move forward existing debates in this area (see e.g., Bloom 2011), as it focuses not upon why individuals join armed groups and terrorist organisations but instead concentrates upon why, through legal philosophy (rather than from the perspectives of sociology or politics), we might excuse them for doing so. The chapter will also explain why we speak of excuse, rather than justification, with regard to the non-punishment of returnees.

As a final point, this chapter focuses on victims of human trafficking who are returning from time spent with terrorist organisations, for ease the term returnee will be used as an umbrella.

Terrorist or Victim of Human Trafficking?

This section looks at whether people recruited to join terrorist organisations could be victims of human trafficking. This in turn can inform how they ought to be treated on return home, for if some recruits fit the definition of human trafficking, it can affect whether the justice system may excuse them through the application of the non-punishment and non-prosecution principle.

This question is particularly interesting as current conflicts are characterised by many complexities that make deciphering who plays what role harder. There are no traditional sides—for example, a State A v State B—and sometimes there are no obvious victims. Terrorist groups and other non-state actors can be the adversary that militaries fight, but it is not always clear who is the fighter. For a soldier going into a new area, this poses legal and moral conundrums; they will ask themselves who is my enemy and who is a victim of my enemy's acts.

People from areas not controlled by terrorist groups, for example, the EU, including a notably large number of women, joined ISIS in large numbers. As stated by Davis, "[w]omen have begun to join the group in shocking numbers; never before in the modern history of terrorism has a group attracted so many women, particularly from the West. Even in comparison to AQI [Al Qaeda in Iraq], the number of women joining ISIL [Islamic State of Iraq and the Levant] is unprecedented. Some of ISIL's most vocal supporters, particularly on social media, are women. They spread the organisation's message and act as recruiters, and, in many instances, they are the face and voice of the Islamic State" (Davis 2017, 123). There is little doubt that many of those who joined the group exercised agency, providing an undisputed basis for criminal responsibility. Yet the matter is rarely black and white; the appropriateness, legitimacy, and even the value of criminal law responses cannot be assumed.

If we look at recruitment methods, who is targeted and what happens upon arrival within the terrorist group, then we will find that for some cases there was no agency in a person's 'choice' to join a group and carry out work on its behalf or supports its cause. The culpability of the people was "significantly diminished or extinguished because of their personal circumstances, in particular their situation of being under the control of the traffickers [terrorists]" (Piotrowicz and Sorrentino 2016, 674).[1] Or at the very least, it becomes questionable whether these persons exercised free will. It is known, for example, that once living within the caliphate, leaving was not an option; women in particular were quickly married off to jihadist fighters and had their daily activities and movements restricted (The Economist 2015). Despite increasing these women's active roles in the caliphate, including in enforcing 'State' rules and regulations, their primary role was as mothers and homemakers. In that capacity, women

[1] Here, presumably, Piotrowicz and Sorrentino write about victims of human trafficking who may have been compelled to commit more "traditional" crimes, such as cultivating cannabis. However, their analogy is borrowed and seen as applicable to those potential victims who are compelled to join terrorist organisations.

were subjected to abuses, including sexual violence and domestic servitude, Factors that are accepted as signs of human trafficking (UNODC date unknown).

Binetti (2015) writes: "[F]actors such as the recruitment tactics that terrorist organizations use, as well as the age of potential recruits, are critical components in the analysis of whether a particular set of facts meets the international definition of human trafficking." In a number of cases those factors are there. It is possible to break down the definition of human trafficking and check each component of that definition against the journey of some people who end themselves in terrorist organisations.

The first element of human trafficking—the *action*—refers to, for example, acts of recruitment, transportation or harbouring. The fact that organisations such as ISIS recruit online, pay for travel to the caliphate and then harbour the people in their homes satisfies the action element. As for the *means* element of the human trafficking definition, this too is present. Deception (as to what awaits or why they must travel) and abuses of positions of power (on the part of the perpetrator) or of vulnerability (on the part of the victim) are common in terrorist recruitment methods. As Binetti (2015) writes, "[r]ecruiters lure girls by painting a 'distorted view' of life inside the Islamic State, falsely advertising the 'joys of sisterhood' and living for a higher purpose." Proving the means and action in a court of law would not be overly complicated. The more problematical question is whether the same is true for the final element of the human trafficking definition, namely that the acts were done for the purpose or intention of exploitation. As exploitation can be sexual and/or include slavery, or practices similar to slavery or servitude, and this is the fate of many people, it can be argued that all elements of the human trafficking definition are met by some of those who joined terrorist groups.

The widely reported case of two Austrian friends provides one of many examples of these realities. Sabina Selimovic and Samra Kesinovic were two teenage (under 18) Austrian nationals who in April 2014 abandoned their family homes in Austria and illegally travelled to Syria to join ISIS. It is believed that they became interested in ISIS after watching propaganda on the Internet and through their attendance at a mosque in Vienna. On arrival in Syria, it is understood that they were married off to Chechen jihadists. In December 2015, a Tunisian woman who had escaped from Islamic State-controlled territory stated that she and Kesinovic had been kept together in a house in Syria, where they were used as sex slaves for Islamic State's newly recruited soldiers. In late 2015, it was reported by the Middle East bureau of the *The Daily Telegraph* that Kesinovic had been beaten to death with a hammer towards the end of 2014 after she was caught by Islamic State enforcers whilst trying to escape from sexual slavery in the Syrian town of Raqqa. A strong case can be made to consider these teenagers as victims of human trafficking, especially, as was mentioned above, the definition of human trafficking dictates that where a child is involved, the specific means (such as coercion and/or fraud) are not required to determine whether or not it is a case of human trafficking; rather, the emphasis is on the nature of the *act* itself and the presence of the *intention* to exploit (see the *2000 UN Protocol to Prevent, Suppress and Punish Trafficking in Persons, especially Women and Children*). Thus, those people under the age of 18 who are recruited to terrorist organisations and exploited could try and make an argument for being victims of human trafficking. As for instance is done in cases of child soldiers. It is also key to note, as Perešin (2015, 22) does, that many of the women who travelled to Syria to join ISIS were minors: "These girls and young women are mainly aged between 16 and 24, but even younger girls have attempted to travel to Syria."

If an individual such as Kesinovic or Selimovic returns home, she could be found guilty of criminal conduct such as constituting a public expression of praise, support for or justification of terrorism. Yet, given the circumstances that led to these girls joining IS, it must be asked whether this conduct conceivably constitutes a crime, and it must also be asked whether, had military actors encountered Kesinovic either on or off the battlefield, they should treat her as a civilian or did she take an active part in hostilities (as per international humanitarian law). Before exploring these issues, it is important at the outset to note that even while a criminal law and philosophical basis can be used to explain why compelled people ought not to bear criminal liability for actions conducted while a victim of human trafficking, the narrative of recruitees as victims may be hard to digest when some of them are seemingly intelligent individuals from relatively comfortable middle-class backgrounds, rather than impoverished and vulnerable persons. As highlighted in the victimology literature and by writers such as Nils Christie (1986), people that do not fit the 'ideal victim' image will have a hard time being categorised as victims. Due to hidden factors at play, including gender biases, there are many *victimological others*, people who are not seen as victims and are therefore excluded from receiving the required protections. Perception is prejudiced by poor media illustrations worldwide, a patriarchal political and justice system, the political climate of a society (e.g., hostile environment for migrants that is increasing in the EU and US), all of which lead to the creation of an ideal victim as the only person entitled to protection, and many potential victims unrecognised. As recalled by Piotrowicz and Sorrentino (2016, 670): "[t]oo often, trafficked people do not receive assistance and protection as victims of a serious crime because they are not recognised as victims. It is more likely that they will be arrested, detained and charged with immigration offences, for soliciting prostitution or engaging in illegal work, making false statements; or else, they are fined for violations of administrative laws and regulations." In our example, it is more likely that they will be arrested, detained and charged with terrorist-related offences.

Excusing the Supposed Wrongdoers

The question of determining whether a crime was committed by a returnee is not something this chapter seeks to address; nor does it explore what constitutes terrorist activities. Certainly, given the plethora of widely interpreted crimes with regard to terrorist-related activities, guilt could be established in many EU states. In France, for instance, "apology for terrorism" has been a crime since November 2014 and "French prosecutors have been aggressively pursuing anyone who speaks positively of a terrorist act or group even if their intention is not to incite violence or promote the group" (Houry 2018). Instead, the enquiry concerns whether the state can, or should, excuse the person recruited to a terrorist organisation for the purpose of exploitation.

Having established that some recruits may be victims of human trafficking, the key argument in this section is based on the principle of non-prosecution and non-punishment as highlighted by the OSCE's Special Representative and Co-ordinator for Combating Trafficking in Human Beings (2013, 12) who notes that we ought to "keep victims immune from punishment where their crime was caused or directly linked to their having been trafficked." This is also enshrined in legislation. Article 8 of EU Directive *2011/36 on preventing and combating trafficking in human beings and protecting its victims*, states:

> Member States shall, in accordance with the basic principles of their legal systems, take the necessary measures to ensure that competent national authorities are entitled not to prosecute or impose penalties on victims of trafficking in human beings for their involvement in criminal activities which they have been compelled to commit as a direct consequence of being subjected to any of the acts referred to in Article 2.

Similarly, Article 26 of the 2005 Council of Europe *Convention on Action Against Trafficking in Human Beings* states:

> Each Party shall, in accordance with the basic principles of its legal system, provide for the possibility of not imposing penalties on victims for their involvement in unlawful activities, to the extent that they have been compelled to do so.

These laws arise out of the realisation that some victims of human trafficking find themselves in circumstances "which have resulted in the victim losing their free will and having no option but to act as they did" (Piotrowicz and Sorrentino 2016, 678). Our current criminal justice system does not punish just because someone committed a bad act, it also considers the accused's mental state, the *mens rea;* on examination of the philosophy of psychology behind the acts, the state may decide to excuse. Here, it is critical to recognise the difference between excuse and justification. Dressler (2001, 202–203) writes: "a justification claim…seeks to show that the act was not wrongful," whereas an excuse "tries to show that the actor is not morally culpable for his wrongful conduct." Similarly, Hart (1968, 23) excuses committed crimes when the person lacks a capacity or fair opportunity to choose their actions. Berman (2003, 4) summarised the difference as: "a justified action is not criminal, whereas an excused defendant has committed a crime but is not punishable." The distinction between justification and excuse has deep roots in moral philosophy, already referred to by Aristotle in *The Nicomachean Ethics;* he recognised that there are pressures which overstrain human nature and which no one could withstand (Dubber and Hörnle 2014, 425).

Embracing the relevance of the concept of excuse within criminal law is in line with a human rights-based approach, which seeks to protect persons from arbitrary use of power by the state and place the individual's rights at the centre.[2] Indeed, human rights preside over the use of criminal law with both a 'shield'—regulating how criminal law is applied—and a 'sword,' which acts to safeguard fundamental rights.[3] It is possible to argue that by accepting a need to excuse some individuals for joining a terrorist organisation, the shield is utilised; the excuse will neutralise the application of criminal law against a vulnerable individual who was compelled into committing a crime. Yet, as stipulated by Hart (2008, 32), "it is clear that not only lawyers, but scientists and plain men differ as to the relevance of some excusing conditions, and this lack of agreement is usually expressed as a difference of view regarding what kind of factor limits the human capacity to control behaviour. Views so expressed have indeed changed with the advance of knowledge about the human mind." Nevertheless, even as our knowledge of the human mind and the effects of compulsion that may induce someone to join a terrorist organisation advances, it is still difficult to establish in court that the person's control and free will were curbed by the acts of others or/and through their own vulnerabilities. Moreover, the law exists in a certain political context, and as much as we wish for it to be blind and independent, it remains a

[2] Importantly, human rights are increasingly prevalent within the military domain. For example, in the UK, the Ministry of Defence formally adopted the concept of human security within defence doctrine, recognising that "protecting civilians from human rights violations is as much a military task as defeating the enemy" (UK Government 2019).

[3] "An example of the sword function can be found in the area of domestic violence, whereby legislative development common to many jurisdictions have been influenced by the recognition of women's and children's rights as human rights at an international level...For example, in the UK, the Family Act 1996 has been amended by the Domestic Violence, Crime and Victims Act 2004, which extends provisions to combat domestic violence by criminalizing certain actions, such as the death of a child or vulnerable adults as a result of neglect or abuse" (Weber et al. 2014, 95).

truism that the interpretation and subsequent application of the law clashes with other values, typically conveyed by the political context (see further below).

For these reasons, it is unsurprising to note that across the world we have seen different responses regarding how to treat returnees who were compelled to joining terrorist organisations and, through their presence, facilitated the groups' activities. Some are allowed to quietly return to their lives—perhaps remaining on a government watch list—whilst others risk being stripped of citizenship, facing trial and incarceration. The lack of consistency is worrying, as is the fact that the state is punishing people whom it should perhaps in some cases be protecting. We need to ask, were the personal circumstances such that the individual was compelled (as per the wording of the principle of non-prosecution and non-punishment) to join a terrorist group? The act of checking the facts needs to be emphasised because, as already stated, not all young and vulnerable persons act without agency and so victimhood is not automatic. With women in particular, we ought not to fall into a gender stereotype that all women who join terrorist groups are inherently vulnerable, perplexed and naïve jihadists. Nor are they always groomed—indeed, some will act out of genuine political commitment and with full agency, as would appear to have been the case with Aqsa Mahmood (a.k.a. Umm Layth), a privately-educated and trained radiologist from the UK who become prolific in spreading ISIS propaganda online. In her online blog and social media accounts, she even praised terror attacks in Tunisia and France (Blaker 2015). Notwithstanding, as shown in the previous section, some people will indisputably have been recruited and compelled in a manner closely resembling victims of human trafficking. Research shows that ISIS, for instance, "use naïve and easily manipulated teenage girls to play a role in territory under its control, inducing them to embrace a cause that they often do not clearly understand" (Perešin 2015, 23).

These people should not necessarily be liable to be punished for terrorist-related offences. For scholars of human trafficking, this is because their free will was significantly curbed or extinguished. If they are punished, then in reality the state is punishing them for being trafficked (Piotrowicz and Sorrentino 2016, p.674). The next section looks into legal philosophy.

Philosophical Justifications of Punishment

Why do we even have laws that excuse the defendant? Fundamentally, different answers to this question will come from the two traditional philosophical justifications of punishment, namely consequentialist and retributivist theories. To reiterate, retributivism appeals to the notion that wrongdoers deserve punishment, while consequentialism suggests that punishing offenders yields better results than not punishing them. The positive results usually comprise (i) reducing the amount of crime by incarcerating criminals; (ii) deterring others from committing crime through using punishment as a threat; and (iii) rehabilitating the criminal. Retributivism is about "seeing to it that people get what they deserve" (Scheid 1983, 264) and it looks back to the crime and the wrongdoer; consequentialism looks to the future and what is best for society.

From the perspective of followers of the Benthamite theory and thus consequentialism, punishment should not be applied because that punishment is wasteful. That is, the existence of the possibility of punishment will not deter other prospective wrongdoers (one of the aims of consequentialism). The theory, in true utilitarian style, looks to maximising overall wellbeing rather than to the state of mind of the defendant. As noted by Hart:

> "once the crime has been committed, the decision to punish or not has nothing to do with any moral claim or right of the criminal to have the features of his case considered, but only with the causal efficacy of his punishment on others. On this view the rationale of excuses is not (to put it shortly) that the accused should, in view of his mental condition, be excused whatever the effect of this on others; it is rather the mere fact that excusing him will not harm society by reducing the efficacy of the law's threats for others" (Hart 2008, 42–43).

On this understanding, punishment should not be used against those who were compelled to join terrorist groups because that punishment will not deter others from doing the same. As Fletcher (2000, 813) writes:

> "there is a good utilitarian explanation for defences based on involuntary conduct. The argument is that involuntary conduct cannot be deterred and therefore it is pointless and wasteful to punish involuntary actors. This theory, which we shall call the theory of pointless punishment, carries considerable weight in current Anglo-American legal thought."

In the case of an 18-year-old female victim of human trafficking who was physically abused and forced into breaking criminal laws, for example, through cultivating drugs, this is of benefit as she would likely not be punished. However, our case is different, because in this instance we are dealing with the heavily politicised arena of terrorism in conflict,[4] where a desperation for deterrence and a blindness to see many of the returnees as victims of human trafficking compelled to commit crimes reigns. In this instance, the consequentialist line of thinking may be turned to argue that we need to punish returnees, because it will in fact deter others and therefore is better for society. This rhetoric would in all likelihood trump any insight into their lack of control over their actions. Yet, to lean on consequentialism in this instance is dangerous and can preclude the full effect of the 'shield' elements of human rights against criminal law. This is because "consequentialism traditionally argues that criminal law should distribute punishment in a way that maximizes some desirable consequences, such as social welfare," and this may come at the cost of sometimes punishing the non-deserving (Bystranowski 2017, 27).

In cases of people recruited and brought to terrorist strongholds, a hypothetical argument could be made that one may think twice about travelling to Syria if the law punished all those who did so; the law might indeed deter. The problem here is that in such an instance we are allowing the state to exercise a punishment 'creep' without proper accord to the *mens rea* element of the crime; which is to say that the state would not be properly examining the person's individual actions. This is punishment that surpasses individual desert and is thus immoral. Indeed, the most common critique of consequentialism is that its advocates would be committed to the punishment of those known to be innocent if it would

[4] In many contemporary conflicts, states fight against non-state actors, including terrorist groups which are unbounded by sovereign territorial boundaries and which are preferring tactics aimed at civilians often far from any traditionally understood battlefield (Blank 2010, 3).

efficiently serve the aim of crime reduction; but this chapter holds that you cannot punish returnees just to teach the rest of society a lesson. On the other hand, some consequentialists would argue, for instance, that "a law enforcer that would choose to frame the innocent individual in such a case would be, at best, a short-sighted consequentialist," and that "cases of this kind are excessively stylised, fanciful, and are not likely to ever happen in the actual world" (Bystranowski 2017, 27). Yet given the politicised world, as exemplified by the unclear reasons behind stripping Shamima Begum[5] of her citizenship, it feels as though the consequentialists are undermined.

For this author, the problem with consequentialism in particular is that it can almost justify anything, and it remains hard to realistically predict what the consequence of punishing will have on society and deterrence; particularly with such an emotive crime. Moreover, consequentialist thinking offers an inadequate consideration of justice for the individual and of his/her desert. This critique springs from the tenet that to punish preventively risks falling foul of the foundations of criminal law, which are to punish harmful activities that a culpable individual committed. Consequently, it is proposed in this chapter that the acts of returnees should be carefully examined; prosecutors/detectives ought to ask about the defendant's actions and conduct their enquiries independently and outside of political agendas to be seen tough on terrorism. The criminal justice system should thoroughly enquire why the defendant joined the group, what was their mental condition and whether their free will was affected. Further avenues of analysis, as per traditional criminal law enquiries, could focus on whether the defendant demonstrated a shortfall of moral judgment that could otherwise be expected of someone in similar circumstances and of similar characteristics. Of course, there is no requirement for heroism or abnormal moral willpower. To borrow

[5]A 19-year-old, who left east London to join the Islamic State group in 2015, and was stripped of her British citizenship in February 2019 when she sought to return home. This was contrary to the UK strategy for Countering Terrorism (CONTEST) for returnees from Syria, which expressly refers to a managed return, potential use of a Temporary Exclusion Order, investigation into criminality and/or rehabilitation and reintegration into society. Moreover, in 2018, an estimated 400 individuals had been allowed to return to the UK after engaging in fighting with groups such as ISIS. It is thus unclear why Shamima Begum was prevented from returning where many others have not (van Ark 2019).

from Simester (2012, 100), we require that the defendant "fall short, not of standards of perfection, but of standards of reasonableness. And excuses require only that his failings be, so to speak, understandable or reasonable ones."

Suppose that a terrorist organisation, over the course of a few months, exploits a position of vulnerability of *J* and persuades *J* that unless she joins them, her God will take vengeance and will send death to her family and they will live out eternity in hell. Suppose *J* truly believes this. Here, *J* is not justified in joining the organisation (as per the discussion on what is a justification above), but we can understand why she travels to join the group; she acts directly out of fear. On arriving in the Caliphate, *J*'s vulnerabilities deepen. She is beaten, abused, turned into a sex slave. She does what is expected of her as a jihadi bride. Because of the so-called duress of circumstances, *J* has an excuse. The concession is reflective of our understanding of the humanity of the individual and not of any greater societal aspirations. We thus operate within the realm of retributive justice, where concepts of desert and justice occupy a dominant place. Understanding how the wrongdoing occurred we can find that punishment is not deserved. This is not a far-fetched scenario: women are known to have joined ISIS having been compelled to believe that religious duty requires them to move to the new 'Caliphate.' As documented by *The Washington Post* (2014), entire families answered that call, 'believing that they are doing the right thing for their children.' Of course, a properly functioning criminal justice system will not excuse everyone who answered this call. There is no argument here for blanket immunity. But the law ought to track the circumstances of how the defendant ended up answering that call, what made them do the things they did and ask whether any excusing conditions that impacted their free will were present; did the person act of their own free will, of their own accord or could they have helped doing what they did?

As explained above, retributive view is that punishment is justified on the grounds that offence deserves punishment. It is morally justified that a person who does wrong should suffer in proportion to their wrongdoing, unless they can be excused. If we can prove that a person who joined a terrorist organisation, such as ISIS, was in fact a victim of human trafficking and that their subsequent support for that organisation and any other connected crimes were a result of compulsion, then it follows they ought to, at the very least, be considered for protection under the non-prosecution and non-punishment principle. This reflects the general concepts of agency and criminal liability on which European criminal law systems are based. With human trafficking, this is made somewhat easier in Europe due to existing provisions: the above cited Article 8; in Directive *2011/36*; and in Article 26 of the *2005 Council of Europe Convention on Action Against Trafficking in Human Beings*.

Conclusion

This chapter raises two key concerns. The first is for the military, namely, how best to react to victims of human trafficking encountered in conflict situations? The second, on which this chapter mainly focused, is for the state's application of criminal justice, and the query of how to respond when potential victims seek to return home. Turning first to the latter, as was shown in this chapter, there should be an increase in the investigative capabilities of the criminal justice system first and foremost. If, through evidence, the returnee is able to demonstrate that they meet the established definition of human trafficking and can show that any crimes they committed were as a result of compulsion, they ought to be excused. This follows the retributivist approach, whereby humans are assumed to have free will and the ability to make rational decisions, such that if they commit a wrongful act they ought to be punished. We ought not to punish, however, returnees who have an excuse, and certainly not for societal reasons, that is, deterring others.

What about the military? The military needs to be sensitised to the reality that some of the adversaries they are fighting may not be there through free will. Consequently, they ought to understand how to spot the signs between an individual who constitutes a genuine adversary versus a victim of human trafficking, and address the latter appropriately. With captured or detained individuals, efforts should be made to understand who belongs under which category. It is also possible that the military—often as the predominant actor in a conflict area, or the actor most proximate to human trafficking victims—may be the only actor able to gather and provide evidence for due process in a domestic court, when trying to determine whether an individual ought to be excused and provided protection through the non-prosecution and non-punishment principle.

References

Berman, Mitchel N. 2003. Justification and Excuse, Law and Morality. *Duke Law Journal* 53 (1): 1–77.

Binetti, Ashley. 2015. A New Frontier: Human Trafficking and ISIS's Recruitment of Women from the West. *Human Trafficking Search*. http://humantraffickingsearch.org/resource/a-new-frontier-human-trafficking-and-isiss-recruitment-of-women-from-the-west/

Blaker, Lisa. 2015. The Islamic State's Use of Online Social Media. *Military Cyber Affairs* 1 (4).

Blank, Laurie R. 2010. Defining the Battlefield in Contemporary Conflict and Counterterrorism: Understanding the Parameters of the Zone of Combat. *Georgia Journal of International and Comparative Law* 39 (1).

Bloom, Mia. 2011. *The Many Faces of Women Terrorists*. London: Hurst & Company.

Bystranowski, Piotr. 2017. Retributivism, Consequentialism, and the Risk of Punishing the Innocent: The Troublesome Case of Proxy Crimes. *Diametros* 53: 26–49.

Christie, Nils. 1986. The Ideal Victim. In *From Crime Policy to Victim Policy*, ed. E. Fattah. New York: St. Martin's Press.

Davis, Jessica. 2017. *Women in Modern Terrorism: From Liberation Wars to Global Jihad and the Islamic State*. Rowman & Littlefield.

Dressler, Joshua. 2001. *Understanding Criminal Law*. New Providence, NJ: Lexis Nexis Publishing.

Dubber, Markus, and Tatjana Hörnle. 2014. *Criminal Law. A Comparative Approach*. Oxford: Oxford University Press.

Fletcher, George P. 2000. *Rethinking Criminal Law*. Oxford University Press.

Hart, Herbert Lionel Adolphus. 1968. *Punishment and Responsibility: Essays in the Philosophy of Law*. Oxford: Clarendon Press.

———. 2008. *Punishment and Responsibility: Essays in the Philosophy of Law*. Oxford University Press.

Houry, Nadim. 2018. France's Creeping Terrorism Laws Restricting Free Speech. *Human Rights Watch,* 30 May 2018. https://www.hrw.org/news/2018/05/30/frances-creeping-terrorism-laws-restricting-free-speech

OSCE Office of the Special Representative and Co-ordinator for Combating Trafficking in Human Beings. 2013. *Policy and legislative recommendations towards the effective implementation of the non-punishment provision with regard to victims of trafficking.* Vienna: OSCE. http://www.osce.org/secretariat/101002?download=true

Perešin, Anita. 2015. Fatal Attraction: Western Muslimas and ISIS. *Perspectives on Terrorism* 9 (3): 21–38.

Piotrowicz, Ryszard., and Liliana Sorrentino. 2016. Human Trafficking and the Emergence of the Non-Punishment Principle. *Human Rights Law Review* 16 (4): 669–699.

Scheid, Don E. 1983. Kant's Retributivism. *Ethics* 93 (2): 262–282.

Simester, Andrew. 2012. On Justifications and Excuses. In *Principles and Values in Criminal Law and Criminal Justice: Essays in Honour of Andrew Ashworth*, ed. L. Zedner and J. Roberts. Oxford: Oxford University Press.

Smith, Amelia. 2014. ISIS Publish Pamphlet on How to Treat Female Slaves. *Newsweek.* https://www.newsweek.com/isis-release-questions-and-answers-pamphlet-how-treat-female-slaves-290511

The Economist. 2015. Caliphate Calling – Women and Jihad. *The Economist*, 26 February 2015. https://www.economist.com/international/2015/02/26/caliphate-calling

The Washington Post. 2014. Hoping to Create a New Society, the Islamic State Recruits Entire Families. *The Washington Post,* 24 December 2014. http://www.washingtonpost.com/world/national-security/hoping-to-create-a-new-homeland-the-islamic-state-recruits-entire-families/2014/12/24/dbff-ceec-8917-11e4-8ff4-fb93129c9c8b_story.html

Van Ark, Rumyana. 2019. *British Citizenship Revoked, Bangladeshi Citizenship Uncertain – What Next for Shamima Begum?* International Centre for Counter Terrorism. https://icct.nl/publication/british-citizenship-revoked-bangladeshi-citizenship-uncertain-what-next-for-shamima-begum/

Watson, Ivan. 2014. Treated Like Cattle: Yazidi Women Sold, Raped, Enslaved by ISIS. *CNN World,* 30 October 2014. http://thecnnfreedomproject.blogs.cnn.com/2014/10/30/treated-like-cattle-yazidi-women-sold-raped-enslaved-by-isis/

Weber, Leanne, Elaine Fishwick, and Marinella Marmo. 2014. *Crime, Justice and Human Rights.* Basingstoke: Palgrave Macmillan.

Julia Muraszkiewicz is a Senior Research Manager at Trilateral Research in the Applied Research and Innovation team and was the research lead of Project Solebay looking at risk assessment methodologies for human trafficking in conflict. She has a publication with Palgrave Macmillan on protecting trafficked persons from liability. Julia in her spare time volunteers with NGOs that directly help victims of human trafficking and labour exploitation. She has a PhD in Law from Vrije University of Brussels.

12

Trafficking and Child Sexual Violence in Afghanistan: The Military's Role in Combating Human Trafficking

Olivia Iannelli

"We must convert a centuries-old culture of impunity into a culture of accountability"—Pramila Patten, Special Representative of the Secretary-General on Sexual Violence in Conflict

Introduction

The last 70 years have seen the increase of protracted conflicts of a non-international character and environmental disasters, which have led to large-scale humanitarian crises. These crises have affected a wide array of countries, across the Middle East, South America, Africa and South Asia. Societies affected by conflict, civil unrest and natural disasters develop into "prime routes for trafficking in both drugs, weapons, natural resources and persons" (Mazurana et al. 2005, 83). These environments

O. Iannelli (✉)
Trilateral Research, London, UK
e-mail: Olivia.Iannelli@trilateralresearch.com

J. Muraszkiewicz et al. (eds.), *Human Trafficking in Conflict*, Crime Prevention and Security Management, https://doi.org/10.1007/978-3-030-40838-1_12

aggravate trafficking trends due to the lack of the rule of law, formal state structures and judicial system, as well as increased displacement of civilians and a loss of livelihood. These conditions create poverty, a breeding ground for corruption, and a culture of impunity (US Department of State 2019), thus further exacerbating vulnerabilities, crime and human rights violations. During armed conflict and post-conflict situations, children are particularly vulnerable due to their age, inexperience and dependence on others. This vulnerability renders them more likely to encounter exploitation, neglect and abuse, resulting in physical, sexual and psychological harm (Sheehan et al. 2012; Spitka 2019, 184). Soldiers International's report on 2018, verified 8185 cases of child soldiers in 15 countries, a significant increase from previous years, and stated that the exploitation of girls was also on the rise (Soldiers International 2019). However, as argued by the International Organisation for Migration in a report published in 2015, human trafficking "remains largely overlooked in crisis situations" (IOM 2015) and young children are not sufficiently protected from exploitation.

There is a critical gap for tackling human trafficking in the humanitarian response system and architecture which must be addressed (Global Protection Cluster 2017). By using Afghanistan as a case study, this chapter will demonstrate that despite strong legislation and an increased awareness and open discussion on children's exploitation in conflict among the international community, a consistent approach to the protection of children in conflict is lacking (Spitka 2019, 184). This lack of protection, it will be argued, is due to the low level of priority that trafficking in conflict is awarded, the lack of understanding of the effect of trafficking on society, compounded by a lack of understanding of some of its indicators.

This chapter seeks to answer the following research question: Does the military have a role in addressing the trafficking of children in conflict, and if so, what does this role look like? Although, the prevention and combat of crime in the context of armed conflicts is not a traditional role undertaken by the military, this chapter will argue that a multi-sectoral response is needed to truly eradicate human trafficking in conflict zones and thus achieve 'durable peace and reconciliation.' Within this multi-sectorial response, the military in Afghanistan, including the North

Atlantic Treaty Organization (NATO), will be proposed as an additional actor in addressing human trafficking in conflict and protecting children. As first responders on the ground, NATO and the Afghan army may be best placed to identify victims of exploitation or individuals at risk and thus help towards their protection and early identification. They may collect evidence and help towards prosecution, in an effort to reduce impunity.

It will conclude that to ensure this multi-sectoral response is successful, human trafficking and more specifically the trafficking of children in conflict, must be included in the growing concept of Human Security. The concept of Human Security is outlined in General Assembly resolution 66/290 which states that "human security calls for people-centred, comprehensive, context-specific and prevention-oriented responses that strengthen the protection and empowerment of all people and all communities" (United Nations General Assembly 2012). Human Security entails "protecting people from critical (severe) and pervasive (widespread) threats and situations" (UN Commission on Human Security 2003). These threats are understood to be multi-sectoral in nature; in other words, they encompass issues related to the economy, personal security, livelihood and food, health, the environment, the community and politics (Office for the Coordination of Humanitarian Affairs 2009, 7). Human trafficking is linked to all of these threats and thus should be "viewed along a conflict and crisis-peace-development continuum" (Inter-Agency Coordination Group against Trafficking in Persons 2017, 3).

In addition to focusing on human security, the chapter calls for greater focus on the Women, Peace and Security (WPS) agenda, which emerged from resolution 1325 (2000) and which has grown significantly since then. Within this resolution it was stated that gender-specific considerations should be brought to the centre of all "United Nations' conflict prevention and resolution, peace-building, peacekeeping, rehabilitation and reconstruction efforts" (United Nations 2002, 1). This includes the gender mainstreaming of military plans and operations; in other words, the inclusion of the perceptions, experience, knowledge and interests of both women and men in policy-making, planning and decision-making (United Nations 2002, 4). The inclusion of gender considerations is key to tackling human trafficking which has various gendered dimensions as will be argued in this chapter. Finally, the chapter argues that to take on an active role in combating human trafficking in conflict, the military must also adopt a child-rights based approach and gain a better understanding of the local context to shape its policy.

Human Trafficking in Conflict: The Case of Afghanistan

In 2018, Afghanistan was listed by the Global Slavery Index as being the country with the fifth highest prevalence of human trafficking (Global Slavery Index 2018). The top ten countries on this list were either countries with highly repressive regimes or countries with ongoing conflicts (ibid). Whilst this author acknowledges the problems with the Index (see Gallagher 2017; Datta et al. 2019), it is true that Afghanistan has been in continuous conflict since 1979, when it was invaded by the Soviet Union. Recent years have also seen rising tensions and violence, which in turn have an impact on the levels of exploitations. The year 2018 saw 3812 casualties, of which over a third were children (The Guardian 2019). The United Nations also stated that July 2019 was one of the deadliest months of the last two years, with 1500 civilians killed or wounded (Abed et al. 2019). The poverty, insecurity and corruption, caused by war and instability, is one of the main reasons (Erdogdu et al. 2016, 6) Afghanistan remains a "source, transit, and destination country" of human trafficking (US Department of State 2018). As mentioned above, conflict amplifies the risks of vulnerabilities to human trafficking as it increases poverty among the community, and thus, desperation for new and improved economic opportunities. Conflicts also lead to a weakening rule of law, the reduction in the accessibility to social services and the breaking down of support systems and communities, thus laying the foundation for a culture of impunity, in which traffickers are able to operate easily without being prosecuted (United Nations Office on Drugs and Crime 2018). In addition, large foreign forces create a demand for human trafficking as was showcased in Kosovo (Smith and Miller-De La Cuesta 2011).

According to the US Trafficking in Persons Report of 2019, which is acknowledged as containing some methodological weaknesses and gaps in data (Gallagher 2017), most of the Afghan trafficking victims are children (United States Department of State 2019). Children in Afghanistan are exploited by carpet making and brick factories, and exposed to other forms of child labour and domestic servitude, such as agricultural labour (United States Department of Labor 2018), forced begging, poppy cultivation, salt mining, transnational drug smuggling and assistant truck driving (United States Department of State 2019). Young boys and girls in Afghanistan are also affected by sex trafficking and sexual exploitation (United Nations Security Council 2015, 10; United Nations Office on Drugs and Crime 2018, 23–24). In 2018, the United Nations Assistance Mission in Afghanistan (UNAMA) documented 37 cases of sexual violence against women and girls (United Nations 2018). Five rapes and one forced marriage were verified as having been committed by parties to the conflict. The previous year, UNAMA documented 53 cases of sexual violence against women and girls, of which three were verified as conflict-related sexual violence committed by members of illegal armed groups and the local police (United Nations 2018). UNAMA also verified four cases of sexual violence against boys and received a further 78 credible allegations of Bacha Bazi (United Nations Regional Information Centre for Western Europe 2014), which for the majority affects young boys. This practice involves abducting, buying or luring young boys with promises of food and money (United Nations Regional Information Centre for Western Europe 2014) and turning them into sex slaves (Ferrie 2018). These victims are forced to dress up as women and dance (Afghanistan Independent Human Rights Commission 2014, 3; United Nations Regional Information Centre for Western Europe 2014) for their 'masters,' who are usually men in position of power, including security forces, government officials, warlords, community leaders (Akhtar 2019, 183; United Nations Regional Information Centre for Western Europe 2014) and terrorist groups (Akhtar 2019, 182). Cases remain widely underreported due to the lack of access to justice, inadequate responses and protection services, social stigma, and shame (ibid., 187).

International organisations, news coverage and reports depict "a picture of systematic, widespread, and continuous sexual abuse of young boys in the forms of Bacha Bazi and child soldiers" (ibid., 182). Indeed, human trafficking in conflict remains largely unnoticed by the military and other organisations, who do not consider it a priority in conflict areas. This is in part due to few cases being reported, as well as a lack of understanding of what human trafficking consists of and its implications for the achievement of long-lasting peace within the community. In addition to this, the military considers it an issue out of its jurisdiction and a 'problem' for national law enforcement to deal with. Tackling human trafficking, in their opinion, does not 'win wars' and thus is not at the top of their agenda.

The US report of 2019, as well as other UN reports, also highlighted the continued forced recruitment and use of children in combat and non-combat roles (United States Department of State 2019; United Nations Office on Drugs and Crime 2018; United Nations Security Council 2015), predominantly by non-state armed groups such as the Taliban and the Islamic State in Khorasan Province (ISILKP). Between September 2010 and December 2014, over 600 children were recruited by the Taliban and ISILKP (United Nations Security Council 2015, 5). In 2016 it was reported that, in the province of Uruzgan, all of its 370 local and national police checkpoints had Bacha Bazis, who were illegally recruited for both sexual purposes and also for active combat (Chopra 2016). A growing practice among terrorist groups is also the use of Bacha Bazi to mount insider attacks on Afghan military bases and police checkpoints. Thus, exploiting young boys and this practice as a tactic of warfare. In 2016, hundreds of policemen were killed after six of these attacks were carried out in the province of Uruzgan (ibid.).

In 2017, the Afghan government made large efforts to counter trafficking by differentiating between smuggling and trafficking and criminalising labour trafficking and sex trafficking, including the practice of Bacha Bazi (United States Department of State 2019). The Afghan government is also setting up a National Referral Mechanism and an online database to counter and respond to human trafficking with support from the US Agency for International Development and the International Organisation for Migration (IOM 2018). Despite these new measures, the Afghan government has upheld minimal law enforcement efforts, allowing traffickers to operate with impunity (United States Department of State 2019; United Nations Security Council 2015, 11). This is partly due to the fact that the perpetrators of Bacha Bazi are high-profile individuals from the Afghan police and security forces, as well as the fact that human trafficking is not given the priority it deserves. This is showcased by Afghan President Hamid Karzai's dismissal of the importance of addressing these issues when he stated: "let us win the war first. Then we will deal with such matters" (Yerman 2012). As a result of this, trafficking in Afghanistan has not only endured but it has thrived (Ferrie 2018). It is suggested here that one cannot successfully win a war and lay the foundation for a peaceful society without paying attention to human security concepts. Issues linked to human security are, in fact, all interconnected and one can often exacerbate the other, creating a domino effect (OCHA 2009, 7). Without addressing root issues and causes, such as discrimination, inequality and human trafficking, conflict will endure.

Legal Framework and NATO's Role in Combatting Human Trafficking in Afghanistan

In order to answer the research question, "does the military have a role in addressing the trafficking of children in conflict, and if so, what does this role look like?" it is important to first outline the legal framework, which is applicable to both NATO and Afghanistan, on combatting and preventing human trafficking. This overview will also help to build a context which favours the inclusion of counter-trafficking actions and activities in the military's missions and planning.

Measures to protect children from exploitation and trafficking during armed conflict are explicitly laid out in international human rights (IHRL), international humanitarian law (IHL) and international criminal Law (CL). *The Convention for the Rights of the Child* (CRC) and its additional protocols, which Afghanistan and NATO member states have signed and ratified, apart from the US, and are therefore obliged to implement, is the main treaty which is applicable to children and remains the most ratified treaty internationally. Article 38 obliges states to respect international humanitarian law and "take all feasible measures to ensure protection and care of children who are affected by an armed conflict" (UN General Assembly 1989, Article 38). The Convention also compels signatories to take "all appropriate legislative, administrative, social and educational measures to protect the child from all forms of physical or mental violence, injury or abuse, neglect or negligent treatment, maltreatment or exploitation, including sexual abuse, while in the care of parent(s), legal guardian(s) or any other person who has the care of the child" (UN General Assembly 1989, Article 19). Article 33 briefly mentions protecting children from trafficking narcotic drugs and psychotropic substances (UN General Assembly 1989, Article 33) and Article 34 compels State Parties to take all appropriate national measures "to protect the child from all forms of sexual exploitation and sexual abuse" (UN General Assembly 1989, Article 34). Although these articles do not explicitly refer to trafficking in conflict, or exploitation during conflict, they clearly underline that States have an obligation to prevent and protect children from exploitation and sexual abuse. Of particular importance within IHRL is also the *UN Protocol to Prevent, Suppress and Punish Trafficking in Persons, Especially Women and Children* (UN General Assembly 2000) which Afghanistan has signed and ratified. Among its provisions, the Protocol Parties calls on States to "establish comprehensive policies, programmes and other measures: to prevent and combat trafficking in persons" (UN General Assembly 2000, Article 9(1)(a)).

Although IHL does not specifically recognise human trafficking, it provides various measures to protect children in conflict and to prevent them from becoming victims of trafficking. This is particularly important in the context of Afghanistan which is a non-international armed conflict (RULAC 2019). Common Article 3 of the four *Geneva Conventions*, which also applies in non-international armed conflict, forbids attacks on anyone not taking an active part in hostilities and states that they shall be treated humanely in all circumstances (ICRC 1949, Article 3). Rule 93 of the *International Committee of Red Cross*, which is considered a rule of customary international law[1] in both international and non-international

[1] Customary international law consists of two components: Opinio juris and State practice. Opinio juris refers to a sense, on behalf of a State that the norm is strong enough to be compelling law. State

armed conflicts, prohibits rape and other forms of sexual violence which is also applicable to children (ibid., Rule 93). Additionally, *Protocol II*, which applies to non-international armed conflicts, provides further protection measures. In particular, Article 4(2)(f) states that "slavery and the slave trade in all their forms" are prohibited at any time and in any place without exception (ICRC 1977, Article 4(2)(f)). Article 4(3) is specific to children and forbids the recruitment of young people under the age of fifteen in armed forces (ICRC 1977, Article 4(3)).

Instances of child sexual exploitation and trafficking in armed conflict may also amount to other violations of international human rights, such as a violation of the right to life, liberty and security of person, prohibition against slavery and slavery-related practices and freedom from torture and other forms of cruel, inhuman or degrading treatment which are both non-derogable, *jus cogens* norms.[2] However, despite the abundance of legislation protecting children from exploitation and trafficking and the rising importance it is being afforded in the international fora, the implementation of these laws remains extremely weak. The challenge, in fact, remains in ensuring that international instruments are translated into practice on the ground. Although criminal law is also important with respect to countering human trafficking, it is beyond the scope of this paper particularly as armed conflicts are unlikely to have the necessary elements in place for its proper implementation, such as respect for the rule of law and an efficient criminal justice system.

Despite the strong legislation in place, child rights continue to be violated in conflict zones by governments as well as non-state actors, as the case of Afghanistan clearly demonstrates. This is partly due to the lack of respect for IHRL and IHL by parties to the armed conflict. It is widely accepted that violations of IHL are not due to the inadequacy of its provisions but rather due to a lack of respect for them (ICRC 2007). There are

---

practice, on the other hand, denotes the acts of States with regard to the norm in question. Once a norm contains these two components, it is considered customary international law and thus, binding on all States, unless they are a persistent objector.

[2] *Jus cogens* norms are defined in Article 53 of the Vienna Convention of the Law of Treaties as norms which are peremptory in nature from which no derogation is permissible, whether by treaty or by objection of a State persistent or otherwise. There is no universal agreement on precisely which norms qualify as *jus cogens*; however, it is generally accepted that these include prohibitions of only the most egregious acts such as torture, genocide and slavery.

various reasons behind this, for instance, IHL lacks effective mechanisms to ensure its rules are respected (ICRC 2016). In addition to this, Bangerter points out that a respect for IHL can vary according to the group's objective, the military advantage they gain by breaking it and what IHL represents to them, which includes their understanding of the law and its implications (Bangerter 2011, 353). Recruiting minors in combat and non-combat roles, for instance, creates a military advantage as it increases the number of fighters. This advantage offsets the disadvantages of having children as combatants (Bangerter 2011, 354). In addition, there are insufficient means to enforce these provisions; a cultural stigma related to sexual and gender-based violence means that incidents often go unreported, with a lack of priority afforded to human trafficking in conflict by first responders, governments and organisations in the field (IOM 2015). This, alongside a lack of enforcement mechanisms, enables state security forces and non-state armed groups to operate with impunity.

The Security Council established the importance of countering human trafficking in conflict in its report on trafficking in persons in armed conflict pursuant to *Security Council resolution 2388* (UN Security Council 2018) and expressed grave concern over the high number of women and children subjected to trafficking in areas affected by armed conflict. Focusing on human trafficking occurring in times of conflict was particularly unusual for the Security Council as the issue was usually addressed by other UN-affiliated actors. Its growing focus, therefore, clearly showcases the shift that has occurred at the international level in considering human trafficking as a security issue.

Within this report, the Security Council called upon Member States to improve their implementation of applicable legal obligations to criminalise, prevent and otherwise combat trafficking in persons and to step up their efforts to investigate, disrupt and dismantle networks engaging in trafficking in persons in areas of conflict (ibid.). The Security Council also reaffirms that trafficking should be addressed within the context of the WPS agenda of the Security Council as it can often amount to conflict-related sexual violence, which has a durable impact on long-lasting peace and reconciliation (UN Security Council 2019). The inclusion of trafficking within this agenda is extremely important as trafficking has various gendered dimensions. The gender of a victim, in fact, informs how they may experience human trafficking. Women are said to be more likely to experience sexual exploitation, whereas men are more likely to experience labour exploitation or trafficking for organ removal (Inter-Agency Coordination Group against Trafficking in Persons 2017, 1). A lack of a gender-specific approach to tackling human trafficking undermines the uniqueness of a victim's experience (Inter-Agency Coordination Group against Trafficking in Persons 2017, 2). Additionally, gender stereotypes may hinder identification processes as well as the provision of appropriate support (ibid). In light of this, the Security Council encouraged "States to design and implement results-oriented national action plans on women, peace and security which include comprehensive measures aimed at preventing and responding to trafficking in persons at the national level and allocate sufficient human and financial resources" to this effort (UN Security Council 2018, 17). The WPS agenda is also instrumental in tackling human trafficking as it requires States to combat gender inequalities and discrimination, which are helping to create and fuel conflicts. Without addressing the core issues of inequality, peace is unlikely to happen. NATO and the Afghan military must, therefore, maintain WPS at the core of their operations and their activities. Although many improvements have been made in realising the WPS agenda, the implementation process is still far from meeting the expectations (Adamczewska 2019, 80).

UN Security Council Resolution 2388 also welcomes a multidimensional approach to trafficking, including the incorporation of information on the risks of trafficking (UN Security Council 2018, 7). This is where the military, specifically NATO, can contribute. NATO's operations in Afghanistan remain their largest operation to date where its principal mission is "to create a stable, peaceful, and prosperous state that will never again become a source of regional insecurity or a wellspring for global terrorism" (NATO 2017). The human trafficking situation in Afghanistan is particularly relevant to NATO and the Afghan military, as such practices bolster the number of adversaries in both combat and non-combat roles, helping to extend the conflict's continuation. Additionally, trafficking and sexual violence continues to be employed in many conflicts as a tactic of war to advance terrorist operations (Akhtar 2019, 183). As demonstrated above, human trafficking in Afghanistan has severely affected the civilian population, in particular, children, who remain the main victims within the conflict (US State Department 2019). Additionally, it is logical to assume that a phenomenon such as human trafficking promotes violence and establishes a status quo wherein violence and, in turn, conflict are normalised, thus creating a perpetual cycle of violence.

The Security Council has further asserted the importance of the military in one of its reports by stating that "measures targeting the capacity of international peacekeepers in active duty or when stationed in areas affected by armed conflict are particularly crucial in addressing trafficking in such areas" (UN Security Council 2018, 6). Additionally, the report recommended increasing specialist training for military personnel on trafficking in persons, the criminal structures involved and their *modi operandi* as part of regular pre-deployment training. As well as, developing and issuing guidelines for the identification and referral of trafficking victims (ibid). *UN Security Council Resolution 2331* in 2016 is also particularly important as it calls on the UN Secretary General to include human trafficking in conflict prevention strategies, conflict analysis, integrated missions' assessment and planning, peacebuilding support and humanitarian response (UN Security Council 2016).

Despite acknowledging that human trafficking is an important issue to address, the focus has mostly been on the army's role as a perpetrator of human trafficking (see Mendelson 2005; Allred 2006). This focus began to emerge particularly following the war in the Balkans and US activities in South Korea, more as a reaction to how the army's involvement in human trafficking may damage its reputation, rather than a genuine concern for human security. In order to truly eradicate this issue, however, there must be an active commitment and understanding that human trafficking is a human security issue. Until now, the army has not been outwardly considered as an active agent in seeking to counter this crime. In fact, in 2015, the *New York Times* released an article in which they looked at the US army's role in reporting incidents of sexual abuse towards boys in Afghanistan. The spokesman for the American command in Afghanistan, Colonel Brian Tribus wrote that: "Generally, allegations of child sexual abuse by Afghan military or police personnel would be a matter of domestic Afghan criminal law" (Goldstein 2015). He added that "there would be no express requirement that U.S. military personnel in Afghanistan report it" (ibid). However, he conceded that an exception to this would be if rape is being used as a weapon of war (ibid).

NATO has affirmed that compliance to international law, including international humanitarian law (IHL) and international human rights law (IHRL), remains central to its operations, missions and other Council-mandated activities (Hill and Manea 2018). Its commitment to maintaining human rights and humanitarian law is evident through the diverse set of policies that NATO has implemented around children and armed conflict, women, peace and security and conflict-related sexual and gender-based violence (ibid). NATO's role and commitment to countering human trafficking, and the exploitation of children, is also somewhat already established in its policy. In 2004, NATO adopted a policy against trafficking (NATOa 2004) in which it stated that human trafficking is a "transnational problem, requiring concerted multilateral action if it is to be defeated" (NATOb 2004). The policy also calls for training and modules, aimed at NATO forces, to raise awareness of issues connected to trafficking and the means to combat it (ibid). It also calls for "support, within their competence and mandate, the efforts of responsible authorities in the host country in combating trafficking in human beings" (ibid). NATO's recent WPS agenda, published in 2018, stated that it will update its Policy on Combatting Trafficking in Human Beings to ensure it reflects the linkage between WPS and human security and it reinforces efforts to protect civilians, in particular women and girls who are the primary victims of trafficking (NATO/EAPC 2018). Additionally, also in 2018, NATO appointed Clare Hutchinson as NATO Secretary General's Special Representative for Women, Peace and Security (WPS), further demonstrating its commitment to pushing this agenda forwards.

NATO has also continued to demonstrate its commitment to the proper implementation of UN Security Council Resolution 1612 and related resolutions on the protection of children affected by armed conflict (Hill and Manea 2018; NATO 2014, para 91) through various policy documents, the most recent being, 'The Protection of Children in Armed Conflict-Way Forward.' Furthermore, at the Wales Summit, NATO stated it would incorporate the issue of children in armed conflict in the training and planning of its operations as well as in the monitoring and reporting of its missions (NATO 2014, para 91). Indeed, according to NATO's Children And Armed Conflict Fact Sheet (NATO 2016), NATO developed standard procedures for monitoring and reporting instances when the six grave violations committed against children[3] occur during its missions and operations, which include trafficking of children. This reporting system is currently in place in Afghanistan, where NATO Commanders are also receiving training on how to better respond when encountering these violations (NATO 2016). A specialised Children and Armed Conflict Adviser was also deployed to Afghanistan in April 2016 (ibid).

Within its Allied Joint Doctrine on stabilisation and reconstruction, NATO also recognises that the military can play a crucial role in the stabilisation and reconstruction of a State during and after crises, when civilian actors are unable to provide support (NATO Standardised Office 2015, 1). In other words, it can help towards maintaining, fostering, or restoring stability to provide the foundation for long-term peace (ibid). This includes, in particular, addressing the sources of instability which fostered the crisis in the first place (NATO Standardised Office 2015, 3). Human trafficking and other human rights violations are often closely connected to conflict escalation (Thoms and Ron 2007, 704) and to a conflict's continuation, as they allow state and non-state actors to propel violence and gain military advantage (be it through finances or through additional manpower), whilst at the same time, weakening their opponents and local communities. Eradicating trafficking, is thus, key to the effort of ending conflict and restoring peace.

In Afghanistan, both state and non-state actors are committing serious violations of both international human rights and humanitarian law, which could amount to crimes against humanity, as exemplified above. These actions are not only in opposition to law but also undermine the prospect of long-term peace and security and are counter to the broader human security agenda. As first responders and often the only responders on the ground, NATO sits in a unique position to advance the agenda of

[3] The six grave violations are as follows: 1. Recruitment and use of children 2. Killing or maiming of children 3. Sexual violence against children 4. Attacks against schools or hospitals 5. Abduction of children 6. Denial of humanitarian access.

protection of civilians in conflict (Hogg 2018, 3), particularly, in conflicts such as Afghanistan, where child trafficking is being used as a weapon of war. NATO can advance protection in numerous ways. Firstly, as first responders on the ground, NATO could be paramount in the collection of evidence, which is of utmost importance to ending impunity. Additionally, NATO could begin to spot signs of trafficking, as well as indicators which may represent an increased risk of trafficking in that area, to improve early prevention and protection of civilians. NATO is best placed to do this in Afghanistan as it has a high level of engagement with the government, it has unique knowledge and understanding of the local context and can gather direct information on the ground (ibid).

Moving Forwards

NATO should be aware of the responsibility that is inherent within this active role in seeking to eradicate trafficking of children in conflict. However, it is not enough to pass legislation and have trainings on countering trafficking. Efforts need to go deeper particularly because the trafficking of children may continue after the armed conflict ends. Thus, intersectional and context-specific considerations linked to trafficking, exploitation and children, should be incorporated in NATO and the Afghan military's efforts. These considerations need to be made because civilians are not all the same, rather they have "intersecting identities (such as race, gender, ethnicity, familial status etc.) and evolving capacities and competencies (related to age, physical abilities, cognition, mental and emotional development, education, and health needs" (Lee-Koo 2019, 54). Thus, children who are victims of human trafficking in conflict have often had widely different experiences and held different roles. These roles may include soldiers, guards, workers, spies, spouses or parents (ibid). The protection programmes should reflect these differences and take on a victim-centred approach by including age-sensitive, gender-sensitive and context-specific measures to ensure they are encapsulating the different needs of boys and girls.

For instance, in 2005, the US and other Western governments pressured the Afghan government to issue an opium ban (Walter 2016, 285).

The abruptness of this ban left many farmers in the Nangarhar province indebted and impoverished. In order to cope, the community resorted to migration of males in search of better opportunities, as well as the selling of livestock, land and women (ibid). In fact, families were reported selling their daughters into early marriages to pay off loans and generate income (ibid). Thus, the programme caused "widespread societal disruption and human insecurity" among the people it was supposed to benefit and enforced Afghanistan's patriarchal gender divides (Walter 2016, 273). This example further illustrates the necessity of maintaining intersectional and context-specific considerations when implementing new policies and programmes.

Although NATO has shown a commitment to this in its policy, as illustrated above, much more needs to be done to ensure that children are protected from trafficking in conflict. This should include a much broader focus on human trafficking in conflict, children's identities and a better understanding of the local context. The WPS agenda is able to offer a framework in which this may happen, rendering it key in facilitating this.

Conclusion

The year 2019, marked the 30th anniversary of the *Convention of the Rights of the Child*, the most ratified treaty internationally, and the 70th anniversary of the Geneva Conventions. However, as evidenced in the case of Afghanistan, despite the strong legislation in place, child trafficking remains prevalent in conflicts across the globe with the near-total impunity of its perpetrators.

This chapter illustrated the current situation in Afghanistan, where children remain the largest percentage of victims of human trafficking (United States State Department 2019). It highlighted some of the current practices in which children are exploited in conflict, such as Bacha Bazi which is used as a weapon of war (Akhtar 2019, 182), and discussed the reasons behind the endurance of human trafficking in Afghanistan, which is exacerbated by conflict. In fact, it argued that despite recent measures taken by the Afghan government, trafficking is still awarded a low level of priority and enforcement efforts remain low, thus leaving children unprotected.

By analysing the legislation in this space, the chapter found significant provision which clearly states that child trafficking in conflict is a violation of both IHL and IHRL and can amount to crimes against humanity under enslavement, sexual slavery and violence and other inhumane acts (Obokata 2005; Allain 2015, 398; *Prosecutor v Kunarac,* para 542). It also showed that NATO's commitment to protecting children and implementing a WPS agenda is evident in its work and the recent policies it has established.

It was argued that to truly combat the trafficking of children, a trans-border, multi-agency and multi-disciplinary response is required. The inclusion of the UN Department of Peacekeeping Operations (DPKO) within the Inter-Agency Coordination Group against Trafficking in Persons (ICAT), for instance, is a vast step forward in this respect. This response "must include mutually reinforcing efforts to prevent and resolve armed conflicts, on the one hand, and to prevent and combat trafficking in persons on the other" (UN Security Council 2018, 6). Against this background, NATO, which currently operates in Afghanistan, was proposed as a key actor in actively combatting human trafficking in conflict. As the sole operator in certain conflict environments, such as Afghanistan, NATO and the Afghan army have the potential to help in identifying patterns and indicators of trafficking to protect victims, as well as the collecting of evidence to increase the prosecution of guilty parties. In order to achieve this, they must ensure their programmes and policies are reconceptualised to include a more nuanced approach to children's identities and victimhood, a broader understanding of gender and of the local context. The WPS agenda, it is proposed, is the most appropriate framework to include these considerations.

References

Abed, Fahim, Faizi, Fatima, and Mashal Mujib. 2019. Violence in Afghanistan Worsens as US-Taliban peace Talks Plod on. *The New York Times*, 7 August 2019. https://www.nytimes.com/2019/08/07/world/asia/kabul-afghanistan-bombing-taliban.html

Adamczewska, Milena. 2019. Strengthening Prevention of Conflict-Related Sexual Violence and Trafficking in Human Beings: Saving the Potential of the Women, Peace and Security Agenda with the Human Rights-Based Approach. *Journal of Trafficking and Human Exploitation* 2019 (1): 61–86.

Afghanistan Independent Human Rights Commission (AIHRC). 2014. *Causes and Consequences of Bacha Bazi in Afghanistan*. 18 August 2014. https://www.refworld.org/docid/5694c3db4.html

Akhtar, Rabia. 2019. The Neglected Boys of War: Trapped in Vicious Cycle of Slavery and Sexual Abuse. *Journal of Trafficking and Human Exploitation* 2019 (1): 179–204.

Allain, Jean. 2015. *The Law and Slavery*, Prohibiting Human Exploitation Leiden: Brill|Nijhoff.

Allred, J. Keith. 2006. Peacekeepers and Prostitutes: How Deployed Forces Fuel the Demand for Trafficked Women and New Hope for Stopping It. *Armed Forced and Society* 33 (1): 5–23.

Bangerter, Olivier. 2011. Reasons Why Armed Groups Choose to Respect International Humanitarian Law or Not. *International Review of the Red Cross* 93 (882): 353–384.

Child Soldiers International. 2019. Child Soldiers Level Doubled Since 2012, and Girls' Exploitation Is Rising. *Child Soldiers International*, 11 February 2019. https://www.child-soldiers.org/news/child-soldier-levels-have-doubled-since-2012-and-girls-exploitation-is-rising

Chopra, Anuj. 2016. Taliban Use of 'Honey Trap' Boys to Kill Afghan Police. *Yahoo News*, 16 June 2016. https://sg.news.yahoo.com/taliban-honey-trap-boys-kill-afghan-police-034032058.html

Datta, Monti Narayan, Olivia Gustafson, Chloe Lubin, Gioia Kelleher, and Rebecca Berg. 2019. Assessing the Global Slavery Index. In *The SAGE Handbook of Human Trafficking and Modern Day Slavery*, ed. Jennifer Bryson Clark and Sasha Poucki. London: SAGE.

Erdogdu, Elif, Sienna McNett, Daniel Winstead, and Ryamond Friend. 2016. Breaking the Stigma against Child Sex Trafficking and Bacha Bazi in Afghanistan. *The Journal of Penn States University* 1 (13).

Ferrie, Jared. 2018. "Human Trafficking on the Rise in Afghanistan Despite New Laws. *Thomson Reuters*, 29 March 2018. https://www.reuters.com/article/us-afghanistan-humantrafficking-laws/human-trafficking-on-the-rise-in-afghanistan-despite-new-laws-idUSKBN1H52U8

Gallagher, T. Anne. 2017. What's Wrong with the Global Slavery Index? *Anti-Trafficking Review* (8): 90–112.

General Assembly. 2012. RES/66/290. Follow-up to Paragraph 143 on Human Security of the 2005 World Summit Outcome, Distr.: General 25 October 2012, Sixty-Sixth Session Agenda Items 14 and 117.

Global Protection Cluster. 2017. Anti-Trafficking in Humanitarian Action. *Global Protection Cluster*, 21 July 2017. http://www.globalprotectioncluster.org/_assets/files/about_us/tors/gpc-task-team-anti-trafficking-tors.pdf

Global Slavery Index. 2018. *Global Findings*. https://www.globalslaveryindex.org/2018/findings/global-findings/

Goldstein, Joseph. 2015. US Soldiers Told to Ignor Sexual Abuse of Boys by Afghan Allies. *The New York Times*, 20 September 2015. https://www.nytimes.com/2015/09/21/world/asia/us-soldiers-told-to-ignore-afghan-allies-abuse-of-boys.html

Guterres, Antonio. 2019. Security Council. Security Council Adopts Resolution Calling Upon Belligerents Worldwide to Adopt Concrete Commitments on Ending Sexual Violence in Conflict, Press Release, SC/13790, 8514th Meeting, 23 April 2019. https://www.un.org/press/en/2019/sc13790.doc.htm

Hill, Steven, and Andreea Manea. 2018. Protection of Civilians: A NATO Perspective. *Utrecht Journal of International and European Law* 34 (2): 146–160.

Hogg, Lata Charu. 2018. Strengthening Responses on Child Protection: The CAAC Framework, Open Publications, 2(3), July 2018. https://www.act.nato.int/images/stories/media/doclibrary/open201803-caac.pdf

ICRC. 1977. *Protocol Additional to the Geneva Conventions of 12 August 1949, and Relating to the Protection of Victims of Non-International Armed Conflicts (Protocol II)*, 8 June 1977, 1125 UNTS 609, Article 4(2)(f).

———. 2016. Strengthening Compliance with International Humanitarian Law: The Work of the ICRC and the Swiss Government. ICRC, 22 July 2016. https://www.icrc.org/en/document/strengthening-compliance-international-humanitarian-law-ihl-work-icrc-and-swiss-government

ICRC, Customary IHL Database. 2007. Rule 93. https://ihl-databases.icrc.org/customary-ihl/eng/docs/v1_rul_rule93#Fn_B4BD78DB_00022,

International Committee of the Red Cross (ICRC). 1949. *Geneva Convention Relative to the Treatment of Prisoners of War (Third Geneva Convention)*, 12 August 1949, 75 UNTS 135, Article 3.

International Organisation for Migration (IOM). 2015. Addressing Human Trafficking and Exploitation in Times of Crisis, Evidence and Recommendations for Further Actions to Protect Vulnerable and Mobile Populations, Geneva, Switzerland, December 2015. https://publications.iom.int/books/addressing-human-trafficking-and-exploitation-times-crisis-evidence-and-recommendations-0

———. 2018. Afghanistan Launches National Referral Mechanism and Online Database to Combat Human Trafficking. *IOM*, 18 December 2018. https://www.iom.int/news/afghanistan-launches-national-referral-mechanism-and-online-database-combat-human-trafficking

Lee-Koo, Katrina. 2019. 'The Intolerable Impact of Armed Conflict on Children': The United Nations Security Council and the Protection of Children in Armed Conflict. In *Children and the Responsibility to Protect*, ed. Bina D'Costa and Luke Glanville. Boston: Brill Nijhoff.

Mazurana, Dyan, Angela Raven-Roberts, and Jane Parpart, eds. 2005. *Gender Conflict and Peace Keeping*. Lanham: Rowman & Littlefield.

Mendelson, E. Sarah. 2005. *Barracks and Brothels: Peacekeepers and Human Trafficking in the Balkans*. Washington, DC: The CIS Press.

NATO. 2014. Wales Summit Declaration, Issued by the Heads of State and Government Participating in the Meeting of the North Atlantic Council in Wales, Issued 05 September 2014. https://www.nato.int/cps/en/natohq/official_texts_112964.htm#unscr1612

———. 2016. NATO and Children in Armed Conflict: Fact Sheet, NATO, July 2016. https://www.nato.int/nato_static_fl2014/assets/pdf/pdf_2016_10/20161018_1610-children-armed-conflict-en.pdf,

———. 2017. NATO Parliamentary Assembly Resolution 438 On Supporting The Afghan National Defense And Security Forces. https://www.nato-pa.int/download-file?filename=sites/default/files/2017-10/2017%20-%20%20RESOLUTION%20438%20-%20AFGHANISTAN%20-%20DAY%20-%20%20216%20DSC%2017%20E.pdf

NATO Standardised Office. 2015. Allied Joint Doctrine for the Military Contribution to Stabilization and Reconstruction, NATO STANDARD AJP-3.4.5, Edition A Version 1. https://assets.publishing.service.gov.uk/government/uploads/system/uploads/attachment_data/file/625763/doctrine_nato_stabilization_reconstruction_ajp_3_4_5.pdf

NATO/EAPC. 2018. Women, Peace and Security Policy and Action Plan. https://www.nato.int/nato_static_fl2014/assets/pdf/pdf_2018_09/20180920_180920-WPS-Action-Plan-2018.pdf

NATOa. 2004. NATO Policy on Combating Trafficking in Human Beings, Policy Document, 29 June 2004. https://www.nato.int/docu/comm/2004/06-istanbul/docu-traffic.htm

NATOb. 2004. NATO Guidelines on Combating Trafficking in Human Beings for Military Forces and Civilian Personnel Deployed in NATO-led Operations, Policy Document, 9 July 2004. https://www.nato.int/docu/comm/2004/06-istanbul/docu-traffic-app1.htm,

Obokata, Tom. 2005. Trafficking of Human Beings as a Crime against Humanity: Some Implications for the International Legal System. *The International and Comparative Law Quarterly*, 54(2) (April, 2005): 445–457.

Office for the Coordination of Humanitarian Affairs (OCHA). 2009. Human Security in Theory and Practice Application of the Human Security Concept and the United Nations Trust Fund for Human Security. https://www.unocha.org/sites/dms/HSU/Publications%20and%20Products/Human%20Security%20Tools/Human%20Security%20in%20Theory%20and%20Practice%20English.pdf,

Rulac. 2019. Non International Armed Conflicts in Afghanistan. http://www.rulac.org/browse/conflicts/non-international-armed-conflicts-in-afghanistan

Security Council resolution 2331. 2016. [On trafficking in persons in armed conflicts] Adopted Unanimously, 7847th Meeting: Issued in: Resolutions and decisions of the Security Council, 1 August 2016–31 July 2017 – S/INF/72 – (SCOR, 72nd year).

Sheehan, Rosemary, Helen Rhoades, and Nicky Stanley, eds. 2012. *Vulnerable Children and the Law: International Evidence for Improving Child Welfare, Child Protection and Children's Rights*, 41–59. London and Philadelphia: Jessica Kingsley Publishers.

Smith, Charles Anthony, and Brandon Miller-De La Cuesta. 2011. Human Trafficking in Conflict Zones: The Role of Peacekeepers in the Formation of Networks. *Human Rights Review* 12 (3): 287–299.

Spitka, Timea. 2019. Children on the Front Lines: Responsibility to Protect in the Israeli/Palestinian Conflict. In *Children and the Responsibility to Protect*, ed. Bina D'Costa and Glanville Luke, 183–210. Leidn, Boston: Brill Nijhoff.

The Guardian. 2019. The Guardian View on Afghanistan: War and Peace Talks. *The Guardian*, 30 July 2019. https://www.theguardian.com/commentisfree/2019/jul/30/the-guardian-view-on-afghanistan-war-and-peace-talks

The Inter-Agency Coordination Group against Trafficking in Persons. 2017. The Gender Dimensions of Human Trafficking, Issue 04, 09/2017. http://icat.network/sites/default/files/publications/documents/ICAT-IB-04-V.1.pdf

Thoms, N. T. Oskar, and Ron, James. 2007. Do Human Rights Violations Cause Internal Conflict? *Human Rights Quarterly*, 29(3) (August, 2007): 674–705.

UN Commission on Human Security. 2003. *Human Security Now,* New York.

UN General Assembly. 1989. *Convention on the Rights of the Child*, 20 November 1989, United Nations, Treaty Series, vol. 1577.

———. 2000. *Protocol to Prevent, Suppress and Punish Trafficking in Persons, Especially Women and Children, Supplementing the United Nations Convention Against Transnational Organized Crime*, 15 November 2000. https://www.refworld.org/docid/4720706c0.html

United Nations. 2002. Women, Peace and Security Study submitted by the Secretary-General pursuant to Security Council resolution 1325 (2000), United Nations Publication. https://www.un.org/ruleoflaw/files/women-peaceandsecurity.pdf

———. 2018. Report of the Secretary General on Conflict-Related Sexual Violence, 16 April 2018. https://www.un.org/sexualviolenceinconflict/wp-content/uploads/reports/sg-reports/SG-REPORT-2017-CRSV-SPREAD.pdf

United Nations Office on Drugs and Crime. 2018. Global Report on Trafficking in Persons – in the Context of Armed Conflict, United Nations, Austria Vienna.

United Nations Regional Information Centre for Western Europe. 2014. The Dancing Boys of Afghanistan. https://www.unric.org/en/latest-un-buzz/29091-thedancing-boys-of-afghanistan

United Nations Security Council. 2015. Report of the Secretary General on Children and Armed Conflict in Afghanistan, S/2015/336, 15 May 2015. https://www.undocs.org/S/2015/336

———. 2018. Report of the Secretary General on Trafficking in Persons in Armed Conflict Pursuant to Security Council Resolution 2388 (2017), S/2018/1042, 21 November 2018. https://www.un.org/sc/ctc/wp-content/uploads/2018/11/N1833923_EN.pdf

United States Department of Labor. 2018. 2017 Findings on the Worst Forms of Child Labor – Afghanistan, 20 September 2018. https://www.refworld.org/docid/5bd05a9e0.html

United States Department of State. 2018. Trafficking in Persons Report – Afghanistan, 28 June 2018. https://www.refworld.org/docid/5b3e0bc5a.html

———. 2019. Trafficking in Persons Report – Afghanistan, 20 June 2019. https://www.state.gov/reports/2019-trafficking-in-persons-report-2/afghanistan/

Walter, B. 2016. The Securitization of Development and Humans' Insecurity in Nangarhar Province, Afghanistan, Global Change, Peace & Security, 28:3, 271–287, pg. 285.

Yerman, G. Marcia. 2012. The Dancing Boys of Afghanistan Examines Sexual Abuse in Afghanistan, The Huffington Post, 2 August 2012. https://www.huffpost.com/entry/the-dancing-boys-of-afghanistan_b_1260667

Olivia Iannelli is a research analyst at Trilateral Research; she holds an LLM in International Human Rights and Humanitarian Law and her expertise lies in Human Trafficking, Children's Rights and Conflict. She has worked for a variety of human rights organisations both in the UK and abroad, including Amnesty International, the Council for At-Risk Academics and Leaders of Tomorrow in Jordan. She also volunteers for Every Child Protected Against Trafficking (ECPAT UK).

13

How Definitions of 'Child Soldiers' Exclude Girls from Demobilisation Efforts

Ally Dunhill and Alicia Kidd

Introduction

Historically, children have been used by states' military forces and armed groups during times of conflict in mostly supportive roles (Embacher et al. 2013). Currently, children in these situations are often referred to as 'child soldiers' and are used in increasing numbers by armed forces and groups in both supportive and combatant roles (United Nations (UN) Security Council 2015). According to Honwana (2006) and Singer (2006), this is largely due to the development and availability of small, light weapons that children can carry and use easily. While it is difficult to ascertain the accurate numbers of 'child soldiers', an estimated 250,000 to 300,000 children and adolescents are involved in armed forces or armed groups around the globe (International Organization for Migration (IOM) 2019), and at least 46 states continue to recruit children under the age of 18 into their armed forces (*Ibid.*). This has become a major

A. Dunhill (✉) • A. Kidd
Wilberforce Institute, University of Hull, Hull, UK
e-mail: alicia.kidd@hull.ac.uk

J. Muraszkiewicz et al. (eds.), *Human Trafficking in Conflict*, Crime Prevention and Security Management, https://doi.org/10.1007/978-3-030-40838-1_13

concern across the world. The UN (2015), through Sustainable Development Goal 8 (SDG8), has called on states to "eradicate [the] recruitment and use of child soldiers … by 2025."

This chapter explores the treatment of children once they have left armed forces and armed groups by focusing on how the remit and outcomes of disarmament, demobilisation and reintegration (DDR) programmes affect these children. The chapter provides an exploration of how girls are overlooked in definitions of 'child soldiers' and highlights the harmful consequences of this. Using examples of DDR programmes, we analyse how children are identified and recruited into such initiatives. We contemplate whether children's experiences as being part of armed forces (belonging to a state) and armed groups (not under the clear control of a state authority) are adequately considered, and whether the gendered treatment in these programmes is conducive to long-term recovery and reintegration into civilian communities. Building on existing literature on female 'child soldiers', the chapter highlights the requirement for further research and concludes with recommendations for more effective and inclusive efforts for female children associated with armed forces or armed groups.

Definitions

The term 'child soldiers' is commonly used by agencies working with children in this context (Wessells 2019). However, there is disagreement over the appropriateness of the term. The United Nations International Children's Emergency Fund (UNICEF) Paris Principles (guidelines for realisation and implementation) and Paris Commitments (political agreement), were adopted in 2007 by UNICEF and States attending the 'Free Children from War' conference organised by France and UNICEF (France Diplomatie 2017). According to UNICEF (2017), 105 countries have endorsed the Paris Principles and Paris Commitments. The objectives of the Paris Principles and Paris Commitments are:

> [preventing] the recruitment of children … gaining the release of children who have been recruited … trying to bring legal sanctions against those

> responsible for recruiting children … and making efforts for effective reintegration programmes for children who have been participants in conflict" (Burchill 2019, no pagination).

Rather than using the term 'child soldiers', the *Paris Principles and Paris Commitments* (UNICEF 2007) use 'children associated with armed forces or armed groups.' According to research by Wessells (2019, 11), the labelling of children as 'child soldiers' focuses on the negative experiences of the child and "can increase stigma and social isolation." From this perspective, the use of such a term can invalidate the child as equally having the right to protection and to participate in all discussions and decisions that will impact them, as is stated in the UN Convention on the Rights of the Child (CRC) (UN 1989). Moreover, notions of 'child soldiers' are often used synonymously with frontline combatants. This is a limited understanding and overlooks a large proportion of children associated with armed forces and armed groups who are not recruited to fight. A generally accepted definition of 'child soldiers' that does not limit inclusion in this way is:

> any person under 18 years of age who is part of any kind of regular or irregular armed force in any capacity, including but not limited to cooks, porters, messengers, and those accompanying such groups, other than purely as family members. It includes girls recruited for sexual purposes and forced marriage. It does not, therefore, only refer to a child who is carrying or has carried arms (UNICEF 1997, 1).

It is this, inclusive, definition of 'child soldiers' that we acknowledge throughout this chapter, ensuring that all children associated with armed forces or armed groups, regardless of the role they play, are recognised as being in need of support. However, it must be recognised that in practice, regardless of this generally accepted definition, the term 'child soldiers' is commonly used purely in reference to child combatants. Further attention is paid to this problem in Recommendation One later in the chapter.

It is also important to note here that the definition above includes all children regardless of whether they were abducted and forced to join the armed forces or armed groups or whether they 'volunteered'. In the majority of cases, children are abducted and forcibly recruited (ICRC 2016; Becker 2017). This often leads them to be understood with a sense of "innocence and passivity" (Wells 2015, 181) whereby they had no agency over their situation. However, children "complicate … conceptions of childhood" (Wells 2015, 181) when they 'volunteer' into armed forces or armed groups. According to Wells, children volunteer:

> to escape poverty, to secure protection, to enact revenge and for political or ideological reasons … War increases the likelihood of children being separated from their parents and this makes them vulnerable to abduction, but can also make the army seem like a safe space; in a situation of conflict children argue (not unreasonably) that it is better to be a soldier with a gun than a civilian being threatened by a soldier with a gun (2015, 170).

While some children may indeed 'volunteer', it is important to consider the context in which they make such choices. Living in an area in which conflict is rife and resources are scarce, choosing to join a group with power and which will offer food, shelter and accommodation may seem like a good decision. However, agency in this sense is constrained by the conflict; it is not an autonomous choice but one limited by a lack of legitimate options (see Wells 2015, 2–3). Importantly, if the victim is under 18, the method through which they are trafficked is irrelevant in meeting the definition of trafficking, as is the case for 'child soldiers'. As such, regardless of their method of recruitment, 'child soldiers' should not be understood as willing, active participants in armed conflict, but as victims of human trafficking. According to the Palermo Protocol:

> 'Trafficking in persons' shall mean the recruitment, transportation, transfer, harbouring or receipt of persons, by means of the threat or use of force or other forms of coercion, of abduction, of fraud, of deception, of the abuse of power or of a position of vulnerability or of the giving or receiving of payments or benefits to achieve the consent of a person having control over another person, for the purpose of exploitation. Exploitation shall include, at a minimum, the exploitation of the prostitution of others or other forms of sexual exploitation, forced labour or services, slavery, servitude, or the removal of organs (UN General Assembly 2000, 2).

To summarise, the term 'child soldiers' refers to anyone under age 18 who plays any role in an armed force or armed group. This is regardless of whether they have a weapon, and regardless of the reasons they joined. They should be recognised as victims of human trafficking as opposed to voluntary contributors to violence.

Female 'Child Soldiers'

The majority of 'child soldiers' are boys; however, girls constitute a significant proportion (Machel 2001; Olsson and Aubert 2018). According to Becker (2017, 113), "in some conflicts, girls make up 30% or more of children recruited into armed groups or forces." However, much of the literature focuses on the experience of boys, and little attention has been paid to the roles and experiences of girls (Mazurana et al. 2002). A report published in 2002 (Mazurana et al.) stated that between 1990 and 2002, girls were present in fighting forces and groups in 54 countries, and their numbers are significant. Therefore, it is questionable as to why they have been so overlooked in the literature. According to Denov (2007, ii) "whether in the heat of conflict or within post-war programming, girls are, for the most part, rendered invisible and marginalized."

Whether they choose to join or are abducted, girls are more vulnerable to sexual exploitation and abuse (UN Security Council 2015). According to Wells (2015, 174), research on female 'child soldiers' has identified that "almost all girls associated with fighting forces in any way—regardless of whether or not they volunteered—report wide-spread sexual violence." Yet the role that children play in a fighting force or group is not always influenced by gender. Thompson exemplifies Liberia and Uganda where most girls were victims of sexual violence, and most boys were used as fighters, but some girls were combatants and some boys were held in sexual servitude (Thompson 1999).

While a significant proportion of the literature on female 'child soldiers' focuses on their roles as 'wives' and their experiences of being sexually exploited by armed forces or armed groups (David 1998; Mazurana et al. 2002; Watchlist 2003; McKay and Mazurana 2004), there is also plenty of evidence that they undertake other roles, including as combatants, porters and cooks (Thompson 1999; McKay and Mazurana 2004; Becker 2017). Often, girls will play more than one role, acting as both fighter and 'wife,' for example. To refer back to the definition, any child under 18 who is part of an armed force or armed group in any capacity is a 'child soldier'. As such, no child associated with armed forces or armed groups should be disregarded as a 'child soldier' based on their gender or the role they undertake.

Disarmament, Demobilisation and Reintegration (DDR) Programmes

DDR programmes exist to encourage soldiers to give up their weapons, to take them out of service, and to resettle them into civilian society. "Formal demobilization, including for child soldiers, usually follows a peace agreement ... Informal occasions include instances where child soldiers escape from or are released by their armed group" (Verhey 2001, 6).

DDR programmes aim to create stability, re-establish security and create the conditions needed for peace. They are aimed at everyone who was involved in armed forces or armed groups, regardless of their role (UNDDR 2019). While the services available in each DDR programme will differ, according to the UN Integrated DDR Standards, all programmes should follow five general principles. They should be: people-centred; flexible, accountable and transparent; nationally owned; integrated; and well planned (Bowd and Özerdem 2013, 456). There is also an expectation that DDR programmes "will prevent further conflict by effectively reintegrating former soldiers into civilian life" (Wells 2015, 180).

While the disarmament and demobilisation aspects of DDR programmes are somewhat self-explanatory, the reintegration of former soldiers is a much more nuanced part of the process, and successful reintegration is problematic to assess. Child reintegration refers to "the process through which children transition into civil society and enter meaningful roles and identities as civilians who are accepted by their families and communities in a context of local and national reconciliation" (UNICEF 2007, 7).

Of course, what is considered 'meaningful' is open to interpretation, and any form of reintegration after an experience as a 'child soldier' is going to have barriers, especially when they are an afterthought in the DDR process. According to Wells (2015, 180), "in the mid-1990s in its first attempt to resolve the conflict in Sierra Leone, the UN made US $34 million available for disarming, demobilizing and reintegrating soldiers; less than $1 million of this was for child soldiers". Bowd and Özerdem (2013, 455) have identified five obstacles to successful reintegration: a lack of confidence and trust, a share in natural resources, access to employment opportunities and land, risk of being involved in criminal activities, and the community's perception of mistrust and insecurity. Further, Newman (2014) identifies some of the consequences when reintegration fails: children are prone to neglect and abuse, they are isolated, and they risk passing these challenges onto the next generation. It is important then that DDR programmes consider these potential barriers in order to ensure the outcomes of the programmes are successful and do not contribute to an endless cycle of struggle that is passed on through the generations (for further information on the impact on future generations, see Newman 2014).

Girls in DDR Programmes

Gender-Specific Needs

Being in an armed force or armed group has physical and psychological effects on 'child soldiers'. Their gender, background, role and duties in the armed forces or armed groups, and the force that they were associated with, will all impact upon their experiences, affecting each child differently. Girls are recruited by armed forces and armed groups to undertake numerous roles. However, many suffer sexual exploitation or are taken as 'wives' by commanders (David 1998; Mazurana et al. 2002; Watchlist 2003; McKay and Mazurana 2004). Therefore, their physical and psychological needs post-conflict are different from boys. Girls who were released or escaped from armed forces or armed groups will have experienced a range of gender and age-related mistreatments. These include:

- The physical and psychological impacts of rape. "In the aftermath of sexual assault, girls experience shock, loss of dignity, shame, low self-esteem, poor concentration and memory, persistent nightmares, depression, and other posttraumatic stress effects" (Mazurana et al. 2002, 115). After sexual assault, girls have been shown to withdraw, while boys respond with aggression (*Ibid.*).
- Having a higher risk of pregnancies, STIs and complications in childbirth (McKay 1998).
- If a girl does become pregnant, she is likely to have no say over whether to keep the baby. She may experience a forced (or 'voluntary') abortion or may have to birth a child which she may deem a constant reminder of her abuse (Peters 2005). Alternatively, she may love and care for the child, but caring for and feeding a baby as a 'child soldier' always on the move, when the mother is likely to be malnourished herself, is a problem in itself (World Health Organisation 2009).
- Having to deal with menstruation. While many 'child soldiers' will suffer malnutrition, this has a specific impact on girls when they become so malnourished that their menses stop (United Nations Population Fund 2019).

The Oversight of Female 'Child Soldiers' by DDR Programmes

UNICEF and NGOs (non-governmental organisations) have established rehabilitation programmes in many countries to provide former 'child soldiers' with medical care and counselling, assist them in locating their families, and provide education or vocational training. But many former 'child soldiers' never benefit from this assistance, while others need more help than the programmes are able to provide (Becker 2017, 113).

UN Security Council Resolutions 1325 (UN Security Council 2000) and 1820 (UN Security Council 2008) specifically include girls and call for their protection and participation in peace processes. Additionally, the Optional Protocol to the Convention on the Rights of the Child (IOM 2019) affirms that "States shall demobilize children under the age of 18 recruited or used in hostilities and provide physical and psychological recovery services and assist their social reintegration." However, this has not been the case. Girls have been almost 'invisible' as they have not been considered when the DDR programmes have been planned (Denov 2007; Salah 2005). According to the Democratic Progress Institute (2015) and Dharmapuri (2017), girls and women are overlooked due to 'gender blindness', where the design focus of the DDR programmes is on male combatants; the role that females play within armed forces or armed groups is often regarded as non-threatening to the peace process. Those girls that do enter DDR programmes often report poor conditions and situations that were clearly not developed with girls in mind. For example, housing girls who were sexually exploited as part of their 'child soldier' experience in centres with a predominantly adult male population is not conducive to an atmosphere of safety and trust. Housing children and adults together also fails to separate demobilised 'child soldiers' from military authority and puts children, regardless of gender, at risk of retribution, re-recruitment or further abuse (Verhey 2001).

For over a decade, professionals working in conflict areas have been raising concerns regarding the low number of DDR programmes being accessed by girls (Olsson and Aubert 2018). Research carried out in the Democratic Republic of Congo (DRC) in 2016, based on interviews with 150 former female 'child soldiers', found that most girls leave or escape armed forces and armed groups by themselves and therefore do not participate in any DDR programmes (Child Soldiers International 2016). Below, we outline a range of reasons why girls are excluded from DDR programmes—both by the programmes and of the girls' own accord.

Girls are Often Not a Priority for DDR Programmes

"Armed, adult male fighters [were] the near exclusive priority for most [DDR] programs, significantly marginalizing all children, but girls in particular" (Mazurana et al. 2002, 116). According to Wells (2015, 180), DDR programmes continue to "marginalize ex-combatants—girls and young children—who are not seen as a security threat." In her research, Wells (2015) identified that boys were more likely to be on a DDR programme than girls. She found that in the DRC "only 23 girls as compared to 1718 boys were demobilized by four international NGOs" (2015, 162). However, according to McKay (2006) (cited in Wells 2015), the number of girls and boys recruited or abducted into the armed forces and armed groups were comparable. This point supports Denov's (2007) comment that girls have been 'invisible or marginalised' not only as 'child soldiers' but within DDR programmes. The numbers of girls recruited into armed forces and armed groups and the roles they play is not proportionate or comparable to the number of opportunities they have to access DDR programmes. Therefore, it can be assumed that girls are not a priority for DDR programmes.

McKay and Mazurana (2004) exemplify a DDR programme established in Sierra Leone in 1999. One of the requirements for acceptance into the programme was to answer a number of questions on how to assemble and disassemble a gun. While, officially, knowledge or possession of arms was not required for a child (under 18) to be accepted into the programme, there was much discrepancy in reports as to whether or not this was the case. The confusion surrounding this meant that many girls believed they were ineligible because they did not have a weapon. This clearly has a fundamental impact on eligibility for those who were members of the armed forces or armed groups but acting in auxiliary roles and therefore did not hold, or have knowledge on how to use, a weapon.

Female 'Child Soldiers' Who Become Child Mothers

Female 'child soldiers' who become mothers are often marginalised (Burman and McKay 2007). Newman (2014) undertook research with Ugandan child mothers who had returned to civilian communities after being abducted by the Lord's Resistance Army to be 'child soldiers'. However, of those girls that passed through formal reception centres after leaving the armed forces, none were provided with counselling, despite their high rates of trauma and the fact that they were children who had borne children and, therefore, victims of rape. While these girls stated that they wanted an education, they were unable to access one because they had to prioritise the needs of their own children, leaving them without the time, money or opportunity to be able to receive this education. Newman describes how some of these girls were not registered as ex-combatants, but rather as child-mothers, meaning that their experiences as 'child soldiers' were ignored.

If given the option, children may be reluctant to leave the armed forces or armed groups for various reasons. One of the main reasons being having no family to return to (often as a result of war), or not knowing the location of their family. Many fear rejection from their communities after being 'child soldiers'. "Their families and home communities may be unwilling to accept them, particularly if they committed atrocities" (Becker 2017, 113, also discussed by Verhey 2001; UN Department of Economic and Social Affairs 2005).

Making Female 'Child Soldiers' Invisible

Armed forces do not want there to be any evidence of them having used girls in their fighting forces (McKay and Mazurana 2004), which is another reason for their exclusion from DDR programmes. Further, armed groups often "consider the females in their ranks property rather than combatants" and these groups then do not admit to having them in their group (Olsson and Aubert 2018, 3). It is clear then that there are many reasons as to why female 'child soldiers' may not partake in DDR programmes. Exclusion may be on the part of the DDR programme, but there is also the possibility that girls choose not to partake in these programmes. As such, echoing McKay and Mazurana (2004), a level of support needs to be built into communities to ensure that there is some degree of care provided to girls returning to them, even if they bypass DDR programmes for any reason. The rejection of girls and women during DDR programmes is documented in the UN Department of Economic and Social Affairs (2005) *World Youth Report* which emphasises how this rejection leads to a lack of physical, economic and emotional support once the conflict has ended. They are left with limited options, which pushes many to remain with their captors, pushed into early marriage or prostitution, or vulnerable to the offers of traffickers. As such, a lack of support after demobilisation locks many girls into an inescapable cycle of exploitation.

Returning to the Community

According to Olsson and Aubert (2018, 2), when former female 'child soldiers' in the DRC were interviewed about their experiences, "it was not the hunger, rape or other horrific experiences of being part of an armed group that caused the most distress to the girls, but the reactions they faced when they got home." Therefore, for these children, the impact of war does not end in their recruitment to the armed forces or groups but continues for the rest of their lives as their pre-war societal connections break down.

"For girl soldiers, return to their home communities is particularly difficult because they suffer additional stigma due to presumed sexual exploitation and may have young children to support" (Becker 2017, 113; see also Kiconco 2019). Some families do not believe that the child was forced into a relationship and consider her a traitor (Newman 2014). This is especially the case if the girl has given birth to children fathered by commanders—children that the family may refuse to accept as related (Mazurana et al. 2002; McKay and Mazurana 2004). In fact, the experiences of girls on return to their families can be so extreme that "in many cases it is easier for a boy to be accepted after amputating the hands of villagers than it is for a girl to be accepted after being the victim of rape" (Shepler 2002, quoted in McKay and Mazurana 2004, 37).

According to Wessells (2019), young mothers who had children while with the armed forces or armed groups reported that they were under constant scrutiny by their community when they returned. These mothers may still be children themselves, but many say that once they have returned, they have no one to look after them and are considered a burden to relatives. "Economically, women are often forced into poorly paid and unprotected work, or into domestic duties, during and after conflicts. This reinforces perceptions of dependence on males" (Ziebell and Goetz 2003, no pagination). If female 'child soldiers' are returning to families that reject them, then they have no one on whom to depend. If there is a culture of dependence on males, this then leaves them with little option but to return to the men who were exploiting them.

Furthermore, "[f]or some girls, belonging to an illegal armed group gives them a sense of power and control that they may not otherwise experience living in a relatively conservative, 'machista' society" (Care

International 2008, 24). This means that returning to civilian communities could feel like a backwards step to girls who lose this sense of power and are socialised into relying on men (War Child 2019). Similarly, because the roles of female 'child soldiers' in armed forces and armed groups are so varied, they are considered highly valuable by such groups and are less likely to be released (*Ibid*). This suggests that it can be difficult for girls to reintegrate into civilian life, where they are often not valued to the same degree, with society dictating that they should rely on men. If their community has rejected them, they are likely to move elsewhere in search of work. With a lack of education and assistance, they can become vulnerable to exploitative offers or, with an absence of alternative options, their only option may be to return to the commanders who were exploiting them (United Nations Organization Stabilization Mission in the Democratic Republic of Congo [MONUSCO] 2015).

Recommendations

We have provided a range of examples of and reasons why female 'child soldiers' are not adequately considered and provided for in DDR programmes. Below, we provide four recommendations for the development of more effective and inclusive efforts going forwards to better assist girls who have been trafficked for use as 'child soldiers'. These recommendations would assist in achieving SDG8 (UN 2015).

Recommendation One

The way in which children are labelled as 'child soldiers' has negative connotations, works contrary to the CRC, and leads to the exclusion of non-fighting children from DDR programmes. When girls predominantly take on non-fighting roles, this can mean that they are disproportionately omitted when DDR programmes are being planned or that they are rejected from attending the programmes. As stated previously, the term 'child soldiers' can escalate "stigma and social isolation" (Wessells 2019, 11). While the term technically includes all children associated with armed forces or groups, regardless of their role, it is often misconstrued to represent only children in fighting roles. Many 'child soldiers'—particularly girls—undertake auxiliary roles in armed forces or armed groups, whereby they may not have access to or training in how to use a weapon. The term 'children associated with armed forces or armed groups' (UNICEF 2007), is less ambiguous than 'child soldiers'. Acknowledging this inclusive definition of 'child soldiers', knowledge or possession of arms should not be a requirement to determine eligibility into DDR programmes. Although the term itself is long to use in practice, it should be adopted by all organisations to ensure the focus is on the child, not the 'soldier'.

Recommendation Two

Every child associated with armed forces or armed groups has unique experiences, depending on their gender and the role they play. Each child should be supported based on his or her particular needs rather than on an understanding of the experiences of 'child soldiers' as presented by adults. Expanding on this, Western notions of childhood may not be suitable to implement on children who have been associated with armed forces or armed groups. Western notions of childhood are historically and culturally specific and are socially constructed (James et al. 2007). Western children are often seen as dependent on adults with no, or very few, responsibilities or duties (Montgomery 2018). However, children from non-western cultures are expected to undertake responsibilities and duties from an early age (Ansell 2017). In view of such differences, former children associated with armed forces or armed groups should be consulted in the development of DDR programmes in order to understand the perspectives of the complex experiences of children from different cultures. This would contribute towards aligning with Article 12 of the CRC (UN 1989): the right of the child to be heard. This level of participation by children could lead to more worthwhile, meaningful and effective DDR programmes for girls.

Recommendation Three

Even with the best efforts of DDR programmes to recruit girls, there will always be some that bypass these programmes for any number of reasons. As advocated by McKay and Mazurana (2004), a level of support needs to be built into the communities that these girls will return to. This includes medical support that may evidently be required, but also financial and psychological support to enable them to restart their lives after having been exploited as victims of trafficking. Receiving support in their communities may also help to tackle some of the ongoing problems facing returnee girls who must support themselves (and often their children born due to their trafficking experience) in a time of post-conflict which often equates to insecurity and a lack of economic opportunities.

Recommendation Four

DDR programmes should recognise that females are part of armed forces and armed groups and should not be excluded from support simply because of their gender. However, the specific needs of girls and women must be recognised within the programmes in order to make them safe and helpful to females. According to Wessells (2019, 5), "By not addressing sexual violence and its distinctive stigma directly, reintegration programmes quietly discriminate against girls and women." Organisers should acknowledge the specific medical, physical and psychological needs of girls who have been exploited as 'child soldiers'. While some of these needs may be similar to the needs of boys, there are gender-specific requirements that are important for girls, including access to menstrual products. Equally, the impact of sexual assault will play out differently, and attention must be paid to the risks of STIs, pregnancies, births and abortions. In addition to the recommendations regarding practice, we hope that this chapter will bring about further research on the experiences of female children associated with armed forces or armed groups and lead to DDR programmes that meet their specific needs.

Conclusion

Governments continue to fail to protect their children from recruitment into armed forces and armed groups, yet simultaneously overlook the experiences of large proportions of those who were exploited by these forces—predominantly girls. In failing to prevent these children being trafficked into becoming 'child soldiers', they are allowing them to be abused for a significant proportion of time; the time in which they will also be developing most rapidly both physically and psychologically. This failure, coupled with the failure to identify female children associated with armed forces or armed groups and offer them the necessary support they need as part of DDR programmes, means that governments are complicit in the continued exploitation of girls over time. This spans from their recruitment into the armed force or armed group to the lack of support received on demobilisation. The lack of support leads to poverty and insecurity which, in turn, has the potential to increase the risk of girls becoming victims of human trafficking. This failure of governments then makes girls vulnerable to entering a continuous and inescapable cycle of exploitation.

References

Ansell, Nicola. 2017. *Children, Youth and Development*. 2nd ed. Abingdon: Routledge.

Becker, Jo. 2017. *Campaigning for Children. Strategies for Advancing Children's Rights*. California: Stanford University Press.

Bowd, Richard, and Alpaslan Özerdem. 2013. How to Assess Social Reintegration of Ex-Combatants. *Journal of Intervention and Statebuilding* 7 (4): 453–475. https://doi.org/10.1080/17502977.2012.727537.

Burchill, Richard. 2019. Protecting Children in Armed Conflict. Insight, TRENDS Research Advisory. April 17, 2019. http://trendsinstitution.org/protecting-children-in-armed-conflict/

Burman, Mary, and Susan McKay. 2007. Marginalization of Girl Mothers During Reintegration from Armed Groups in Sierra Leone. *International Nursing Review* 54 (4): 316–323.

Care International. 2008. *Overcoming Lost Childhoods – Lessons Learned from the Rehabilitation and Reintegration of Former Child Soldiers in Colombia*. London: Care International.

Child Soldiers International. 2016. What the Girls Say: Improving Practices for the Demobilization and Reintegration of Girls in DRC. https://www.child-soldiers.org/Handlers/Download.ashx?IDMF=e57e9cb2-cd70-4dc2-8681-e29bc6f3622b

David, Kelly. 1998. *The Disarmament, Demobilisation and Reintegration of Child Soldiers in Liberia. 1994–1997. The Process and Lessons Learned*. New York: UNICEF.

Democratic Progress Institute. 2015. *DDR and Former Female Combatants*. London: Democratic Progress Institute.

Denov, Myriam. 2007. *Girls in Fighting Forces: Moving Beyond Victimhood*. Canadian International Development Agency (CIDA). https://gsdrc.org/document-library/girls-in-fighting-forces-moving-beyond-victimhood/

Dharmapuri, Sahana. 2017. Back to Basics: Gender Blindness Negativity Impacts Security. *Our Secure Future*. https://oursecurefuture.org/blog/back-basics-gender-blindness-negatively-impacts-security

Embacher, Helga, Gratzia Prontera, Albert Lichblau, Johannes-Dieter Steinert, Wolfgang Aschauer, Darek Galasinki, and John Buckley, eds. 2013. *Children and War*. Solihull: Helion & Company.

France Diplomatie. 2017. What are the Paris Principles and Paris Commitments? https://www.diplomatie.gouv.fr/en/french-foreign-policy/human-rights/children-s-rights/protecting-children-from-war-conference-21-february-2017/article/what-are-the-paris-principles-and-paris-commitments

Honwana, Alcinda. 2006. *Child Soldiers in Africa*. Philadelphia: University of Pennsylvania Press.

ICRC. 2016. Customary IHL. Rule 136 Recruitment of Child Soldiers. https://ihl-databases.icrc.org/customary-ihl/eng/docs/v1_cha_chapter39

IOM. 2019. Spotlight: Recruitment of Children and Adolescents: Retention as Slow Violence. February–March 2019. https://repository.oim.org.co/bitstream/handle/20.500.11788/2177/33.%20RPR%20Spotlight%20Recruitment%20of%20CHAY_Feb-Mar2019.pdf?sequence=1&isAllowed=y

James, Allison, Chris Jenks, and Alan Prout. 2007. *Theorizing Childhood*. Cambridge: Polity Press.

Kiconco, Allen. 2019. Speaking about violence in Sierra Leone. *Beyond Slavery and Trafficking, OpenDemocracy June* 26, 2019. https://www.opendemocracy.net/en/beyond-trafficking-and-slavery/speaking-about-violence-sierra-leone/

Machel, Gracia. 2001. *The Impact of War on Children*. London: Hurst & Co.
Mazurana, Dyan, Susan McKay, Khristopher Carlson, and Janel Kasper. 2002. Girls in Fighting Forces and Groups: Their Recruitment, Participation, Demobilization, and Reintegration. *Peace and Conflict: Journal of Peace Psychology* 8 (2): 97–123. https://doi.org/10.1207/s15327949pac1003_8.
McKay, Susan. 1998. The Effects of Armed Conflict on Girls and Women. *Peace and Conflict: Journal of Peace Psychology* 4 (4): 381–392.
———. 2006. The Inversion of Girlhood: Girl Combatants During and After Armed Conflict. In *A World Turned Upside Down: The Social Ecologies of Children in Armed Conflict*, ed. Niel Boothby, Allison Strang, and Michael Wessells, 89–109. Bloomfield, CT: Kumarian Press.
McKay, Susan, and Dyan Mazurana. 2004. *Where Are the Girls? Girls in Fighting Forces in Northern Uganda, Sierra Leone and Mozambique: Their Lives During and After War*. Montreal: International Centre for Human Rights and Democratic Development.
Montgomery, Heather. 2018. *Children's Rights and Cultural Relativism*. Bristol: Policy Press.
MONUSCO. 2015. Invisible Survivors. Girls in Armed Groups in the Democratic Republic of Congo. From 2009–2015. https://childrenandarmedconflict.un.org/wp-content/uploads/2015/11/151123-Girls-in-Armed-Groups-2009-2015-Final.pdf
Newman, Carter. 2014. No One to Stand by Us: Reintegrating Formerly Abducted Child-Mothers in Uganda. *Journal of Intervention and Statebuilding* 8 (4): 357–380.
Olsson, Sandra, and V̂eronique Aubert. 2018. Reintegrating Returned Girl Soldiers in the DRC. Africa Programme Meeting Summary. January 25, 2018. London: Chatham House. https://www.chathamhouse.org/event/reintegrating-returned-girl-soldiers-drc
Peters, Lilian. 2005. *War is No Child's Play: Child Soldiers from Battlefield to Playground*. Geneva: Centre for the Democratic Control of Armed Forces.
Salah, Rima. 2005. *The Impact of Conflict on Women and Girls in West and Central Africa and the UNICEF Response*. UNICEF. https://www.unicef.org/publications/index_25262.html
Shepler, Susan. 2002. Les filles-soldats: Trajectoires d'après-guerre en Sierra Leone [Girl soldiers: Post-war trajectories in Sierra Leone]. *Politique Africaine* 4 (88): 49–62.
Singer, Peter Warren. 2006. *Children at War*. Berkley: University of California Press.

Thompson, Carol B. 1999. Beyond Civil Society: Child Soldiers as Citizens in Mozambique. *Review of African Political Economy* 26 (80): 191–206.
UN. 1989. The Convention on the Rights of the Child. https://www.ohchr.org/en/professionalinterest/pages/crc.aspx
———. 2015. Sustainable Development Goals. https://sustainabledevelopment.un.org/sdgs
UN General Assembly. 2000. *Protocol to Prevent, Suppress and Punish Trafficking in Persons, Especially Women and Children, Supplementing the UN Convention Against Transnational Organized Crime* (15 November 2000, Res 55/25). http://www.ohchr.org/EN/ProfessionalInterest/Pages/ProtocolTraffickingInPersons.aspx
UN. Department of Economic and Social Affairs. 2005. *World Youth Report: Young People Today and in 2015*. July 30, 2005, ST/ESA/301. New York: United Nations.
UN. Security Council. 2000. S/RES/1325. https://documents-dds-ny.un.org/doc/UNDOC/GEN/N00/720/18/pdf/N0072018.pdf?OpenElement
———. 2008. Women and Peace and Security. S/RES/1820 (2008). https://www.un.org/ruleoflaw/files/women_peace_security_resolution1820.pdf
———. 2015. Resolution 2225. S/RES/2225(2015). https://undocs.org/S/RES/2225(2015)
UNDDR. 2019. *What is DDR?* http://www.unddr.org/what-is-ddr/introduction_1.aspx
UNICEF. 1997. Cape Town Annotated Principles and Best Practices. April 30, 1997. Cape Town: UNICEF.
———. 2007. The Paris Principles and Guidelines on Children Associated with Armed Forces or Armed Groups. https://www.unicef.org/emerg/files/ParisPrinciples310107English.pdf
———. 2017. At least 65,000 Children Released from Armed Forces and Groups Over the last 10 Years, UNICEF. Press Release, 20 February 2017. https://www.unicef.org/press-releases/least-65000-children-released-armed-forces-and-groups-over-last-10-years-unicef
United Nations Population Fund. 2019. *Menstruation and Human Rights – Frequently Asked Questions*. https://www.unfpa.org/menstruationfaq
Verhey, Beth. 2001. Child Soldiers: Preventing, Demobilizing and Reintegrating. *Africa Region Working Paper Series,* 23: 1–31. http://web.worldbank.org/archive/website00523/WEB/PDF/CHILD_SO.PDF
War Child. 2019. Rethink Child Soldiers. In *A New Approach to the Integration of All Children Associated with Armed Forces and Groups*. London: War Child.

Watchlist. 2003. *The Impact of Armed Conflict on Children in the Democratic Republic of Congo (DRC)*. New York: Watchlist.
Wells, Karen. 2015. *Childhood in a Global Perspective*. 2nd ed. Cambridge: Polity Press.
Wessells, Michael. 2019. Do No Harm: How Reintegration Programmes for Former Child Soldiers Can Cause Unintended Harm. In *Research Handbook on Child Soldiers*, ed. Mark A. Drumbl and Jastine C. Barrett. Washington: Edward Elgar.
World Health Organisation. 2009. Healing Child Soldiers. *Bulletin of the World Health Organization*, 87(5): 325–404. https://www.who.int/bulletin/volumes/87/5/09-020509/en/
Ziebell, Stephanie, and Anne Marie Goetz. 2003. *Gender-Aware Disarmament, Demobilization and Reintegration (DDR): A Checklist*. New York: UNIFEM.

Ally Dunhill is an independent researcher and consultant, focusing on the human rights of children. She is Honorary Fellow of the Wilberforce Institute in Hull, Non-Resident Fellow of TRENDS Research & Advisory in the UAE and Visiting Researcher at the Energy and Environment Institute at the University of Hull.

Alicia Kidd is a postdoctoral researcher at the Wilberforce Institute, part of the University of Hull. Her PhD focused on identifying the links between conflict and contemporary slavery, and she continues to undertake research on exploitation, human trafficking and 'modern slavery.' Alicia also works with practitioners through her role as Vice Chair of the Humber Modern Slavery Partnership.

14

The Role of Regional Organizations in Addressing Human Trafficking in Conflict: The Cases of NATO and the EU

Lucas J. Ruiz-Díaz

Introduction

The challenges of irregular migration and human trafficking are both directly and indirectly relevant to multilateral peace operations. They are directly relevant because a mission may be confronted with the task of protecting displaced populations or because human trafficking may support spoilers to evade a peace process. They are indirectly relevant because irregular migration or human trafficking may increase demands on scarce state resources in an already weak state or fuel a conflict in other ways and, as such, decrease the effectiveness of a peace operation (Van der Lijn 2019, 3).

I would like to thank the reviewer of this chapter and the coordinator of the book for their valuable comments, which contributed to the improvement of the original draft.

This chapter presents some of the findings from my postdoctoral research stay at the Institute for European Studies of the Vrije Universiteit Brussel (IES, VUB) during the academic year 2017–2018.

L. J. Ruiz-Díaz (✉)
Universidad de Granada, Granada, Spain
e-mail: lucasruiz@ugr.es

J. Muraszkiewicz et al. (eds.), *Human Trafficking in Conflict*, Crime Prevention and Security Management, https://doi.org/10.1007/978-3-030-40838-1_14

Regional organizations (ROs) have traditionally deployed civilian missions and military operations as an operative means to support on the ground the United Nations (UN) in the maintenance of international peace and security. Particularly since the 1990s, their support has demonstrated to be strategic in assisting the UN at the regional level, either assuming their "traditional" roles (e.g. observing and implementing ceasefires after inter-State wars) or policing crime in support of, or in substitution for, local authorities in post-conflict environments—among other non-traditional roles that these peace operations have undertaken in the last decades (Bellamy et al. 2010). The examples of both the North Atlantic Treaty Organization (NATO) and the European Union (EU) illustrate well the synergies between the UN and ROs in the maintenance of international peace and security, in particular in those challenging scenarios in which ceasefires are not fully respected or where transnational organized crime (TOC) operates—blurring the lines between armed conflict and other forms of organized violence.

Because of these blurred lines, TOC can be seen as a spoiler of peace processes (Cockayne and Pfister 2008, 30), influencing peace operations and post-conflict reconstruction, or engaging directly in conflict dynamics (Van der Lijn 2019, 3). Peacekeeping operations (PKOs) have, thus, developed different responsibilities within their mandates to fight TOC involved in human and other illicit trafficking in conflict and post-conflict scenarios, in line with a clear evolution of this concept in the last three decades. As stated in the Brahimi Report:

> United Nations peace operations entail three principal activities: conflict prevention and peacemaking; peacekeeping; and peace-building. (…) Peacekeeping is a 50-year-old enterprise that has evolved rapidly in the past decade from a traditional, primarily military model of observing ceasefires and force separations after inter-State wars, to incorporate a complex model of many elements, military and civilian, working together to build peace in the dangerous aftermath of civil wars. (Brahimi Report 2000, 2–3).

Therefore, in this chapter—unless otherwise specified—we will use PKOs as the general term to refer to these kinds of operations, irrespective of the mandate that they have (conflict prevention, peacemaking, peacekeeping, peace enforcement or peace building). The reason for this choice is twofold: it is the term traditionally used within the UN for the so-called "classic" peace operations since the beginning of their set-up in the early 1950s, and it is still commonly used to name the institutional framework and in the official documents, such as the renowned *Capstone Doctrine* (UN 2008) or the UN Secretary-General initiative, *Action for Peacekeeping* (UNSG 2018).

That said, the intervention of both NATO and the EU in the Western Balkans under the UN mandate illustrate well this evolution in terms. Furthermore, and notwithstanding some scandals,[1] these ROs exemplify how these PKOs have executed policing activities in the absence of well-established institutions in order to support peace processes and ensure human rights protection of human trafficking victims, at the same time that they helped local authorities to halt and prosecute traffickers operating in the region and build their capacities.

Despite the good records of this kind of cooperation between the UN and ROs, several legal and institutional gaps undermine the full potential of these strategic partnerships. The aim of this chapter is to analyse the role of both NATO and the EU in policing crime within the context of PKOs. In particular, this chapter will examine their contribution to the prevention and repression of human trafficking, acting either under a given international UN mandate to intervene or, irrespective of the mandate, under International Law and UN Security Council Resolutions.

---

[1] Despite the good records, there have been several scandals related to the misconduct of the UN peacekeepers in the theatre of operations that have come to the attention of the organization and the media, some of which involved NATO troops. For instance, a report from Prince Zeid Ra'ad Zeid Al-Hussein, Permanent Representative of Jordan, entitled *A comprehensive strategy to eliminate future sexual exploitation and abuse in United Nations peacekeeping operations* (A/59/710), recognized that "[s]exual exploitation and abuse by military, civilian police and civilian peacekeeping personnel is not a new phenomenon [...] ranging from those [operations] in Bosnia and Herzegovina and Kosovo in the early 1990s to Cambodia and Timor-Leste in the early and late 1990s to West Africa in 2002 and the Democratic Republic of the Congo in 2004." (p. 7). Moreover, the report pointed out with regret the lack of adequate investigation mechanisms to punish those who violate UN standards of conduct, and proposed the establishment of a professional investigative capacity to investigate those allegations. This report, endorsed by the Secretary-General, was discussed by the UN Security Council at its 5379th Meeting, on the 23 February 2006. Today, the UN has reinforced its zero-tolerance policy, and has developed a three-pronged strategy to address all form of misconduct: prevention of misconduct, enforcement of UN standards and remedial action. See for additional information: https://peacekeeping.un.org/en/standards-of-conduct

Firstly, we will briefly describe the legal framework of the UN Charter (section 2), and analyse how the role of PKOs undertaken by ROs has progressively evolved to tackle human trafficking on the ground, taking the examples of NATO and the EU (section 3). As we will observe, even if both ROs differ in the way they deal with human trafficking[2]—due *inter alia* to their very different nature and scope of cooperation, fighting human trafficking has been part of their common agenda since the 2004 NATO Istanbul Summit, at which the EU was represented by Javier Solana, the then High Representative for Foreign Affairs and Security Policy, along with those States taking part in both organizations that attended this meeting. This commitment has been further confirmed on the occasion of the Alliance meetings of 8 July 2016 and 10 July 2018, in Warsaw and Brussels, respectively. As a consequence of this joint undertaking, the PKOs led by both organizations have included responsibilities to fight human trafficking within their mandates, providing examples of best practice in the conduct of their operations, as well as other areas that need further improvement to overcome certain lacunae (section 4), either derived from the ambiguities of the Charter as regard the relation with the UN in *crisis management*—that is, "preventing a crisis from occurring, responding to an ongoing crisis, or assisting in the consolidation of peace (or order) once the acute phase of a crisis has passed" (Tardy 2015, 9)—or concerning their complex bilateral cooperation on the ground.

Some Preliminary Remarks on Chapter VIII

Possibly due to its ambiguous and succinct wording, as well as the reluctance of some ROs to be categorized as such, Chapter VIII of the UN Charter (articles 52 to 54) has been traditionally underused. The chapter *consents*[3] that "regional arrangements or agencies" deal with crisis man-

[2] For space constraints, in this study we will examine only the policies of both organizations, irrespective of the anti-human trafficking policies developed by their member States individually considered.

[3] "*Nothing* in the present Charter *precludes the existence* of regional arrangements or agencies for dealing with such matters relating to the maintenance of international peace and security as are appropriate for regional action …" (art. 52.1 of the UN Charter; italics are mine).

agement, "provided that such arrangements or agencies and their activities are consistent with the Purposes and Principles of the United Nations" (art. 52.1 of the UN Charter). Indeed, it promotes their role as first-instance authorities for the pacific settlement of any local dispute that might arise (art. 52.2 and 3), and, if required, it provides that the Security Council (UNSC) "shall (...) utilize such regional arrangements and agencies for enforcement action under its authority" (art. 53.1). Therefore, even if the UN Charter enshrines the centrality of the UN system in the maintenance of international peace and security, Chapter VIII allows for the option of "outsourcing" this task to ROs where necessary.

Nevertheless, certain conditions apply. Generally speaking,[4] ROs are in a *complementary* and *subordinate* position as regards, in particular, the UNSC (Villani 2002, 537), which remains the ultimate responsible body for the maintenance of international peace and security (art. 24 of the UN Charter). Complementarity has been the leitmotiv of the UN-ROs cooperation since the beginning,[5] and has been confirmed by subsequent political declarations[6] and the practice followed by most ROs in crisis management. Subordination is clear since the UNSC has the right to authorize any potential use of force (art. 53.1), and must "be kept fully

[4] For instance, NATO has clearly challenged this subordination principle, and, unlike the OSCE, has traditionally avoided being characterized as a RO acting under Chapter VIII to keep its (political and military) autonomy vis-à-vis the UN. For that reason, the UNSC Resolutions authorizing a NATO-led operation has been adopted using a general reference to Chapter VII instead.

[5] During the draft of the UN Charter, there was a strong debate between *universalists* and *regionalists* on the position that ROs should play in the maintenance of international peace and security. The result of those debates is a compromise text in which the existence and role of ROs in crisis management should be subject to the UN principles and objectives as defined by the Charter.

For a detailed analysis of these debates, see for instance: Arend, Anthony Clark. 1996. "The United Nations, Regional Organizations, and Military Operations: the Past and the Present". *Duke Journal of Comparative and Internacional Law* 7, no. 1 (Fall): 3–33; Cot, Jean Pierre and Pellet, Alain. 1991. *La Charte des Nations Unies. Commentaire article par article.* Paris: Economica; Kamto, Maurice. 2007. "Le role des 'accords et organismes regionaux' en matière de maintien de la paix et la sécurité internationales à la lumière de la Charte des Nations Unies et de la pratique international". *Revue Générale de Droit International Public* 111, no. 4: 771–802.

[6] See, for instance, *Declaration on the Enhancement of Cooperation between the United Nations and Regional Arrangements or Agencies in the Maintenance of International Peace and Security*, A/RES/49/57, 17 February 1995; Strengthening the role of mediation in the peaceful settlement of disputes, conflict prevention and resolution, A/RES/68/303, 13 August 2014; *Political declaration on strengthening cooperation between the United Nations and regional and subregional organizations*, A/RES/69/277, 27 May 2015.

informed" of the activities carried out by ROs (art. 54), being either under the peaceful settlement of local disputes or in the framework of a given coercive measure. International praxis has shown that ROs have fully respected this subordination principle when deploying PKOs in the last decades, in particular when they involved the authorization for the use of force by the UNSC, acting under Chapters VIII or—most of the time—VII of the Charter. For instance, the UNSC has authorized Member States "acting nationally or through regional organizations, including the EU" to use "all measures commensurate to the specific circumstances in confronting migrant smugglers or human traffickers" carrying out these illegal activities "on the high seas off the coast of Libya" (UNSC Res. 2240 (2015), paragraphs 2, 10 and 11). This pattern has also been used in other areas under different circumstances, such as in South Sudan (e.g. Resolution 2304 (2016)) and Somalia (e.g. Resolutions 1846 (2008) and 2316 (2016)), where the UNSC has authorized ROs to act using all the necessary means to guarantee their mandates. That said, the case of NATO's intervention in Kosovo demonstrated that, however, this subordination principle on paper has not always been respected in practice, challenging the centrality of the UN system. Robert Kolb, for instance, voiced concerns over the intervention of NATO in Kosovo in the late 1990s, arguing that it challenged the centrality of the UNSC in the maintenance of international peace and security, and even "dismantled" it (Kolb 2005, 49). This unilateral action in its search for autonomy was, somehow, in contravention of articles 1, 5 and 7 of its own founding Treaty (Allain 2004, 250–252).

Despite this apparent subordination principle, and the several legal and operational "loopholes" identified during the last decades (Ruiz Díaz 2018, 267–72), the relevance of ROs in crisis management should not be underestimated. ROs have gained extensive experience and knowledge in the field, implementing diverse mandates that have evolved over the years to adapt to the conflict or post-conflict scenarios in which they have been deployed. Nowadays, policing crime may be perceived as one of main tasks to be undertaken by PKOs on the ground, in particular, to halt people smuggling and other illicit trafficking—including human trafficking—when operating in a post-conflict scenario. The cases of NATO and the EU illustrate well this evolution of PKOs' mandates, particularly since the end of the Cold War. Moreover, ROs might be seen as being geographically, socially and politically closer to the parties in a given local dispute, and should not be perceived as a Western interference in regional affairs by the parties in conflict. For that reason, several ROs (e.g. NATO and the EU) have lately backed the strengthening of their counterparts in other areas of the world as the necessary complement to foster international peace and security, because global security starts at the local level. As we will observe—while it is still an unfinished business, vertical and horizontal coordination among ROS and the UN in this shared commitment remains essential for the success of PKOs in fighting human trafficking on the ground.

The Role of Regional Organizations in Addressing Human Trafficking in Conflict: NATO and the EU's Different Approaches

Both NATO and the EU have adopted their own, different approaches. Although earlier in time, their strategies are in line with the duty to protect the civilians affected by armed conflicts and post-conflict situations, in particular those victims of human trafficking, as mandated inter alia by UNSC Resolutions 2331 (2016a) and 2388 (2017a). The focus and experiences differ, however. While the EU has traditionally followed a more comprehensive and proactive role, making fighting human trafficking part of its external (normative) diplomacy, NATO's commitment has been limited to fighting human trafficking within the mandate of its operations, both as part of the code of conduct of its personnel and in the running of its operations. In their efforts, both ROs share, nevertheless, some common grounds for action, acknowledging for instance the negative impact that PKOs might have on local populations and human trafficking (Westendorf and Searle 2017; Mendelson 2005).

The Case of NATO. The First Steps of a Policy Still in Its Infancy

At the Istanbul Summit, in June 2004, NATO leaders adopted the Alliance policy against human trafficking. As embraced by the Heads of State and Government taking part in the meeting, NATO recognized that:

> This NATO policy takes into account the universal condemnation of the crime of trafficking in human beings and reiterates that it constitutes a serious abuse of human rights, especially affecting women and children. It is a transnational problem, requiring concerted multilateral action if it is to be defeated. Trafficking in human beings, affects countries of origin, countries of transit and countries of destination. This modern day slave trade fuels corruption and organised crime. It has the potential to weaken and destabilise fragile governments and runs counter to the goals of NATO-led efforts especially in South Eastern Europe. A zero-tolerance policy regarding trafficking in human beings by NATO forces and staff, combined with education and training, is required. (NATO 2004a).

This zero-tolerance policy on human trafficking is, thus, addressed by NATO in four main interrelated areas: (i) guaranteeing the appropriateness of the conduct of the personnel deployed in NATO-led operations and its staff by setting the basic standards of behaviour, (ii) halting human trafficking in the conduct of NATO-led operations in the field, (iii) developing training and educational programmes to raise awareness among the military and civilian personnel of the contributing nations, and (iv) promoting the prevention and repression of human trafficking in national legislation, among other initiatives, by encouraging all contributing nations "to ratify, accept or approve" the UN Palermo Convention and its First Protocol on Human Trafficking (United Nations 2000) and adhere to the OSCE Code of Conduct (OSCE 2003). Three guidelines were additionally adopted to guide NATO staff on preventing the promotion and facilitation of human trafficking and its deployed forces on combating it in the conduct of operations, as well as for the development of training and educational programs at NATO and national levels (NATO 2004b).

This policy, thus, promotes NATO's commitment to fight human trafficking by setting forth the code of conduct to which its staff and the personnel deployed under its commandment and control must adhere. It also encourages supporting the responsible authorities in the host country to stop human trafficking in the field during their operations "within their competence and respective mandate". Accordingly, NATO has developed specific provisions for the protection of victims of human trafficking or conflict-related physical violence within the planning and conduct of its operations as part of its efforts to enhance its international credibility and legitimacy in the conduct of PKOs (NATO 2019, 15). Moreover, any breach of this zero-tolerance policy by a member of a force or of a civilian component of a NATO-led operation should be subject to prosecution at national level according to the clauses of the NATO Status of Forces, in particular its Article VII (NATO 1951). We might assume, therefore, that the Alliance's anti-human trafficking policy is complementary to the main purposes of the organization, as pointed out by the 2010 Strategic Concept—that is, collective defence, crisis management and cooperative security, and constitutes an attempt to provide the Alliance with a more comprehensive approach to (human) security for the twenty-first century in the conduct of operations, in which "trafficking in people" might be perceived as one of the consequences of instability and conflict that threatens NATO's security (NATO 2010).

This zero-tolerance policy, on the ground, has been translated not only in the conduct of its troops and staff in accordance with these standards but also in the mandates of the NATO-led PKOs deployed in the twenty-first century. For instance, neither the Stabilization Force (SFOR) nor the Kosovo Force (KFOR), which were established in the 1990s, included under their main responsibilities fighting human trafficking; only a general mandate to protect the civilians and promote human rights was added to their core duties—linked to the traditional interstate warfare (UNSC 1996, 1999). Indeed, "both SFOR and KFOR maintain[ed] an 'assistance only' role in combating crime in general and human trafficking in particular" (DoD/IG 2003, 23). Nowadays, some of the current NATO-led PKOs have been particularly devoted to halt people smuggling and human trafficking. These are the cases of two operations deployed in the Mediterranean in the late 2010s. Firstly, the Operation

Sea Guardian, a non-Article 5 maritime operation launched in November 2016 to replace Operation Active Endeavour, which contributes to counter terrorism and to maritime security capacity-building in the Mediterranean Sea. Secondly, the presence of NATO's Standing Maritime Group 2 (SNMG2) in the Aegean Sea and at the Turkish-Syrian border to help prevent human trafficking and illegal migration through intelligence, surveillance and reconnaissance. As we will analyse further, these operations are coordinated with, and support the EU's missions and operations in the Mediterranean—including those coordinated by the European Border and Coast Guard Agency (Frontex), constituting a valuable example of collaboration between ROs in crisis management.

Finally, this zero-tolerance policy has also been embedded in the relationships that the Alliance has established with third countries. As part of its projecting stability goal, NATO advices and trains the military personnel of third countries on security issues (e.g. NATO Mission Iraq, NMI), and has signed partnership agreements with third countries to foster dialogue and cooperation on shared security challenges, some of them engaged in the Mediterranean Dialogue launched in 1994 by the North Atlantic Council (for instance, Colombia, Algeria, Mauritania, and Morocco[7]). At regional level, NATO has also established cooperation with the UN, the Organization for Security and Cooperation in Europe (OSCE) and the African Union (AU). It has assisted the latter, for instance, by providing for logistics and airlift support in the deployment of its mission in Darfur between 2005 and 2007, and assisting its mission in Somalia (AMISOM). The collaboration established with the EU deserves specific attention (see section 3.3 below).

The EU's Normative Power in Practice

Since the late 1990s, with the adoption of the 1997 Joint Action, but particularly in the twenty-first century, the EU has pursued a proactive, comprehensive role in fighting human trafficking in its external action,

[7] With this country, NATO even signed a Tactical Memorandum of Understanding for Morocco's contribution to NATO's counter-terrorism mission, Operation Active Endeavour, which included from information exchange to Moroccan contribution of naval and air assets to the operation.

singularly through its Common Security and Defence Policy (CSDP) missions and operations. Being part of its external role against human trafficking, defined primarily in an Action Oriented Paper (Council of the EU, 2009), the EU has urged third States to ratify the relevant international conventions or adopt its *acquis* in the framework of its Enlargement Policy, including the 2011 Directive (European Parliament and Council of the EU, 2011). Moreover, its anti-human trafficking policy has been part of its agenda in international fora and bilateral summits with partner countries, constituting an example of what Ian Manners called its *normative power* (Manners 2002). Its policy against human trafficking has had, however, an evident securitarian dimension for years (Ruiz Díaz 2014), somehow influenced by the misleading connection among EU policy-makers between "external" criminal organizations and human trafficking, and between human trafficking and people smuggling or irregular migration—one of the clearest shortcomings of the EU's approach even today despite its good intentions.

As far the CSDP is concerned, EU missions and operations have incorporated, directly or indirectly, fighting TOC and human trafficking within the scope of their mandates since it was declared operational in 2001. The first mission to integrate policing crime within its mandate was the European Union Police Mission (EUPM) in Bosnia and Herzegovina (2002–2012), followed by other missions and operations that supported these efforts in the field, such as EUFOR Althea (since 2004) in the same country. More recently, in the 2010s, another example of this kind of operation deployed in its neighbourhood to stop human trafficking and people smuggling is Operation Sophia in the Mediterranean Sea, which has patrolling functions against traffickers and smugglers, along with the joint operations coordinated by Frontex at the external borders within the scope of its competences in the Area of Freedom, Security and Justice. This naval operation, launched on 22 June 2015 to fight people smuggling and human trafficking, however, symbolizes the divisions among EU member States on the common migration policy, and, since March 2019, has no vessels patrolling the Central Mediterranean because of the Italian government's refusal to receive more migrants and the lack of solidarity among the other member States to share the burden. Despite this major setback, since "internal and external security are ever more intertwined" (High Representative 2016, 7), it soon become clear that the near abroad would be the first line of defence for the EU. At the same time, it also become clear that EU-led PKOs are a relevant instrument for exporting (human) security and stability in post-conflict areas according to the priorities identified in the EU Global Strategy (EUGS).

These missions and operations, thus, do not only police crime in the field in support of local authorities, or in their absence. They also train third States' police and military forces to promote a longer engagement against human trafficking in post-conflict and reconstruction environments. Being part of its comprehensive approach, the EU has also deployed civilian missions and non-executive military operations to underpin international and local efforts in the security sector reform and the consolidation of the rule of law in post-conflict scenarios. Once again, the Western Balkans and Libya exemplify well this commitment with the deployment of EULEX Kosovo and the EU Integrated Border Assistance Mission in Libya (EUBAM Libya) to instruct local authorities to be able and capable of disrupting TOC involved in people smuggling, human trafficking and terrorism. These training missions, together with the military operations and other instruments at disposal of the EU's external action—e.g. migration policy—help to stabilize its near abroad and, as a consequence, reinforce its own internal security, having the fight against human trafficking as backdrop.

Forging the EU-NATO Cooperation for the Twenty-First Century

NATO and the EU may be considered strategic partners. The relevance of this partnership for the European security has been repeatedly emphasized by both the EU institutions (Council of the EU 2016, 2019) and its NATO counterparts (NATO 2014). As far as human trafficking is concerned, at the NATO Istanbul summit (2004) the members already pointed out the need for a closer information exchange between both ROs. This joint commitment was further underlined more recently on the occasion of the Alliance meetings of 8 July 2016 and 10 July 2018 in Warsaw and Brussels, respectively, and endorsed by their foreign ministers soon after, when the NATO Allies and EU member States adopted 74 specific actions altogether to foster the seven identified areas of information sharing and operational cooperation, comprising inter alia operative cooperation including maritime and migration issues and supporting Eastern and Southern partners' capacity-building efforts.

On the ground, the strategic partnership between the two organizations goes beyond their usual area of cooperation—the Western Balkans—and has been recently reflected in the cooperation and coordination between Operation Sophia and NATO's Operation Sea Guardian in the Central Mediterranean at tactical and operational levels. Along with the CSDP training mission EUBAM Libya and the joint operations coordinated by Frontex in the Mediterranean (e.g. Operation Poseidon), as well as NATO surveillance mission in the Aegean sea, both operations are providing capacity and training to the Libyan Coast Guard and Navy, and support the implementation of the UN arms embargo on the high seas off the Libyan coast, following UNSC Resolutions 1970 (2011), 2292 (2016b) and 2357 (2017b). Nevertheless, despite the good records and the complementarity between both operations—in particular since NATO can help to fill the gaps identified within the EU on intelligence gathering (Dibenedetto 2016, 12)—the uncertainty over the continuation of Operation Sophia might have an impact on this cooperation against traffickers in the Mediterranean.

This blurring line between cooperation and competition is likely to continue in the short term, as it has been particularly the case of the EU-OSCE relationship since the 2000s (Ruiz Díaz 2018). The operations in the Mediterranean against traffickers are not the only examples of this lack of capacity—and political will—to cooperate between NATO and the EU due mainly to their different approaches as regards (human) security and the very nature of their foundations and leitmotivs in the international scene. That was also the case of the CSDP Operation Atalanta (since December 2008) and the NATO Operation Ocean Shield (2008–2016) carrying out anti-piracy tasks off the coast of Somalia. There, too, both ROs conducted their respective operation without operational or strategic cooperation, and even before, during their planning, both entered into competition in the deployment of an operation to respond to the UN Secretary-General's request. In fact, instead of succeeding NATO's Operation Allied Provider (October–December 2008) as initially defended by the UK Prime Minister, Gordon Brown,[8] Europeans decided to launch their own first-ever naval force without taking into account the Berlin Plus arrangements, "a political victory for the entire Union, but especially for France" (Nováky 2018, 140). Indeed, although strategic partners, NATO and the EU still want to keep their autonomy vis-à-vis the other in deciding not only where to intervene but also in the conduct of operations.

Successful Stories, Lessons Learnt?

Chapter VIII has been traditionally underused. Generally speaking, the UNSC has proceeded under Chapter VII when authorizing the deployment of a RO-led PKO. Legal and institutional lacunae have contributed to the praxis followed by the UNSC, but also the reticence of ROs to be categorized under this chapter. For example, NATO and the EU—unlike the OSCE—have traditionally avoided falling under the umbrella of Chapter VIII, and the collaboration that they have both established with the UN system, as well as between them, has been built upon common ad hoc commitments on shared security challenges and values. Otherwise, *complementarity* and *autonomy* have been reiterated inside NATO and particularly the EU Institutions as the new mantra in Brussels, especially now that the EU is pushing for taking the first steps to Europeanize national defence policies, among other multilateral initiatives, through the launch of the permanent structured cooperation (Tocci 2018; Fiott et al. 2017), and has allocated for the first time its own funds for research and development on defence issues to back what has been called in the EUGS its *strategic autonomy* (High Representative 2016, 4). Stronger coordination is thus needed in the short term to put in practice the good intentions at the political level to fight human trafficking on the ground.

[8] "Asked about a possible EU force in the Gulf of Aden to combat piracy, the PMS emphasized that this was something that had been under consideration (…). Planning was under way for an EU mission to the region to help combat pirating as a successor to the NATO mission." House of Lords. 2009. *Select Committee on Communications. 1st Report of Session 2008–09. Government Communications*, p. 52. https://publications.parliament.uk

Fighting and preventing human trafficking constitutes one of these areas of common interests where NATO and the EU have cooperated along the lines written by the UNSC. In fact, both ROs have undertaken operations that, directly or indirectly, have dealt with human trafficking in conflict or post-conflict scenarios. In both cases, capacity-building and policing crime have been an integral part of their activities in the conduct of operations. Moreover, in the case of NATO, its staff and the personnel under its command and control must adhere to its zero-tolerance policy on human trafficking when deployed on the ground. However, differences remain. Firstly, the EU's approach is more comprehensive than that of NATO, limited to its nature as defensive organization. CSDP military operations are complemented by civilian missions and non-executive military operations to train local forces in post-conflict environments, dealing with a broad set of issues in the security sector reform and the consolidation of the rule of law—exceeding, thus, the tasks assigned to NATO operations traditionally rooted in the military aspects of capacity-building. Secondly, the EU has pursued a new approach to human trafficking since the adoption of the 2011 Directive, favouring a human-centred, holistic approach that—at least, theoretically—puts the victim at the centre of its intervention. This is simply not the aim of NATO's involvement in crisis management since fighting human trafficking is not considered a top security priority in its 2010 Strategic Concept. Thirdly, the EU's anti-trafficking policy is mainstreamed in every policy having an external dimension. Therefore, the Union seeks fighting and preventing human trafficking not only in the framework of its Enlargement and Neighbourhood policies but also as part of its bilateral relations with other third countries or inside international fora. That said, it is worth noting that, nowadays, NATO is the only RO with the institutional and operational capabilities to lead a rapid response when a crisis arises—an unfinished business within the EU to date.

Despite these differences—or because of that, the EU and NATO have been complementary to each other and have positively contributed to fighting and preventing human trafficking on the ground, as practice has shown. Effective operational and tactical coordination is, however, still lacking in areas of cooperation other than the maritime domain, and strongly relies upon *ad hoc* structures and informal staff meetings. As briefly portrayed above, political will is essential in the planning and conduct of operations since there is neither a compulsory nor voluntary provision in the Charter to compel ROs to cooperate on the ground. Now that the EUGS calls for the EU's strategic autonomy and the complementarity of the European defence with NATO—not the duplication of efforts, the time has come to transcend these differences and foster coordination at all the relevant levels for the sake of responding effectively to the common security challenges that both ROs face, including human trafficking.

References

Allain, Jean. 2004. The True Challenge to the United Nations System of the Use of Force: The Failures of Kosovo and Iraq and the Emergence of the African Union. *Max Planck Yearbook of United Nations Law* 8 (1): 237–289.

Bellamy, Alex, Paul Williams, and Stuart Griffin. 2010. *Understanding Peacekeeping*. 2nd ed. Cambridge: Polity Press.

Cockayne, James, and Daniel Pfister. 2008. *"Peace Operations and Organised Crime". Geneva Papers, no. 2*. Geneva: Geneva Centre for Security Policy—International Peace Institute.

Council of the European Union. 2009. *Action Oriented Paper on Strengthening the EU External Dimension Against Trafficking in Human Beings*, 11450/5/09 REV 5, Brussels, 19 November 2009.

———. 2016. *Implementation Plan on Security and Defence*, 14392/16, Brussels, 14 November 2016.

———. 2019. *Council Conclusions on Security and Defence in the context of the EU Global Strategy – Council Conclusions (17 June 2019)*, 10048/19, Luxembourg, 17 June 2019.

Department of Defense Office of Inspector General (DoD IG). 2003. *Assessment of DoD Efforts to Combat Trafficking in Persons – Phase II – Bosnia-Herzegovina and Kosovo*. Prepared by the Directorate for Investigations of Senior Officials, Office of Deputy Inspector General for Investigations, Case No. H03L88433128, December, 8, 2003.

Dibenedetto, Alessandra. 2016. Implementing the Alliance Maritime Strategy in the Mediterranean: NATO's Operation Sea Guardian. Research Paper, Research Division—NATO Defense College, No. 134, December 2016.

European Parliament and Council of the European Union. 2011. Directive 2011/36/EU of the European Parliament and the European Council, of 5 April 2011, on Preventing and Combating Trafficking in Human Beings and Protecting Its Victims, and Replacing Council Framework Decision 2002/629/JHA, OJ, No. L 101, 15.4.2011:1–11.

Fiott, Daniel, Missiroli, Antonio, and Tardy, Thierry. 2017. Permanent Structured Cooperation: What's in a Name?. *Chaillot Papers*, No. 142, November 2017. Paris: European Union Institute for Security Studies.

General Assembly— Security Council. 2000. *Comprehensive Review of the Whole Question of Peacekeeping Operations in All Their Aspects*, A/55/305–S/2000/809, 21 August 2000 (Brahimi Report).

High Representative of the Union for Foreign Affairs and Security Policy. 2016. Shared Vision, Common Action: A Stronger Europe. A Global Strategy for the European Union's Foreign and Security Policy.

Kolb, Robert. 2005. Le droit relatif au maintien de la paix international. In *Evolution historique, valeurs fondatrices et tendances actuelles*. Paris: Pedone.

Manners, Ian. 2002. Normative Power Europe: A Contradiction in Terms? *Journal of Common Market Law Studies* 40 (2): 235–258.

Mendelson, Sarah E. 2005. *Barracks and Brothels. Peacekeepers and Human Trafficking in the Balkans*. Washington, DC: Center for Strategic and International Studies.

North Atlantic Treaty Organization (NATO). 1951. *Agreement Between the Parties to the North Atlantic Treaty Regarding the Status of Their Forces*, London, June 19, 1951.

———. 2004a. *NATO Policy on Combating Trafficking in Human Beings*, 29 June 2004. https://www.nato.int/cps/en/natohq/official_texts_71856.htm?selectedLocale=en

———. 2004b. *NATO Guidelines on Combating Trafficking in Human Beings for Military Forces and Civilian Personnel Deployed in NATO-led Operations*, *NATO Guidance for the Development of Training and Educational Programmes to Support the Policy on Combating the Trafficking in Human Beings*, and *Guidelines for NATO Staff on Preventing the Promotion and Facilitation of Trafficking in Human Beings*. https://www.nato.int/docu/comm/2004/06-istanbul/docu-traffic.htm

———. 2010. *Strategic Concept for the Defence and Security of the Members of the North Atlantic Treaty Organization*, Adopted by Heads of State and Government at the NATO Summit in Lisbon 19–20 November 2010.

———. 2014. *Wales Declaration on the Transatlantic Bond*, Press Release (2014) 122, Issued on 5 September 2014. https://www.nato.int/cps/en/natohq/official_texts_112985.htm
———. 2019. *NATO Standard AJP-3 Allied Doctrine for the Conduct of Operations. Edition C, Version 1*, February 2019.
Nováky, Niklas. 2018. *European Union Military Operations. A Collective Action Perspective*. Oxon: Routledge.
Organization for Security and Co-operation in Europe (OSCE). 2003. *Code of Conduct for Staff/Mission Members*, Appendix 1 to the OSCE Staff Regulations and Staff Rules, Permanent Council Decision 550/Corr.1, 27 June 2003.
Ruiz Díaz, Lucas. 2014. La especial protección de las víctimas de la trata de seres humanos: las novedades de la Directiva 2011/36/UE. In *Derecho internacional y protección de mujeres migrantes en situación de especial vulnerabilidad*, ed. Carmen Pérez González, 91–129. Valencia: Tirant lo Blanch.
———. 2018. The Role of Regional Organizations in Peacekeeping: Shared Responsibilities, New Roles, and Old Uncertainties. In *Peacekeeping: Global Perspectives, Challenges and Impact*, ed. Pablo Antonio Fernández Sánchez, 265–282. New York: Nova Science.
Tardy, Thierry. 2015. CSDP in Action— What Contribution to International Security?. *Chaillot Papers*, No. 134, May 2015. Paris: EU Institute for Security Studies.
Tocci, Natalie. 2018. Towards a European Security and Defence Union: Was 2017 a Watershed? *Journal of Common Market Studies* 56 (1): 131–141.
United Nations. 2000. United Nations Convention against Transnational Organized Crime (Palermo Convention), and the Protocol to Prevent, Suppress and Punish Trafficking in Persons, especially Women and Children, both adopted by General Assembly Resolution 55/25 of 15 November 2000.
———. 2008. *United Nations Peacekeeping Operations. Principles and Guidelines* (Capstone Doctrine). New York. https://www.un.org/ruleoflaw/files/Capstone_Doctrine_ENG.pdf
United Nations Secretary-General (UNSG). 2018. *Action for Peace. Declaration of Shared Commitments on UN Peacekeeping Operations*. [Online] https://peacekeeping.un.org/en/action-for-peacekeeping-a4p
United Nations Security Council (UNSC). 1996. Resolution 1088 (1996), Adopted by the Security Council at Its 3723rd Meeting, on 12 December 1996.
———. 1999. Resolution 1244 (1999), Adopted by the Security Council at Its 4011th Meeting, on 10 June 1999.

———. 2011. Resolution 2017 (2011), Adopted by the Security Council at Its 6644th Meeting, on 31 October 2011.
———. 2016a. Resolution 2331 (2016), Adopted by the Security Council at Its 7847th Meeting, on 20 December 2016.
———. 2016b. Resolution 2292 (2016), Adopted by the Security Council at Its 7715th Meeting, on 14 June 2016.
———. 2017a. Resolution 2388 (2017), Adopted by the Security Council at Its 8111th Meeting, on 21 November 2017.
———. 2017b. Resolution 2357 (2017), Adopted by the Security Council at Its 7964th Meeting, on 12 June 2017.
Van der Lijn, Jaïr. 2019. Multilateral Peace Operations and the Challenges of Irregular Migration and Human Trafficking. *SIPRI Background Paper.*
Villani, Ugo. 2002. The Security Council's Authorization of Enforcement Action by Regional Organizations. *Max Planck Yearbook of United Nations Law* 6 (1): 535–555.
Westendorf, Jasmine-Kim, and Louise Searle. 2017. Sexual Exploitation and Abuse in Peace Operations: Trends, Policy Responses and Future Directions. *International Affairs* 93 (2): 365–387.

Lucas J. Ruiz-Díaz has a sound knowledge of European affairs and law, in particular relating to the external dimension of EU Justice and Home Affairs and the Common Security and Defence Policy (CSDP). He obtained his PhD in Public International Law and International Relations from the University of Granada in 2015. He is currently Assistant Lecturer at the Universidad de Granada.

15

Human Security Analysis for Military Planning: Lessons Learnt from Developing a Risk Assessment on Human Trafficking

Hayley Watson, Toby Fenton, and Stephen Anning

Human Trafficking as a Human Security Risk

As this volume demonstrates, there is ample evidence of the trafficking of human beings in conflict. Considering the activities of the so-called Islamic State of Iraq and al-Sham (ISIS, also known as ISIL) in relation to the selling of Yazidi women in Iraq, human trafficking not only involves grave human rights violations, but can also be seen as offering tactical benefits in terms of yielding financial gain for ISIS combatants and furthering the group's strategic goals in relation to the development of the caliphate (see for instance, Ahram 2015; Binetti 2015; Besenyő 2016). Furthermore, the forced conversion and recruitment of Yazidi children as

H. Watson (✉) • T. Fenton
Trilateral Research, London, UK
e-mail: hayley.watson@trilateralresearch.com;
toby.fenton@trilateralresearch.com

S. Anning
University of Southampton, Southampton, UK

J. Muraszkiewicz et al. (eds.), *Human Trafficking in Conflict*, Crime Prevention and Security Management, https://doi.org/10.1007/978-3-030-40838-1_15

child soldiers points to the added manpower for operational purposes. Such deliberate targeting of civilians by ISIS has led to significant levels of displacement, which can result in mass migration and places greater emphasis on the need to understand how human security risks can alter the behaviours of populations, which in turn, can impact the military's operational and tactical planning considerations (e.g., the movement of troops and selection of targets). Elsewhere, armed groups such as Boko Haram in Nigeria are exploiting women and girls for operational purposes (see for instance, Zenn and Pearson 2014; Bloom and Matfess 2016). As such, it is necessary to understand the risks related to human trafficking as part of military planning. Doing so will not only support the achievement of military objectives concerning the protection of citizens and the promotion of human security and wider stability but will support military actors in understanding and analysing the use of human trafficking as a tactic of warfare.

But where does human trafficking[1] fit within military considerations? For the UK Ministry of Defence (MOD), human trafficking is recognised as a human security issue within UK military doctrine under Joint Service Publication (JSP) 1325: *Human Security in Military Operations*, which was published in January 2019. Traditional conceptualisations of security prioritise the nation-state through the rubric of *national security*, which captures "the imperative of defending territory against, and deterring, 'external' military threats" (Newman 2001, 240). However, human security "seeks to place the individual—or people collectively—as the referent of security, rather than, although not necessarily in opposition to, institutions such as territory and state sovereignty" (Ibid, 239). In JSP 1325, the conceptualisation adopted is that by the United Nations Development Programme, which includes "seven areas of threat to the individual; economic, food, health, environmental, political, community and personal. The latter being understood as protection from physical violence, from the state or external states, from violent individuals and sub-state actors" (JSP 1325 2019, 2). JSP 1325 focuses on the threats to personal security, including considerations around "empowerment and access to equal rights for women and girls; the prevention of conflict and

[1] Within this chapter, the authors rely on the definition of human trafficking set out within the United Nations Palermo Protocol (2000), as described in the introduction to this book.

human rights violations and the protection of women, men, girls and boys from human rights violations such as rape in conflict, abduction and forced recruitment of children and human trafficking" (Ibid). Threats to human security are not simply a consequence of conflict but can also contribute to establishing the conditions for conflict in the first place and in enabling an environment in which conflict can continue. Indeed, there exists various linkages between the human security paradigm and other well-established areas of military activity. For instance, the military can contribute to civilian-led stabilisation and reconstruction (S&R) activities, which "include support to establishing long-term stability and strengthened governance, local capacity building, re-establishment of the rule of law", and ultimately seek to establish "the basis for economic, human, health and social development. The long-term goal [of S&R] is to promote those processes which lead to lasting stability and self-sustaining peace" (NATO 2019a, 51–52).

Four months prior to the release of JSP 1325, a small-scale innovation project began, Project Solebay, to develop a proof of concept for a risk-assessment methodology to support the UK military in understanding human trafficking in conflict. This chapter discusses Project Solebay's approach to assessing human trafficking risk and explores a number of core lessons learnt throughout the project that have important implications for wider efforts at developing human security analysis capabilities.

As this chapter will show, developing a proof of concept regarding a risk assessment for human trafficking in conflict was not without its challenges given the significant complexity of the issue at hand and the lack of appropriate data from the field. Importantly, the approach taken to develop the risk assessment offers important lessons, as revealed in this chapter, for the development of methods to further understand threats and vulnerabilities within the wider human security landscape. In turn, this requires a partnership approach to assessing and planning for the risks related to human trafficking as part of military operations. As discussed below, this partnership approach could be usefully advanced through the existing framework of civil-military cooperation (CIMIC).

Conflict, Security and Civil-Military Cooperation

Although some military actors, such as the US Army, have maintained 'civil affairs' units since at least the Second World War, the formal military function known as CIMIC is primarily a NATO product. NATO (2018, 37) defines CIMIC as "a joint function comprising a set of capabilities integral to supporting the achievement of mission objectives and enabling NATO commands to participate effectively in a broad spectrum of civil-military interaction with diverse non-military actors". As a NATO member, the CIMIC framework forms part of UK defence doctrine. It has a particular saliency regarding military activities in the context of stabilisation efforts (e.g., MOD 2016, 13; MOD 2012). Although CIMIC is a complex and multifaceted concept, the essential focus is upon the military's engagement and cooperation with non-military (i.e., civilian) actors to support mission objectives. This cooperation is crucial due to changes in the evolving character of conflict and of contemporary security challenges over at least the past two decades.

For much of modern history, conflict was essentially seen to involve a military contest—'warfare'—between two opposing states. However, the decline in inter-state warfare since 1945 has changed the character of the contemporary defence and security landscape. As Smith (2006) notes, this decline in inter-state warfare—or 'industrial warfare,' characterised by the mass deployment of soldiers and machines—has paralleled the rise of intra-state conflict as 'wars among the people' reflecting a shift from the enemy-centric character of industrial warfare to a more population-centric approach to operations. This more population-centric approach necessitates the consideration of terrorist and criminal activity as a military concern. Kaldor (1999, 2) makes a similar observation, describing intrastate conflict as 'new wars' characterised as a blurring of distinctions between war, organised crime and large-scale human rights violations. The awareness of human rights abuses as a weapon of war has gained significant traction in the public consciousness, particularly in the domain of Women, Peace and Security.

This evolution in the evolving character of conflict and the re-conceptualisation of security represent an expansion in the complexity of the military's operating environment, which in turn has provided the impetus for a re-formulation of the way the military conducts operations. From NATO's (2018, 1) perspective, the strategic context for CIMIC is a recognition that security challenges "will come from a wide variety of threats, both military and non-military"; these challenges may include "ethnic, political and religious rivalries, territorial disputes, conflict over resources, inadequate or failed efforts at reform, the violation of human rights and the weakening of states". Similarly, the "contemporary operating environment involves a myriad of ethnic, religious, ideological and technological issues, which require sustainable solutions in societies disrupted by conflicts, disasters or humanitarian catastrophes" (ibid). Thus, while applications of hard and soft military power will still be necessary, alone they are insufficient. CIMIC recognises the requirement for a "comprehensive approach from the international community", which will "depend on cooperation and coordination based on a common sense of purpose and resolve, mutual understanding, collaboration and appropriate resourcing", and will be "founded on a shared situational awareness, understanding and recognition that sometimes non-military actors may support the military and *vice versa*" (Ibid, 2).

As argued in this chapter, developing a robust and systematic risk-assessment approach to human trafficking in conflict—as part of wider human security analysis capabilities—will require (at least) cooperation, collaboration, information sharing and mutual resourcing between military and non-military actors, as CIMIC advocates.

Assessing the Risk of Human Trafficking in Conflict

Conceptually, risk is composed of three components: *occurrence* (or scenario), *likelihood* and *consequences* (or impact) (Kaplan 1997, 408). Assessing risk involves asking: "What can happen? How likely is that to happen? If it does happen, what are the consequences?" (Ibid). The dual-dimensional nature of risk assessment—*likelihood and consequences*—is crucial in the context of military planning and decision-making because the military is not an anti-slavery organisation, despite the myriad ways in which human trafficking intersects with military operations. Unlike, for instance, an NGO, which might wish to assess the *likelihood* of human trafficking or the *vulnerability* of certain populations for the purpose of safeguarding, advocacy, the military must seek to understand the varying *consequences* of human trafficking. Within the context of the military, assessing the consequences includes the consequences for local populations but also those for military personnel, military operations—whether warfighting, peacekeeping, stabilisation and reconstruction (S&R) or other activities—and longer-term strategic goals in order to balance the resulting risks against a variety of other tactical, operational, strategic, logistical, procurement, political, diplomatic and other priorities.

In the military domain, risk has different implications at the *strategic*, *operational* and *tactical* levels. Identification, assessment and management of risk is integral to the planning of military operations (NATO 2019b, 33).

- Strategic risk focuses on "events that impact upon or change the overall strategic context … in the worst-case jeopardising achieving strategic objectives or attaining the [operation's desired] end state" (NATO 2019a, 137).
- Operational risk "is associated with the relationship between strategic objectives and tactical activity"; these risks arise due to planning decisions or through external events or influences (Ibid).
- Tactical risk "arises from the results of both planned activity and other anticipated events, and the unplanned and unforeseen" (Ibid, 138).

The British Army's *Field Manual* for *Land Operations* differentiates between two types of operational risks. *Risk to force* contains two subsets of risk: the "risk of loss of the force"; and the risk of "damage to fighting power", which refers to loss of personnel, equipment and materiel (MOD 2017, 182). The second type of operational risk is *Risk to mission*, which refers to "the possibility that the mission will not succeed"; causes of this risk include adversary actions, environmental factors, and the actions of the military force itself, which may increase its vulnerabilities (Ibid, 183).

Against this backdrop, Project Solebay, sought to develop first-of-its-kind proof of concept for a risk assessment that would enable the UK military to assess the strategic impact of the risk of human trafficking in conflict on military operations. In addition, Project Solebay was concerned with demonstrating how open data could be used to inform risk-assessment processes in order to work towards a data-driven approach to supporting the analyst to assess risk, rather than solely relying on professional-based risk assessment. What follows is an overview of the methodology used to develop the risk assessment and lessons learnt.

Methodological Approach to Developing a Risk Assessment

Prior to presenting the lessons of the experience of conducting the project to develop the risk assessment, it is necessary to understand the methods used by the research team to ensure the risk assessment was designed in collaboration with the needs of the end users. It is worth noting that the research team deemed it necessary to shape the risk factors component within the risk assessment in a manner that was grounded in evidence of how human trafficking manifests in conflict, thereby enhancing its validity, as such a research-based approach to developing the risk assessment was critical.

The project entailed an interdisciplinary team from social science, law, human rights, defence studies and data science. This team worked in a co-design manner with UK-MOD representatives to develop the proof of concept of a risk assessment that was fit-for-purpose in the defence domain. In this regard, co-design involved the process of working together to identify a problem (i.e., understanding risk of human trafficking to the military) and solutions (i.e., a fit-for-purpose risk-assessment methodology). Within this co-design setting, the team used a mixed-methods approach to develop the risk assessment and associated open data dashboards to demonstrate how data can support the analyst in assessing risk.

Methods used included a literature review of over 70 documents (peer-reviewed articles, books and edited books, government and civil society reports) to assess: (1) how human trafficking is understood and features in a military context, (2) risk factors associated with human trafficking in a military context, (3) critical analysis of existing risk-assessment models across an array of domains; (4) analysis of open data human trafficking-related risk factors. Further, the research team undertook 28 semi-structured interviews, using snowball methods, with non-Government organisations, law enforcement authorities, military personnel and research institutes that undertake risk assessments in other fields (e.g., corruption or supply chain). Further, in order to show how open data could be used to support analysts in assessing risk, the research team used the risk factors associated with human trafficking in a military context (e.g., rule of law, corruption, gender-based violence etc.) and examined corresponding open data sets. For instance, one data visualisation on human trafficking risk factors drew on 11 data sets (e.g., Transparency International Corruption Index, World Bank GDP Per Capita, International Labour Organisation—Youth Unemployment, United Nations Development Programme—Education Index, Freedom House—Functioning Government Index *among others*), which were then linked to 15 risk factors identified during the desk-based research and interviews, across 183 countries (Fenton et al. 2019). For the research team, a data-driven approach to assessing risk is not intended to replace the work of the analyst but to support them in their efforts in a complementary fashion.

The risk assessment was validated using in-person workshops with the UK-MOD, cross-government bodies, academia and civil society representatives. The mixed-methods approach enabled the research team to validate findings in the absence of field-based data on human trafficking in conflict. As such, lessons from literature, case studies of human trafficking in conflict and consultation with experts served as an evidence base for the development of the risk-assessment methodology. The co-design approach enabled a risk assessment that was fit for purpose with the end user (i.e., UK-MOD) in mind. It is important to note that the project was limited in terms of access to field-based intelligence of direct observation of human trafficking in the field; in part, this was due to the novelty of considerations around human trafficking from the perspective of the UK-MOD (*as with other national militaries*). In the future, to get to a more granular level of risk assessment at the operational and tactical level, field-based data is critical. To achieve this goal, it is necessary to improve field-based data-collection methods within UK-military day-to-day operations.

Lessons in Developing a Risk Assessment and Threat/Vulnerability Analysis

Following consideration of the methods used to develop the risk assessment, the following section provides some instrumental lessons that the research team experienced and were forced to overcome in order to arrive at a proof-of-concept for a risk-assessment methodology in this space.

In the process of distilling potential risk factors for human trafficking, the team came up against the classic causation versus correlation problem. Assessing risk requires understanding which phenomena in the environment can cause certain occurrences to arise in the first place or to increase in likelihood. However, differentiating between factors that drive or cause human trafficking, against those that merely appear to be present alongside or that correlate with human trafficking is problematic. This issue was not unique to Project Solebay; during the research, interviewees raised the same issue. One interviewee, a UN employee, remarked that when looking at these kinds of risks there are "challenging causal chains that you have to establish" and that far more analysis and field work is needed "to make these kinds of links" (cited in Fenton et al. 2019, 20). An employee from an NGO said that for her organisation it remained impossible to "say for certain that the variables we're identifying are causal for slavery" (cited in Ibid). Such problems remain at the heart of efforts to study and model human trafficking. For instance, Diego-Rosell and Larsen (2018, 18) write that "[w]e cannot ascertain the direction of causality between variables and risk factors and that unfortunately the field of [modern slavery and human trafficking] lacks a unifying causal theory that can be used to inform variable selection".

According to Renn (2006), risks can be classified in terms of the level of knowledge that can be obtained about them. Based on these variations in knowledge, risks can range from the simple to the complex. The "difficulty of identifying and quantifying causal links between a multitude of potential causal agents and specific observed effects", writes Renn (2006, 29–30), "may be traced back to interactive effects among these agents (synergism and antagonisms), long delay periods between cause and effect, inter-individual variation, intervening variables, and others". Human trafficking certainly fits this description of complexity—especially within the context of a highly contested, fragmented and multidimensional conflict environment—which has implications for the extent to which resulting risks can be inferred causally from preceding events, hazards, or combinations of contextual factors and drivers. As Quigley et al. (2015, 29) note, "[w]hereas simple risks are associated with phenomena that are relatively frequent with fairly well understood causal links, extending these rational quantitative methods can become increasingly unreliable as the risk situation becomes more complex", especially within systems that are "characterized by non-linear interactions and delayed feedback".

The approach chosen by the team to work with this level of complexity[2] was the division of the risk-assessment tool into two primary components: a *threat/vulnerability assessment* component, and a *scenario-based impact-assessment* component. Within the first component, the question sets were re-formulated and re-grouped under either 'Threats' or 'Vulnerabilities' as applicable, thereby supporting the generation of a richer and, from the perspective of the project's MOD representatives, more useful and useable representation of the operating environment, while severing the erroneously and speciously deterministic connection between *likelihood* questions and certain risk scenarios.

Regarding the second component (i.e., impact), discussions with MOD representatives had emphasised the requirement to understand what the output of the risk assessment means in practice for military

[2] Readers should note that these aforementioned issues were not solely responsible for the subsequent design direction of the risk assessment, as this was also informed by on-going engagements with UK MOD (as part of the co-design approach to the project) and changes in UK defence policy and doctrine.

planning and prioritisation. Through these discussions, it was realised that attempting to assess the *impact* of forced labour *per se*, or of child soldiers *per se*, or of sex slavery/trafficking *per se*, made little practical or conceptual sense; one cannot meaningfully assess the *impact* of an occurrence without knowing the nature of the occurrence with sufficient specificity. In other words, the question "what is the impact of child soldiers" is meaningless in the absence of additional knowledge about the particular ways in which the phenomena (recruitment and use of child soldiers) is or might be manifesting. As such, the team produced several evidence-based risk scenarios that would represent, with sufficient uniqueness and military relevance, the ways in which each type of human trafficking might manifest in conflict. The scenarios were based on a combination of historical cases (e.g., the kidnapping of British soldiers by the West Side Boys militia in Sierra Leone), relevant areas of risk-assessment practice (e.g., forced labour and supply chain risk), and, reflecting the strong element of creativity inherent in the process of risk identification and assessment (e.g. Renn 2006, 23), creative thinking within the team.

Impact, Impact, Impact

Integral to any risk assessment is an assessment of the *consequences* or *impact* of the occurrence. However, understanding the extent and severity to which a particular type of human trafficking would manifest depends greatly upon the intrinsic qualities of—to use traditional risk jargon—the 'asset' being impacted, whether this refers to the local civilian population, or the 'level' of human security (however that is determined) or the military itself. Moreover, it is inadequate merely to say that a certain type of human trafficking can have a certain type of impact. Developing a more nuanced question set requires being able to say *how* this impact is made operative, *what* type of impact it is, and *under what conditions* the severity of that impact changes. The impact on the military itself may vary depending on the specific characteristics of the warfighting environment, while the impact may be different yet again in the context of stabilisation and reconstruction (S&R) activities, or during peacekeeping operations, and so on. Similarly, the impact on the individual and upon the community may vary greatly depending upon a broad range of inter-related personal, environmental and social factors. Indeed, one of the project's interviewees, an anti-slavery and anti-trafficking expert formerly with the UNODC, remarked that the *consequences* dimension of most human trafficking-related risk assessments (particularly in a policing context) is very generic and that further consideration is needed to determine how the *consequences* of any instance of human trafficking should be judged and scored (cited in Muraszkiewicz et al. 2019, 27). Another interviewee discussed how it is hard to say what *consequences* actually means in a human trafficking context, not least because the variables that affect risk at the individual level "play out differently in different regions" (cited in Ibid, 29).

Aside from the well-recognised lack of human trafficking data—especially as pertains to conflict situations—one might expect to be able to determine, with at least reasonable degree of validity, the *likelihood* of human trafficking manifesting in Country X based on, for instance, the number and strength of risk factors present, the reported prevalence of human trafficking there, and the frequency of new victims of human trafficking. However, determining the consequences of human trafficking for the population, with any degree of accuracy and diagnostic validity, would be a gargantuan undertaking. To start, it would be necessary to understand the various consequences, in principal, for a given population—while remembering that each population is unique—whether these consequences are physical, psychological, social, financial, educational, and so on. Then the assessment would need to link particular types of human trafficking to each consequence, asking, for instance, what are the physical consequences of being a victim of forced labour, what are the psychological consequences of being a victim of sex trafficking, or of becoming a child soldier, and so on. The assessment would then arrive at the most difficult and controversial line of enquiry: are the physical consequences of forced labour more or less severe than the psychological consequences? What about the comparative severity of the different consequences related to becoming a child soldier, or of entering into sexual exploitation?

Any attempt to accurately and comprehensively determine the nature of all these *consequences* would require posing questions such as the following: 'What's worse—being a child soldier or being a forced labourer?' Moreover, this occurs before even beginning to consider the consequences of human trafficking within the context of the risks to the UK military itself—for whom, following the same processes, one would arrive at questions such as: 'What's more consequential for the UK military—child soldiers, or forced suicide bombers, or forced labourers, and so on?' The difficulty in answering (and indeed asking) such questions places a greater emphasis on the professional judgement and nuanced professional experience of those individuals undertaking the risk assessment.

Because of the challenges in conceptualising and assessing the effects of human trafficking upon the civilian population, along with the recognition that the focus of the project revolved around understanding the *impact* dimension of human trafficking risk from the perspective of a military actor, the decision was made to wrap these population effects into a 'human security' risk category. Thus, to bridge the gap between the types of risks that the military is concerned about and the ways in which human trafficking can manifest in conflict situations, the team opted to use a standardised impact table (see Muraszkiewicz et al. 2019, 67–68). This is a framework common amongst military planners for assessing the impact severity of occurrences across different impact categories. The table used includes several impact categories with which military stakeholders will already be familiar, such as 'Life', 'Performance/Mission', 'Financial' and 'Reputation.' However, it is supplemented with categories derived from the project's research into human trafficking and human security, namely 'Mental Health, Wellbeing and Morale' and 'Human Security'. During the validation workshop, this was well-received because of the ease with which it would align with the way that military planners currently conceptualise and assess impact.

However, judging from the project's research efforts, interviews, stakeholder conversations and workshops, quantifying the *consequences* dimension of human trafficking risks is likely to remain a particular challenge within a complex, fragmented, multidimensional, dynamic environment—that is, conflict—and any assessment of this dimension will remain largely dependent upon the viewpoint of the observer, pending further research breakthroughs. As such, Project Solebay's adoption of the impact table implicitly captures the nuances mentioned above through direct input from the user.

Data and Collaboration

Because of the difficulty in identifying which factors are drivers, indicators, and/or those that merely have a tendency to correlate with human trafficking in a statistically insignificant minority of cases, the devised *threat* and *vulnerability* question sets remained at the macro level. For instance, it is possible to say that organised crime, weak rule of law, corruption, cross-border smuggling, gender-based discrimination, mass migration, and limited employment opportunities, amongst other factors, are drivers of human trafficking in conflict. However, it is difficult to be more specific than this. As discussed in the methodology section, with the absence of data it is challenging to 'dig deeper' into the problem in a way that would enable the generation of more granular or higher resolution question sets. To illustrate, while mass migration is a risk factor for human trafficking in conflict, it is difficult to pinpoint *why exactly*, *when exactly*, *under what circumstances exactly*, and *for which population groups* migration is a more or less salient risk factor. Further research is required to overcome this challenge. From the perspective of the team, future efforts must engage with a more granular level of data, which may be accessed via collaborative efforts through the CIMIC function (i.e., through targeted engagement between military and civilian actors).

Determining which chain of events or which combination of factors has a greater or lesser causal effect on the likelihood of a particular risk is not possible given the lack of sufficiently large and granular datasets. As such, making further advances in understanding the complexities of human trafficking will require the gathering of much more comprehensive in-depth data. As new data is gathered and analysed for patterns, this will generate requirements for further data collection as efforts are taken to build an increasingly reliable data model of human trafficking in conflict. Further, there will need to be greater collaboration between the military and the civil-humanitarian sectors. While humanitarian actors are often somewhat reluctant to work closely with the military and share information gathered from conflict-afflicted areas, such impediments to collaboration will need to be overcome going forward. As discussed earlier in this chapter, the CIMIC function provides a useful pre-existing model through which to advance this required collaboration and cooperation between military and non-military actors supporting the collection of appropriate intelligence.

Conclusion: Lessons for Human Security Analysis

While the issue of human trafficking in conflict might not at first glance be a primary military objective, its military relevance is increasingly recognised through the lens of human security. By locating the individual (and the local community) as the focus of security planning, the concept of human security provides the conceptual and analytical framework to consider the multitude of non-traditional, inter-connected and cross-cutting issues that undermine societal stability and individuals' wellbeing, and that can ultimately drive, exacerbate and prolong many of today's contemporary conflicts. In terms of advancing the state-of-the-art in human security analysis, there are some core lessons to be taken forward from Project Solebay.

First, it is crucial to understand what the purpose of human security analysis is. To inform responses, it is unlikely to be adequate to say merely that the objective is to 'analyse human security'. Instead, it is critical to understanding what the *output* is intended to be used for. This, in turn, requires understanding how the various human security issues at hand intersect with the roles, functions, capabilities and interests of various actors. A human security analysis conducted by (or for) a military actor may well differ in terms of insights and outputs than a human security analysis intended for a particular civil society actor. It is apparent that the military and its civilian partners can make progress here by working more closely together (e.g., through the CIMIC framework) to ensure that each actor is able to provide, and is provided with, the tools and resources necessary to effectively understand and address the range of human security issues to support them in their activities, both individually and collectively.

Second, from the perspective of risk assessment, further research is required to better conceptualise the dimension of *impact* upon the civilian population, and to devise methods for assessing that impact. As highlighted above, this task is by no means simple; it will require rigorous approach to both research and methodological development. Regardless of the conceptualisation(s) offered for this *impact* dimension, the result is unlikely to satisfy every stakeholder's ethical criteria. The objective, therefore, will not be to devise the 'right' approach but rather to devise an approach which is iteratively 'more right' than the previous. When assessing the impact of any form of human insecurity upon the civilian population, the focus should remain upon understanding and improving the on-the-ground reality experienced by that population.

Third, greater efforts are required to overcome the prevailing lack of data on human trafficking (and other human security issues) in conflict. To better inform military planning, not only is it necessary to more comprehensively map the currently available datasets and determine their utility in supporting the assessment of human security-related risks, but it is also crucial to understand what kind of data needs to be collected, from which sources, at which level of analysis (e.g., strategic, operational and tactical levels), and who is best placed to reliably collect the most accurate data. It is likely that both military and civilian actors will be well-placed to fill various of these information gaps, yet it is the combining of multiple datasets from various sources that will likely prove most useful in supporting human security analysis.

The time has come where there is increasing attention within a military setting on engaging with the concept of human security. Taking such a human security lens, Project Solebay sought to develop a risk-assessment methodology to support the UK-MOD in better understanding the issue of human trafficking. The result involved an assessment of human trafficking threats and vulnerabilities, along with an assessment of the impact of certain pre-defined but evidence-based risk scenarios. Being able to develop a proof-of-concept risk-assessment methodology regarding human trafficking for military purposes was largely due to the adoption of a co-design approach and the enthusiastic engagement from a large number of stakeholders including the MOD itself. Such levels of engagement will be key in continuing to drive forward R&D initiatives on human security. Similarly, partnerships between the military, civil society, private sector and the research arena is essential in developing appropriate means to inform and support decision-making. For the Project Solebay team, emphasis is on a socio-technical approach to data-driven innovation in human security analysis, and the lessons from Project Solebay, as well as others in this field, are instrumental in informing future efforts.

References

Ahram, Ariel I. 2015. Sexual Violence and the Making of ISIS. *Survival* 57 (3): 57–78.

Besenyő, János. 2016. The Islamic State and Its Human Trafficking Practice. *Strategic Impact* 60 (3): 15–21.

Binetti, Ashley. 2015. A New Frontier: Human Trafficking and ISIS's Recruitment of Women from the West. Information 2 Action.

Bloom, Mia, and Hilary Matfess. 2016. Women as Symbols and Swords in Boko Haram's Terror. *PRism* 6 (1): 104–121.

Diego-Rosell, Pablo, and Jacqueline Joudo Larsen. 2018. Modelling the Risk of Modern Slavery. https://papers.ssrn.com/sol3/papers.cfm?abstract_id=3215368

Fenton, Toby, Muraszkiewicz, Julia, Watson, Hayley, Maio, Giuseppe, Hesketh, Graham, and Wadhwa, Kush, 2019. Project Solebay: Modern Slavery Risk Assessment and Methodological Description. London: Trilateral Research. https://trilateralresearch.co.uk/project/project-solebay/

Kaldor, Mary. 1999. *New and Old Wars: Organized Violence in a Global Era*. 1st ed. Stanford University Press.

Kaplan, Stan. 1997. The Words of Risk Analysis. *Risk Analysis* 17 (4): 407–417.

MOD. 2012. *Structure of the Military Stabilisation Support Group*. https://www.gov.uk/government/publications/structure-of-the-military-stabilisation-support-group

———. 2016. *Joint Doctrine Publication 05. Shaping a Stable World: the Military Contribution*. The Development, Concepts and Doctrine Centre. https://assets.publishing.service.gov.uk/government/uploads/system/uploads/attachment_data/file/516849/20160302-Stable_world_JDP_05.pdf

———. 2017. Army Doctrine Publication Land Operations. The Development, Concepts and Doctrine Centre. https://assets.publishing.service.gov.uk/government/uploads/system/uploads/attachment_data/file/605298/Army_Field_Manual__AFM__A5_Master_ADP_Interactive_Gov_Web.pdf

———. 2019. JSP 1325: Human Security in Military Operations. Ministry of Defence. https://assets.publishing.service.gov.uk/government/uploads/system/uploads/attachment_data/file/770919/JSP_1325_Part_1_2019_O.PDF

Muraszkiewicz, Julia, Fenton, Toby, Watson, Hayley, Maio, Giuseppe, and Hesketh, Graham. 2019. Considerations for a UK Military-based approach to Assessing the Risk of Modern Slavery. London: Trilateral Research. https://trilateralresearch.co.uk/project/project-solebay/

NATO. 2018. *Allied Joint Doctrine (AJP)-3.19 for Civil-Military Cooperation.* https://www.gov.uk/government/publications/allied-joint-doctrine-for-civil-military-cooperation-ajp-319

———. 2019a. *Allied Joint Doctrine (AJP)-3 for the Conduct of Operations.* https://www.gov.uk/government/publications/allied-joint-doctrine-for-the-conduct-of-operations-ajp-3b

———. 2019b. *Allied Joint Doctrine (AJP)-5 for the Planning of Operations.* https://www.gov.uk/government/publications/allied-joint-publication-ajp-05a-allied-joint-doctrine-for-the-planning-of-operations

Newman, Edward. 2001. Human Security and Constructivism. *International Studies Perspectives* 2: 239–251.

Quigley, Kevin, Ronald Pelot, Colin Macdonald, and Lynne Genik. 2015. *Conceptual/Contextual Framework for Critical Infrastructure Protection Supply Chain Issues.* http://cradpdf.drdc-rddc.gc.ca/PDFS/unc193/p802230_A1b.pdf

Renn, Ortwin. 2006. *Risk Governance: Towards an Integrative Approach.* http://www.irgc.org/wp-content/uploads/2012/04/IRGC_WP_No_1_Risk_Governance__reprinted_version_3.pdf

Smith, Rupert. 2006. *The Utility of Force: The Art of War in the Modern World.* New York: Penguin.

United Nations. 2000. *Protocol to Prevent, Suppress and Punish Trafficking in Persons Especially Women and Children, supplementing the United Nations Convention against Transnational Organized Crime.* https://www.ohchr.org/en/professionalinterest/pages/protocoltraffickinginpersons.aspx

Zenn, Jacob, and Elizabeth Pearson. 2014. Women, Gender and the evolving tactics of Boko Haram. *Journal of Terrorism Research* 5 (1): 46–57.

Hayley Watson is Senior Practice Manager at Trilateral Research, managing business units around Applied Research & Innovation and the provision of interdisciplinary technical and research services to support data-driven decision making. Hayley's core background lies in social research that examines the positioning of citizens in relation to security-related issues. She has conducted research on the public's response to security issues (including crises), public vulnerabilities stemming from the impact of security-related issues, considerations for improving the resilience of the public, among other research projects. Hayley has a PhD in Sociology from the University of Kent.

Toby Fenton is an Associate Product Manager at Trilateral Research, where he works to understand the perspectives and needs of decision-makers and other stakeholders in the defence and security sectors to support innovation, applied research and technology development. From 2018–2019 he worked on Project Solebay which developed a proof-of-concept risk assessment to support the UK military's response to modern slavery and human trafficking (MSHT) as a human security issue. Toby's background lies in research and consultancy within the defence and security space. He holds a BSc in International Relations and an MA in International Peace & Security.

Stephen Anning is a PhD candidate at the University of Southampton conducting interdisciplinary research into Peace Studies and Computer Science. Following a career as an Infantry Officer in the Regular Army he is now a reservist and was the military lead for Project Solebay.

16

Incorporating Human Security Considerations into Military Planning: Some Suggestions

Toby Fenton, Peter Wieltschnig, and Julia Muraszkiewicz

Introduction

This book has sought to explore the various ways in which human trafficking and its related harms manifest particularly during times of conflict and crisis, along with its plethora of nebulous drivers and the policy levers and actors that could help address its impacts. Noting the prevalence of trafficking in persons in conflict, as the final part of this book, the current chapter turns to discuss the extent to which human trafficking, as a human security issue, might be better incorporated into military planning and analysis frameworks, and the ways in which such frameworks

T. Fenton (✉) • P. Wieltschnig • J. Muraszkiewicz
Trilateral Research, London, UK
e-mail: toby.fenton@trilateralresearch.com; peter.wieltschnig@trilateralresearch.com; julia.muraszkiewicz@trilateralresearch.com

J. Muraszkiewicz et al. (eds.), *Human Trafficking in Conflict*, Crime Prevention and Security Management, https://doi.org/10.1007/978-3-030-40838-1_16

might be augmented. The need to better account for human security considerations—or to take a human security perspective—during the planning of military operations is increasingly prominent in military thinking, along with key lessons learnt from headline military experience over the past nearly three decades. In discussing frameworks for military planning and situational analysis, this chapter mainly focuses on the NATO context due to the volume and accessibility of NATO (and its member states') documentation on this matter. That said, it is intended that this discussion might contribute to debates both within and without NATO regarding the incorporation of human security considerations within the planning of military operations.

As noted elsewhere in this book, human trafficking is an issue that generates a particular interest in the context of armed conflict when viewed through the prism of human security. As a "people-centred, comprehensive, context-specific and prevention-oriented" approach, the concept of human security aims to foster "responses that strengthen the protection and empowerment of all people" (UN General Assembly 2012, para 3(b)) prior to, during and after times of crisis. Resultantly, it can provide a strong conceptual and analytical basis for addressing the complexities of human trafficking during conflict. Indeed, the harms and insecurities faced by victims of human trafficking intersect and interact within multiple other human security issues, infringing on the freedoms from fear, from want, and from indignity—and limiting people's ability to make individual choices (MacLean 2006, 90; King and Murray 2001, 593; Commission on Human Security 2003, 10).

Given the complexities and multifaceted nature of human trafficking, and the manner in which is it situated amongst a range of security issues, a broad scope and sufficient depth of analysis is required to adequately account for human trafficking within a human security approach to military planning. As with other human security concerns and themes, human trafficking should not be assessed as a single, siloed issue, but rather—as indeed is fundamental to the concept of human security—in terms of the cumulative effects of the interactions between a range of threats, vulnerabilities and insecurities (OCHA 2009, 6). This chapter proceeds first by reviewing a selection of select military planning and analysis frameworks to explore their potential utility for assessing human trafficking within the rubric of human security; and second, by focussing specifically on the PMESII/PMESII-PT framework (explained below), which has been adopted by a number of NATO militaries and which may provide a starting point for further incorporating human security into military planning and situational analysis.

Human Trafficking and Human Security in Policy and Practice

Militaries have been increasingly attuned to non-traditional security threats and challenges since at least the end of the Cold War. Military actors, such as the UK Ministry of Defence (MOD) and NATO, are currently seeking to further develop guidelines, policies and practices to address the issue of human trafficking within the wider approach to incorporating human security concerns within the planning and conduct of military operations (MOD 2019b). Through a greater understanding of the ways in which the human security of various population groups (including cultural, ethnic, gender, age and other demographic dimensions) is affected differently during conflict and crisis situations, militaries are fostering a more nuanced and intersectional understanding of human security (see e.g. MOD 2013; 2019b). Military thinking captured in publications from the UK MOD and NATO provide a useful illustration here.

As already mentioned in this book, in 2004 NATO formalised its zero-tolerance *Policy on Combating Trafficking In Human Beings*. This policy held that personnel involved in NATO-led operations should "receive appropriate training to make them aware of the problem of trafficking and how this modern day slave trade impacts on human rights, stability and security, as well as being informed of their own responsibilities and duties and the respective responsibilities of International Organisations in this field" (NATO 2004). More recently, in 2019 the UK MOD released *Joint Security Publication (JSP) 1325* on *Human Security in Military Operations*, which highlights the importance of countering human trafficking as part of the wider incorporation of human security into military activities. *JSP 1325* recognises the need to "ensure that anti-trafficking responses are systematically included in military planning and execution of operations," and also "to enhance the knowledge base of human trafficking. In particular, collecting data, monitoring, and analysing trafficking in the context of crises, including protective and risk factors, as these can support stronger responses" (MOD 2019b, 42). However, it should be noted that these NATO and UK MOD documents are both defence policy, rather than military doctrine, and thus express statements of political intent. Indeed, as declared in the preface to *JSP 1325* (MOD 2019b, ii), that document constitutes "a statement of policy for the implementation of United Nations Security Council Resolution (UNSCR) 1325 and additional UNSCRs on women, peace and security (WPS), children in armed conflict (CAAC), Protection of Civilians (POC) and human trafficking into military activity."

The utility of considering issues like human trafficking in conflict within the rubric of human security has touchpoints with wider discussions around improvements to military planning. For instance, to clarify the essential points of the lessons learnt from the 2016 Iraq Inquiry (or Chilcott Inquiry) into the UK's involvement in the 2003 Iraq War, in 2018 the UK MOD published a document called *The Good Operation* (MOD 2018, 5) which sought to "prompt its readers to ask the right questions as they plan for and execute a military operation." As noted in *The Good Operation*, the Iraq Inquiry's report had suggested that in the years prior to, during and after the 2003 invasion of Iraq (the Report covered the period 2001–2009), the UK government, amongst other things, "[d]idn't properly understand the situation it was getting involved in," "[d]idn't exercise sufficient foresight about the way in which events would develop, particularly in planning for the post-warfighting phase of the operation," and that governments in general "have a responsibility to make every effort to understand the effects of their military action on civilian populations" (ibid., 7–8). The resulting *Chilcott Checklist* thus calls on military and political decision-makers to take a number of factors into account, including analysing "what is happening now [during a conflict or crisis] in terms of its root causes and likely evolution?"; understanding "[t]he likely impact of this operation on the country and its populace, including factors such as protection of non-combatants and gender issues. What do local communities want"; and, more expansively, to understand:

> The political, economic and social structures you are dealing with in the theatre of operations; the culture, including religious, ethnic or ideological drivers; and the principal personalities, their motivations, how they interconnect and where our priorities lie in terms of engaging them.

This emphasis on understanding the underlying reality (or 'ground truth') of a complex operating environment—including the underlying drivers, issues, dynamics, structures and intersections—has strong resonance with a human security-based approach to planning military activities (and also echo's efforts of understanding human trafficking). As some military actors already have policies in place (to various extents and degrees of effectiveness, although predominantly focusing on ensuring that troops do not engage in sexual exploitation) to help tackle human trafficking in conflict, the question arises as to how these policies can be better operationalised in order to safeguard and promote the human security of the population.

Through developing a stronger understanding of these underlying drivers of insecurity, military actors may be able to better target their efforts to support a baseline level of human security that allows for UN agencies, humanitarian organisations and other development actors to begin delivering more comprehensive development and security programming. Looking at the example of human trafficking, for instance, this stronger understanding of the 'human aspects' of a conflict-affected or otherwise fragile environment may enable the military to support the elimination of the conditions—threats, vulnerabilities, drivers, and so on—that allow human trafficking to prosper. For instance, establishing a safe and secure environment (SASE) in which the population has the ability to pursue daily activities without fear of persistent or large-scale violence, may allow for better economic stability, thereby reducing drivers of human trafficking within the area (NATO 2015, sections 0102 & 0203). Alternatively, it may be used in amending internal processes to account for the indirect impacts on individuals, such as ISAF's (International Security Assistance Force) targeting of poppy fields in Afghanistan to the detriment of the economic security of the local populace, for example, where the economic challenges faced by population ultimately led to an increase in the number of forced marriages (Walter 2016, 283).

Whilst militaries possess methodologies and techniques for attaining a situational awareness of the operating environment that already include a consideration of non-traditional security threats alongside more traditional ones, it is possible there is scope to further augment these in order to help better incorporate a human security approach into military planning that will account for different types of insecurities, including human trafficking.

Locating Human Security Within Military Planning and Analysis

While one can recognise the obligations for military actors arising from the Palermo Protocol, as detailed in other parts of this book, the complex web of drivers and manifestations of human trafficking will ultimately provide difficulties in the operationalisation of protective responses. In attempting to overcome this, one can look towards military planning and analysis, in a manner that aims to capture the human security dimensions of human trafficking for the military context. As noted above, adopting a human security approach can provide a lens through which to examine the particular characteristics—drivers, consequences, interdependencies with other related issues—of human trafficking in a way that is relevant for military planners to better understand the operating environment. This chapter suggests that a starting point for inserting all this into military planning may take the form of something akin to a 'human security analysis'.

While multiple models and frameworks exist to support military planning and analysis for situational awareness, the question for the purpose of this chapter—taking human trafficking as the primary reference point—concerns the extent to which these frameworks, in their current form, can sufficiently capture the relevant human security considerations. Although it is beyond the scope of this chapter to offer a comprehensive and fully international overview of assessment frameworks for military planning, nevertheless those developed within the NATO ecosystem provide some insight into the nature of these frameworks. These frameworks include, but are not limited to, those identified in the list below (MOD 2019a, section 3–21).

- *PESTLE*—political, economic, social, technological, legal and environmental perspectives. This framework can assist with the identification of the political and socio-economic dynamics present, whilst also capturing the level of technological strength, the strength of the legal system in place as well as the environmental considerations of the operating environment.
- *STEEPLEM*—social, technological, economic, environmental, political, legal, ethical and military perspectives. Expanding on the issues contained within the PESTL model, STEEPLEM is perhaps of greater operational utility. By including environmental, ethical and military perspectives within the analysis, it can allow militaries to enhance their understanding of how to engage in the operational environment, beyond the identifications of systems.
- *PMESII/PMESII-PT*—political, military, economic, social, information and infrastructure, with a more expansive version also encompassing the physical environment and time. This model is widely used by western militaries and has now been incorporated into NATO doctrine, for instance in *NATO Allied Joint Doctrine for the Planning of Operations* (NATO 2019). It was originally developed to provide an assessment framework for the systems involved with nation building (Ducote 2010, 6).
- *Constituents of a Nation*—rule of law, education, commercial, humanitarian, health, information, military, economic, diplomacy, administration, governance. The Constituents of a Nation is orientated towards the long-term stability of the operational environment, placing a particular emphasis on the capacity of the state as a whole.
- *ASCOPE*—area, structure, capabilities, organisation, people and events. This model has also been heavily used by western militaries, including the International Security Assistance Force in Afghanistan. The ASCOPE model provides a practical model for operational purposes, helping to hone military responses and enhance the effectiveness

of their efforts. It is frequently used together with the PMESII framework to provide an enhanced analysis of PMESII factors across the ASCOPE sectors.

Each of the above frameworks aims to facilitate a structured assessment of threats and risks pursuant to each of their thematic sub-headings. From a military perspective, these frameworks do appear to provide value as a suitable starting point for fostering a more robust and systematic incorporation of human security considerations. This is because they force the military to focus on human security. To put differently, these frameworks are fundamentally effects-based in their orientation, and furthermore largely locate the population as the focal point for assessment, recognising the importance of the systems that affect and influence their lives and are fundamental to operational planning. Moreover, depending on the model used, the concerns that are considered may be broad and include the long-term impacts (both intended and unintended) of military actions.

The remainder of this chapter focusses discussion on the PMESII-PT framework, for two reasons. First, it enjoys prominence within the military planning processes of a number of NATO members. Second, relative to the other frameworks outlined above, PMESII-PT by its nature implies the assessment of human security-related concerns, such as economic well-being, and therefore contains a useful degree of pre-existing analytical potential for thinking about how human security considerations might be further incorporated into military planning.

PMESII-PT: A Starting Point for Human Security Analysis?

Borne out of a discontent with ASCOPE and a desire to target nation-building systems, the US military originally devised PMESII in order to improve their decisions on who and what to target, as opposed to creating a tool for the analysis of the wider operating environment (Ducote 2010, 6). Despite this original purpose, PMESII was later reconfigured to allow the US military to understand complex environments (ibid). To achieve this, the physical environment (P) and time (T) were added to PMESII, thus creating PMESII-PT. This was intended to improve the military's ability to understand the diversity of factors that influence the changing nature of a complex operating environment, beyond the systems initially present in the environment (ibid).

The updated PMESII-PT methodology has since been adopted by NATO, in the sense that they still use the original PMESII model but recognise that additional issues or 'dimensions' may be used to expand the analysis, therefore paving the way for the physical environment and time to be added into their assessments (NATO 2013, section 1–6, fn 7). In utilising the PMESII/PMESII-PT framework, military planners at the operational level can undertake a review of the goals, strength, weaknesses and interdependencies of key actors in the environment across these headings to understand how these actors may perceive and respond to the issues captured under each heading, and thus how their behaviours may be influenced positively (US Army 2009, 7). The result from a PMESII/PMESII-PT analysis is used to inform how military activities can be shaped to achieve wider strategic aims (NATO 2013, sections 1-8-1-9). By placing individual people as the subjects of analysis, militaries can gain a stronger understanding of the root causes of instability at the individual and community level (this being the level of analysis fostered through a human security lens), and thereby design strategies and activities that help promote the security and well-being of the population.

Additionally, the PMESII/PMESII-PT framework can be incorporated into effects modelling (i.e. the measurement of the anticipated effects resulting from military measures) to ensure that the variables sufficiently capture the complex nature of the operating environment. This augmented PMESII/PMESII-PT framework, tailored to incorporate human security considerations, attempts to provide a realisable approach for militaries similar NATO's military concept on the *Protection of Civilians*, which seeks to achieve four objectives: understand the human environment (UHE) including culture, history, demographics, strengths and vulnerabilities; safeguard civilians from harm by belligerents; facilitate access to basic needs and services to the population; and to contribute to establishing a safe and secure environment (SASE) through support to local government and its institutions (NATO 2018 *The PoC*). Ultimately, this can allow for a framework capable of fostering and understanding of the underlying dynamics that may contribute to human trafficking.

Potential Changes to PMESII/PMESII-PT

This chapter has so far sought to identify the potential of PMESII-PT as a starting point for incorporating human security considerations into military planning and the analysis of the operating environment. Taking this inquiry forward, the challenge is to determine what changes may be required within PMESII-PT to enable a structured analysis of human security issues. Readers should note that the changes outlined below are intended to explore how this might work in practice; they should not be interpreted as the authors' declaration on what the military 'should' do, but rather are being put forward for wider consideration, critique, and revision; nor are the issues captured below exhaustive. On this basis, it thus appears that the PMESII-PT headings could be provisionally adapted as follows:

- *Political*—This would include an understanding of formal and informal power structures (national, regional and local levels), including key actors and the political dynamics characterising the operating environment. This may include the strength, relationships and positioning of tribes, ethnic groups and familial groups, and others. Beyond this, the rule of law (or the ability to establish the rule of law) is an important consideration, potentially involving looking at the capacity of local political systems to provide an environment where the human rights of the population are secured. As such, it is worth analysing issues such as corruption, discrimination in all its forms, respect of human rights (including political groups' respect for human rights), the presence and extent of a free media, the nature of interest-based politics and exclusionary politics, and the extent of the militarisation of informal and formal power structures. With respect to human trafficking, one would look at legislation in relation to this crime, enforcement of such legislation (including conviction rates), as well as political commitment to fighting the exploitation of persons.

- *Military*—This would focus on developing an awareness of the capabilities of all state and non-state armed actors within the operating environment, including the deployment of the local or foreign armed forces. This could include a quantitative and qualitative analysis of military personnel, equipment, technology, organisational structures, culture, ethos, and resources. With respect to human trafficking, one would also enquire into the level of training/awareness on the issue of human trafficking, including for the purposes of sexual exploitation. Military planners would also seek to improve their understanding of the possible impacts of their own military activities upon the local population and the potential negative security effects—including second- and third-order effects. This latter consideration would likely involve, for instance, looking at the impacts of military activities upon the maintenance or promotion of human rights, along with the environmental consequences (e.g. pollution of water/food supplies, resource depletion, or environmental degradation) resulting from the deployment of military forces in various geographic areas. Moreover, military planners may in fact consider the relative utility, or lack thereof, of different forms of military activity for the purpose of addressing aspects of human insecurity in the first place. In this sense, planners could seek to assess whether they currently possess the necessary capabilities to address the range of identified human security issues (such as human trafficking) and thus whether additional resources or collaborative efforts are needed, such as closer cooperation with civilian humanitarian actors.
- *Economic*—Analysing the economic dimension though a human security lens could involve looking at trade, development, finance, policies, capabilities, and legal constraints relating to the production, distribution, and consumption of resources, and the ways in which they affect economic behaviours. This would likely involve the assessment of a vast range of factors, including the overarching economic system, the geographic and demographic distribution of resources (including food), employment levels, income distribution, external investment, taxation policy, consumption patterns, port authorities, the movement

of goods, consumer issues, border controls, corruption, standards of living, black-market and underground economies, and the distribution of labour. Such issues are of relevance in military planning, as the economic well-being of the population will have a huge bearing on the ways in which effects manifest. In this sense, the economic conditions in which the population live will affect their resilience in the face of harm, including human trafficking, or may be relevant in the choice of the means and methods of warfare where they impact economic practices. Indeed, poverty which is tied to economics, is one of the biggest drivers of human trafficking and broader economic structures impact labour exploitation.

The military already uses what might be described as a human security lens for this dimension of the PMESII/PMESII-PT analysis, as it is reflects the fact that a country's economic conditions are directly related to security and stability. Additionally, this dimension of analysis can lend itself to an appreciation of the non-kinetic aspects of the operating environment and the importance of a collaborative approach with aid agencies, for example, to ensure economic and indeed general stability and security. However, additional considerations could be incorporated into this dimension analysis to strengthen human security considerations. For instance, military planners could look closer at issues such as child labour, economic resource (and access thereto) inequality, availability of access to credit lines, discrimination in economic practices, resource depletion, sudden rises in food prices, economic shocks, indicators pointing to the potential collapse of the economy, the extent of social supports, and threats to agricultural practices.

- *Social*—The social dimension of the PMESII analysis is particularly important in taking a people-centred approach to understanding the operating environment. Here, it seems likely that military planners would seek to develop an awareness of the cultural identities of local populations, community demographics (including ethnic, gender, religious and identity-based groupings), the languages used, education levels and attendance, traditions and culture, and the cohesiveness and potential points of tension between different groups. Additional considerations would include migration trends, the level of urbanisation, and standards of living. That said, whilst these issues are essential for developing a more human security-orientated understanding of the operating environment, and would also contribute to a better understanding of human trafficking or its potential in the theatre of conflict, the concept of human security places a premium on individual security. As such, the social dimension of PMESII/PMESII-PT could be further divided into two sub-dimensions—physical well-being and social well-being—in order to capture these essential features of human security, often articulated as the freedom from fear and the freedom from want, and provide space for the full assessment of non-traditional threats to individuals' physical well-being, e.g. through disease. Readers should note that whilst some of the relevant threats will necessarily intersect across both sections, the exact way in which they manifest to impact an individual's physical or social well-being will take different forms. Nevertheless, the two sub-dimensions are outlined as separate issues in order to provide clarity for operational planners, as it is not necessarily intuitive that social well-being would also include aspects of physical well-being. In this respect, the creation of a specific subdivision is intended to direct military attention to these issues, as well as the desire to emphasise the importance of physical well-being. The relevant human security concerns under the physical well-being and social well-being considerations will entail the following considerations:

- *Physical well-being*—This sub-dimension could include threats directly affecting individuals' physical security and well-being, such as the physical threats arising out of crime and street violence, human trafficking, terrorism, child abuse, child labour, and sexual and gender-based violence will be of relevance. Further, issues such as the lack of access to healthcare, lack of access to safe food, disruption of food supplies, lack of access to safe water, disease, malnutrition, psycho-social trauma, FGM practices, the lack of shelter, poor housing conditions, drug use, natural disaster, pollution, unsanitary conditions will be relevant issues that militaries may choose to consider.

- *Social well-being*—This sub-dimension could include threats that affect individuals' social security and social well-being, encompassing non-survival issues that are nevertheless essential for fulfilling existence. These could include threats stemming from the lack of education, ethnic, religious and other identity-based tensions, weakened cultural life, discrimination, lack of social support, lack of access to justice, the destruction or limitation of agricultural and other economic practices, child abuse, child labour, threats to indigenous communities, sexual and gender-based violence, other forms of exploitation, lack of free media, economic inequality, inequality in the access to resources, poverty, crime, the lack of shelter, poor housing conditions, destruction of property (including cultural property), drug use, and weakened cultural diversity.

- *Information*—The information dimension of PMESII/PMESII-PT could be augmented to enable military planners to better understand, for instance, the relevant communications systems present within the operating environment, as well as the extent and nature of media coverage (sub-national, national and international) both of the crisis area itself and of the planned or on-going military activities. Considerations in this dimension could also include the military's, its allies' and adversaries' abilities to access communication systems and information, as well as their ability to disseminate, manipulate, assess, store and act on information. The military's reliance on certain forms or sources of information will be an important consideration under PMESII/PMESII-PT, as will the population's own access to communications systems such as the internet or radio. With respect to human trafficking, information would also include ease of access to knowledge on human trafficking laws as well as organisations offering protection and assistance. Owing to the centrality of information communications systems in almost all societies today, this dimension of PMESII/PMESII-PT would also prompt military planners to look at the potential effects of military activities on the security, maintenance and accessibility of these systems.

Additionally, this dimension may be viewed within a human security approach as highlighting the importance of gaining information on issues across the various PMESII/PMESII-PT headings from all levels of society, including the input of the local community within the operating environment. In the example of Afghanistan, the Chief of Coalition Intelligence noted that such information can be gathered through the collection of:

- Census data and patrol debriefs;
- Minutes from consultations with local communities and community representatives;
- After-action reports from civil affairs officers and Provincial Reconstruction Teams (PRTs);
- Polling data and atmospherics reports from psychological operations and female engagement teams;
- Translated summaries of radio broadcasts that are influential to the local community, Field observations of Afghan soldiers, United Nations officials, and NGOs (Flynn and Pottinger 2010).

Throughout any information-gathering activities, it is important from a human security perspective that all information is sufficiently disaggregated so that military planners are provided with an awareness of the intersectional and cross-cutting impacts of threats posed to communities. Here, information would be disaggregated to account for demographics such as age, gender, ethnic, religious and social class, disability and any other marker that is believed to potentially affect an individual's vulnerability. The information dimension would also look at the presence and/or extent of a free media and the level of respect for human rights, particularly the freedom of expression, opinion and assembly.

- *Infrastructure*—This could include an analysis of the basic facilities, services, installations and other infrastructure required for the society to function, as well as the population's abilities to access the related services, particularly in relation to healthcare services, and access to food and water. It is noted that poor infrastructure could lead to a rise in the informal job sector which can attract human trafficking for the purpose of labour exploitation.

Demographically disaggregated information will be vital, as individuals may be impacted in different ways depending on their particular characteristics. For example, persons with disabilities are likely to be severely affected when access to services is reduced. Consideration could also be paid to threats arising from the destruction of property (including cultural property), lack of shelter (including shelter for victims of human trafficking), poor housing conditions, lack of irrigation systems, unsanitary conditions, and lack of education. Once again, military planners would also look closely at the potential negative effects of planned military activities upon this range of issues. This dimension of PMESII-PT may be supported by using the SWEAT-MSO framework for assessment:

- *Sewers*—Collection and treatment of sewage;
- *Water*—Production and distribution of water;
- *Electricity*—Generation and distribution of electricity;
- *Academic*—Facilities and services related to education;
- *Trash*—Collection and disposal of waste;
- *Medical Facilities*—Facilities and services related to healthcare;
- *Safety*—Facilities and services related to public safety (e.g. police and fire-fighting services) (US Army 2008, sections 4–57).
- *Other*—Such as transportation (including the distance to roads; traffic levels) and the society's level of technological development.

- *Physical Environment*—Analysing the physical environment would include looking at the local terrain (both natural and man-made) as well as the climate and weather to understand the environmental constraints on military activities. Moreover, military planners would look at issues such as environmental degradation, climate change/catastrophe, natural disasters, pollution, drought, famine, flooding, resource depletion and, in particular, the use of any military munitions (such as landmines) that may impede people's ability to interact with their physical environment. Understanding, for instance, the nature and impact of climate change could help predict potential migration flows, and in turn identify a risk of human trafficking amongst migration routes.

- *Time*—This dimension refers largely to a consideration of the impact of the conflict/crisis and the militaries' activities over time, including the effect upon public support (within the operating environment and abroad) for military activities. It also includes looking at the temporal aspects of military activity, including the timing of actions in relation to civil activities that result in more densely populated areas, such as when and where festivities take place and how this may change behaviours and sentiments amongst the population. This dimension of PMESII/PMESII-PT may also provide a practical contribution to operationalising human security, in the sense of prompting military planners to look closely at community and individual levels of resilience to human security threats across time.

A Resilience-Based Approach to Human Security Impacts

Adopting a resilience-based approach for analysing human security impacts can enable military planners to better demarcate the line between possible threats to consider and actual human security concerns in a manner that accommodates the accumulative impact of threats. Here, we can recognise 'resilience' as the population's ability to withstand, mitigate or adapt to negative impacts to their security (or 'harms'), and may include the access to reserve supplies, the ability to conduct repairs or the strength of civil society efforts to response, for instance. This approach may help to create a more realisable understanding of civilian harm—one that does not, for analytical convenience, rely disproportionately on *freedom from fear* considerations to the detriment of wider *freedom from want* considerations (Owen 2004, 382). Here, the full range of potential harms may be considered without reducing human security to a limited number of discrete threats. Instead, human insecurity arises when the threat or manifestation of the harm is of a particular severity and the community or individual's capacity to withstand, mitigate or adapt to the harm is limited (*ibid*). Resilience capacities will determine the severity of the threat or manifestation of harm and identify whether human security has been or will be impacted. In conducting this assessment, attention should be paid to the immediate severity of harm, individual or community vulnerability of the community, and the resilience of the individual or community over time. The immediate severity of the damage likely to be caused by the threat is an essential consideration for determining the impact of a threat. To take an extreme illustration, a hydrogen bomb clearly poses a greater immediate threat than the gradual desertification of terrain.

Weight should therefore be given to the characteristics of an individual or community to assess how threats may intersect and compound to impact human security. Here, demographically disaggregated data becomes particularly useful, as noted above, as does location-based data that can help prioritise those people who are in closer proximity to potential threats. This may require the assessment of their existing capabilities as well as coping behaviours to determine their abilities to withstand, mitigate or adapt to harms.

In regard to the threshold itself, there are various approaches that may help chart the relevant standards. Quantitative data may be obtained, for example, on the number of deaths within the operating environment, or living standards within an area. However, any quantitative approaches will ultimately return to subjective determinations in the importance of each impact when aggregating information. Owen suggests that the threshold should ultimately be determined politically, by international organisations, national governments and NGOs with the level of political priority, will and capacity informing the determination (*ibid.*, 384).

Concluding Remarks

Operationalising human security within military planning is challenging in any form, given the complexities and ill-defined nature of the concept of human security. Similar complexities and problems of poor definition also arise with regard to human trafficking, whether in conflict or during peace time. Better understanding the nature of particular human security issues—as the other chapters in this book have sought to do in relation to human trafficking in conflict—is a necessary early step in this journey. With regard to human trafficking, we are in need of concrete legal guidance as to what the military obligations are—as chapter nine by Milano, chapter ten by Chadimova and Chap. 14 by Ruiz-Diaz have sought to do—in addition to stronger explication of how the military can contribute towards anti-human trafficking efforts, including in relation to human security. This book hopes to further provoke such discussions.

A subsequent step will be in developing processes to enable military actors to better incorporate human security considerations within the planning and conduct of military activities. The suggestions outlined in this chapter have been intended to contribute to on-going discussions about how to tackle this latter (though by no means final) step. Expanding the existing military PMESII/PMESII-PT analytical framework to account for a number of human security issues, including trafficking of persons, may support military planners in making meaningful and useful advances here.

The suggested augmentations to PMESII/PMESII-PT capture a parallel requirement related to military efforts at understanding the environments in which they operate. Namely, the insights required will be frustrated so long as planners and decision-makers continue to be hamstrung by a lack of accurate, granular, sub-national level data on the range of human security issues, threats, vulnerabilities, and dimensions outlined above—and which have been embodied throughout this book through a focus on human trafficking in conflict. This 'data challenge' is a particularly acute and perennial one. Chapters three and 12 of this book, for instance, noted the lack of accurate statistics on child soldiers. There are multiple ways to explain the lack of data on this and other points. One explanation is the sheer difficulty in obtaining accurate data regarding any issue during times of conflict and crisis. Beyond the very real threats to researchers, humanitarians and others—including, of course, frontline military forces—seeking to obtain survey data during conflict situations, it is likely to be the case for many actors that the delivery of aid and relief, rather than the collection of data, is the primary concern—at least until such a time as the environment has become sufficiently 'safe and secure'. As such, data collection may often be relegated to post-conflict, stabilisation, and reconstruction phases, which can require piecing information together from testimonies, eyewitnesses, official and unofficial records, and population surveys. At the same time, the acquisition of comprehensive and accurate figures and data on the extent and types of different human security issues is compounded by their nebulousness, especially in conflict; as van Rij, Mohay and Bileišis note in Chap. 5, the "cunningness" of human traffickers, and the modes and methods of exploitation, are constantly evolving.

One particularly interesting example of the use of more granular data to understand human trafficking dynamics in conflict situations was found in the example conveyed in chapter six. Here, Maio, Hurtado, Hesketh and Wadhwa discussed the use of sub-national level data from the department of Antioquia, Colombia, to understand the particular factors and combinations thereof which underlie the decisions of children to join armed groups. In addition to sourcing the relevant data from local public offices, the authors described the use of statistical analysis techniques to generate and test a model for children's decisions to enlist. Such approaches to analyse human trafficking dynamics in conflict provide a promising basis on which to continue developing more data-driven human security policies and strategies for political, military and humanitarian planners alike.

The book has presented other barriers that the military faces when trying to understand and contribute towards human security in conflict. In the context of human trafficking, these problems are namely in relation to understanding who a victim of human trafficking is and who is a perpetrator, as exemplified by Dunhill and Kidd in Chap. 13, Muraszkiewicz in Chap. 11 and by van Rij, Mohay and Bileišis in Chapter fice. Yet, as was mentioned in the introduction to this book, enabling the military to develop a stronger understanding human trafficking in conflict is key, especially as the phenomenon greatly impacts their ability to promote and sustain security and stability, including through the financial empowerment of adversarial actors as we saw in chapter four. In situations where the military itself becomes involved in the practice of human trafficking in some way, as discussed in chapter seven by Pehlic and chapter eight by Greer and Cates, this can seriously impacting their reputation, their perceived legitimacy, and, ultimately, their ability to achieve broader security and stability objectives.

In a sense, one could argue that conflict and security has always been 'people-centred'. It is individual people or groups of individuals who start conflicts; it is individuals and groups who engage in conflicts; and it is large numbers of people, many of whom are civilians, who suffer when conflict rages around them or cuts a swath through entire communities; whether it is because they are directly impacted by violence or by conflict-propelled phenomenon like human trafficking. By strengthening the understanding of the human side of conflict through a deeper analysis of the issues and dynamics that threaten the security of the individual, and which often propel people towards violence and societies towards instability, military planners and decision-makers may therefore be able to better select the most effective security measures and activities, mitigate the potentially negative impacts of military interventions upon the population, reduce the likelihood that post-conflict societies will relapse into instability, and ultimately promote a more sustainable security.

References

Commission on Human Security. 2003. *Human Security Now*. New York: Commission on Human Security.

Ducote, Brian. M. 2010. *Challenging the Application of PMESII-PT in a Complex Environment*. Fort Leavenworth, Kansas: School of Advanced Military Studies United States Army Command and General Staff College. https://apps.dtic.mil/dtic/tr/fulltext/u2/a523040.pdf

Flynn, Michael, and Pottinger, Matt. 2010. *Fixing Intel: A Blueprint for Making Intelligence Relevant in Afghanistan*. Working Paper, 4 January 2010. Washington DC: Center for a New American Security (CNAS).

King, Gary, and Christopher Murray. 2001. Rethinking Human Security. *Political Science Quarterly* 116 (4): 585–610.

MacLean, George. 2006. Human Security and the Globalization of International Security: Mutual Vulnerability, and Sustainable Development, a Critical View. *Whitehead Journal of Diplomacy and International Relations* 7 (2): 89–99.

MOD. 2013. *Joint Doctrine Note 4/13 Culture and Human Terrain*. Wiltshire: Development, Concepts and Doctrine Centre, MOD. https://assets.publishing.service.gov.uk/government/uploads/system/uploads/attachment_data/file/256043/20131008-_JDN_4_13_CultureU.pdf

———. 2018. *The Good Operation*. London: MOD. https://www.gov.uk/government/publications/the-good-operation
———. 2019a. AJP-5 Allied Joint Doctrine for the Planning of Operations (Edition A Version 2 with UK National Elements). London: MOD. https://assets.publishing.service.gov.uk/government/uploads/system/uploads/attachment_data/file/837082/dcdc_doctrine_nato_planning_of_ops_ajp_5.pdf
———. 2019b. JSP 1325 Human Security in Military Operations. London: MOD. https://assets.publishing.service.gov.uk/government/uploads/system/uploads/attachment_data/file/770919/JSP_1325_Part_1_2019_O.PDF
NATO. 2004. *NATO Policy on Combating Trafficking in Human Beings*. https://www.nato.int/docu/comm/2004/06-istanbul/docu-traffic.htm
———. 2013. *Allied Command Operations Comprehensive Operations Planning Directive*. Belgium: Supreme Headquarters Allied Powers Europe.
———. 2015. AJP-3.4.5: *Allied Joint Doctrine for the Military Contribution to Stabilization and Reconstruction*. Belgium: NATO Standardisation Office.
———. 2018. *The Protection of Civilians*. https://www.nato.int/cps/en/natohq/topics_135998.htm
———. 2019. *Allied Joint Doctrine for the Planning of Operations (Edited A Version 2)*. Brussels: NATO Standardisation Office.
OCHA. 2009. *Human Security in Theory & Practice: Application of the Human Security Concept and the United Nations Trust Fund for Human Security*. New York: UN Human Security Unit.
Owen, Taylor. 2004. Human Security—Conflict, Critique and Consensus: Colloquium Remarks and a Proposal for a Threshold-Based Definition. *Security Dialogue* 35 (3): 373–387.
UN General Assembly. 2012. Follow-up to Paragraph 143 on Human Security of the 2005 World Summit Outcome. A/RES/66/290, 25 October 2012.
US Army. 2008. *Field Manual 3–07 Stability*. Washington, DC: Headquarters, Department of the Army. https://www.globalsecurity.org/military/library/policy/army/fm/3-07/fm3-07_2014.pdf
———. 2009. *Training and Doctrine Command, G2, 'The Operational Environment'*. https://www.hsdl.org/?abstract&did=35592
Walter, Ben. 2016. The Securitization of Development and Humans' Insecurity in Nangarhar Province, Afghanistan. *Global Change, Peace & Security* 28 (3): 271–287.

Toby Fenton is an Associate Product Manager at Trilateral Research, where he works to understand the perspectives and needs of decision-makers and other stakeholders in the defence and security sectors to support innovation, applied research and technology development. From 2018–2019 he worked on Project Solebay which developed a proof-of-concept risk assessment to support the UK military's response to modern slavery and human trafficking (MSHT) as a human security issue. Toby's background lies in research and consultancy within the defence and security space. He holds a BSc in International Relations and an MA in International Peace & Security.

Peter Wieltschnig is a research analyst at Trilateral Research. He holds an LLB in Law & Human Rights and an LLM in International Humanitarian Law. He has experience working within human rights research as he has a background in criminal defence work in the north of Ireland. His research interests relate to the protection of economic, social and cultural rights in armed conflict.

Julia Muraszkiewicz is a Senior Research Manager at Trilateral Research in the Applied Research and Innovation team and was the research lead of Project Solebay looking at risk assessment methodologies for human trafficking in conflict. She has a publication with Palgrave Macmillan on protecting trafficked persons from liability. Julia in her spare time volunteers with NGOs that directly help victims of human trafficking and labour exploitation. She has a PhD in Law from Vrije University of Brussels.

Index[1]

A

Afghanistan, x, 14, 147, 151, 152, 158, 161, 212, 233–249, 321, 323, 331
Analysis, 12, 14, 43, 69, 92, 108–110, 125, 156–164, 189, 198, 209, 212, 219, 227, 244, 297–313, 317–319, 322–334, 336, 337
Armed groups, 2, 8, 10–12, 24, 26–31, 34, 36, 61, 64, 66, 74, 84, 85, 92, 101–117, 179, 189, 216, 217, 237, 238, 242, 257–263, 265–272, 298, 336
Army, 67, 90, 134, 153, 162, 235, 244, 249, 260, 300, 302, 325

B

Boko Haram, viii, 2, 26, 29, 32, 67, 71, 215, 298
Bosnia and Herzegovina (B&H), vii, 12, 51, 123–129, 131–139, 279n1, 287

C

Children in armed conflict (CAAC), 14, 245, 320
Child soldier, vii, ix, x, 2, 5, 14, 15, 29–31, 34, 43–49, 52, 83–85, 90, 91, 93–95, 102, 102n3, 103, 106–109, 220, 234, 238, 257–272, 297, 307–309, 335

[1] Note: Page numbers followed by ‘n’ refer to notes.

J. Muraszkiewicz et al. (eds.), *Human Trafficking in Conflict*, Crime Prevention and Security Management, https://doi.org/10.1007/978-3-030-40838-1

Civil-military cooperation (CIMIC), 299–301, 310, 311
Colombia, 12, 30, 45, 101–117, 174, 189, 286, 336
Conflict, v–vii, x, 2–5, 7–16, 21–32, 34, 36–38, 43–57, 61–75, 84–87, 89–94, 96, 101, 102, 102n3, 113, 123–139, 143, 173, 174, 178–184, 186, 188–192, 199, 200, 202, 211, 212, 216, 217, 226, 226n4, 229, 233–249, 257, 259–263, 265, 267, 268, 278–292, 297–304, 306–312, 317–321, 329, 333–337
Corruption, 10, 31, 50, 51, 63, 124, 130–132, 138, 234, 236, 284, 304, 310, 326, 328
Cultural property, 330, 332

D

Data, vi, 3, 11, 12, 21, 72–74, 88, 96, 104, 106–112, 111n6, 114, 116, 132, 152, 237, 299, 303–305, 308, 310–312, 320, 331, 334–336
Democratic Republic of Congo (DRC), vii, 3, 26, 31, 65, 130, 174, 265, 266, 268, 269, 279n1
Disarmament, demobilisation and reintegration (DDR), 14, 15, 137, 258, 262–267, 269–272
Doctrine, 298, 300, 306n2, 320, 323

E

European Court of Human Rights (ECtHR), 94, 176, 177, 180, 186
Exploitation, v–vii, x, 2, 4, 6, 9, 12, 14, 22, 32, 34, 36, 37, 43–57, 62–67, 73–75, 85–89, 91, 96, 124, 125, 127, 128, 131, 133, 136, 137, 143–145, 150, 151, 154, 161–165, 173, 187, 188, 216, 219, 221, 234–237, 239–241, 243, 245, 247, 260, 261, 263, 267, 268, 272, 279n1, 308, 321, 327, 328, 330, 332, 336

F

Finance, 173, 246, 327
Forced combat, 34–35

G

Gender, 5, 9, 50, 53, 109, 113, 221, 224, 235, 242, 243, 247–249, 261–263, 265, 270, 271, 319, 320, 328, 331

H

Humanitarian law, 29, 30, 245, 246
Human rights, 3, 5, 9, 13, 25, 27, 30, 33, 65, 87, 93, 94, 115, 128, 130n1, 135, 137, 138, 165, 174–177, 179, 180, 188, 189, 217, 223, 223n2, 223n3, 226, 234, 241, 245, 246, 279, 284, 285, 297, 298, 300, 301, 303, 319, 326, 327, 331

Human security, v–viii, 3, 4, 6–8, 15, 25, 27, 38, 223n2, 235, 239, 244–246, 285, 288, 289, 297–313, 317–336
Human trafficking, v–x, 2–7, 9–16, 21–27, 32–35, 37–38, 43–57, 61–75, 83–96, 104, 123–139, 143, 144, 146–148, 150, 159–162, 164, 173–192, 197–212, 215–222, 224, 226, 228, 229, 233–249, 260, 261, 272, 278–292, 297–313, 317–322, 326–330, 332–337

I

Impunity, 14, 27, 31, 125, 126, 132, 234–236, 238, 247, 248
International Criminal Court (ICC), vii, 31, 32, 89, 93, 197–199, 201, 206, 210, 211
International humanitarian law (IHL), 92–94, 175, 207, 220, 239–242, 245, 249
Iraq, 2, 36, 91, 147, 151, 152, 156, 157, 159–161, 212, 297, 320
Islamic State (or ISIS, ISIL), viii, 2, 26, 29, 30, 35, 36, 64, 66, 67, 71, 215, 216, 218–220, 224, 227n5, 228, 297

K

Kosovo, 36, 130, 130n1, 174, 236, 279n1, 282, 288

L

Legal responsibility, 13, 197–212
Libya, 65, 66, 212, 282, 288, 289

M

Military, v, viii–x, 3–6, 10–16, 23, 25, 27, 28, 30, 31, 50, 52, 64, 66–68, 70, 74, 83–96, 123–125, 128–130, 143–165, 173–192, 197–212, 218, 220, 223n2, 229, 233–249, 257, 265, 278, 279n1, 281n4, 284, 286, 288, 291, 297–313, 317–337

N

Nigeria, 2, 32, 52, 298
North Atlantic Treaty Organisation (NATO), vii, x, 3, 5, 14, 15, 23, 25, 95, 127, 130, 178, 183, 184, 186, 190, 235, 239–249, 278–292, 299–302, 318–321, 323–326

P

Palermo Protocol, 2, 6, 14, 22, 48, 87, 175, 177, 179, 180, 184–186, 260, 298n1, 322
Peacekeeping, 12, 15, 23, 25, 26, 28, 124, 125, 134–137, 139, 143, 182, 183, 191, 212, 235, 278, 279, 279n1, 302, 307
PMESII, 319, 323–333, 335
Poverty, x, 4, 9, 21, 46, 50–54, 103, 104, 115, 138, 139, 173, 188, 234, 236, 260, 272, 328, 330

Prevention, 4, 15, 21, 103, 104, 145, 148–150, 159, 175, 176, 178, 187, 189, 234, 235, 244, 247, 278, 279, 279n1, 281n6, 284, 298
Private military & security company (PMSCs), 11, 84–86, 90–96
Punishment, x, 14, 47, 134, 149, 153, 162, 203n8, 217, 222, 225–229

R

Ransom, 33–34, 64, 66, 68
Regional organisations, 6, 15, 278–292
Risk, vi, vii, 9, 11, 15, 28, 37, 43, 44, 46, 49, 51–57, 67, 68, 70, 71, 73, 74, 85, 91, 102, 104, 113–117, 124, 148, 157, 180, 182, 186–191, 224, 227, 235, 236, 243, 247, 263–265, 271, 272, 297–299, 301–310, 312, 320, 324, 333
Risk assessment, viii, 15, 23, 70, 297–313
Rome Statute, 13, 32, 197–212
Russia, ix, 35, 83–96, 127

S

Sexual abuse, 23, 103, 128, 163, 237, 240, 244
Sexual exploitation, vii, 4, 22–29, 48, 49, 52, 53, 65, 73, 87, 89, 90, 125, 127, 137, 144, 145, 150, 154, 161–165, 173, 237, 240, 241, 243, 260, 261, 263, 268, 308, 321, 327
Sexual violence, 26, 28, 29, 33, 67, 189, 219, 233–249, 261, 271
Slavery, v, vii, 6, 26, 29, 32–33, 44n1, 48, 87, 88, 93, 137, 143, 165, 175, 176, 189, 197, 199n2, 203, 219, 220, 241, 241n2, 249, 260, 305, 307
Soldiers, vii–ix, 33, 45–47, 49, 104, 128, 130, 135, 145, 162, 164, 165, 182, 183, 218, 220, 247, 260, 262, 263, 270, 300, 331
Solebay, 23, 299, 303, 305, 309, 311–313
South Korea, 145, 147, 244
Stabilisation, 3, 15, 246, 299, 300, 302, 307, 335
Syria, viii, 2, 26, 30, 37, 67, 86, 89, 90, 212, 219, 220, 226, 227n5

T

Terrorism, 2, 28, 64, 67, 69–72, 165, 173, 216, 218, 220, 221, 226, 227, 243, 286, 288, 329
Threat, 6, 8–10, 48, 56, 72, 87, 88, 133, 144, 147, 148, 153, 225, 235, 260, 265, 298, 299, 301, 305–307, 312, 318, 319, 321, 322, 324, 328–335
Trafficking Victims Protection Act (TVPA), 144, 149, 150, 156–158, 165
Typology, 21–38, 70, 72, 73, 75, 106, 107

U

UN Charter, 280, 280n3, 281, 281n5

United Nations (UN), 25, 26, 63–70, 128, 130n1, 138, 139, 182, 235–237, 278, 279n1
United Nations Office on Drugs and Crime (UNODC), vii, 4, 23, 24, 34, 35, 62–65, 67–69, 88, 108, 114, 173, 174, 178–180, 219, 237, 238, 308
United States of America (USA), ix, 86, 128, 143–165

V

Victim, vi, vii, x, 2–4, 6, 7, 9, 13–15, 21, 22, 24, 27–29, 34, 35, 43–45, 47–57, 62–64, 67, 73, 74, 88, 89, 95, 102n2, 106, 124–126, 129–133, 135–138, 144, 149, 150, 158, 161, 163, 173–192, 216–222, 224, 226, 228, 229, 235, 237, 240, 242–245, 247–249, 260, 261, 266, 268, 271, 272, 279, 283, 285, 291, 308, 318, 332, 336
Violence against women, 237
Vulnerability, 2, 6, 15, 21, 23, 24, 28, 35–38, 45, 48–50, 52–54, 64, 74, 86–88, 91, 123, 135, 138, 143, 173, 188–191, 216, 219, 223, 228, 234, 236, 260, 299, 302, 303, 305–307, 310, 312, 318, 321, 325, 331, 334, 335

W

War, vii, ix, 4, 7, 27, 30, 31, 45, 46, 50, 52, 54, 55, 85–87, 89, 93, 95, 104, 123, 124, 126, 127, 134, 137, 138, 143, 173, 189, 197–200, 199n2, 207, 236, 238, 239, 243–245, 247, 248, 260, 267, 268, 278, 300
Women Peace and Security (WPS), 14, 235, 242, 243, 245, 248, 249, 300, 320

Y

Yazidi, viii, 2, 27, 32, 34, 64, 67, 216, 297

The manufacturer's authorised representative in the EU is Springer Nature Customer Service Centre GmbH, Europaplatz 3, 69115 Heidelberg, Germany. If you have any concerns regarding our products, please contact ProductSafety@springernature.com

Printed and bound by CPI Group (UK) Ltd, Croydon, CR0 4YY
05/10/2026
02227638-0002